About the Editors

Professor Bill Roche is Dean of the Graduate School of Business at University College Dublin and Director of Research. He holds a doctorate from the University of Oxford where he was a Research Fellow of Nuffield College. He has published extensively in the areas of human resource management and industrial relations in leading international journals. He is a member of the Council of the Economic and Social Research Institute and of the National Committee on Economics and Social Science of the Royal Irish Academy.

Dr. Kathy Monks is Associate Dean for Research at Dublin City University Business School and Director of the Masters Programme in Human Resource Strategies. Her research interests include human resource practice, organisational learning and managerial careers and she has published extensively in these areas.

Dr. James Walsh is College Lecturer in management at the Department of Management and Marketing at University College, Cork and Director of the Strategic Learning Programme. His research and teaching interests are in firm growth processes, strategic human resource development and organisational learning and he has published extensively in these areas.

Irish Studies in Management

Editors:

W.K. Roche
Graduate School of Business
University College Dublin

David Givens
Oak Tree Press

Irish Studies in Management is a new series of texts and research-based monographs covering management and business studies. Published by Oak Tree Press in association with the Graduate School of Business at University College Dublin, the series aims to publish significant contributions to the study of management and business in Ireland, especially where they address issues of major relevance to Irish management in the context of international developments, particularly within the European Union. Mindful that most texts and studies in current use in Irish business education take little direct account of Irish or European conditions, the series seeks to make available to the specialist and general reader works of high quality which comprehend issues and concerns arising from the practice of management and business in Ireland. The series aims to cover subjects ranging from accountancy to marketing, industrial relations/human resource management, international business, business ethics and economics. Studies of public policy and public affairs of relevance to business and economic life will also be published in the series.

Human Resource Strategies

Policy and Practice
in Ireland

Edited by
William K. Roche
Kathy Monks
and James Walsh

Oak Tree Press
Dublin
in association with
Graduate School of Business
University College Dublin

Oak Tree Press
Merrion Building
Lower Merrion Street
Dublin 2, Ireland

A catalogue record of this book is
available from the British Library.

ISBN 1-86076-101 1

Printed in Britain by MPG, Bodmin, Cornwall

Contents

List of Tables

List of Figures

List of Boxes

ABOUT THE CONTRIBUTORS

FINIAN BUCKLEY is Lecturer in Organisational Psychology at Dublin City University Business School.

ANNE COUGHLAN is Executive in the Survey & Business Information Unit at the Irish Business and Employers' Confederation.

NOELLE DONNELLY is CRH Newman Scholar in International Human Resource Management at the Graduate School of Business, University College Dublin and a doctoral student at the Warwick Business School, University of Warwick.

CHARLES GEANEY is Lecturer in the Department of Business Administration at University College, Dublin.

JOHN GEARY is Lecturer in Human Resource Management and Industrial Relations at University College, Dublin.

PAULINE GRACE is a doctoral student at Templeton College, University of Oxford and a former Lecturer in Human Resource Management at University College, Dublin.

PATRICK GUNNIGLE is Professor of Business Studies at the University of Limerick.

TIM HASTINGS is ESB Business Journalist Research Fellow at the Graduate School of Business, University College, Dublin and Industrial Correspondent of Independent Newspapers.

NOREEN HERATY is Lecturer in Human Resource Management at the University of Limerick.

PAUL McGRATH is Lecturer in the Department of Business Administration at University College, Dublin.

GERARD McMAHON is Lecturer in Human Resource Management at the Dublin Institute of Technology.

MICHAEL MORLEY is Lecturer in Human Resource Management and Industrial Relations at the University of Limerick.

GERALDINE O'BRIEN is Lecturer in Human Resource Management at University College, Dublin.

JOHN O'DOWD is Co-director of the National Centre for Partnership, Department of the Taoiseach.

HUGH SCULLION is Reader in International Human Resource Management at the School of Management and Finance, University of Nottingham.

ANNE SINNOTT is Lecturer in Marketing at Dublin City University Business School.

ANGELA M. TRIPOLI is Lecturer in Business Administration at University College, Dublin.

THOMAS TURNER is Lecturer in Industrial Relations and Organisational Behaviour at the University of Limerick.

Introduction

During the last decade and a half the field of human resource management (HRM) has emerged as a major area of general management. In the increasingly competitive and turbulent markets of the 1980s and 1990s organisations have subjected long-established approaches to the management of people to critical review and shown increasing signs of experimentation with new principles, strategies and policies. The management of people, traditionally viewed as a residual concern of general management and organisational strategy, has assumed growing significance and priority. Demand has risen sharply for courses in HRM in undergraduate, post-graduate and executive programmes in business and management. The international research literature on HRM has also grown explosively.

A large number of HRM texts are now available. These range from those which focus on the basic principles and policies underpinning how HRM professionals do their work to those which consider how the management of people fits into the overall business strategy. However, there is no text aimed at general management concerns which also takes account of HRM strategies and policies in an Irish context and their impact in practice.

Human Resource Strategies: Policy and Practice in Ireland aims to make good this deficiency. The chapters in the text address the major aspects of HRM strategy and policy as these are understood internationally, but also consider developments in organisations in Ireland. Indigenous and multinational firms are covered, as are organisations located in the public sector.

All chapters have been specially written for the text. Contributors were chosen on the basis of their academic or professional expertise in the areas covered by their contributions. They draw extensively on research which has been carried out in Ireland and utilise Irish cases to illustrate trends and developments. They adopt a critical perspective on HRM, aware that while well-developed strategies and professionally validated policies contribute to the effective management of people, there are no panaceas or easy remedies. Too often the flood of management writing in the area of HRM proceeds on strongly prescriptive lines, putting forward solutions and models without a balanced assessment of their effects in practice in different types of organisations or different regional and national settings.

The appearance of a text on HRM for a general management readership marks an important milestone in the development of the academic field in Ireland. Over the past decade, Irish academics have gained considerable experience of how students and executives respond to central principles of HRM in an Irish context and how they assess a range of policies in practice. This experience is captured in the ways in which issues are reviewed in the chapters of the text. As more organisations have experimented with HRM and sought to develop well-articulated HRM strategies, evidence has become available which indicates what is being attempted in significant companies and public agencies and with what practical consequences. The fact that so many multinational, particularly US companies, synonymous with the concept of HRM have chosen to locate in Ireland also provides a rich natural laboratory for examining HR issues and studying the ways in which principles originating in very different business and cultural conditions may be transplanted to another national context. The growth in both the volume and quality of research HRM in Ireland over the past decade also provides a rich source of information on the character and effects of HRM policies. While this research commonly appears in journals and technical monographs it is important that it also informs management education and professional debate in the field in Ireland. This text therefore draws extensively on research in order to foster in practising managers, whether working in HRM or general management, the critical perspective and balance that are essential qualities shared by well-conducted research and effective management practice.

In Chapter 1 Patrick Gunnigle traces the development of the personnel and HR function in Ireland from its inception to the present day. This analysis explores the economic and social factors which have fashioned the structure and operation of the HR function and considers the issues facing the function in the future.

In Chapter 2, Angela Tripoli focuses on non-union companies and the employee voice and involvement mechanisms that they have adopted as part of their management of employee relations.

Chapter 3 extends the analysis of employee relations to the unionised firm. Bill Roche and Tom Turner consider the ways in which HRM policies and practices affect trade union representation and the conduct of collective bargaining by examining, in particular, the major theme of "workplace partnership".

The issue of recruitment and selection is examined by Noreen Heraty and Michael Morley in Chapter 4. They use data from the Price Waterhouse/Cranfield study to examine changes that have occurred in the ways in which companies recruit and select employees in Ireland.

James Walsh utilises survey research to consider the status of management development in Ireland and options for its growth and expansion in Chapter 5.

In Chapter 6, Kathy Monks traces the development of employment equality initiatives, including the current emphasis on managing diversity, and considers the impact of HRM on these initiatives.

Kathy Monks, Finian Buckley and Anne Sinnott trace the development of total quality management in Chapter 7 and consider the role played by the HR manager in the implementation of quality initiatives, including communications programmes.

In Chapter 8, Pauline Grace and Anne Coughlan outline the alternative reward systems available to companies and draw on an IBEC survey to examine the incidence of various reward systems in companies in Ireland. The chapter also examines the wider strategic context of reward systems and considers current debates on reward systems in the HRM literature and trends in their adoption. In Chapter 9 Gerry McMahon extends the analysis of reward systems to include the issues of performance-related pay and performance appraisal.

John Geary considers the area of work and its reorganisation in Chapter 10. He discusses new forms of work organisation and draws on case study evidence and several major research studies to examine the diffusion of task participation, its impact on employees' lives and its place in employee management relations.

Paul McGrath and Charles Geaney, Chapter 11, review the organisational change literature, consider recent trends and developments and suggest roles for the HR manager in managing complex change processes.

In Chapter 12, Hugh Scullion and Noelle Donnelly explore the area of international human resource management in the context of the internationalisation of Irish businesses.

The public sector is the focus of Chapter 13. John O'Dowd and Tim Hastings consider the impact of private sector models of HRM and employee relations on change strategies in the public sector and commercial semi-state companies.

In the final chapter Geraldine O'Brien, sets out the key issues surrounding the concepts of business strategy and human resource management strategy and explores the linkages between these two areas.

The editors would like to acknowledge the advice and assistance of David Givens, who encouraged this project from its inception. Jenna Dowds, Production Manager at Oak Tree, handled the translation of complex manuscript to book with great efficiency and good humour. Geraldine McEvoy and Susan Neilson of the Business Research Programme at the UCD Graduate School of Business, handled the administration associated with the book and technical work on a number of chapters with the utmost professionalism and skill.

Bill Roche

Kathy Monks

James Walsh

August 1998

1

HUMAN RESOURCE MANAGEMENT AND THE PERSONNEL FUNCTION[1]

Patrick Gunnigle

INTRODUCTION

A significant aspect of human resource management practice concerns the role of the specialist personnel management function. This chapter considers that role in Ireland. It reviews its development and current role and considers some key contemporary challenges facing the personnel function.

THE LESSONS OF HISTORY

As a starting point, it is useful to review the historical development of the personnel management function to evaluate what this tells us about the current state of the function. While much of the early literature is based on developments in Britain, these events have considerable relevance for Ireland and the growth of the personnel management function here.

Early Developments: From Caring to Control

It is widely accepted that the origins of personnel management may be traced back to the so-called *welfare tradition*. Starting in

[1] I would like to thank Kathy Monks (Dublin City University), Mike Morley and Tom Turner (University of Limerick) for comments on earlier drafts of this chapter.

Britain in the 1890s, this phase saw the appointment of the first welfare officers, mostly in Quaker-owned food and confectionery firms (Niven, 1967). By the early 1900s the welfare tradition reached Ireland with the appointment of welfare officers by firms such as Jacobs and Maguire & Paterson (Byrne, 1988). Welfare officers are generally regarded as the forerunners of the modern personnel practitioner. Welfare is inextricably linked to a paternalistic "caring" approach to employees, dealing with issues such as safety standards and working conditions problems. It is also the source of an ongoing ambiguity as to the managerial status of personnel practitioners: welfare officers occupied a semi-independent position in the factory system with employees being the main beneficiaries of their role. This led in large measure to the so-called "middle man" perception of personnel practitioners.

Another significant early influence on personnel management was the adoption of *scientific management* and the associated notion that "improved" approaches to workforce management led to greater organisational efficiency. Scientific management encouraged employers to adopt more systematic approaches in the areas such as job design and payment systems. Its historical significance from a personnel perspective was to shift the emphasis of personnel work away from the employee-oriented "caring/ do-gooding" agenda of the welfare tradition towards a managerial "efficiency/profitability" agenda.

A third strand in the initial development of the personnel management function was the emergence of interest in the *behavioural sciences*. This provided an important impetus for the fledgling personnel function by establishing a body of knowledge to underpin many aspects of personnel work such as employee selection and work systems design. It also served to focus attention on some of the problems created by work organisation in the "factory system", such as worker monotony and low morale.

These early developments had a profound impact on the personnel function. Possibly the most significant legacy was to highlight two contrasting orientations in the role of personnel function, *caring* and *managing*. The *caring orientation* reflects the welfare influence: in this model, the personnel practitioner's role is employee- (not management-) oriented. This role manifests itself today in the employee assistance focus of personnel work and, most particularly, in employee perceptions — generally misplaced — of the personnel function as one of looking after the interests of workers. The *management orientation* is based on an efficiency motive, and places the personnel role firmly in the management hierarchy, with primary responsibilities in selecting and training workers to "fit" particular job roles and in establishing various control systems to oversee the work of such employees. It is interesting that as the management orientation replaced the welfare role, participation of women in the function decreased (see Legge, 1995). Early welfare workers were mostly women (in a role which was stereotypically female: see Niven, 1967). However, as efficiency motives replaced caring motives, men tended to replace women in the function. This trend was accentuated as industrial relations became the dominant concern of the personnel function. Recent Irish evidence indicates that while the overall ratio of males to females working in personnel is now similar, men still dominate when it comes to senior personnel roles (Gunnigle et al., 1997).

Industrial Relations as *the* Key Personnel Activity

A second critical theme emerging from a review of the historical development of the personnel function is the predominance of industrial relations as *the* most significant area of personnel activity (O'Mahony, 1958; Shivanath, 1987). The growth of an industrial relations emphasis in personnel work was a direct result of the increasing influence of *trade unions*. After some initial opposition, employers came to accommodate the reality of organised labour and responded through multi-employer bargaining via employer associations and the employment of personnel practitioners whose primary role was to deal with industrial relations matters at enterprise level. The primacy of industrial relations within the personnel role reflected a widespread acceptance of the "pluralist model" incorporating primary reliance on adversarial collective bargaining.

The pluralist tradition was underpinned by public policy support and employer acceptance of trade union recognition and collective bargaining. For the personnel function, industrial relations became *the* priority with personnel practitioners vested with the responsibility to negotiate and police agreements. Industrial harmony was the objective and personnel specialists through their negotiating, interpersonal, and procedural skills had responsibility for its achievement. This industrial relations emphasis helped position the personnel function in a more central management role, albeit a largely reactive one.

Other Important Factors

Other factors helped consolidate the personnel function as an important feature of the Irish management landscape. A major growth of *employment legislation* in the 1970s — primarily focused on extending the individual employment rights of workers — was instrumental in providing another string to the personnel practitioner's bow. Personnel practitioners assumed a degree of "expert power": helping their organisations come grips with such legislation.

A related and significant development, particularly since the late 1970s, was a increasing emphasis on the formal *education and training* of personnel specialists. This was somewhat of a new departure. Traditionally, Irish organisations recruited their personnel practitioners from the line or, indeed, from the unions. The major selection criterion was collective bargaining experience: one was expected to have served one's time in the "trenches". However, many of the newer multinational and some indigenous firms increasingly emphasised the appointment of formally qualified personnel practitioners. This trend was related to a broadening of the personnel role into areas such as training and development and manpower planning. Of course the reverse effect is also important. This new *cadre* of personnel practitioners, whose development was more influenced by the "benches" than the "trenches", were keen to apply their academic knowledge across a broader sphere of personnel activities. The fact that such individuals were less likely to emanate from a trade union tradition was also to have an increasing effect as the decade progressed.

A final important factor worthy of mention in the context of the development of the personnel function in Ireland is the impact of *multinational companies* (MNCs). Direct foreign investment is critical feature of Irish industry and foreign-owned firms account for 50 per cent of manufactured output and three quarters of industrial exports. Possibly the most notable legacy of MNCs was their emphasis on the role of personnel function. Among larger MNCs, this was generally manifested in a well developed personnel department, which operated at a senior management level, and through comprehensive policies and procedures covering various aspects of personnel management (McMahon et al., 1988; Gunnigle, 1993). Another important contribution of MNCs was the diffusion of new personnel techniques. In areas such as selection testing, training methods and reward systems, MNCs have often led the way in introducing new developments and approaches.

In evaluating the historical development of the personnel function in Ireland, it appears that growth in industrialisation, direct foreign investment and semi-state activity contributed to the establishment of personnel as a discrete management function. By the late 1970s the personnel management role was firmly established in most larger Irish organisations. Personnel departments operated as a distinct management function with responsibility for a well defined range of personnel tasks. Industrial relations was the key activity area with most emphasis on collective bargaining.

THE LESSONS OF THE MARKET

While the historical development of the personnel function has helped shape its role, the most salient challenges for personnel management in recent years emanate from changes in market forces (see, for example, Beaumont, 1995).

The 1980s heralded a period of considerable turmoil for personnel management. A depressed economic climate together with increased competitive pressures, helped change both the focus of personnel management and the nature of personnel activities. Competitive pressures combined to set new priorities, forcing the personnel function to act under tighter cost controls and to undertake a wider range of activities. The harsh economic climate dramatically changed the industrial relations environment. Widespread redundancies and high unemployment significantly altered the bargaining context. Increasingly, employers sought to address issues such as payment structures and levels of wage increases, the extent of demarcation and restrictive work practices and, ultimately, the erosion of managerial prerogative. In Ireland, trade union membership fell significantly and industrial unrest also declined. At the same time increased market competition forced many organisations to seek ways of establishing competitive advantage. One apparent source of such improvements lay in the better utilisation of human resources.

Possibly the most pervasive contemporary issue impacting on organisational approaches to personnel management is increased product market pressures. In evaluating the specific impact of market developments on personnel management, Marchington (1990) identifies two useful dimensions to evaluate an organisation's product market position, namely that of (i) monopoly power and (ii) monopsony power. *Monopoly power* refers to the degree to which an organisation has power to dictate market terms (particularly price) to customers. High monopoly power may be the result of factors such as cartel arrangements, regulated (e.g. state) monopolies, high barriers to entry, or unique product or technology. In contrast, *monopsony power* refers to the extent to which customers exert power over the organisation. High monopsony power may occur as a result of high levels of market competition (numerous competitors) or because of the existence of powerful customers who can exert considerable control over price and other factors (e.g. credit terms, service). In such situations, supplying organisations may be forced to accept the market terms, particularly price, dictated by customers.

The relative levels of monopoly and monopsony power which an organisation experiences influences the degree of management discretion in decision making in all functional areas, including personnel management. Where monopoly power is high, organisations have greater scope to adopt "investment-oriented styles". Such favourable market conditions are conducive to the application of benign HR practices such as comprehensive employee development policies, tenure commitments and gain-sharing. This does not imply that employers will always adopt "resource"-type policies in favourable product market conditions. Rather, such conditions provide management with greater scope to choose from the full range of HR policy choices. On the other hand, organisations operating under high levels of monopsony power (market pressure) have considerably less scope for choice, and a more traditional cost and labour control approach may be more appropriate. In evaluating contemporary developments, one can discern a pattern of reduced monopoly power and increased monopsony power across a range of industrial sectors and sub-sectors.

The Irish Context: External Challenge

Turning specifically to the Irish context, there is little doubt that "traditional" approaches to personnel management have come under immense challenge in recent years (Roche & Gunnigle, 1995; also see Beaumont, 1995). In the Irish context, developments in the wider business context have acted as the key catalyst in stimulating changes in personnel management. The most widely accepted explanation of changes in traditional approaches to personnel management is the increasingly competitive nature of product markets. In attempting to disaggregate the sources of *increased competitiveness* one can point to an amalgam of factors, most particularly the (i) liberalisation of European and world trade; (ii) deregulation in capital, product and service markets;

(iii) improved communication and transport infrastructures; (iv) developments in technology and (v) greater market penetration by emerging economies. These developments have particularly significant implications for Ireland due to its status as a small, open economy which is heavily reliant on export performance.

The impact of increased competitive pressures has been to focus attention on both cost *and* product innovation/quality as factors impacting on competitive positioning. For many firms, this creates a "flexibility imperative" whereby companies have to be increasingly responsive to consumer demand on dimensions such as customisation, delivery and support services. The overall implication of these developments seems to have all but diluted the concept that companies compete on either a price (low cost) or a product differentiation (premium price) basis. Increasingly, it appears that all companies, and not just the low-cost producers, must tightly control their cost structures. While the need to control labour and pay costs may be more intense in labour-intensive sectors, it is also important in other sectors as product and service market competition increases and profit margins tighten.

It is also significant that these competitive trends are increasingly penetrating the State-owned sector. A major reason for this development is the erosion of state monopolies as a result of developments at European Union level. An early example of a state company having to deal with increased competitiveness was that of Aer Lingus. Deregulation in the airline industry meant that the company was faced with increased competition on key routes. Resultant restructuring led to significant changes in employee numbers, employment patterns and reward systems. The ESB and Telecom Eireann are now faced with EU-sponsored initiatives aimed at de-regulating the electricity and telecommunications markets. Such changes are likely to have profound effects on personnel management in these companies. The conditions imposed by the Maastricht Treaty for entry to the third phase of economic and monetary union on issues such as interest rate convergence and the debt/GDP ratio pose considerable challenges for Government, not least the issue of public sector expenditure (see Hourihan, 1994). The completion of the internal market and removal of trade barriers also serves to expose many Irish organisations to increased international competition with attendant implications for personnel management at the level of the enterprise (see, for example, Hastings, 1995).

THE HUMAN RESOURCE MANAGEMENT PHENOMENON

By far the most widely debated development in personnel management during this past decade or so is that of Human Resource Management (HRM). This was seen by many as a new development which contrasted with "traditional" personnel management. Its apparently proactive stance was viewed as a major departure from the traditionally reactive "industrial relations" focus associated with established approaches. The central contention underpinning HRM is that organisations incorporate human resource considerations into strategic decision-making, establish a corporate human resource philosophy and develop a complementary and coherent set of personnel strategies and policies to improve human resource utilisation.

The implications of HRM for the personnel function remain unclear. Some contributors argue that it merely involves a re-titling exercise. Others argue that its implications are more substantive, involving a complete reorientation of the role of the personnel function. In evaluating the application of HRM, David Guest (1987) argues that companies will be more successful if they pursue four key HRM goals, namely: (i) strategic integration; (ii) employee commitment; (iii) flexibility and (iv) quality. He suggests that these HRM goals can be optimally achieved through coherent HRM policy choices in the areas of organisation/job design, management of change, recruitment, selection and socialisation, appraisal, training and development, rewards and communications. Guest identifies five necessary conditions for the effective operation of HRM, namely:

- **Corporate leadership**: to ensure that the values inherent in HRM are championed and implemented

- **Strategic vision**: to ensure the integration of HRM as a key component of the corporate strategy

- **Technological/production feasibility**: Guest suggests that heavy investment in short-cycle, repetitive production assembly-line equipment militates against the job design principles and autonomous team-working necessary for HRM

- **Employee relations feasibility**: Guest suggests that multi-union status, low-trust management/employee relations and an adversarial employee relations orientation militate against the implementation of HRM

- **Management capacity**: to implement appropriate policies.

Problems with the HRM Concept

Several commentators have identified a number of inherent contradictions and inconsistencies in HRM, particularly the "soft" variant (see, especially, Cradden, 1992). For example, Legge (1995) highlights the apparent paradox between the traditional commodity status of labour under the capitalist framework and the essentially unitarist perspective of HRM which sees no conflict of interests between management and employees. It has traditionally been accepted that there is an inherent conflict of interest between management and employees over the price of labour. Indeed, this is the very basis for the existence of industrial relations as a key concern of workers and management. However, the HRM perspective appears to ignore the "inherency" of a conflict of interests, but rather focuses on the achievement of congruence between management and employee interests and on achieving high levels of employee commitment.

In particular, the HRM focus on employee commitment not only seems incongruent with the pluralist perspective of the organisation but also appears to conflict with another basic tenet of HRM, namely that personnel management policies should be integrated with, and complement, business strategy. Clearly, many decisions which complement business strategy may not develop employee commitment. If, for example, an organisation's business strategy is to maximise short-term returns to owners/shareholders, this may well involve decisions which do not develop employee commitment; for example, replacing labour with technology, contracting out, or intensifying work flow.

A related issue on this theme is the suggestion that HRM involves the simultaneous achievement of higher levels of individualism and teamwork. These twin goals have tremendous potential for conflict. For example, performance-related pay based on individual employee performance may indeed conflict with teamwork, as can individual communications/negotiations.

High levels of flexibility are seen as a core objective of HRM. However, the difficulties in achieving congruence between different flexibility forms (numerical, functional and financial) are widely evident. It is clearly difficult to achieve high levels of functional flexibility (such as multi-skilling) where employees have a tenuous relationship with the organisation, as may result from attempts to improve numerical flexibility (see, for example, Pollert, 1991).

A further difficulty in the HRM argument that personnel policies must be internally consistent arises in relation to job security. A prominent theme in the HRM debate is that for HRM to be effective, management must provide implicit job tenure guarantees for employees. Indeed, it is argued that job tenure commitments are a necessary precondition in achieving a mutuality of management and worker interests. However, it is patently evident that high levels of competition and volatility in product markets have made job security increasingly difficult to achieve. Indeed, job security may itself be incompatible with broader business goals attributed to HRM, such as increased flexibility in responding to rapid changes in demand. In practice, it would appear that some organisations seek to achieve such flexibility by policies which actually reduce the likelihood of job tenure commitments — for example, by using atypical employment forms.

On the issue of the practicability of achieving a fit between business strategy and HRM policies (e.g. job tenure commitments), this is clearly problematic in highly competitive or recessionary conditions where the "needs of the business" are likely to undermine any internal fit with "soft" HRM values. As Blyton and Turnbull (1992: 10) comment: "shedding labour . . . will severely challenge, if not destroy, an organisation's HRM image of caring for the needs and security of its employees."

Another apparent inconsistency in HRM is the focus on achieving greater individualism in management/employee relations. As we have seen, personnel management practice in Ireland has been characterised by a highly collectivist emphasis as manifested in, for example, relatively high levels of trade union density and much reliance on collective bargaining. The "soft" human resource management approach places the managerial emphasis on achieving high-trust relations between management and employees, and appears to have a preference for pursuing this goal in a non-union environment. Within the "soft" HRM model, high-trust relations are pursued through managerial initiatives to increase individual employee involvement and motivation, and the adoption of techniques such as performance appraisal and performance-related pay. Thus, such organisations attempt to create close management/employee ties and break down the traditional management/worker dichotomy, of which collective bargaining is seen as the principal manifestation. Such initiatives are indicative of a unitarist management perspective, albeit a sophisticated variant, and have potential for significant conflict with the pluralist perspective characteristic of industrial relations in Ireland.

HRM in Practice

While the wider debate places much emphasis on the strategic nature of HRM, there is limited empirical evidence on the extent to which strategic approaches to HRM are actually adopted in practice. Indeed, recent Irish research questions the extent of strategic HRM (Roche & Turner, 1994). Research on high performing British organisations by Tyson, Witcher & Doherty (1994) sought to examine whether organisations attempt to achieve a fit between the business and HRM strategy, and if so, how. The research discovered three distinct approaches to corporate and business strategy formation and found common elements in the HR strategies adopted by the sample companies in the fields of *management and employee development, employee relations* and *organisation development*. However, the integration of HR and business strategies occurs more naturally where there are core values and explicit mission, thus suggesting, according to the authors, that integration is "easier in more simple businesses". At the strategic level, the study failed to find any distinctive approach to human resource management, but it did find that financially successful companies, in different ways, took human resource issues seriously. Thus, according to Guest & Hoque (1994: 44), while the link between practices and outcomes is tenuous:

> The key is strategic integration. What this means is that personnel strategy must fit the business strategy, the personnel policies must be fully integrated with each other and the values of the line managers must be sufficiently integrated or aligned with the personnel philosophy to ensure that they will implement the personnel policy and practice. . . . Where this can be achieved, there is growing evidence that a distinctive set of human resource practices results in superior performance.

As indicated earlier, personnel management practice in Ireland has traditionally been associated with a strong "industrial relations" emphasis. As such, personnel management practice is seen as essentially reactive, dealing with various problematic aspects of workforce management. Thus, personnel policies and activities tend to focus on short-term issues with little conscious attempt to develop linkages with business policy. A key manifestation of the pluralist tradition at establishment level was a primary emphasis focus on *industrial* relations, with collective bargaining and related activities being the key role of the specialist personnel management function. However, we have also seen that the 1980s were a decade of reappraisal for personnel management, both in Ireland and abroad. In Ireland, the onset of recession lessened the need for many core personnel activities such as recruitment and, particularly, industrial relations. At the same time increased market competition forced many organisations to seek ways of establishing competitive advantage including improved approaches to workforce management.

Looking at contemporary developments, it appears that recession and subsequent recovery have led to a change in traditional approaches to workforce management, a greater devolution of personnel management activities to line management and the emergence of a greater strategic role for personnel management issues in a number of Irish companies (Turner & Morley, 1995).

The final section of this chapter reviews the implications for the personnel function, considers alternative models of personnel management and evaluates the prospects for the personnel function in Ireland.

THE PERSONNEL MANAGEMENT FUNCTION: MODELS AND PROSPECTS

As noted earlier, a critical aspect of organisational approaches to HR management concerns the role of the personnel function. For example, it is suggested that a key feature of the so-called "strategic" human resource management (HRM) approach is that the major responsibility for personnel management be assumed by line managers. However, we have noted above that a specialist personnel function with a reasonably well-defined range of responsibilities is an established feature of workforce management in most larger Irish organisations.

Recognising that considerable variation can arise in the role that the personnel function may play in organisations, Tyson and Fell (1986) provide us with probably the most useful categorisation of models of the personnel function, as outlined in Table 1.1.

TABLE 1.1: MODELS OF THE SPECIALIST PERSONNEL FUNCTION

a. **Clerk of Works:** Within this model personnel management is a low-level activity operating in an administrative support mode to line management. It is responsible for basic administration and welfare provision.

b. **Contracts Manager:** Within this model personnel management is a high-level function with a key role in handling industrial relations and developing policies and procedures in other core areas. The role is largely reactive, dealing with the personnel management implications of business decisions. This model incorporates a strong "policing" component where the personnel department is concerned with securing adherence to agreed systems and procedures.

c. **Architect:** Within this role personnel management is a top-level management function involved in establishing and adjusting corporate objectives and developing strategic personnel policies designed to facilitate the achievement of long-term business goals. Personnel management considerations are recognised as an integral component of corporate success with the personnel director best placed to assess how the organisation's human resources can best contribute to this goal. Routine personnel activities are delegated allowing senior practitioners adopt the broad strategic outlook of a "business manager".

Source: Tyson & Fell, 1986.

The Irish Context

A study by Shivanath (1987) considered the relevance of Tyson's role models for personnel management practice in a cross section of large organisations in Ireland. In relation to the *clerk of works model*, the survey evidence found that the vast majority of Irish personnel practitioners were not limited to this role. While personnel departments were, of necessity, concerned with routine clerical/administrative tasks, these were generally delegated allowing senior practitioners deal with more strategic matters. The description of the personnel practitioner within the *contracts manager* model seemed to most accurately reflect the roles of the majority of Irish practitioners. Industrial relations was identified by the bulk of respondents as the most crucial area of their work. The study also found that the *architect model* was prominent in a number of organisations.

In assessing contemporary developments, the last decade may be typified as a period of both continuity and change for the specialist personnel function in Ireland (see Monks 1992; Foley & Gunnigle 1994, 1995). The continuity dimension is manifested in the widespread presence of a specialist personnel function in Irish organisations and a continuing emphasis on industrial relations as a significant aspect of the personnel role (see Gunnigle et al. 1997).

However, we can also point to evidence of important changes such as greater strategic integration of the personnel/HR function, some movement away from traditional *industrial* relations and collective bargaining to a more individual approach, a growth in atypical forms of employment and greater emphasis on other aspects of personnel activity, particularly training and development (see Gunnigle et al., 1997 a & b). Many commentators have noted an increasing opposition to trade union recognition while still others have alluded to some (limited) examples of organisations seeking to increase the extent of labour/management participation (see chapter 3 in this book). Existing research provides evidence of a more individual approach to workforce management, replacing traditional pluralism, particularly among newer organisations. Recent research also identifies training and development as an increasingly important area in the work of the personnel function (Heraty et al., 1994). Still more evidence indicates significant managerial initiatives designed to dismantle accepted procedures and custom and practice in personnel management. Thus, contemporary practices indicates there is an increasing proliferation of personnel management types with no apparent convergence to any dominant model.

LOOKING TO THE FUTURE: A SEARCH FOR ORTHODOXY

In tracing the development of the personnel function in Ireland over recent decades one can identify a predictable pattern of evolution. From somewhat humble beginnings, the specialist personnel function developed to a stage where it became accepted as an integral part of the management structure of larger organisations. This pattern of evolution saw convergence to a *prevailing orthodoxy* of the role of the personnel function. This orthodoxy was grounded in the belief that *the* key employer concern in workforce management was the establishment and maintenance of stable industrial relations. Cornerstones of this approach were trade union recognition, adversarial collective bargaining and a degree of procedural formalisation. Thus, the personnel function assumed responsibility for managing relations with the unions. While more reactive rather than strategic, this *industrial relations* role was nonetheless significant: it served to both define what personnel work involved and position the personnel management function as an important aspect of the managerial infrastructure.

This role reached its heyday in the 1970s. By the early 1980s we began to witness the initial dismantling of industrial relations orthodoxy. As we have seen earlier, the roots of such change can be traced to numerous sources but most particularly to the increased competitive pressures on organisations. For the personnel function these changes have heralded a period which essentially appears to be devoid of orthodoxy. What we see emerging is a range of different roles for the personnel function so that, as Paauwe (1996: 227) comments, "it is almost impossible to speak of *the* personnel function". It appears that contingency approaches are the order of the day with the role, and even the existence, of the personnel function varying according to industrial segment, managerial philosophy, product market performance and so on. It is therefore useful to consider some of the more common *organisational context/personnel function* models which are apparent today. Four such models are discussed below, viz.: (i) the commitment model; (ii) the transaction cost model; (iii) the traditional adversarial model; and (iv) the partnership model.

Organisational Context-Personnel Function Models

The Commitment Model

Often labelled "soft" HRM, this was the first model to challenge seriously industrial relations orthodoxy. It is characterised by a resource perspective of employees, incorporating the view that there is an organisational pay-off in performance terms from a combination of "sophisticated" personnel policies designed to develop employee commitment and emphasise the mutuality of management and employee interests. In this model, the personnel function is high-powered and well-resourced with a significant change agent role. This model appears to characterise core business organisations whose competitive strategy is based on a product differentiation/premium price approach, often on a "first to market" basis. Such organisations may employ significant numbers of highly trained technical and engineering staffs whose development and retention are critical to organisational success. This model generally relies on a *union substitution* premise: although organisations with union recognition but where the union role is essentially peripheral also fall within this category. While the commitment model has received much attention, its viability has increasingly come under scrutiny in recent years. In particular, exemplars of the commitment model (e.g. Wang & Digital) have come under intense competitive pressures from low cost producers.

The Transaction Cost Model

The transaction cost model places the workforce management emphasis on minimising operating costs. Thus, outsourcing becomes an important strategy, particularly in using contracted labour and other forms of "atypical" employment. This approach is also associated with an intensification of the pace of work flow and an increased range of work tasks. This model may rely on a *union suppression* premise: often linked to the (management) suggestion that unions inhibit the development of necessary flexibility levels to ensure competitiveness. In this model the key role of the personnel function is cost-effective labour supply. The personnel role is essentially reactive: dealing with the operational workforce management consequences of a low cost competitive strategy. This model is likely to prosper in more deregulated environments and thus poses much challenge for the European Union's "social market" philosophy.

The Traditional Adversarial Model

This model equates to "industrial relations orthodoxy" discussed above and was traditionally the predominant personnel function type in Ireland. It is grounded in low trust management/employee relations and primary reliance on adversarial collective bargaining. It equates to Tyson and Fell's (1986) contracts manager model.

The Partnership Model

The development of union/management partnerships has been the focus of much recent debate in Ireland. The proponents of partnership often point to perceived deficiencies of the adversarial model, in particular the apparent dominance of distributive bargaining with its emphasis on dividing limited resources. It is argued that this approach leads the parties to develop adversarial positions believing that any gains can only be made by inflicting losses on the other party. Based on recent analyses of industrial change, it is widely argued that there is a need for a new partnership model of employee relations which incorporates a strong trade union role. It is further argued that this new model allows both sides to break out of the traditional adversarial relationship through the adoption of a new industrial relations model based on "mutual gains" principles. The essential "deal" is that employers and trade unions enter into a set of mutual commitments as follows:

- employers recognise and facilitate worker and trade union involvement in strategic decision making;

- workers/trade unions commit themselves actively to productivity improvements;

- the gains of productivity improvements are shared between employers and workers;

- productivity improvements do not result in redundancies but rather employers actively seek new markets to keep workers gainfully employed.

In essence the mutual gains argument is that workers and trade unions actively pursue *with* management solutions to business problems and appropriate work reorganisation in return for greater involvement in business decisions and in the process of work reorganisation. Within this model, the personnel function becomes an important strategic lever in developing the partnership agenda. It also assumes an important role in implementing a range of personnel policy initiatives to underpin this new orientation, specifically in areas such as reward systems, management/employee communications, job design and employee development.

Managing Without a Personnel Function

While the focus of this chapter is the changing role of the personnel function, it is useful to consider briefly the issue of managing without a traditional personnel function. As many organisations move to "leaner" organisational structures, it is clear that the establishment of a traditional personnel function is no longer an inevitable consequence of increases in organisation scale.

In essence, there appears to be two principal means of replacing the traditional personnel function: (i) devolvement to the line (internal devolution) and (ii) outsourcing (external devolution) (see Paauwe, 1996). The first route is not particularly novel: indeed line management have always had a key role in day-to-day personnel issues. What is somewhat novel is the argument that line managers should play a greater role in policy development and interpretation. This theme has developed concurrently with changes towards flatter organisation structures and teamworking. Undoubtedly this development is important and will lead to a changing division of labour between personnel and line management. However, it is unlikely to lead to a widespread abolition of the personnel function.

Possibly the greatest threat to the personnel function is that of outsourcing. The transaction cost model, discussed above, places considerable emphasis on the "make" or "buy" decision. If a particular department does not make a demonstrable added value contribution when compared to outsourcing, so the argument goes, then such services should be contracted in. Two other factors make this option even more attractive: (i) on the demand side, the trend towards smaller organisation scale combined with growth of contracted-in labour means that organisations have fewer "employees" to manage and (ii) on the supply side, the proliferation of management consultants provides a buoyant source of relatively inexpensive contracted-in personnel services.

CONCLUSION

This chapter has focused on the development of the personnel/HR function in Ireland. It considered some of the key challenges facing the function and outlined some typologies which reflect alternative role models of the personnel function. A key theme of this paper is that up to the late 1970s the development of the personnel function was characterised by *convergence* to a common model of industrial relations orthodoxy. However, since then a combination of environmental changes have questioned the appropriateness of this model. In particular, increased competitive pressures have stimulated significant *divergence* in relation to acceptable models of personnel management. Such differences reflect the changes in the concept of the organisation and employment.

References

Beaumont, P.B. (1995): "The European Union and Developments in Industrial relations" in Gunnigle, P. and Roche, W.K. (eds.) *New Challenges to Irish Industrial Relations*, Dublin: Oak Tree Press in association with the Labour Relations Commssion.

Blyton, P. and Turnbull, P. (1992): *Reassessing Human Resource Management*, London: Sage.

Byrne, T.P. (1988): "IPM in Ireland", *IPM News*, 3(2).

Cradden, T. (1992): "Trade Unionism and HRM: The Incompatibles", *Irish Business and Administrative Research*, 13: 36–47.

Foley, K. and Gunnigle, P. (1994): "The Personnel/Human resource Function and Employee Relations" in Gunnigle, P. et al. (eds.) *Continuity and Change in Irish Employee Relations*, Dublin: Oak Tree Press.

Foley, K. and Gunnigle, P. (1995) "The Personnel Function — Change or Continuity" in Turner, T. and Morley, M. (eds.) *Industrial Relations and the New Order*, Dublin: Oak Tree Press.

Guest, D. (1987), "Human Resource Management and Industrial Relations", *Journal of Management Studies*, 24(5): 503–521.

Guest, D. and Hoque, K. (1994): "Yes, Personnel Does Make a Difference", *Personnel Management*, November, 40–44.

Gunnigle, P. (1993): "The Case of Ireland", Paper presented to Organisation for Economic Co-operation and Development (OECD) Seminar, *Labour/Management Relations and Human Resource Practices in Foreign and Multinational Enterprises: The Experience of Four OECD Countries*, Budapest, Hungary, June.

Gunnigle, P., Morley, M., Clifford, N. and Turner, T. (1997a): *Human Resource Management in Irish Organisations: Practice in Perspective*, Dublin: Oak Tree Press.

Gunnigle, P., Morley, M. and Turner, T. (1997b): "Challenging Collectivist Traditions: Individualism and the Management of Industrial Relations in Greenfield Sites", *Economic and Social Review*, 28(2).

Hastings, T. (1994): *Semi-states in Crisis: The Challenge for Industrial Relations in the ESB and Other Major Semi-state Companies*, Dublin: Oak Tree Press.

Heraty, N., Morley, M. & Turner, T. (1994): "Trends and Developments in the Organisation of the Employment Relationship", in Gunnigle, P. et al (eds.) *Continuity and Change in Irish Employee Relations*, Dublin: Oak Tree Press.

Hourihan, F. (1994): "The European Union and Industrial Relations" in Murphy, T.V. and Roche, W.K. *Irish Industrial Relations in Practice*, Dublin: Oak Tree Press.

Legge, K. (1995): *Human Resource Management: Rhetorics and Realities*, London: Macmillan.

Marchington, M. (1990): "Analysing the Links Between Product Markets and the Management of Employee Relations", *Journal of Management Studies*, 27(2): 111–132.

McMahon, G., Neary, C. and O'Connor, K. (1988): "Multinationals in Ireland: Three Decades on", *Industrial Relations News*, 6(11) Feb: 15–17.

Monks, K. (1992): "Personnel Management Practices: Uniformity or Diversity? Evidence from Some Irish Organisatons", *Irish Business and Administrative Research*, 13: 74–86.

Niven, M. (1967): *Personnel Management 1913–1963*, London: Institute of Personnel Management.

O'Mahony, D. (1958) *Industrial Relations in Ireland*, Dublin: Economic and Social Research Institute.

Paauwe, J. (1996): "Personnel Management without Personnel Managers", in Flood, P., Gannon, M.J. and Paauwe, J. (eds.) *Managing without Traditional Methods: International Innovations in Human Resource Management*, Wokingham, England: Addison-Wesley.

Pollert, A. (1991): *Farewell to Flexibility*, Oxford: Blackwell.

Roche, W.K. and Gunnigle, P. (1995): "Competition and the New Industrial Relations Agenda" in Gunnigle, P. and Roche, W.K. (eds.) *New Challenges to Irish Industrial Relations*, Dublin: Oak Tree Press in association with the Labour Relations Commission.

Roche, W.K. and Turner, T. (1994): "Testing Alternative Models of Human Resource Policy Effects on Trade Union Recognition in the Republic of Ireland", *International Journal of Human Resource Management*, 5(3): 721–753.

Shivanath, G. (1987): "Personnel Practitioners: Their Role and Status in Irish Industry", Unpublished MBS Thesis, University of Limerick.

Turner, T. and Morley, M. (1995): *Industrial Relations and the New Order*, Dublin: Oak Tree Press.

Tyson, S. (1987): "The Management of the Personnel Function", *Journal of Management Studies*, 24(5): 523–532.

Tyson, S. and Fell, A. (1986): *Evaluating the Personnel Function*, London: Hutchinson.

Tyson, S., Witcher, M. and Doherty, N. (1994): *Different Routes to Excellence*, Cranfield University School of Management, Human Resource Research Centre.

2

"Employee Voice" and Involvement in Non-Union Companies

Angela M. Tripoli

In all organisations, there are numerous channels for downward communication from management to employees. *Employee voice* captures the idea of systems which allow communication to flow upward. The origin of the concept of "employee voice" in the employment relationship is attributed to Hirschman's (1970) exit-voice-loyalty model (Lewin and Mitchell, 1992) which identifies the viable alternatives available to employees who are dissatisfied with their organisation. One option is for the aggrieved employee to leave the firm in reaction to their discontent. According to Hirschman's model, the exercise of voice is framed as an alternative to exit.

Two types of voice systems have emerged internationally. First, grievance systems provide a mechanism for employees to have complaints or problems heard and potentially resolved. Involvement systems offer employees the opportunity share their ideas and opinions on some aspect of the work process or organisation practices.

This chapter begins with a discussion of the reasons why organisations choose to establish voice and involvement systems. The next two sections describe the primary grievance and involvement systems in use within organisations internationally and examine the effects of these systems on organisations, employees, and employee/management relations. While the research evidence suggests that many of these effects have been positive (although not overwhelmingly so), there appear to be numerous challenges in implementing a set of voice programmes to fully capture the benefits and minimise the problems. The chapter concludes with a view that while individual voice practices seem to offer some distinct challenges and opportunities, a more meaningful understanding of voice management may be derived by analysing a set of practices embedded in the larger context of an organisation's structure, management practices, employment relations, and culture.

WHY VOICE SYSTEMS?

Why would a non-union firm choose to adopt or not adopt particular voice mechanisms for employees? Lewin and Mitchell (1992) suggest several factors that may motivate a firm to create voice systems for their employees.

Firstly, establishing voice systems can be motivated by the desire of the firm to remain non-union. Unionism has been viewed as a mechanism for collective employee voice (Freeman and Medoff, 1984). For non-union firms to retain their status, the belief has been that substitute systems must be used to provide employees with the opportunity to voice complaints. How well this strategy has worked in avoiding unionisation is not known, but a study by Drago and Wooden (1991) found that employees who participated in low-level decisions related to the shop floor were less interested in becoming involved in higher level decisions. In assessing the implications of these results Drago and Wooden (1991: 196) comment that

> Low-level participation programmes may work to the advantage of management by improving productivity, and may disadvantage unions by deflecting worker desires for involvement in more strategic decisions.

They conclude that increasing the amounts of involvement in low-level issues among non-union employees might offer a "profitable strategy for union avoidance" (p. 196). Earlier research by Toner

(1987) suggests that grievance systems in non-union firms can be quite satisfactory from the employees' perspective. Toner (1987) surveyed employee attitudes in four union and three non-union electronics firms in Ireland. There was greater satisfaction with the grievance procedures among employees in the non-union companies than among those workers in the unionised firms. As well, more of the non-union employees felt that their complaints were taken seriously.

Secondly, many organisations introduce participative voice programmes for performance/productivity reasons. This is grounded in the belief that employees can capably and substantively contribute to the improvement of organisation performance through their input (Lawler, 1986; Miller and Monge, 1986; Wagner, 1994). This was the most commonly reported motive of European managers in the European Foundation's EPOC survey of involvement practices in organisations throughout ten European countries (European Foundation for the Improvement of Living and Working Conditions, 1997).

Thirdly, both participation and grievance systems may be established for ideological reasons. A high proportion of the firms in the EPOC survey claimed that their motives for adoption of involvement practices were grounded in the belief that employees have a right to involvement and the organisation wants to improve the quality of working life for employees. For contemporary non-union organisations, attention to employee voice systems may become almost *de rigueur* in the wake of increasing expectations for participation. From an institutional theory perspective, firms risk losing legitimacy if they provide no method for dealing with employee grievances. Yet, only between 8 and 13 per cent of the non-union European firms in the EPOC survey claimed that current employee demands had motivated the introduction of direct participation practices.

Fourth, organisational size seems to play a role in the voice strategies a firm can and needs to adopt. The size of a firm:

> is a proxy for many characteristics that might be associated
> with voice. And conversely, it is the smaller enterprise
> which is least likely to offer a voice option . . . voice may
> exist in small firms, but not in the form of explicit ar-
> rangements. (Lewin and Mitchell, 1992: 106).

This may in part explain the dearth of formal systems in indigenous Irish SMEs.

Finally, the industry and culture of an organisation may determine the use of voice and involvement channels. Firms with
high rates of employee turnover and intermittent employment at-
tachments are likely to see little point in establishing and operating voice mechanisms. For example, industries that have highly
seasonal market cycles may shy away from elaborate and involved
voice systems because the employee/organisation relationship is
tenuous. Likewise, firms are also less willing to involve contract
and other peripheral workers in organisational decision making.

GRIEVANCE SYSTEMS

> For many people, the most critical right of employees is the
> right to due process (Velasquez, 1982: 327).

Grievance systems are mechanisms for employees to voice problems, complaints or disputes within the organisation. McCabe
(1988) argues that grievance systems are essential within organisations to ensure due process. However he goes on to stress that
"the greater necessity is to have a grievance-prevention procedure" (1988: 8) because a truly just system would avoid putting
employees through the stress involved in the pushing to get their
complaints resolved. Yet, even in the best of organisations, problems are inevitable and thus so are employee grievances. It is not
the existence of complaints per se that spells trouble for industrial
relations within an organisation; it is the lack of due process to
resolve the grievances. Complaints, while indicators of underlying
problems, have the benefit of offering the organisation information to enable it to improve.

With these issues in mind, a grievance system can be seen to serve three primary functions. It can allow employees to air their complaints, thus operating as an "escape valve" to vent issues of concern to employees. It can provide the organisation with an opportunity to resolve the grievances and ensure that employees' rights are upheld. Thirdly, the grievance process can offer the organisation rich insights into the nature of organisational problems. These insights emerge partly from the grievance process itself when it forces a deep analysis of specific focal problems, but also from an analysis of the broad pattern of issues which emerge over time.

Currently, the most common formalised non-union grievance systems include: open-door policies, corporate ombudspersons, and formal appeal systems (i.e. hierarchical appeal procedures, internal tribunals and peer reviews, and arbitration). These practices are not mutually exclusive. In fact, most larger companies would use more than one formal practice, in conjunction, as part of their overall system for grievance management. Open-door policies, and in some cases ombudspersons, can be useful for handling grievances at an early stage. They offer employees a relatively quick and informal outlet for voicing complaints or concerns with management decisions or organisational practices. Formal appeal systems differ from open-door policies in that they provide employees with the opportunity to have their grievances reviewed in a systematic process. Each of these grievance systems is described below.

Open-door Policies

The "open-door" policy is a pervasive practice in non-union firms. It appears to be the most common method of hearing employee complaints (McCabe, 1988). A study of 78 US leading non-union manufacturing companies found that 80 per cent of the firms had a formal open-door policy which was documented in their employee handbooks (McCabe, 1988), while another study suggests that almost all managers claim to have an "open door", whether or not a formal policy exists in their firms (Balfour, 1984).

The actual open-door practice in place within organisations varies widely. At one extreme, is the full open-door policy which claims that managers are accessible without exception. That approach was summed up by the manager of one US manufacturing company as: "Employees can talk to anyone at anytime about anything" (McCabe, 1988: 120). Such a policy is merely an ideal that is difficult and often impractical to implement due to the pressure on management time. At the other end of the continuum we see companies attempting to manage these difficulties by limiting the times management are accessible and limiting the levels of management (e.g. immediate supervisor only) which employees may approach. A danger in this approach is the message it may send to employees regarding management's true openness. Herein lies a key challenge in maintaining an open-door policy: creating a system which conveys management's openness and willingness to listen, but which is still feasible and practical in terms of management time spent on employee relations.

In McCabe's (1988) study, the employee handbook descriptions of the open-door policies seem to implicitly reflect this challenge. The descriptions state that the doors of management are open, but almost always add that employees are strongly encouraged to see their supervisor first and to use the formal appeal process if their problem is still unresolved. Thus, the extreme open-door policy is usually symbolic only. How effective that symbolism is in creating the desired impression is debatable since employees very soon figure out just how "open" those doors are.

Evaluations regarding the outcomes of open-door policies are mixed. In theory the method can offer several important benefits. It can act as a quick and efficient mechanism for hearing complaints; it maintains informality in employee relations, and can build employee morale (McCabe, 1988). But these benefits only accrue if managers are seen as responsive and trustworthy (Carrell and Kuzmits, 1986). Otherwise, the system loses credibility. Employees will not use it and employee relations may be damaged, rather than enhanced.

One major concern with the open-door system is that it has no external input or third party monitoring to provide objectivity and ensure fairness. This is especially troublesome if the supervisor with the open door is part of the problem (Gordon, 1986). In such a case many employees are hesitant to use that open door to air their complaints. A full open-door policy in which employees may bypass their own supervisor and go directly to any higher level management might seem to offer a solution. Yet, many employees fear reprisal for going over the boss's head (Rowe and Baker, 1984). In general, there appears to be a natural scepticism on the part of employees who perceive that complaining can lead to stigma, retribution, or merely a waste of time.

Open-door policies which allow employees to bypass their supervisors have also been criticised for having potentially detrimental effects on supervisors' ability to manage. Pigors and Myers (1981) offer several arguments. First, bypassing the supervisor interferes with his or her need for information. As noted earlier, complaints contain vital information about organisational problems and current employee relations sentiment. If supervisors are left out of the communication chain, they get delayed second hand information and lose the opportunity to set things right on their own. Finally, the supervisor may also lose the respect of other subordinates or managers.

A counter-argument is that a full open-door system can provide useful information to top management about "problem" supervisors. If a supervisor is continually bypassed, it may signal a problem with that supervisor's management approach. As well, despite the criticisms, it seems clear that the need for a full open-door system remains strong for non-union firms. When disgruntled employees have little faith in their supervisor, an alternative channel must be offered if voice is to be meaningfully provided to all employees.

Some employee handbooks explicitly state that the employee need not fear reprisal for using the open-door system. However, the trust of employees is ultimately grounded in the actions of managers who handle complaints within the open-door system.

"At the first sign that the policy can backfire on an employee, it will lose its usefulness." (Suters, 1987: 102). All supervisors should be aware that if very few complaints are brought to them, this may be a positive sign of general contentment or it may signal that employees have lost faith in the open-door system and your role in it (Suters, 1987).

Ombudspersons

A corporate ombudsperson is an individual outside of the line management structure who is there is to listen to employees' concerns and to assist them in getting their problems resolved (Rowe, 1986). The form of assistance may involve merely facilitating the employee in using the appropriate formal channels for grievance resolution. Alternatively, the ombudsperson's assistance may extend to actually becoming involved in the resolution of the problem by counselling, advising, fact-finding, mediating, and acting as a go-between (Rowe, 1986).

The ombudsperson role may exist alone or in conjunction with a formal grievance procedure. In either case it provides a confidential and informal opportunity for employees to discuss problems they have in relation to the organisation. Common issues dealt with by ombudspersons include:

> promotion and demotion, performance appraisals, salary and fringe benefits, job security, company policies, discipline, termination, personality conflict, and management practices (Rowe, 1986).

The ombudsperson's role seems to become more important in larger firms where formal systems have become the primary channel for employee voice (Foegen, 1972). These formal systems can become slow and frustrating to an aggrieved employee. Ombudspersons provide an immediate, human response and can expedite the formal process. While an "open-door" policy may seem to offer the same benefits, the ombudsperson differs in that confidentiality is maintained, something which may be critical in the case of sensitive issues such as harassment or problems with management.

To be effective, an ombudsperson must be explicitly supported by the organisation and trusted and respected by employees. It may pose a challenge to achieve both simultaneously, since the fact that the ombudsperson is employed by the organisation may diminish his or her perceived objectivity. At Elan Pharmaceutical Technologies, a division of the Irish company, Elan Corporation, plc, this challenge seems to have been met in that the current ombudsman is viewed by management and employees alike as objective and level-headed. While it is difficult to pinpoint the source of his credibility, it may in part derive from the fact that he was promoted from within, having originally worked in R and D. Also, of the cases he has taken so far, the decisions have been roughly equally divided in favour of employees and management. Intel has also managed the challenge of dual credibility at its Irish plants by deliberately separating the roles of management advisors and employee advisors in any grievance issue. Employees are supported and advised through a grievance procedure by employee relations specialists who act as employee advocates. Management are advised by a separate group of human resource development representatives. Furthermore the ombudsperson (i.e. the overall site employee relations advisor) reports directly to the legal department in the US, rather than to the site manager. This may further enhance employee perceptions of the objectivity of the ombudsperson.

Formal Appeal Systems

Formal appeal systems usually include multiple stages. Most require that the employee first discuss and or file the appeal with their immediate supervisor. If not satisfied with the response, the employee can push their appeal to the next stage of the process which may involve review by a higher level of management, or the personnel officer or hearing officer. It is in the final stages that appeal systems in various firms distinctly differ. The final deci-

sion is made by either top management, an internal tribunal, or
arbitration. The distinct benefit of formal appeal systems is that
they can offer a clear, efficient and final resolution. Open-door
policies provide channels for employees to voice complaints and
assistance through fact-finding and mediation, but there is usually no formal requirement with these systems to provide a definitive response to an employee's grievance.

In an in depth case study of the appeal systems in three large
non-union firms in the US, Lewin (1987) found some interesting
patterns related to who uses the formal appeal system and what
types of appeals are most prevalent. Over a four-year period, the
most common set of issues taken up in appeals were related to *pay
and work assignments* (including pay rate, grade or level, overtime assignment, job classification, work standards, job assignment, work hours and safety and health). These accounted for
roughly one-third of the appeals. Almost as common in two of the
firms were *performance and mobility* issues (including performance evaluation, promotion, transfer, layoff, recall, and training).
The next most appealed issues were *discipline* (including suspen-
sion, demotion and discharge) and *benefits* (including holidays,
personal leave, seniority, and insurance benefits). The remainder
of the appeals involved issues of *discrimination* or *supervisory relations,* and interestingly, each accounted for less than 10 per cent
of the total appeals in each firm.

Although each grievance system allowed for four steps, the vast
majority of the cases (approximately 83 per cent) were settled in
the first or second step of the process. The most protracted appeals centred on discipline, discrimination, and performance and
mobility. These issues tended to go through more appeal stages,
which may reflect both the difficulty in making clear judgements
on these issues and the seriousness of the outcomes for both parties.

Now we turn to specific features of three different approaches
to the multi-stage formal appeal process.

Hierarchical Appeal Process

In a hierarchical appeal process, an employee appeal goes through several layers of management with a written response at each stage. If the grievance is still not solved to the employee's satisfaction, he or she may take the appeal to a final stage in which a designated member of top management — typically the chief executive officer, managing director, or the company vice president of human resources — makes a final decision.

One clear advantage of this approach to companies is that management retains control of all grievance resolutions within the firm. Therefore, management can strive for consistent decisions which support company goals. Yet, the system also has a distinct liability. It requires that managers sometimes go against decisions made by their own subordinate managers. They naturally would have a reluctance to do this because they might lose the loyalty of those who work for them. Even if this weren't actually the case very often in practice, the perception is still prevalent among employees using the grievance system (Caras, 1986). A hierarchical appeal system can thus lose credibility. It is partly for this reason that General Electric established a peer review panel in their Columbia plant.

Peer Review Panels and Internal Tribunals

Internal tribunals are panels which review grievance cases and recommend judgements. The membership of internal tribunals may be composed solely of representatives from management or employee peers of the grievant. However the most common composition is a mixed panel with a majority of peers. "Peer review panels" is the name given to the specific form of internal tribunal which includes peers. A new panel is usually formed for each case, although one member of management may be a continuing member.

Internal tribunals are typically added as an option or step in a grievance system, rather than a stand-alone. As with most formal appeal systems employees must first try to resolve the issue with their supervisor or higher management. When other methods fail, they have the opportunity to use a tribunal. The decisions of tribunals are usually binding and many human resource managers who have implemented these systems claim that this finality is important for maintaining credibility in the process (McCabe and Lewin, 1992). The argument is that if either management or peers could overturn a disappointing decision, the process would quickly lose legitimacy as a true mechanism for due process.

As a voice system to handle grievances, internal tribunals seem to be fairly successful. Some employees see peer review panels as more legitimate than a traditional hierarchical grievance system. In the traditional system a manager would have to go against a decision made by a manager below them. The founders of the peer review systems at Control Data and at General Electric's Columbia plant found that managers were reluctant to do this. Managers were concerned about losing the loyalty of their subordinate managers if they ruled against them (Caras, 1986). Another "flaw" in the system is the lack of independence among the levels of management. An executive of Control Data explains:

> . . . if I'm a middle manager and a grievance comes across my desk, I'm probably going to review it with my supervisor, explain how I plan to handle it, and solicit his or her support (Olson, 1984: 59).

This naturally reduces the likelihood that a superior will come to a different decision if the grievance gets pushed up to his or her level. In contrast, a panel of peers and randomly chosen management would be viewed as more objective assessors.

The positive effects of peer reviews do not seem to be limited to providing a fair and factual review. Comments from those who have implemented peer review systems indicate broad ranging positive effects on employee relations, including greater employee commitment and trust, and reduced employee/management conflict (Caras, 1986). Another very beneficial effect of the peer review system is that they can encourage managers to be more careful in following company policy and communicating effectively with their employees (Coombe, 1984) because they realise that their decisions and actions may be exposed to outside scrutiny. In this sense, they can provide a kind of preventative health mechanism.

While many companies view the internal tribunal as a viable and effective method "for providing employees with a real and truly legitimate voice" (McCabe, 1988), there are potential downsides which must be considered. Some companies have found the system to be costly and time-consuming. Especially costly are the lost work hours from panel members, and in the case of geographically dispersed firms, the cost of travel for panel members. This latter issue would be less problematic for most firms in Ireland. One perceived problem of peer review panels that peers will not be objective in their reviews and will always side with the grievant. Yet current evidence suggests that this has not been the case in practice. One assessment of peer review panels found that they decided in favour of upper management about 60 per cent to 70 per cent of the time (Reibstein, 1986). McCabe (1988) also found employee members to be stricter in their judgement of the behaviour of their peers than of managers. This is particularly interesting given that some companies allow the grievant to choose at least one of the peers, and they have the option of choosing an employee who is a friend. Even if objectivity is not a significant problem, are there no residual bad feelings between panel members and the grievant following a decision in favour of management? The survey research evidence and case studies are silent on this issue. Another perceived problem with peer review panels is that they impose on management rights (e.g. by ruling on policy), but this has not proven to be a real issue for most firms adopting peer systems because they simply delimit the scope of issues which can be brought before the panel. In other words, organisations choose to keep company policy outside the realm of appealable issues, but allow the appeal of the application of policy (McCabe, 1988).

Arbitration

Arbitration is necessarily the last step in any formal appeal system because its decisions are binding. McCabe (1988) describes a typical arbitration system. The employee must first discuss the grievance with his or her supervisor, as is the case with all formal appeal systems. Then he or she can consult with personnel who will try some form of mediation. If an employee's problem has not been solved at these earlier stages by management, personnel, or through mediation then the employee can have his or her problem reviewed by an arbitrator or a group of three arbitrators. The arbitrators may be people internal to the organisation or may be professional arbitrators.

Arbitration is at present one of the least common means of resolving employee grievances within non-union firms (McCabe and Lewin, 1992). Two large studies of US firms in the last decade found between eight and 20 per cent of the firms with a formal appeal system offered arbitration as a final step (Delaney, Lewin, and Ichniowski 1989; McCabe, 1988). It is not clear that its relatively scarce existence is due solely to inherent difficulties with the system. McCabe (1988) conjectures that arbitration may suffer some from a poor image. Some management view arbitration as an invasion of management rights because management "must relinquish their control over their own destinies into the hands of a third party" (McCabe, 1988: 66). It seems that while management realise the necessity of some check in the organisational system to ensure due process, they still want to retain their right to keep some issues non-negotiable. However, in practice this has not been a problem. As is done with internal tribunals, most companies narrow the scope by allowing the arbitrator to rule only on whether their existing procedures and policies have been followed properly, rather than whether the existing procedure/policy itself is unfair. Therefore the companies retain their right to establish and maintain their own policies and rules. To further delimit the issues open to arbitration, some firms allow arbitration only for specific appeals, dismissal being the most common.

One might view the existence of third party adjudication as a strength of arbitration because it increases perceptions of objectivity in the process. From that perspective, McCabe (1988: 78) argues that the availability of arbitration in an organisation "should assure employees that their company is fair-minded to the degree of willingness to have their grievance settled on neutral ground". Yet, the independence of the arbitrators from the disputants may simultaneously be seen as troublesome. Can fair judgements about "local" issues be made by those outside the system who do not understand the context in which the dispute arose? These two opposing viewpoints may reflect one of the inherent challenges in gaining widespread acceptance of arbitration.

Beyond its role in serving due process following disputes, arbitration has been found to have a useful influence in shaping better policies and practices within the firm (McCabe and Lewin, 1992). The Northrup Corporation's director of industrial relations in 1982 commented that the existence of arbitration can force the clarification of rules, procedures and documentation to ensure that grievances don't arise; and it can encourage managers to be more consistent and careful in exercising good judgement knowing that their behaviour may be put to review (cited in McCabe, 1988)

However, as with all current complaint systems there are disadvantages with arbitration. The most severe downside seems to be the high costs associated with the process. The organisation is usually responsible for paying the arbitrator, and perhaps the employee's representative. Travel for witnesses has also been a major cost in the past, but deliberation can now be accomplished through teleconferencing in firms with such resources. One must also factor in the cost of time in preparing the case. Despite all of these costs, arbitration is still much less expensive than a lawsuit, and quicker to resolve (McCabe, 1988). Thus, for serious disputes, it may be a viable alternative.

The Overall Effects of Grievance Systems of Voice

Having described the specific grievance systems in current practice, a summary and categorisation of the overall benefits and costs of these systems can be made. Firms which choose to adopt a system of voice for employees to put forward complaints or grievances can expect impacts on at least four aspects of the organisation:

- The first impact is a direct effect on *due process*. A well-designed grievance system "offers the employee security in knowing that the organisation is less likely to make arbitrary decisions" (Luthans, Hodgetts, and Thompson, 1980: 137–38). The grievance system provides a method for resolving employee complaints which is "prompt, just, and consistent" (O'Brien and Drost, 1984: 67). Litigation can be an alternative mechanism for establishing due process, but it is more costly to the employer and results in much-delayed decisions. If "justice delayed is justice denied" then an internal grievance system offers a better chance of due process (McCabe, 1988). There doesn't appear to be any evidence that grievance systems are abused by employees taking frivolous or false grievances forward.

- Second, the establishment of a grievance resolution system within a firm can have important symbolic effects on employee relations. A well designed and credible system sends a message to employees that the organisation is serious about due process and considers employee rights to be paramount (McCabe and Lewin, 1992). Thus it can be "valuable for morale" (Ewing, 1982) and positive employee management relations. A grievance system can improve and facilitate communication between employees and management and it can minimise rumours by "clearing the air" (Ewing, 1982). Finally, grievance systems which provide real voice and fair resolution can eliminate many of the problems and conditions which lead employees to seek union representation (O'Brien and Drost, 1984).

- A third impact of grievance systems is their role in preventative health and organisational learning. Current perspectives on the positive effects of conflict suggest that bringing conflict out into the open can improve innovation and organisation learning by increasing the number of ideas and providing deeper insight into organisational problems (Baron, 1991). Complaint systems can provide opportunities to solve problems before they develop into larger more difficult ones (Gill and Loftus, 1984). Intel's operation within Ireland has recently redesigned their employee grievance system and added a strategic role for the ombudsperson. This role includes analysing the emergent pattern of grievances to identify ways in which management can improve and hopefully preclude many future complaints. For example, a recent review indicated that first-line managers might benefit from training in handling employee complaints at that early stage. The grievance evidence suggested that poor handling of the grievant's complaint early on by supervisors sometimes escalated the grievant's concerns and dissatisfaction. Grievance systems can also keep managers "in check", knowing that a problem may be brought to a neutral investigator (Ewing, 1982). The Site Employee Relations Advisor at the Intel operation in Ireland observes that this is one of the challenges of the system for managers. They may have to work much harder to resolve issues at their level to avoid being investigated through the grievance system.

- The fourth and perhaps most complex effect of formal grievance systems is their role in influencing employee turnover and performance. Access to a grievance system seems to positively affect employee willingness to stay in the organisation (Olson-Buchanan, 1996; Spencer, 1986). Spencer (1986) also found that the number of voice mechanisms seems to be important. He found that a high number of mechanisms was associated with employees' perceptions that they would be able to resolve problems with the organisation and perceptions of the effectiveness of the organisation's procedures for dispute resolution.

However, these findings only reflect employees' reactions to the *existence* of a grievance system. When we look at the outcomes for employees after they have actually used the system, a different and more complicated picture emerges. Lewin (1987) conducted probably the first systematic study of the consequences of grievance filing and found some perhaps disturbing results. In a sample of three large US-based companies (representing financial services, aerospace and computer manufacturing), employees who filed a grievance were more likely than non-grievance filers to lose their job in the following year through layoff or discharge or other involuntary separation. They were also significantly less likely to be promoted than non-filers. Furthermore, those who took their cases to the final stages of the appeal process received lower performance ratings than other employees, even though the grievance filers actually had slightly higher performance ratings than their peers prior to the grievance process. Finally, those who filed a grievance were also more likely to leave of their own accord. In addition to these negative effects for employees who used the system, there were similar results for the supervisors/managers of the employees who filed the grievances.

Lewin (1987) interprets these findings as evidence that a system of reprisal might be in effect, whereby those who avail of the voice system and those who supervise them are later punished with the loss of job and promotion opportunities. He cautions that a grievance system may appear to be effective because it generates a quick settlement and relatively equal wins for both sides, yet the effectiveness of the system as measured by its ability to ensure due process is called into question if the users suffer retribution.

Lewin's study only looked at the effects on employees one year later, so we don't know the long-term effects on employees who file grievances. Yet the outcomes in that first year would suggest that those employees would not fare as well as their peers. Looking beyond the direct effect on grievance filers, there may also be a secondary effect on those employees who witness the results of the grievance system. If employees perceive that filing a grievance leads to retaliation, they will likely hesitate to use the system themselves. Lewin (1987) found supplementary data to support this conjecture. He surveyed a broad sample of employees in each of the firms in his study to ascertain why people might not use the appeal system. The most common reason for not filing appeals was "fear of management reprisal". This was true even for management/administrative employees. Yet, "three-quarters of this group believed that they had one or more work-related issues that merited appeal filing" (Lewin, 1987: 499).

Evidence for possible punishment effects of grievance filing was also found in a field study conducted by Klaas and DeNisi (1989). They found that performance ratings were lower for those who filed grievances which targeted the managers' actions or decisions, rather than a more general grievance with the organisation. This was particularly true if the employee won the dispute. To further isolate these apparent effects of filing an appeal, Carnevale, Olson, and O'Connor (1992) conducted a laboratory study. They found that managers seemed to punish grievance filers by giving them lower performance ratings, even though objective performance was held constant by having confederates turn in exactly the same work.

Despite this evidence, it could be argued that punishment is not necessarily the only explanation for the low performance ratings of grievance filers subsequent to the grievance. Rather, their low performance ratings may reflect, in part, real performance drops due to lowered motivation following the appeal process. Olson-Buchanan (1996) designed a laboratory study to test this hypothesis. She found that when given access to an appeal system, those who chose to file a grievance had significantly lower objective job performance than those who didn't file (including those who had a reason to dispute). In other words, those who "suffered in silence" contributed more to their jobs than those who took the opportunity to exercise their voice. She also found that those who had a bona fide grievance but were not given access to a grievance system had similarly low performance to that of the filers.

In summary, it appears that access to a voice mechanism seems to be important for maintaining employee performance, but paradoxically, when employees actually avail of the system the employee/management relationship is disturbed. Drops in performance occur which are not necessarily or wholly due to the conflict that precipitated the grievance. Could it be that the trauma of the grievance activity itself (compare with civil litigation cases for harassment) damages employee relations, or perhaps the filing of the grievance increases the salience of the conflict and prevents the parties from putting the issue behind them? Taking the above studies as whole, the performance differences seem to be attributed to both real performance differences and punishment effects. Perhaps an interaction among the two is at play (Olson-Buchanan, 1996). For example, an employee may drop their performance, the supervisor punishes, and it spirals downward. Alternatively, the supervisor may initiate the spiral. In either case, both parties are probably in a state of increased sensitivity after the grievance filing and may be more likely to look for evidence of negative behaviour on the part of the other.

Challenges in Implementing Grievance Systems in Ireland

While internationally there are many lessons regarding the implementation of effective grievance systems, the practical relevance of these lessons for the Irish context need to be considered carefully. Two key features of many grievance systems, especially hierarchical appeal systems, internal tribunals and arbitration are their formality and impersonal nature. These features have been considered strengths of the systems in some respects because they are assumed to contribute to objectivity and confidentiality. Yet, formality and impersonal administration may not always suit the values and norms within the Irish context. Nor are they always necessary in particular organisational contexts. For example, the formal grievance system has rarely been utilised at the Dell sales and marketing operation in Bray, Ireland, which has been in existence since 1993. But rather than this being a sign that the system is not credible or useful, it appears to reflect more on the utility of the informal systems of voice within the firm. Employee surveys indicate that employees feel that management are easily accessible (all employees work in the same building in an open-space plan). Employees have respect for management and feel comfortable approaching them in an informal way about any issue or complaint. Similarly, informality is valued at Elan Pharmaceutical Technologies. The Human Resource Director suggested developing a hotline for employees to voice issues or concerns of a general nature. Employees could call the number anytime and leave their issue/concern on the voice mail. To keep it anonymous, yet open, responses to the issues would be posted on a notice board. Currently, there is little support for the idea which is seen as "very American". Employees are not accustomed to using an impersonal system such as that and want to be able to go in to their supervisor and chat about their problem.

Another key challenge is to create a system that is credible and useful to both employees and management. With these objectives in mind, Intel recently established an innovative redesign of their human resources department along with their grievance system.

BOX 2.1: INTEL IRELAND'S GRIEVANCE SYSTEM

Intel Ireland has developed a new human resources structure aimed at providing a better service to their customers (i.e. the employees). Although there were no employee complaints about the old system, the human resources department viewed the old structure as flawed because the same people who advised employees on problems with management were also advising the management on the same problems.

To develop the new human resources structure, a team of employees from different areas of the business was formed to give input. Their ideas were taken on board in the new design. The new structure is comprised of two "organisations", one which provides advice to managers and the other to employees. Human resource development representatives advise managers on problems and other issues such as training for staff.

For employees, advice is offered in a tiered system:

- At the first level, a call center with a toll free number is available for employees to call from work or home to get any queries answered. As well, employees are encouraged to discuss any problems with their supervisor, as in a typical open-door or hierarchical appeal process.

- At the next level, employee relations specialists deal with problems which are not satisfactorily resolved at the first level or problems which are more complex — for example when an employee feels he or she are being harassed by another employee or a supervisor. The specialists may act as an employee advocate, as a coach, and as an intermediary.

- Finally, problems that have not been resolved at the department level are investigated by the site employee relations advisor who acts as a type of ombudsperson. She investigates the problem from scratch and interviews all involved. This position reports directly to Human Resources Legal in the United States. This reporting structure allows the ombudsperson the freedom to judge cases on their merit without undue pressure to appease the management on site.

- The open-door data is tracked and analysed twice yearly to see if any trends are emerging and to develop preventative measures. The information is published to employees through department/shift meetings and through the company newsletter.

This new system has been in place for a little over one year and the feedback has been quite positive. Employees now feel that there is a place for them to have their queries and concerns resolved. Human resources believes that with the introduction of the new system employees seem to be opening up much more. While it was not apparent at the time, under the previous system employees were more reticent about discussing the real issues behind a problem. Thus, even though employees never complained about the old system, it appears that they may have been wary.

Ewing (1982) warns companies not to even introduce due process mechanisms unless they are committed to non-autocratic management. Such systems inevitably bring management decisions into question. Managers who do not embrace a participative approach may suffer "wounded pride". Furthermore, introducing a system then balking when it exposes a problematic or faulty management decision might merely have the effect of bringing vividly into the open the desired autocracy of management, and in turn disturb the trust and morale of employees (Ewing, 1982). It is to this issue of participative management that we now turn.

INVOLVEMENT SYSTEMS

Involvement programmes can be viewed as mechanisms which invite and encourage employee voice in organisational decision-making. Involvement programmes can function as grievance channels also. But they go beyond merely providing systems to resolve individual complaints; they have the potential to offer a real opportunity to change and alter policies and practices of the firm. Some have argued that many forms of top-down communication (e.g., explaining to employees the reasons behind decisions) are also forms of employee involvement (e.g. Webb, 1989). Yet, if we include all forms of communication, even those in which employees have no real opportunity to contribute to decision making in any meaningful way, then the employee involvement label is at risk of being so diluted as to be synonymous with communication in general. Here the view of employee involvement encompasses channels of upward and two-way communication only.

As with grievance systems, a diverse array of involvement systems are currently in practice in non-union companies internationally. These include both direct and indirect involvement of employees. In indirect involvement schemes, employees gain voice through representation, rather than direct participation. Direct employee involvement programmes can be categorised into two types: delegative participation and consultative participation (Geary, 1998). Consultative participation offers employees the opportunity to offer suggestions and ideas regarding organisational decisions, but management is left with the prerogative to incorporate these ideas or not. Delegative participation, sometimes referred to as "on-line" participation, goes beyond mere voice to actually allowing employees an active role in organisational decision making by empowering them to make decisions in the course of their work (Batt and Appelbaum, 1995). For example, current systems include job enrichment and self-managing work teams. These forms of *delegative* participation are covered at length in Chapter 10, "Managing Work Organisation: Moving Towards Task Participation". In this chapter the focus is on *indirect* involvement and *consultative* forms of direct participation which have collectively been referred to as "off-line" participation (Batt and Appelbaum, 1995). Specifically, our purpose here is to assess the capability of these participation systems to enable effective employee voice and the impact of that voice on employees and the organisation as a whole.

Indirect Participation

Indirect participation within non-union companies typically takes the form of joint employee/management committees whose purpose is to provide a forum in which employee ideas and concerns are discussed and negotiated with management. The participation is indirect in that only representatives of various employee groups within the firm speak on behalf of all employees. Such a system offers the benefit of creating a regular and consistent forum to resolve issues of concern both to management and to employees, and to reduce uncertainty for employees regarding organisational decisions. However, there is also a potential inherent in these representative forums to create effects which reach beyond the resolution of specific issues. One personnel director of an Irish firm has observed that their representative forum seems to make managers more aware of their actions. They recognise the need to be more careful now that there is a relatively public forum in which their actions may be reviewed. However, he also notes a potential downside. Managers may be more hesitant to give a warning to an employee with a true performance or disciplinary problem. Thus the increased conservatism may be beneficial in preventing managers from being capricious, but may also inhibit them from giving negative feedback or even from making difficult or contentious decisions where they adversely affect their employees.

Consultative Forms of Direct Participation

Consultative forms of direct participation vary quite significantly in their structure and in the degree of real voice offered by the practice. The most extensive study to date of direct participation practices within Europe, including Ireland, is the EPOC survey conducted by the European Foundation (European Foundation for the Improvement of Living and Working Conditions, 1997). Here we draw on their typology and describe three distinct forms of consultative direct participation currently in use.

"Face-to-face" Systems

The term "face-to-face" systems is used to describe formal communication forums which create opportunities for direct discussion and feedback between management and individual employees. Some forums are designed with a relatively open agenda which allows employees to bring up any ideas of interest to them. One example is open-door policies which allow informal communication between supervisor and employee. Another increasingly used face-to-face forum is the performance appraisal and development meeting. The current trend toward performance management has encouraged a shift in the focus of appraisals — away from a one-way communication of evaluative information to a two-way dialogue aimed at employee development (e.g. Neale, 1991). Thus, performance appraisal and development meetings under performance management systems become one-on-one channels of voice for employees. For example, in theory, employees may raise issues regarding resources, work systems or management structure which may be affecting their work performance. In practice, the employee's willingness to use this channel to voice such issues depends on the trust inherent in the management/employee relationship which in turn rests on the foundation of trust created by the larger network of management and voice systems.

A recent complement to the supervisor/employee face-to-face meeting is the "skip-level interview". Here the organisation legitimises one-on-one meetings between an employee and his or her manager's manager. At the IBM operations in Ireland, such meetings can be requested by the employee, or the employee may be asked to attend one. Not all employees would experience one of these every year. The meetings are usually initiated on an ad hoc basis to get information regarding some issue. For example, employees may request a meeting because they are interested in other opportunities outside their current department and thus feel uncomfortable talking to their current manager. A manager may request one to get feedback on ideas for changes in the department.

"Arms-length" Systems

"Arms-length" systems provide employees with mechanisms to offer ideas and express opinions, but in a less exposed or even anonymous channel. Typical examples include suggestion schemes and opinion surveys. According to the EPOC study, "arms-length" systems were the least common form of direct participation in Ireland. Yet companies operating within Ireland who currently run such programmes have experienced some strong benefits. IBM has a long history of employee surveys. Results of the surveys are fed back to employees and the data is analysed to determine where improvements in organisational functioning can be made. According to an IBM human resources consultant within the firm's Ireland operations, surveys enable the organisation to increase their knowledge and understanding of issues affecting employees. For example, a recent survey was designed to help the company better understand the challenges employees face in balancing the demands of both work and personal life. The results indicated that many employees were responsible not only for children, but also for adult dependants. IBM is continually developing its existing range of work/life programmes to facilitate employees to balance work/life demands.

Yet surveys are not without their challenges. Chris Argyris (1994) has provocatively argued that surveys gather useful information but fail to deal with the more fundamental issue of why the problems raised in the surveys have not surfaced and been resolved in the course of day-to-day work. Argyris asks the question, What is it about the structure and nature of the organisation that prevents people from openly voicing ideas and concerns and taking initiative to get them implemented or resolved. Furthermore, the very nature of the survey as a voice channel (impersonal and one-directional) leaves the employee respondent free from responsibility for the problems uncovered. Argyris's (1994) arguments are a fair criticism of surveys used as the primary or sole voice channel in an organisation — if the organisation wants to create true involvement. Specifically when used in isolation, surveys may stem from a culture of low participation, and they ensure that that state is perpetuated. However, used in conjunction with a set of voice channels, surveys can be viewed as a complementary component which offers the advantage of confidentiality, access by all employees (rather than a privileged few), and a comparative perspective on issues facing employees in different departments.

Suggestion schemes, like surveys, can be created as an anonymous system to allow employees freedom to suggest ideas that might give insult to the current management. For example, IBM in Ireland runs a "Speak up" programme in which employees can voice opinions, suggestions and criticisms anonymously by contacting the "Speak up" co-ordinator. The co-ordinator then finds someone to answer the query or investigate the issue. Employees get feedback on their query from the co-ordinator. Some suggestion systems are specifically non-confidential because they offer awards for profitable ideas (e.g. Scanlon systems). Here the system is used as a mechanism for encouraging innovation and providing incentives to employees.

"Group Consultation"

"Group consultation" forms of participation are typically comprised of problem-solving groups which are asked to provide ideas on particular issues or practices within the organisation. Current examples include regular employee/management meetings (e.g., team briefings, departmental meetings, and annual employee forums), temporary groups such as ad hoc non-management task forces and focus groups, and more "permanent" groups such as quality circles which meet on a regular basis. In each of these forums, employees meet in groups, usually with their supervisor and/or facilitator, to solve specific work problems and discuss ways of improving products, services or processes of the organisation.

Probably the most well-know of these forums is the quality circle which became popular in the 1970s and 1980s in the USA and Europe. Although the idea was initially developed in the USA, the technique was refined and popularised in Japan, then imported back into the US (Hayes, 1981) and to Europe. While the impetus and spread of the technique is probably attributable to the increase in global competition and increased market demands for improved quality (Poole, 1986), the side benefit for employees has been the legitimacy of a direct channel for employee voice, and the increased power that may accrue to workers through this system. However, the perceived success of quality circles has often fallen short of early expectations. Despite initial enthusiasm on the part of top management and employees actually involved in the circles, the life cycle of the groups often fades into disillusionment and in some cases abandonment. A seven-year study of French organisations adopting quality circles suggests that, like many management fads, circles wane when their development is unsupported and isolated from the larger organisational context and human resource practice (Chevalier, 1993). For example, quality circles may not be actively supported by the management hierarchy and may end up working on problems which have not been clearly linked to organisational goals. The recommendations of the groups may extend to other departments and thereby infringe on the domain of other managers who may have no incentive to co-operate.

Finally, employees within the circles may initially be motivated by the novel opportunity for voice and change, but their enthusiasm declines in the face of lack of progress and nothing more than symbolic rewards for their investment. Chevalier (1993) found that quality circle groups that did eventually work through their life cycle and come out successful were those that were well integrated into a supportive organisational system.

Perhaps due to the disillusionment with quality circles, many organisations are using other forms of problem-solving forums such as focus groups and task forces, along with regular employee/management meetings, including regular team briefing, departmental and site-wide employee meetings. Dell, in its Bray operation in Ireland, uses all of these forums in an integrated system designed to deal with a range of challenges from localised short-term problems to organisation-wide long-range issues.

BOX 2.2: VOICE SYSTEMS AT DELL IRELAND

Dell Direct in Bray, Ireland has established an extensive array of voice channels which together form a system of complementary components. Such a system not only provides multiple channels for employees to voice their ideas and concerns, but also ensures that the organisation receives input on issues ranging from individual performance problems to organisation-wide operational issues. The components of Dell's voice system would normally include:

- *Weekly meetings:* Teams of usually ten to twelve people meet with their immediate manager to discuss challenges related to meeting short-term goals. They tackle the operational issues of how they are doing against their targets and what they can do to improve. The communication during the meetings is two-way, rather than being run as a management information/directive session.

- *Monthly meetings:* Once a month, all of the teams within a given department would meet to address broader issues affecting the operations of the entire department. Here communication travels both upward and across project teams.

- *Quarterly site meetings:* Every three months a meeting of all employees from the site is organised. These meetings are designed to combine both business and some fun, and are usually held off-site. Employees get briefed on how the business is doing and the strategic direction of the company. Employees themselves fully participate in these events by delivering some of the information.

Not surprisingly, with each successively larger group, the opportunity for individual voice becomes increasingly difficult, thus creating more voice in operational rather than strategic decision making. However, several additional voice channels are offered which increase employees' opportunities to become involved in the organisation:

- *"Viewpoint":* An employee opinion survey is regularly conducted. It covers a wide range of issues including: employee perceptions of how the company is satisfying their customers, perceptions of product quality and range, how teams are working together, accessibility of management, trust, fairness, etc. The results are analysed for two sets of themes: those that pervade the entire site and those that relate to specific departments.

- *Focus Groups and Action Plans:* Following the administration and analysis of the "Viewpoint" surveys, departmental themes are fed back to employees and employee focus groups are formed. These focus groups meet to discuss the opportunities to improve and are then sent off to get more information and feedback from fellow employees to gain more ideas for exactly how to improve things. The senior management team meets with all focus groups to agree action plans. The plans may involve tasks for teams, for managers and for the focus groups. After the action plans are in the implementation phase, follow up meetings are held with the focus groups to assess how well the implementation is going.

In addition to all of these channels for groups of employees to voice ideas and concerns, Dell has established a system which offers individual employees the opportunity to offer their input in a more intimate environment.

- *Performance appraisal system:* Every quarter, each employee has a one on one meeting with his or her team leader. They discuss how well the employee has met objectives for the previous quarter. They set future objectives, and discuss any developmental needs — e.g., training the employee may require. In between each formal quarterly meeting, employees and team leaders are encouraged to meet regularly to assess progress. These quarterly appraisals feed into an annual performance appraisal which is linked to the compensation system.

With respect to voice management, one of the biggest challenges Dell sees right now is not the issue of providing more channels of communication, but communicating effectively and consistently. There is the potential for employees to be overloaded with communication. The challenge is to ensure that the important issues are not lost in the wealth of information being passed along several media. With this in mind, Dell is constantly reviewing its communication channels and exploring other alternatives to ensure that its communications are effective.

Prevalence and Scope of Consultative Direct Participation

The EPOC study provides us with rich data on the extent to which these participation practices have been adopted in Ireland and across nine other European countries. The survey sample included both unionised and non-unionised organisations. However, the results indicated that in Ireland, as well as the majority of the other European countries surveyed, the existence of a union, or any form of employee representation, seemed to play no role in the introduction of direct participation. Organisations without representation were just as likely to adopt direct participation as those with representation. This finding is consistent with other similar research on U.K. practices (Wood and de Menezes, 1998).

Across the workplaces in the ten countries surveyed, 82 per cent had some form of direct participation. However, the number of workplaces adopting each individual practice was considerably lower. Roughly one-third of the workplaces adopted any given consultative participation practice. Many of the organisations practised more than one form of participation, yet in almost one-half of the workplaces they practised only one or two forms. Equally important as the incidence of these various forms of participation is the level of involvement afforded by each. The EPOC study was able to assess the scope of participation by asking about the number of issues employees were consulted on within each form of participation. The scope was measured in terms of high, medium, and low. In approximately one-half of the workplaces practising participation, the scope of participation was low. Looking at all firms in the survey, only between five and eight per cent had adopted consultative participation practices which allowed a high scope of issues on which employees were consulted. In short, while the large majority of European companies appear to be engaging in at least one involvement practice, the actual breadth of practices and scope of involvement is significantly smaller.

Within Ireland, the incidence and scope of participation are quite close to the European average. It appears that "face-to-face" forms of consultative participation are the most popular, followed by permanent group consultation, such as quality circles. Interestingly, delegative forms of participation proved to be more common than any of the consultative forms. As well, the scope of participation was somewhat higher where delegative participation was adopted.

The Overall Effects of Participation on Organisations and the Workforce

Participation, in its various forms, has been reported to have a number of important effects on employees, organisation performance, and workforce rationalisation. First looking at the effects on employees, active opportunities for participation seem to shape employee attitudes and performance. Recent reviews of the participation literature have found consistent evidence to suggest that consultative participation in its various forms is related to employee satisfaction and productivity (Miller and Monge, 1986; Wagner, 1994). These relationships held true for different types of organisations (i.e. service, manufacturing, research) and different job levels. Still, the positive impacts on employee performance and satisfaction, as well as employee commitment, appear to be stronger for delegative participation than for consultative or indirect participation (Batt and Appelbaum, 1995). What may be key in the relationship between participation and employee satisfaction is the effect on job characteristics. Batt and Appelbaum (1995) found that where participation (regardless of whether it was delegative, consultative or indirect) provided the job characteristics of *task identity* and *task significance*, satisfaction was increased. Task identity exists when the job allows the employee to complete a whole and identifiable piece of work. Task significance is the perception that the job is important and makes a meaningful contribution to the organisation or society.

Interestingly, it appears that a participative climate has a greater effect on employee satisfaction than the existence of participation in specific decisions (Miller and Monge, 1986). This may have more to do with the pervasiveness of the participation and the openness it encourages when there is a general climate of participation, rather than any inherent disadvantages with programmes which solicit participation in specific decisions. Finally, participation can also reduce feelings of alienation (Zeffane and Macdonald, 1993). This may be increasingly critical in contemporary organisation contexts in which the workforce is faced with uncertainties due to changes brought about by competitive pressures.

The EPOC study provides findings concerning management's perceptions of the effects of participation on the economic performance of organisations based in Ireland. It is interesting to note that only 57 per cent of the respondents answered the questions regarding impacts. The researchers comment that this may reflect the difficulty managers have in determining the effects of direct participation. Among the surveyed firms in Ireland, 95 per cent of those using direct participation reported an improvement in the quality of their product or service. Over half (57 per cent) of the organisations reported a reduction in their costs, and 64 per cent saw reductions of their throughput time. Finally, Ireland ranked third highest among the ten countries in terms of the number of workplaces (79 per cent) that indicated their output had increased since the introduction of direct participation.

In addition to these positive effects on economic performance, a significant concern may be the effects of participation on the rationalisation of the workforce. Across the ten countries surveyed, the majority suffered no reduction in employees or managers in the short term, and had a stable or positive medium-term employment pattern. In approximately one-third of the organisations adopting direct participation there were layoffs in the short term. However, half of these organisations were able to make up for these losses in the medium term with increased employment, sometimes beyond the original level. Within the Irish organisations, only 22 per cent suffered any short-term layoffs and more than half of those were able to compensate for the losses with increased employment in the medium term.

Challenges in Implementing Participation Programmes

In keeping with the concern of this chapter, a key issue to consider in establishing a participation system is the degree of real voice and involvement created by the system. In an extensive survey of private-sector employees in Australia and New Zealand, Drago and Wooden (1991) found that the formal participation programmes such as quality circles, employee involvement groups, and productivity improvement teams did provide real influence, as perceived by employees. However, not all formal participation programmes will be viewed by employees as real and substantive voice channels. The level of employee involvement depends both on the potential inherent in the mechanism itself, and the manner in which the system is implemented. This may account for Miller and Monge's (1986) finding of a stronger effect on employee satisfaction from perceived versus actual participation. In other words, many existing practices provide voice in name only.

The perception of voice develops where employees can detect a link between their input into the voice channel and decision making by the organisation. With delegative participation, this

link is inherent in the voice channel because employees, by definition, make organisation decisions in the course of their work. With
consultative participation, there is a discontinuity between employee input and organisation decision making because management retains the right to use the input as it sees fit. Thus, the
challenge of implementing a voice system which is perceived as
more than a channel for employee venting is significantly greater
with consultative participation.

AN INTEGRATED APPROACH TO VOICE AND INVOLVEMENT

Many recent studies have looked at an array of voice and involvement practices in combination with other human resource
practices (e.g. Cooke, 1994; Delaney and Huselid, 1996; Huselid,
1995; Huselid, Jackson, and Schuler, 1997; MacDuffie, 1995;
Schuster, et al., 1997). An interesting finding from this research is
that voice and involvement practices tend to correlate with other
progressive human resource practices, and that the entire "bundle" or configuration strongly impacts on firm performance. Thus,
while this chapter has sought to describe the unique challenges
and benefits of individual voice practices, the net effects of these
practices probably can be understood more fully by analysing the
entire configuration of management practices within an organisation system. Each voice channel is embedded within a larger set of
voice channels, and in turn, that set is embedded in the larger
context of the organisation's structure, culture, management practices, and employment relations. The argument here is that employee reactions to, and use of, any individual voice channel are
shaped by the context within which the channel is embedded.

Looking at individual voice channels existing within a network
of channels, a number of potential synergies may emerge. First,
one voice channel can shape and support others. For example, information gained through surveys and suggestion systems can be
used to modify the nature of grievance systems or performance
and development meetings. At Dell, survey data were used to form
focus groups, which in turn were used to develop action plans

which then led to the adaptation of other organisation practices. Second, a sheer variety of channels provides insurance that ideas and concerns will not remain filtered at the lower ranks. IBM currently has a broad network of voice systems (including: a grievance process, a suggestion system, skip-level interviews, employee/management forums, performance appraisal and development, employee surveys, and newsletters). IBM's belief is that multiple channels ensure that each employee will find at least one mechanism with which they are comfortable. One employee may choose to voice ideas in a survey if he or she prefers anonymity; whereas another may be more comfortable using a focus group if he or she is encouraged by social support.

We would also expect unique effects arising from the integration between voice and involvement channels and the organisation's management practices, structure, culture, and employment relations. Voice and involvement systems rely on other management practices to provide support. For example, training may be necessary for both management and employees to enable both to understand the grievance process or participation practice and to implement it. The structure and culture of the organisation may facilitate or neutralise the effects of any voice and involvement system. A highly bureaucratic organisation with a culture of authoritarianism and defensiveness will inevitably create a true test for the organisation's commitment to voice and involvement. For example, introducing quality circles or "skip level" meetings and then getting management resistance to any ideas that emerge will serve to expose management's entrenched philosophy of bureaucracy and control, and to weaken the tenuous bonds of trust between employees and management. If employment relations deteriorate on any issue, the success and credibility of any individual systems becomes tenuous (Storey, 1992: 111).

SUMMARY

A wide variety of voice and involvement practices are in use by contemporary organisations. There is little data on the prevalence of grievance practices in non-union firms in Ireland. Those that exist appear to be more informal and less elaborate than those used in large US organisations. Involvement practices do appear to be common in firms in Ireland, yet the range and scope of such practices within any individual organisation are fairly restricted. Although many small companies here may actually have substantive involvement, yet not have a "formal" programme in place.

The evidence is clear that both grievance and involvement practices shape behaviour and attitudes within organisations. Employee complaint systems not only provide a vehicle for employees to vent and seek due process, they also generate useful information to management about problem areas within the organisation. For example, these systems expose policies that are viewed as unfair or ambiguous, managers who may be acting inappropriately, or education and training which may be useful to employees. Thus, grievance systems can create some of the same benefits as participation systems. At the same time, participation by employees can help to develop and operate a useful and acceptable grievance system. In fact, for any firm that claims participative management, soliciting employee ideas on the design of a grievance system is a natural, if not necessary, approach (McCabe, 1988).

The challenges involved in adopting voice systems are also numerous. In the Irish context, organisations may be concerned about creating a grievance process which is objective and consistent, yet not overly formalised and impersonal. Other challenges include avoiding negative repercussions for employees who file grievances and minimising any perceived threat by management to their power and discretion. Reprisals for employees who complain may result in employees refusing to use the grievance system. While the lower number of complaints may give the appearance of success, it may actually reflect apathy and distrust. Implementing participation practices poses the challenge of not merely providing channels for employee voice to be heard, but simultaneously puts the onus on management to demonstrate that the ideas are somehow incorporated in management decision making. A participation system that does not provide meaningful voice will likely suffer disuse. Finally it is argued that the entirety of the voice and involvement network integrated within the larger organisation system sends a message about the openness of management to employee voice. An integrated system conveys a clear philosophy, rather than a few token practices.

References

Argyris, C. (1994): "Good Communication that Blocks Learning", Harvard Business Review, July–August: 77-84.

Balfour, A. (1984): "Five Types of Non-union Grievance Systems", *Personnel*, 61: 67–76.

Baron, R.A. (1991): "Positive Effects of Conflict: A Cognitive Perspective", *Employee Rights and Responsibilities Journal*, 4: 25–36.

Batt, R. and Appelbaum, E. (1995): "Worker Participation in Diverse Settings: Does the Form Affect the Outcome, and If So, Who Benefits?", *British Journal of Industrial Relations*, 33: 353–78.

Caras, H.S. (1986): *Peer Grievance Review — A Proven Approach to Employee Problem Resolution*, Washington, DC: CUE — An Organisation for Positive Employee Relations, National Association of Manufacturers, No. 41 — Studies in Employee Relations.

Carnevale, P.J., Olson, J.B. and O'Connor, K.M. (1992): "Formality and Informality in a Laboratory Grievance System" in Lind, E.A. (Chair), Analyzing Organisational Grievance Systems. Symposium conducted at the conference of the International Association for Conflict Management, Minneapolis, MN. Cited in Olson-Buchanan, J.B. (1996): "Voicing Discontent: What Happens to the Grievance Filer After the Grievance?", *Journal of Applied Psychology*, 81: 52–63.

Carrell, M.R. and Kuzmits, F.E. (1986): "Grievance handling in Nonunion Organisations", in *Personnel: Human Resource Management*, (second edition), Columbus, OH: Merrill Publishing.

Chevalier, F. (1993): *Managerial Fads and Longitudinal Research — Focus on Quality Circle Programs*, Presented at European Group for Organisational Studies, 11th Colloquium, Paris, July 6–8.

Cooke, W.N. (1994): "Employee Participation Programs, Group-Based Incentives, and Company Performance: A Union/Non-union Comparison", *Industrial and Labor Relations Review*, 47: 594–609.

Coombe, J.D. (1984): "Peer Review: The Emerging Successful Application", *Employee Relations Law Journal*, 9: 659–71.

Delaney, J.T. and Huselid, M.A. (1996): "The Impact of Human Resource Practices on Perceptions of Organisational Performance", *Academy of Management Journal*, 39: 949–69.

Delaney, J.T., Lewin, D. and Ichniowski, C. (1989): "Human Resource Management Policies and Practices of American Firms", BLMR No. 137, Washington, DC: US Department of Labor, Bureau of Labor/Management Relations and Cooperative Programs. Cited in McCabe, D. M. and Lewin, D. (1992): "Employee Voice: A Human Resource Management Perspective", *California Management Review*, 34: 112–23.

Drago, R. and Wooden, M. (1991): "The Determinants of Participatory Management", *British Journal of Industrial Relations*, 29: 177–204.

European Foundation for the Improvement of Living and Working Conditions (1997): "Towards New Forms of Work Organisation — Can Europe Realise its Innovative Potential?: An Interim Report of the Results of the EPOC Questionnaire Survey of Direct Employee Participation in Europe". Luxembourg: Office for the Official Publications of the European Communities.

Ewing, D.W. (1982): "Due Process: Will Business Default?", *Harvard Business Review*, 60: 114–22.

Foegen, J.H. (1972): "An Ombudsman as Complement to the Grievance Procedure," *Labor Law Journal*, 23: 289–94.

Freeman, R.B. and Medoff, J.L. (1984): *What Do Unions Do?*, New York: Basic Books.

Geary, J. (1998) "Managing Work Organisation: Moving Towards Task Participation?" in Chapter 10 of this volume.

Gill, B.W. and Loftus, D.B. (1984): *Union-Free Complaint Procedures — 25 Samples*, Washington, D.C.: CUE — An Organisation for Positive Employee Relations, National Association of Manufacturers, Number 41 — Studies in Employee Relations.

Gordon, J.R. (1986): "Approaches to Resolving Grievances in Non-union Organisations", in *Human Resources Management: A Practical Approach*, Boston: Allyn and Bacon.

Hayes, R.H. (1981): "Why Japanese Factories Work", *Harvard Business Review*, July–August: 57–66.

Hirschman, A.O. (1970): *Exit, Voice, and Loyalty*, Cambridge, Mass.: Harvard University Press.

Huselid, M.A. (1995): "The Impact of Human Resource Practices on Turnover, Productivity and Corporate Financial Performance", *Academy of Management Journal*, 38: 635–72.

Huselid, M.A., Jackson, S.E. and Schuler, R.S. (1997): "Technical and Strategic Human Resource Management Effectiveness as Determinants of Firm Performance", *Academy of Management Journal*, 40: 171–88.

Klaas, B.S. and DeNisi, A.S. (1989): "Managerial Reactions to Employee Dissent: The Impact of Grievance Activity on Performance Ratings", *Academy of Management Journal*, 32: 705–17.

Lawler, E.E. III (1986): *High Involvement Management*, San Francisco, CA: Jossey-Bass.

Lewin, D. (1987): "Dispute Resolution in the Non-union Firm", *Journal of Conflict Resolution*, 31: 465–502.

Lewin, D. and Mitchell, D.J.B. (1992): "Systems of Employee Voice: Theoretical and Empirical Perspectives", *California Management Review*, 34: 95–111.

Luthans, F., Hodgetts, R.M. and Thompson, K.R. (1980): "Dispute Resolution and Procedures for Employee Justice" in *Social Issues in Business*, third edition, New York: Macmillan.

McCabe, D.M. (1988): *Corporate Non-union Complaint Procedures and Systems: A Strategic Human Resources Management Analysis*, New York: Praeger.

McCabe, D.M. and Lewin, D. (1992): "Employee Voice: A Human Resource Management Perspective", *California Management Review*, 34: 112–23.

MacDuffie, J.P. (1995): "Human Resource Bundles and Manufacturing Performance: Organisational Logic and Flexible Production Systems in the Auto Industry", *Industrial and Labour Relations Review*, 48: 197–221.

Miller, K.I. and Monge, P.R. (1986): "Participation, Satisfaction, and Productivity: A Meta-analytic Review", *Academy of Management Journal*, 29: 727–53.

Neale, F. (1991): *The Handbook of Performance Management*, London: Institute of Personnel Management.

O'Brien, F.P. and Drost, D.A. (1984): "Non-union Grievance Procedures: Not Just an Anti-union Strategy", *Personnel*, 61: 61–9.

Olson, F.C. (1984): "How Peer Review Works at Control Data", *Harvard Business Review*, 62: 58–64.

Olson-Buchanan, J.B. (1996): "Voicing Discontent: What Happens to the Grievance Filer After the Grievance?", *Journal of Applied Psychology*, 81: 52–63.

Pigors, P. and Myers, C.A. (1981): "Complaints and Grievances", in *Personnel Administration: A Point of View and a Method*, ninth edition, New York: McGraw-Hill.

Poole, M. (1986): *Towards a New Industrial Democracy: Workers Participation in Industry*, London: Routledge and Kegan Paul.

Reibstein, L. (1986): "More Firms Use Peer Review Panel to Resolve Employees' Grievances", *The Wall Street Journal*, 3 December, sec. 2, 29, cited in McCabe, D.M. (1988): *Corporate Non-union Complaint Procedures and Systems: A Strategic Human Resources Management Analysis*, New York: Praeger.

Rowe, (1986): cited in McCabe, D.M., 1988, *Corporate Non-union Complaint Procedures and Systems: A Strategic Human Resources Management Analysis*, New York: Praeger.

Rowe, M.P. and Baker, M. (1984): "Are You Hearing Enough Employee Concerns", *Harvard Business Review*, 62: 127–35.

Schuster, F.E., Morden, D.L., Baker, T.E., McKay, I.S., Dunning, K. and Hagan, C.M. (1997): "Management Practice, Organisation Climate, and Performance", *Journal of Applied Behavioural Science*, 33: 209–226.

Spencer, D.G. (1986): "Employee Voice and Employee Retention", *Academy of Management Journal*, 29: 488–502.

Storey, J. (1992): *Developments in the Management of Human Resources*, Oxford: Blackwell Publishers.

Suters, E.T. (1987): "Hazards of an Open-Door Policy," *Inc.: The Magazine for Growing Companies*, January: 99–102.

Toner, W.P. (1987): Union or Non-Union? — Contemporary Employee Relations Strategies in the Republic of Ireland, unpublished D.Phil. thesis, University of London.

Velasquez, M. (1982): "The Right to Due Process" in Business Ethics: Concepts and Cases, Englewood Cliffs, NJ: Prentice Hall.

Wagner, J.A. III (1994): "Participation's Effect on Performance and Satisfaction: A Reconsideration of Research Evidence", Academy of Management Review, 19: 312–30.

Webb, S. (1989): "Feedback", *Industrial Society*, 21(2): 14–16.

Wood, S. and de Menezes, L. (1998): "High Commitment Management in the U.K: Evidence from the Workplace Industrial Relations Survey, and Employers' Manpower and Skills Practices Survey", *Human Relations*, 51: 485–515.

Zeffane, R. and Macdonald, D. (1993): "Uncertainty, Participation and Alienation: Lessons for Workplace Restructuring", *International Journal of Sociology and Social Policy*, 13: 22–52.

HUMAN RESOURCE MANAGEMENT AND INDUSTRIAL RELATIONS: SUBSTITUTION, DUALISM AND PARTNERSHIP

William K. Roche and *Thomas Turner*

The objective of this chapter is to outline the ways in which human resource management policies and practices come to bear on trade union representation and the conduct of collective bargaining between unionised employees and management. This is demonstrably a major issue in the Irish as in the wider European context. Ireland is a strongly unionised country, with long and deeply established traditions of trade union representation and collective bargaining. Unions enjoy considerable public and political legitimacy. Since 1987 they have played a pivotal role at national level under four successive tripartite national programmes covering pay determination, public policy, public spending and a range of areas of economic and social policy. In such a context a number of obvious questions arise as to the interface between HRM and trade unions.

Can HRM policies provide an effective means of assisting company strategies of union avoidance? How does HRM accommodate to trade unions and collective representation in companies where unions are strongly organised at workplace or enterprise levels? Can HRM policies operate effectively in such settings without reaching a rapprochement with collective representation? Can cases be identified where earnest attempts are being made to coordinate in some way HRM policies and collective bargaining?

What models of co-ordination are evident and what factors influence their adoption by the managements and unions involved? These are the major questions which guide the chapter. In seeking to answer them our focus will be on Ireland and we will attempt to use, where possible, data and research on the recent Irish experience of the diffusion of HRM-inspired policies and principles in a national context marked by extensive unionisation and high levels of union influence in public policy making.

We identify three broad ways in which HRM policies interface with trade unions and collective representation in companies and workplaces in Ireland. The first involves the adoption of HRM policies by companies as part of a strategy of union avoidance or "union substitution". The second involves the adoption of HRM policies in a manner which avoids co-ordination with collective bargaining and trade union representation, an approach which has become known in the literature as "dualism". The third involves the adoption of HRM policies in ways which seek explicitly to come to an accommodation with collective representation, by co-opting trade unions to joint programmes of change or workplace governance — a process which in Ireland has come to be known as the promotion of "partnership" at the level of the workplace and enterprise. We will discuss each of these three approaches in turn and conclude by considering the prospects of each approach.

THE ADOPTION OF HRM POLICIES AS PART OF A STRATEGY OF "UNION SUBSTITUTION"

HRM policies can be used to exclude unions either through the use of *suppression* tactics or *substitution* tactics (Kochan et al., 1986). In the former case, management vigorously resists union recognition and utilises "hard" HRM practices to suppress any tendencies towards unionisation (Storey, 1989). This approach is selective in its treatment of employees often distinguishing between core and peripheral employees and, in general, emphasises the use of labour in a flexible and cost-effective manner. A union suppression strategy is likely to occur in circumstances charac-

terised by a low threat of unionisation, such as in highly competitive sectors of the economy; where firms are small; where the
work is low skill; and where there is an unfavourable legal
framework for trade unions (Flood and Toner, 1997). A union substitution strategy focuses on removing the triggers to unionisation
through the use of so-called "soft" HRM practices. The "soft" version views employees as a resource to be developed, motivated and
integrated into the firm. This type of strategy is generally associated with large companies in profitable sectors of the economy
which have sufficient resources to ensure employees are relatively
well paid and elaborate employee voice and due process procedures are in place (Foulkes, 1980).

Here we shall focus chiefly on those companies which use HRM
policies as a union substitution strategy. In Ireland, substitution
strategies are almost wholly associated with greenfield sites
where companies set up with an explicit policy of remaining non-
union. There is little evidence at present to suggest that unionised
companies in established brownfield sites are attempting to de-
recognise and exclude trade unions on any significant scale. In
relatively highly unionised countries, such as Ireland, union exclusion strategies are more likely to be high-risk strategies for
employers, and there is always the possibility of a resurgence in
union strength in the long term (Storey, 1992). According to
Smith and Morton (1993: 101) in Britain, "the more common policy of employers is the implementation of partial exclusion policies
the object of which is to marginalise trade unions even while recognising their continued right to operate". Marginalisation is
achieved through the strategic management of certain critical
employee processes. The emphasis on more direct communication
with individual employees can, for example, be viewed as a usur-
pation of the "voice" function of trade unions (Storey, 1992). It is
appropriate, therefore, to view the marginalisation of unions in
the unionised sector as essentially similar in aim to union substitution strategies in greenfield sites. However, our focus in the
following sections is on the characteristics of companies in the
non-union sector, the specific human resource practices used in

medium and large non-union companies, and the management
advantages or outcomes of such a strategy.

A survey of 225 Irish enterprises with more than 50 employees
in 1995 indicated that 80 per cent of firms recognised trade unions
for collective bargaining purposes (Gunnigle et al., 1997a). Excluding public sector organisations, the figure for union recognition in the 195 private sector firms remained relatively high at 77
per cent, while 35 percent, or 45 firms, did not recognise a trade
union. However, as Roche and Turner (1994: 740) note, cross-
sectional surveys do not detect long-run trends. A study of companies with more than 100 employees setting up in greenfield sites
in the manufacturing and internationally traded services sectors
in the period 1987 to 1992 reveals a different picture (Gunnigle,
1995). Out of the 53 companies surveyed, 28 were non-union and
23 of these companies were of US origin, located mainly in the hi-
tech sector. Gunnigle concluded that non-unionism is increasing
dramatically in start-up companies and is particularly closely associated with US ownership. More recent evidence for the period
after 1992 appears to confirm this trend. In the period January
1994 to November 1995, a total of 32 new foreign owned companies employing more than 100 employees established subsidiaries
in Ireland. Only two of these companies recognised a trade union
and none of the US owned firms which accounted for 20 of the
companies, recognised a union (Hourihan, 1996). However, there
is some evidence to suggest that the increase in non-union companies is not just a function of US corporate preferences but is a
feature of a growing proportion of companies regardless of country
of origin. According to Turner et al. (1997) more recently established companies are more likely to be non-union than older established companies. While there is a need for more comprehensive longitudinal studies it appears that non-unionism is associated with country of origin and the date of establishment of the
company, with more recent companies having a greater propensity to remain non-union.

A common perception of large non-union companies is that
they are subsidiaries of multi-nationals, are generally character-

ised by good pay and conditions, have well-staffed personnel departments and sophisticated personnel policies which are devised in part to remove or substitute the triggers for unionisation (Foulkes, 1980; Kochan et al., 1986). Well known household names associated with sophisticated human resource approaches in Ireland are IBM, Hewlett Packard, Intel, Digital, Motorola and Verbatim (see Box 3.1).

According to Freeman and Medoff (1984) unions can provide an effective voice for employees with beneficial outcomes for the employer. The provision of a collective voice mechanism can improve the attitudes, morale and motivation of the work force by, for example, the use of a seniority mechanism for rewards, promotions and layoffs; the reduction of rivalry among workers allowing experienced workers to train and assist new workers; and ensuring a sense of fairness through formal due process grievance and discipline systems. However, it can be argued that large non-union companies with sophisticated HRM policies effectively substitute for union voice by providing a similar function. Such companies provide substantial information on how the company is performing, substantial investment in training and developing employees, often above average wages and conditions, apply seniority criteria in the case of redundancies, prioritise security of employment and provide formal discipline and grievance procedures (see Kochan et al., 1986; Flood and Toner, 1997). In a survey of 144 blue collar workers in 3 unionised firms and 101 workers in 4 non-union firms employing more than 200 in the hi-tech sector, Toner (1985) reported that morale was rated higher in the non-union companies. Labour turnover rates were similar in the union and non-union companies, and the reasons for leaving were broadly similar in both cases. Employee opinions on pay were similar but fringe benefits were rated higher in the non-union companies. Communication and consultation were rated better in the non-union firms, as employees felt that complaining about grievances was taken more seriously. Toner (1985) concluded that the four non-union companies appeared to enjoy more voice, better working conditions and higher morale.

BOX 3.1: "ELECTRONIC GIANTS KEEP UNIONS AT ARM'S LENGTH"

At the Intel factory in Leixlip, workers enjoy an "open door" policy in employee relations. Managers and shop floor workers have
the same dress code and business is conducted on first name
terms in an open plan environment. If workers have a grievance,
they can go straight to the superior of their superior. There are
business update meetings, staff lunches and a process of employee reward called FOCAL. The door, however, is closed to
trade unions. . . . Apart from the sophisticated communications
and grievance procedures, companies like Intel and Hewlett
Packard also offer considerable incentives to employees. Intel
workers have the opportunity to purchase Intel shares, up to a
value of 10 per cent of salary, at a discount of 15 per cent. The
shares can be cashed in within six months. . . .

Unions claim to have a "sleeping" membership in a number of
US electronics companies, one union official claimed to have 200
members at a factory in Cork, the union is not recognised by the
company. The membership is seen as a kind of insurance policy.
If times turn hard, the union membership will become active —
or so the theory goes. . . .

But evidence suggests that the human resources systems built
by the more powerful US electronics companies are robust
enough to sustain blips on the horizon. When Digital pulled out of
Clonmel, it did not prompt unionisation at the Galway factory.
Digital remains non-union despite the complete withdrawal of
hardware manufacturing in Ireland. Hewlett Packard survived a
major retrenchment in 1985 when pay cuts of 5 per cent were implemented in British factories. The company even withdrew complimentary ground coffee and biscuits from staff "think-ins". The
harsh measures did not ferment pro-union feelings.

Source: Excerpted from "Electronic Giants Keep Unions at Arm's Length",
Brian Carey, *Sunday Business Post*, 24 December 1995.

A more direct substitute for union voice is a company-based representation structure, such as a staff association or works council,
sponsored by the company itself. How independent such structures are is often difficult to assess, particularly as non-union
companies are not noted for providing access to academic researchers. However, a number of cases have arisen in recent years

where a staff association or works council have taken a company to the Labour Court in disputes over pay and conditions, indicating some degree of independence from management control. A notable feature of each of the cases is that the development of the representative structure occurred as a measure to block union recognition (Box 3.2).

BOX 3.2: UNION SUBSTITUTION AND STAFF ASSOCIATIONS — HOW ARE THEY ORGANISED AND WHAT DO THEY DO?

Saehan Media

When Saehan Media in Sligo was originally established in 1991, many of the employees joined SIPTU, but management refused recognition. Strike notice was given at one point, although it was later withdrawn, and the issue was the subject of a Labour Court recommendation in 1993, in which the Court took the traditional pro-recognition stance.

The employee council was formed to deal with negotiations on pay and conditions and took the company to the Court on a pay claim for terms above the PCW (LCR14866). In 1994 it negotiated 1 per cent more than the PCW increase. The following year it claimed 14.5 per cent for a one-year agreement, although the company offered 10.5 per cent over three years. At the hearing, the council showed its confidence about criticising the company, when referring to its "paltry wage policy", which had "increased in-house pressure from staff for trade union membership and recognition".

Elan Corporation

Elan Corporation's "Representative Council" was formed about 12 months ago, a few months before a Labour court hearing on union recognition. It has 22 members — four of which are management representatives. Each department or area across the plant (and a number of R&D staff based in Trinity College) elect the employee members, and the chairperson is elected by this group of 18. The chair rotates on a six-monthly basis, and council members are elected for a term of two years by secret ballot. Fifty per cent of the council members retire each year, so elections will be held each year in the first week of December.

> Each member represents a constituency of 40 to 50 people. A spokesman for Elan said that the council had discussed issues such as career progression, paternity leave, productivity bonuses, and a new share option scheme. It has also been used by management as a means of communicating product and business updates. He added that the council was not seen as a body with which to negotiate agreements, as much as a way for employees to have "an input into decisions".

Source: "Staff Associations — How are They Organised?", *Industrial Relations News*, 1996, 46: 17–20.

There is sufficient evidence to indicate that a number of well-known large non-union companies in Ireland have been successful in substituting comprehensive human resource practices for the traditional trade union voice. However, it is arguable as to what extent these companies are representative of the non-union sector. Gunnigle et al. (1997b) claim that only 7 of the 53 companies starting up between 1987 and 1992 had in place a comprehensive set of HRM policies which could be labelled as a sophisticated HRM strategy. Union avoidance in these greenfield sites, Gunnigle et al. (1997b: 123–124) argue, was predominantly achieved through extensive use of outsourcing, subcontracted labour and other forms of a typical labour. Blyton and Turnbull (1994: 252) in a review of HRM policies in non-union firms in the UK reached a similar conclusion and argued that non-union companies such as Marks and Spencer and IBM are the exception rather than the rule and that most non-union firms do not *need*, nor could the majority *afford*, to adopt a substitution strategy (italics in original).

Advantages and Outcomes of Union Substitution

There has been a large volume of empirical studies on the economic effects of trade unions, chiefly on labour productivity, but also on company profits and investment (see Freeman and Medoff 1984; Belman 1992). While the empirical results on union effects on productivity are inconclusive, the evidence appears to indicate that unions in manufacturing industries, particularly in the

United States, can reduce firm profitability by magnitudes that are economically significant. Thus it is plausible to assume that large non-union firms who invest in HR policies to avoid unionisation have rational economic grounds for believing that there are substantial advantages to remaining non-union. In a highly unionised country like Ireland, remaining non-union nevertheless carries a number of costs. Supervisors interviewed in union and non-union firms by Toner (1987) listed a number of disadvantages of a non-union strategy (quoted in Flood and Toner, 1997: 261):

- A non-union company has to offer pay and benefits at least as good as those offered by similar unionised companies.

- Management is afraid to enforce discipline.

- There is a lack of structure for dealing with grievances, safety issues etc.

- The fear of unionisation is a constant worry.

- The supervisors are monitored too closely.

- The non-union plant has to work harder at communication.

- Human resource policies are too costly in terms of the size and requirements of the personnel department (e.g. setting up appraisal systems etc.).

These constraints on managing without unions are referred to by Flood and Toner (1997) as a "catch 22" situation in which large non-union firms cannot take advantage of the absence of unions to reduce wages or benefits, ignore grievances or dismiss unsatisfactory workers at will for fear of bringing in unions. However, management in non-union firms believe there are a number of disadvantages associated with a union presence in a firm. The following main perceived disadvantages of unionisation emerged from Toner's (1987) interviews with supervisors in non-union and union firms:

- Communication with employees becomes more difficult.

- Unions make changes in work organisation more difficult.

- Unions give rise to demarcation problems.

- Unions impose restrictions on production.

- Unions impose higher staffing levels.

- Unions protect unsatisfactory workers.

- Unions inhibit individual reward systems.

- Unions promote an adversarial climate.

- Unions encourage the pursuit of trivial grievances.

- Unions cause strikes and stoppages.

These perceived disadvantages were however difficult, if not impossible, to substantiate and Flood and Toner (1997: 270) conclude that the major advantage of excluding a union is that it allows a company more scope to develop a "unitary culture" and to foster "warm personal relations" between management and employees. While it is difficult to quantify the advantages of these factors in economic terms, the economic research discussed above indicates that the presence of a union may adversely affect profit levels. This provides a plausible rationale for new firms, particularly of US origin, to adopt a union avoidance strategy. The perception that trade unions impact negatively on company performance allied to the strong anti-union values of US management are well illustrated in the comments of managers listed in Box 3.3.

"DUALISM": THE UNCOORDINATED ADOPTION OF HRM POLICIES IN PARALLEL WITH ADVERSARIAL INDUSTRIAL RELATIONS

Much the most common practice in Irish companies to date, the evidence suggests, has been for managements to adopt HRM policies in an essentially piecemeal or fragmented manner, without any attempt to use these policies to promote union substitution, co-ordinate these policies with collective bargaining or to involve unions in their uptake or implementation. Unions for their part at local or plant level appear often to have been predisposed to watch management innovations from the wings, adopting an unenthusiastic, vigilant or defensive posture.

BOX 3.3: RESPONSES FROM SENIOR MANAGERS IN FIVE NON-UNION US COMPANIES

"We are strongly anti-union. We will bend rules (corporate policy) to keep unions out. We had a recent flare up and went to the Labour Court. Up to 40 workers may now be in the union and we have several letters from the union. Corporate say they will pull out if the union is recognised: they feel unionisation here will also jeopardise jobs in the States. The senior vice-president came to XXX (Irish regional plant) to tell workers that they won't recognise a union — if that happens they will pull out. He said we have 70,000 employees in the US who are non-union — this cannot be risked." — Personnel Administrator

"We want to be non-union at all costs. XXXX (company name) is unionised in the States. They have had union problems there which prompted the decision to go non-union in Ireland: the decision was based on business reasons, particularly labour costs. We pay £10.00 an hour in the US and £4.50 an hour here." — Employee Relations Manager

"Our senior management in the US have a very strong non-union feeling. They have a fear of unions — possibly because they have no experience of dealing with them. We place a strong emphasis on direct communications as a key device in seeking to avoid union recognition. No-union status is part of our corporate philosophy." — Financial Controller

"We are not madly anti-union. However, non-union status is very much our preferred strategy as it is felt that unions impinge on our flexibility in work arrangements and operations. Also corporate management would react very badly if a union was recognised. We have a conscious non-union strategy and manage this very carefully. Key considerations in managing non-union status which have guided our activities are: (i) sector/location/scale, (ii) culture (iii) reward management: we shift emphasis away from group reward structures to individual rewards and (iv) single status." — Chief Executive

> "Maintaining non-union status is part of our corporate policy. The issue of union recognition has come up via an indirect approach from the SIPTU branch official and worker disquiet over low pay. The workers had a meeting, took advice from other unionised employees and decided not to join. We used the grapevine to communicate to workers that corporate HQ would not tolerate union recognition. At the same time we told the workers that we were improving pay and benefits. Labour turnover was 35 per cent at the start — now it's down to 5 per cent." — HR Manager

Source: P. Gunnigle, *Management Styles and Employee Relations in Greenfield Sites: Challenging a Collectivist Tradition*, Unpublished Ph.D. thesis, Cranfield. 1997: 139–141.

Survey Evidence

Evidence that such an approach has dominated the response of managers and unions in unionised companies to HRM can be found in a variety of studies and sources. First evidence from surveys of HRM in practice are consistent with the view that, on the whole, Irish companies have tended to adopt HRM policies selectively and opportunistically, with little apparent concern with the overall coherence of those policies, and that they have shown greater enthusiasm for policy innovations which pose least threat to areas traditionally regulated by collective bargaining. Roche and Kochan (1996) and Roche and Turner (1997) conducted secondary analyses of the data collected from 270 company-level HRM respondents (or their equivalents in the public sector) to the 1992 Irish survey conducted in association with the Price Waterhouse/Cranfield International Survey of Human Resource Management (cf. Gunnigle et al. 1994 for details of the survey). These studies show that it has not been common for companies in general to adopt consistent sets of HRM policies across the spectrum of HRM policy innovations. Few companies in the sample, for example, appeared simultaneously to have adopted performance-related payment systems, flexible models of work organisation, sophisticated recruitment and performance management systems, internal promotion policies, and active policies of communicating with their workforces on areas like company strategy or financial performance. Much more common was a pattern in which companies have adopted HRM policy innovations in one or several discrete policy areas only.

Moreover, the survey evidence suggests that the incidence of HRM policy innovations was lowest in those policy areas which traditionally have been most heavily regulated by collective bargaining and thus of greatest concern to trade unions. Less than 10 per cent of the organisations surveyed operated individual performance-related pay systems for all categories of staff, while 40 per cent had no individual performance-related pay for any category of staff. Similarly, 56 per cent of organisations operated no form of group performance-related pay systems, profit sharing or share ownership for any category of staff. Nearly half of the organisations surveyed reported that they had undertaken no initiatives to make jobs broader or more flexible in the case of any category of staff. Only 15 per cent reported that they had engaged in such flexible work organisation initiatives in the case of managerial, professional, clerical and manual staff categories. Considerably more common were HRM innovations in areas like communication, the use of suggestion schemes, quality circles etc. and in such areas of "flow" management as internal recruitment to promotional positions and performance appraisal, planned job rotation (cf. Roche and Kochan, 1996: 34).

Roche and Turner (1997) attribute such differences in the uptake of HRM innovations across the range of policy areas to the constraints, perceived or real, flowing from established traditions of industrial relations and collective bargaining in Ireland. Managements show greatest conservatism in adopting HRM innovations in the areas of pay and work organisation as these in practice tend to be most heavily regulated by trade unions. A significant change in these areas is likely to run into strong union resistance, or to require the active co-operation of trade unions. In contrast, unions are likely to be least resistant to management innovations in areas like communications, provided that they are not seen to threaten collective bargaining. In such areas management may enjoy scope to press ahead without engaging unions in their new policies. The same broadly holds for innovations in "flow" policies. Unions have not traditionally tended to negotiate over selection policies and techniques, other than perhaps by seeking to defend established recruitment channels. Nor have they attempted to negotiate over performance appraisal systems, other than possibly by trying to regulate the use to which appraisal records are put.

Reviews of Published and Unpublished Studies

Other sources of evidence are consistent with this broad picture. A document prepared for the National Economic and Social Council (NESC, 1995) summarises all Irish studies relevant to the theme of innovation in HRM and associated new manufacturing concepts and systems. Evidence is reviewed on the incidence of a wide range of innovations, including "world class manufacturing", buyer-supplier relationships, total quality management and quality circles, training and the involvement of employees and unions in dialogue over the introduction and use of new technology. Such evidence as exists on the attitudes of union members and officials to these innovations and the manner of their introduction is also examined. The study concludes that there was evidence of considerable innovation across Irish business. However, the pattern of innovation appeared uneven and fragmented, characterised by what the NESC document described as "cherry picking" or "sipping and tasting". Unions, by and large, were seen to have played a marginal role in total quality management and world class manufacturing (cf. Roche and Kochan, 1996: 35–7). A study conducted by Charles Sabel for the OECD (OECD, 1996) also concluded that innovation in HRM and new manufacturing concepts appeared widespread in Ireland but that the pattern of change was incremental and new techniques and traditional approaches often existed side by side. The study suggested that innovations in such areas as production systems, training, work organisation, compensation systems and information sharing arrangements usually occurred without the direct involvement of trade unions (OECD, 1996: 32). Changes in industrial relations structures and postures which might accord unions a more central role in overall processes of innovation were seen to have lagged behind other innovations in human resource management and work organisation. As active union involvement in innovation was uncommon, it is hardly surprising that union attitudes to innovations reflected mistrust and the adoption of a traditional adversarial posture. A survey by SIPTU of 50 instances in which world class manufacturing or related innovations were introduced between 1991 and 1995 concluded that employees and their union representatives believed that these innovations were primarily in the owners'/managements' interests and that some form of compensation was warranted if employees were expected to co-operate (SIPTU, 1995). An internal discussion paper on HRM in Ireland issued by SIPTU reflected the union's concern that in practice HRM policies commonly reflected a managerial change agenda which posed considerable threats to trade union representation and organisation (SIPTU, 1993).

In many ways Tim Hastings' study of the attempted restructuring of industrial relations and human resource management in the ESB in the early 1990s represents a case study in microcosm of incremental HRM innovation uncoordinated with collective bargaining and trade union representation. The study is summarised in Box 3.4.

As will be clear from the sections on "partnership" below, in more recent years the ESB sought to overcome dualism by promoting a more integrated programme of change with the co-operation of their trade unions.

Box 3.4: The Adoption of HRM Innovations Uncoordinated with Collective Bargaining: The Case of the ESB in the Early 1990s

Growing competitive pressure rooted in the EU-led liberalisation of the electricity market in the 1980s spurred the uptake of HRM principles and innovations by the managers in the power generation side of the company's business. The personnel department remained largely wedded to the established adversarial model of industrial relations and maintained traditional relations with trade unions. In the aftermath of a serious strike in the Board in 1991, the HRM change agenda was in the ascendant, championed still for the most part by line management in generation. Both HRM and traditional industrial relations postures continued to exist side by side and the HRM agenda was largely unco-ordinated with collective bargaining and relations with trade unions. This "dualism" was present both at the level of the company and at the level of individual establishments. For Hastings, a case study of a change management programme at the Board's key Moneypoint power station well illustrated both the prevailing approach in the company generally and the major tensions which inevitably arise where HRM-inspired initiatives are adopted in parallel to established adversarial collective bargaining in a highly unionised company:

"The evidence from Moneypoint pinpoints the major pitfalls in launching a human resource type initiative in an environment with a deeply embedded adversarial industrial relations system and culture. . . . The "dualistic" tensions between both pillars of the initiative, the industrial relations arm and efforts at opening up communication/trust/participation, threw up several neutralising factors. Staff were simultaneously being asked to share a future agenda with management for station co-operation, while at the same time [being asked to] face reductions in numbers, cuts in overtime and an era of almost constant change through benchmarking with operations elsewhere" (Hastings, 1994: 152–3).

Source: T. Hastings, *Semi-States in Crisis: The Challenge for Industrial Relations in the ESB and Other Major Semi-State Companies*, Dublin, Oak Tree Press, 1994.

Irish Evidence in Comparative Context

The Irish evidence of widespread but incremental innovation through HRM-type policies, frequently without the involvement of unions, is similar to evidence on prevailing patterns on change in the United States, Europe and the United Kingdom. In the case of the US, a review of workplace innovation over the past decade points to widespread but piecemeal experimentation with new forms of work organisation (teamwork, quality circles, TQM programmes etc.), new compensation systems and new selection and performance management systems (Ichniowski et al., 1996). One of the reasons given for the lack of coherence in change programmes and their often observed failure to take root is labour-management distrust, sometimes intensified by employer attempts to win union support for change programmes in existing unionised facilities, while engaging in union avoidance strategies in other sites (Ichniowski et al., 1996: 327–9). John Storey's research on change programmes in major UK companies in the private and public sectors during the 1980s and early 1990s pointed to a "dualism" in management postures which commonly involved innovations in policy areas least amenable to union influence or resistance and a "war of attrition" in relations with unions in areas where they were capable of exerting control (Storey, 1992). Marino Regini's research on innovation in major European companies also concluded that the dominant management response to intensified competition was to engage unions in change initiatives when necessary while stopping well short of any attempt to restructure the overall character of relations between unions and employers. Regini refers to this posture as "pragmatic eclecticism" or "secluded co-operation" (Regini, 1995: Ch. 7).

Possible Effects of Uncoordinated HRM Innovations

The common view of commentators internationally is that for HRM innovations to prove effective in enhancing company performance, they must first involve coherent sets of policy changes, and secondly, dovetail with attempts to build new and more co-operative relations with unions (cf. Kochan and Osterman, 1994; Pfeffer, 1994). Substantial empirical evidence in support of these propositions has been reported in the United States (Kochan and Useem, 1992; Huselid, 1995; Ichniowski et al., 1996). Evidence also exists for the United Kingdom that cohesive sets of human resource policies enhance organisational performance (Guest and Hoque, 1996). Whether the impact of HRM policies is moderated in unionised companies by the manner in which they are co-ordinated with collective bargaining has not been addressed directly in quantitative research. UK research evidence does however suggest that multiple unionism — which clearly adds to the task of articulating HRM policy innovations effectively with collective bargaining — exerts a significant drag on performance. Surprisingly, single union recognition arrangements, which are often taken to reflect union involvement in an integrated package of HRM initiatives, also seem to exert a modest drag on performance, as compared with non-union companies (Guest and Hoque, 1996: 25–8).

Hastings' study of the ESB experience in the early 1990s and the SIPTU survey of employee and union responses to change programmes point to the dangers that HRM and related innovations which fail to take account of relations with unions may prove ineffective and even intensify mistrust and adversarialism. A paradigm case of an instance in which HRM-related innovations were originally both poorly co-ordinated in themselves and uncoordinated with collective bargaining was provided by the subject of a study by the advisory service of the Labour Relations Commission. The company attempted to introduce world class manufacturing in 1995, with what the LRC saw as an inappropriate combination of policies, and without seeking to co-ordinate WCM innovations with collective bargaining. The result was a serious deterioration in industrial relations and an increased reliance on third parties to resolve resulting grievances and disputes (see Box 3.5). These problems were tackled through the negotiation of a "partnership agreement" between the company and the unions in 1998.

BOX 3.5 WORLD CLASS MANUFACTURING UNCOORDINATED WITH COLLECTIVE BARGAINING

Using consultants, the manufacturing company began implementing WCM in 1995 to move to a more customer-driven and competitive approach to production. The WCM initiative involved a new shop floor management structure which provided for an operations manager, four production group leaders and one maintenance group leader per shift. In order to facilitate the target performance level, employees could be required to work on two machines, a practice known as "machine banking".

The LRC found that many staff interviewed during the course of their review appeared not to know that the changes undertaken were part of a WCM programme. The principles underpinning WCM were not understood, and communications generally at the plant were such that significant changes in a range of areas led to "fear, mistrust and suspicion", resulting in resistance to change. In spite of the philosophy of continuous improvement supposed to underpin WCM, staff accused management of what the LRC report described as an "uncompromising, dictatorial" style. New team leaders were seen as having been promoted to positions of leadership without being accorded the necessary authority. The quality improvement programme was seen to have led to increased responsibilities for staff in the areas of paperwork and quality measurement. "Machine banking", particularly on machines which were not located close together, resulted, according to staff, in increased pressure, wastage and reduced quality.

As management saw it, the WCM programme met with a "culture of non-cooperation". A large increase was registered in the processing of grievance and disciplinary issues. Management accused the union of resisting change through the excessive use of procedure. It was alleged that petty issues were routinely processed through company procedures. Absenteeism was also seen as a major problem. Incidents of unofficial industrial action also occurred at the plant.

In 1998 the company and its union entered a "partnership agreement" to tackle the shortcomings identified.

Source: *Industrial Relations News*.

It would be invalid, however, to propose in any simple, deterministic manner that HRM innovations un-coordinated with collective bargaining will necessarily have negligible or negative effects on organisational performance. Cases can be found of high performance companies which emphasise direct staff involvement in HRM-type initiatives and policies, but choose to maintain traditional arms-length adversarial relations with unions. The viability of such an approach, and in particular the degree to which it impairs the effectiveness of HRM initiatives, is likely to be moderated by a number of factors. Among the most important of these will be the level of union organisation at workplace level, the level of attachment of employees to unions and the degree of influence unions have exercised over areas of employment central to HRM policies and innovations. The higher the level of union organisation, the greater the level of employees' attachment to unions and the more influence or control unions have gained over areas of employment which HRM policies and innovations seek to address, the greater the likelihood that such policies and innovations will be at best ineffective if they are not co-ordinated with collective bargaining.

THE ADOPTION OF HRM POLICIES AS PART OF A STRATEGY OF PROMOTING "PARTNERSHIP"

Very much less common in Ireland to date are attempts by management and unions to co-operate in the implementation of HRM and associated innovations through explicit initiatives to link HRM policies with change in the conduct of industrial relations. In recent years, however, there has been growing interest in what is now commonly referred to as the promotion of "partnership" at enterprise and workplace levels through joint management/union programmes of change. In one way or another, these programmes involve the co-ordinatation of HRM initiatives with the conduct of collective representation and with collective bargaining.

"Partnership" and New Industrial Relations

The concept of "partnership" has also been referred to in the wider literature, under the rubric of terms such as the "mutual gains model", "jointism", "joint decision-making", "joint governance" or "new industrial relations" (Kochan et al., 1986; Verma and Cutcher-Gershenfeld, 1993; Cutcher-Gershenfeld and Verma, 1994; Kochan and Osterman, 1994). The central principles common to this approach can be outlined as follows.

- Management seeks to win the consent of unions to change, innovation, the introduction and operation of HRM and related policies and wider managerial and business decisions, by granting unions a voice in decision-making on a non-adversarial or consensual basis.

- To this end managerial policies commonly seek to meet central union concerns, particularly in areas such as employment security, the preservation of good pay and conditions and the underwriting of union recognition and security.

- The scope of union voice may be narrow (confined to specific levels, areas or issues) or broad (possibly encompassing business strategy and a wide range of levels and aspects of enterprise and workplace governance); and the channels through which it is given expression will vary from case to case.

- Unions are willing, in return, to work co-operatively with management plans and policies and encourage their members to co-operate with HRM policy innovations, new principles of work organisation and management initiatives to promote competitiveness.

Models of Partnership in Ireland

Three broad models of partnership are apparent in recent Irish experience. These exemplify the principles outlined above to varying degrees, and in different ways, but all reflect an underlying concern on the part of management to integrate HRM policies and related innovations in work organisation and production systems with collective representation through trade unions. In each case unions have also shown a willingness to co-operate with programmes of change and innovation, or to work through non-traditional and non-adversarial channels to explore with management possible blueprints for the reconstruction of industrial relations.

A Consultation-focused Model

This model approaches the co-ordination of HRM policies with collective representation and bargaining through the medium of consultative arrangements with trade unions. Unions are involved in company policies and operations through regular briefings of shop stewards and union officials on management plans and their implications; through the routine provision of information on company plans and performance; through regular consultation and possibly through involvement on task forces and project teams. No new joint management/union structures (e.g. plant or works councils or committees) are established, however, to give institutional expression to "partnership", and no new ground-rules are agreed which give unions formal or de facto rights of co-decision making over any areas of company policy. Consultative channels may exist side by side with collective bargaining. The information and security provided by extensive consultation may encourage unions to support — and certainly not to fear — direct employee participation in quality circles, continuous improvement programmes, teams, project groups etc. and to accept performance management and appraisal systems, performance-based pay and other HRM policies.

This model equates with partnership as practised in some companies in manufacturing, healthcare and electronics industries in Ireland. Aughinish Alumina, in Limerick, provides one such example, where management has embarked on a programme of innovation and change focused on "de-layering", facilitative and leadership-oriented supervision, a shift from individual working to team working and a wider programme of culture change emphasising the replacement of an "adversarial culture" with a "collaborative culture" (Sweeney and Mulcahy, 1997). Relations with unions in the context of the new approach emphasise ongoing consultation and information exchange through established channels. In addition, a joint management/union evaluation of self-managed work teams has been undertaken. The Shannon-based German fine chemicals manufacturer, SIFA Ltd, concluded an agreement with SIPTU in early 1997 which formally endorsed a "partnership" approach to relations between the company and the union. The SIFA/SIPTU agreement provides for a TQM programme at the 150 employee plant, fully flexible working practices, a performance management and appraisal system and team working (IRN, 1997, 3: 18–9). The company acknowledged the union's key role in supporting its business plan. The parties declared themselves committed to giving "operational meaning" to partnership through the union adopting a "supportive and participative role" on behalf of its members, extending to an annual review of the company's plans and goals. While no new joint management/union structures are identified, the agreement specifies that the union will explore a role in a company-wide representational framework, providing for what is described as "more streamlined company-wide communications and dialogue with employees" (IRN, 1997, 3: 18).

SmithKline Beecham's plant in Carrigaline, Co. Cork concluded an agreement with SIPTU in 1994–95 which made provision for the introduction of world class manufacturing, skill-based pay, performance management and appraisal and team working. The company committed itself to support the new production model through heavy investment in training and development (IRN, 1995, 7: 14–6) The agreement was concluded with SIPTU, and the company planned to extend the principles involved to relations with craft workers and their unions. The agreement and its implementation were predicated on ongoing co-operative relations with the unions and contained provision for the establishment of joint review teams to monitor progress towards world class manufacturing. These teams were explicitly intended to

concern themselves with "business issues" and to channel industrial relations issues to the appropriate forum (IRN, 1995, 16: 15).
The agreement brought to an end a long-running industrial relations saga at the company (formerly known as Penn Chemicals)
which arose when management offered individual contracts to
employees on terms more favourable to those negotiated by
SIPTU. As a result, a dual payment system developed, and the
unions believed that the rewards strategy was an attempt to bring
about de-recognition.

The international literature on partnership might be disposed
to describe such a consultation-focused model as a relatively weak
version of partnership in that it relies primarily on the active
maintenance of co-operative relations with trade unions through
information exchange and consultation and stops short of structures or arrangements which accord unions a more active voice in
company decision-making, other than perhaps on an ad hoc basis.
For the companies involved, however, the model provides a viable
and highly effective basis for winning both employee and trade
union acceptance of HRM policies, flexible working arrangements
and high levels of staff involvement in work. Several companies
adopting this model are viewed as exemplary cases of highly effective employee relations in which harmonious relations with trade
unions are seen to benefit both the company and employees.

Joint Decision-making Models

A second approach to co-ordinating HRM and related innovations
with collective representation involves the establishment of new
joint management/union structures of varying scope to give employees, through their trade union representatives, a formal voice
in company decision-making. These structures, which might cover
specific areas of decision-making (for example, training or product
policy) or a wide spectrum of issues (for example, plant operations, or competitive strategy and business unit strategy) accord
unions formal, or de facto, joint decision-making powers. The parties are expected to make decisions through consensus, or unions
enjoy parity or near parity of membership on joint committees.

Again formal partnership arrangements of this type are likely to endorse, support or otherwise smooth the path of initiatives focused on direct employee involvement. Collective bargaining channels continue to co-exist with the joint structures, but the lines between the two channels may become blurred in ways that neither party finds unacceptable. For example, once decisions have been reached in the joint forum, it may prove easier for the sides to reach agreement in subsequent rounds of negotiations on the issues involved. Likewise, grievances and disputes which might otherwise have sparked rounds of negotiations can be reduced in frequency or intensity.

Such joint decision-making arrangements are as yet uncommon in Ireland. The "steering team" at the Bausch and Lomb sunglasses plant, located in Waterford, and the "task group" in Waterford Crystal provide significant and contrasting examples. The Bausch and Lomb initiative with SIPTU represents a joint decision-making or joint governance arrangement of wide scope which oversees the operation of the plant's production system (IRN, 1995, 19: 12–14). The Waterford Crystal initiative with the ATGWU and other unions is narrower in scope, focusing mainly on joint decision-making on product strategy — an area of manifest importance for the company and its employees (see Box 3.6).

BOX 3.6: JOINT DECISION-MAKING ON PRODUCTS AT WATERFORD CRYSTAL

Waterford Crystal manufactures high quality stemware and giftware at manufacturing plants in Waterford city and county. Products in the Waterford range are also outsourced from various European locations. For much of its history the company had a long tradition of "paternalistic" industrial relations: wages and benefits were high, while technology and productivity compared poorly with many key competitors. This regime was supported by buoyant demand, particularly in the key North American market. During the 1980s the company experienced severe competitive problems, spurred by a weakening in the dollar. Every ten cent fall in the value of the dollar translated into a £4 million loss of revenue to Waterford.

Waterford's competitive position was further weakened by a rationalisation programme which undermined the craft-based production system. A new management team took over in 1989. Amid severe industrial relations turbulence, they launched a new competitive strategy and a tight programme of cost control, involving pay cuts, a prolonged pay freeze, severe job cuts, work re-organisation and the ending of the bartered piecework system of compensation for skilled blowers and cutters. A new product range, the "Marquis" range, was introduced, selling at lower price points than traditional products. Marquis products were outsourced, as were a small proportion of traditional products.

As management viewed it, the new HRM and industrial relations strategy was based on supporting high wages and conditions through advanced technology and high productivity. The company sought to stabilise its cost structure and industrial relations framework to win further investment in technology. Of particular importance was the acquisition of a high-technology tank furnace for the production of stemware products.

After the highly conflictual dealings between management unions surrounding the programme of wage cuts and rationalisation, management sought to institute "partnership" as a guiding concept for future relations between the company and its unions. A range of policy changes was adopted in the interest of promoting was described by the human resource manager as the "co-operative route" involving the creation of a "high trust" environment." A key aspect of this strategy was the establishment of the "task group".

The task group is a joint management/union group which meets regularly to review the product range and examine whether existing products could continue to be produced competitively at the Waterford plants, or should be outsourced. New product range options and their production, technological and work practice implications can also be considered at this forum. The group operates through consensus and is not a collective bargaining forum. Parallel negotiations are conducted through the enterprise-level joint negotiating committee. Other joint management/union committees monitor industrial relations, seeking to avoid flash-points wherever possible, handle pensions, health and safety and manage the company's profit sharing scheme. Periodic information briefings by senior management are held and line managers conduct "cascade briefings".

Team work is emphasised, particularly on the new tank furnace technology and the company has sought to create a new facilitative style of supervision. The company and unions have agreed a new disputes resolution procedure in which Labour Court recommendations are binding on both sides. The company's main union, the ATGWU, has sought to extend the partnership approach underpinning the task group to other areas of company operations.

Sources: *Industrial Relations News*, various issues 1987–95; *Industrial Relations News*, Industrial Relations Conference — "Restructuring and Culture Change to Meet Today's Reality", Dublin: IRN, 1994; J.S. Walsh and M. Linehan, "Strategic Change in Employment Relations: The Case of Waterford Crystal", Report prepared for the Labour Relations Commission, 1996.

In the international literature on voluntary partnership arrangements, initiatives such as these are viewed as particularly significant. More so than in relations between management and unions built around consultative arrangements, the parties bear *joint* responsibility for decisions. As decisions are arrived at, wherever possible, on a consensual basis, or through joint groups with parity of union and management representation, each of the parties — and not management alone — enjoys considerable power (cf. Cutcher-Gershenfeld and Verma, 1994: 551–2). In the United States it is these types of joint governance arrangements which have attracted major attention from academics and professional managers. In North America, where such arrangements are also notably rare, several cases of joint governance, most notably the General Motors Saturn production facility, the Shell refinery at Sarnia in Canada and management/union relations at Xerox, are viewed as providing world-class standards for voluntary joint management/union decision-making.

Transitional Models

A number of companies have embarked with trade unions on exploratory dialogue as to the form partnership might take in relations between the parties. This dialogue is conducted outside established collective bargaining, or encompasses alternative channels for management/union decision-making. The parties view such talks and arrangements as a first step, or transitional stage, in a process intended to transform industrial relations, even though the final shape of any future partnership arrangements remains to be determined. In such instances, partnership is recognisable first and foremost in the emergence of new procedural ground-rules for the conduct of dialogue, the purpose of dialogue and the scope of dialogue. In a manner that is not compatible with established collective bargaining, the parties are free to explore alternative models for management/union relations on an open basis. They may seek agreement on a common set of principles to guide their mutual dealings, for example the pursuit of competitiveness as a means of preserving jobs and supporting good pay and conditions; and they may address whether issues beyond the scope of traditional collective bargaining should come within the scope of new partnership arrangements, for example, business plans, product strategies and the introduction of new technologies etc. While dialogue is proceeding along non-traditional lines, the parties continue to deal with each other through parallel collective bargaining postures and arrangements. Cases where partnership finds expression in exploratory but earnest dialogue focused on new management/union relations will be referred to as examples of a "transitional model".

Three contrasting instances of transitional arrangements will be given. In the first of these, involving the ESB and its unions from about the mid-1990s, exploratory talks on new industrial relations arrangements were interrupted by a major programme of reorganisation and rationalisation (see Box 3.7). The attempt to address the changes involved through a nascent partnership process imposed severe strain on the parties and resulted in them switching back and forth between partnership and adversarial collective bargaining. The second example is provided by the attempt of the main banking groups and the IBOA to move away from the bitter and highly conflictual postures which characterised relations in the aftermath of a serious strike in the early 1990s (Box 3.8). The third example, involves a radical initiative embarked on by Aer Rianta and its unions aimed at instituting "constructive participation" at all levels of the company, as it prepares for the major commercial challenge posed by the EU-instigated ending of duty-free shopping and other major changes in commercial circumstances (Box 3.9).

BOX 3.7: RATIONALISATION IN THE CONTEXT OF A NASCENT PARTNERSHIP PROCESS IN THE ESB

Following the dramatic strike by electricians in 1991, which resulted in a serious power crisis, the ESB and unions in the company embarked on a joint review of relationships. The review, chaired by ICTU general secretary, Peter Cassells, identified the broad strands of change required in industrial relations as the ESB prepared for growing liberalisation of the European electricity market. The new industrial relations model proposed by the review committee was based on partnership principles. Before the committee's implementation plan could be carried forward, however, the parties were faced with the most profound set of changes in the company's history.

As the review committee's work was proceeding, the Government was examining the structure of the electricity industry, with a view to ending the ESB's monopoly. EU proposals to open European electricity markets to competition were also gaining momentum.

The ESB's chief executive proposed that the company's management and unions should undertake a review of ESB's cost structure and competitive position on a partnership basis. The Cost and Competitiveness Review (CCR), which began in 1994, represented a severe test of the nascent partnership process at a very early stage: the parties were seeking to manage on a partnership basis the most significant set of commercial and industrial relations challenges in the Board's history. In addition to senior union officials and managers, senior civil servants from the Department of Transport Energy and Communications sat on the CCR steering committee. The committee engaged McKinsey consultants as analysts and advisors. Joint management/union groups examined ESB's costs and operations against top performing electricity utilities in Europe and the United States. This joint review included staffing, organisation and work practices.

The review process concluded that in order to operate competitively the ESB needed to generate annual savings of £100 million and to reduce employment levels by 2,900 people. These targets had clear ramifications for staffing, work practices, job content, grading and industrial relations generally.

It had been hoped — certainly by management — that partnership might extend beyond a common understanding of the commercial and staffing changes required to embrace a joint approach to implementing change. Such was the scale of the changes involved, however, that relations between the parties increasingly pivoted on category-level bargaining of a traditional and adversarial kind. Each major category of ESB staff in the generating stations and commercial districts now looked to their unions to drive the best possible deal on severance payments, working practices and related matters. The category-level negotiating process prolonged the CCR exercise beyond its original target completion date of May 1995 to April 1996. Union ballots showed acceptance of final terms by 61 of the 63 categories of staff involved and by 95 per cent of all staff.

The parties jointly campaigned for acceptance of the package and moved back, albeit informally, towards a partnership approach to securing the programme in the face of non-acceptance by remaining key categories. The cost of the severance and other payments resulting from the CCR were the subject of public controversy, and there is little doubt that by involving trade unions in the change process the company was in a stronger position to win Government acceptance of its proposals for meeting new commercial imperatives. However, through the CCR, the ESB and its unions had brought about the most radical set of changes in the company's history without work stoppages. Unions and management in ESB are committed to working to find a partnership model for the new commercial circumstances of the company and its staff in the slimmed down organisation. The shape of future partnership arrangements in the company remain to be determined. Profit sharing, grade integrations and job flexibility are being introduced, as provided for in the CCR.

Sources: *Industrial Relations News*, various issues, 1994–96; Electricity Supply Board, *Review of Relationships in the ESB: Final Report of the Joint Steering Committee, Dublin, ESB*, 1993; L. Donald, "The Cost and Competitiveness Review in the ESB — A Case Study", *Partnership: Myth or Reality*, Dublin: *Industrial Relations News*, 1997.

BOX 3.8: IN SEARCH OF PARTNERSHIP IN THE BANKS

The bitter 1992 dispute between the major banking groups and the Irish Bank Officials Association was a watershed in industrial relations in the banking industry. The immediate cause of the dispute was a difference of views over flexible and extended opening hours. The dispute however arose in the context of a sequence of changes in human resource management and industrial relations in the industry. These involved management grades opting out of collective bargaining and union membership in favour of performance-related remuneration; growing management insistence on the need for flexibility in response to intensifying competition; the introduction of junior grades at the base of the grading structure, with very limited scope for career progression, and mounting union anxiety over the security of collective representation.

The 1992 dispute was a watershed for the industry. For the first time in a national bank strike the banks remained open for business. In the aftermath of the dispute considerable bitterness ensued between staff who had sided with the union and those who remained at work. The IBOA expelled members who crossed the picket line, suffering a serious loss of membership in the process. The union also affiliated to the Irish Congress of Trade Unions. The banks were faced with setting up new employee relations channels and policies for staff who had left, or had been expelled from, the union, while simultaneously dealing with a diminished but still far from broken union.

The highly publicised bitterness and recrimination surrounding the strike, and its effects on morale and industrial relations led both sides to consider the options now open. The union had been weakened but nevertheless remained a formidable force in the industry. In the prevailing business and public climate, the option of breaking the union must have appeared unattractive or unviable. The union had resorted to what historically had been its most potent weapon, the national strike, and had failed. Both sides had to contend with a changing and increasingly uncertain industry. In the mid-1990s separate rounds of talks commenced with the IBOA in Bank of Ireland and AIB to explore a new industrial relations framework. The IBOA's stance was influenced by the ICTU policy of encouraging partnership wherever local circumstances warranted. The talks increasingly focused on partnership principles.

The Bank of Ireland review also explored the option of introducing binding arbitration in disputes. The talks are ongoing and the future shape of any new industrial relations model remains to be determined.

Sources: *Industrial Relations News*, various issues 1992–96; "Binding Arbitration Mechanism Agreed in Bank of Ireland Review", Dublin, *Industrial Relations News*, 24: 2–3, 1996.

BOX 3.9: IN PURSUIT OF "CONSTRUCTIVE PARTICIPATION" IN AER RIANTA

Aer Rianta has long been viewed as a progressive company in the areas of human resource management and industrial relations. The airports authority gains a major share of its revenue from duty-free shopping in the domestic airports. In line with EU policy, duty-free shopping is due to end for European passengers in 1999. While passenger numbers through Irish airports have grown very sharply over the past decade, deregulation has led to intense competition between airlines, with consequent pressure on landing charges. Debate on the possible privatisation of remaining semi-state companies, including Aer Rianta, is also ongoing. These factors provide the main commercial context of proposals to change industrial relations at Aer Rianta.

From the early 1990s management and the group of unions in Aer Rianta have conducted talks to explore ways to institute more participative and involvement-based forms of work organisation and decision-making at all levels of the company. Under the rubric of "constructive participation" a joint union/company group has sought to promote staff and trade union involvement throughout the company at levels ranging from "natural work groups" to the formulation of corporate and business unit strategy. Pilot groups were established at the airports and at head office to explore the issues arising. The publication in 1994 of a joint "compact" outlining the shared principles of the parties for future arrangements was a milestone in the process. The compact states that employment security will be a priority objective of the company and rejects competing on the basis of a low wage policy.

Work continues on the implementation of the constructive participation project, guided by the shared ethos and commitment to "jointness" outlined in the compact. The parties are committed to

> no preconceived structural arrangements or solutions for partnership, but recognise that policy changes in various areas of HRM, including compensation systems, will be necessary to support partnership and mutual gains.

Sources: Aer Rianta Joint Union/Company Group on Constructive Participation, *Requisite Arrangements Towards Constructive Participation, and Towards Constructive Participation: A Positive Approach to Management/Union Relationships*, Dublin: Aer Rianta, 1994; G. O'Connor and B. Browne, "Constructive Participation: An Approach to Partnership", *Partnership: Myth or Reality*, Dublin: Industrial Relations News, 1997.

Partnership in Context: Influences and Consequences

The conceptual models outlined above cannot be applied rigidly in understanding the complex and changing industrial relations reality involved in management and union efforts to find new ways of conducting industrial relations at plant and company level. Arrangements between unions and management in some companies may contain elements of both consultation-focused and joint decision-making models. For example, some companies and unions operating consultation-focused models make use of joint teams or task forces to tackle specific problems or issues. Transitional models typically establish joint monitoring groups or steering committees to explore partnership arrangements or to monitor movement to new industrial relations arrangements. Management/union dealings may also move from one broad partnership model to another, or back to adversarialism. Transitional models may not succeed in bringing into being new industrial relations arrangements and may slide backwards into adversarial industrial relations.

Notwithstanding these caveats, partnership arrangements are most likely to develop in certain contexts and consultation-focused and joint decision-making models are likely to reflect the influences of different sets of contextual factors.

- The impetus for partnership is most likely to develop where the parties experience an acute commercial crisis, seek to make the case for further investment from a parent company, or anticipate a major change in a company's future commercial circumstances. The effect of such forces on perceptions of the continuing viability of established industrial relations arrangements will be clear from the examples outlined above. Crisis or major impending external change has long been known to be a powerful catalyst for internal change.

• Partnership is more likely to develop where union organisation is strong, at least in "density" terms, and where bypassing the union, marginalisation or de-recognition are not perceived as viable change options by management.

• Consultation-based arrangements are more likely to emerge where union members are less heavily committed to, or involved in, plant-level union affairs, whereas joint decision-making arrangements are more likely to reflect strong pre-existing traditions of union activism and solidarity at plant levels and possibly in the wider industrial community in which the plant is located.

• Other factors can also play an important role in the emergence and development of partnership arrangements. On the management side these include the values and ethos of senior human resource managers, the influence of the human resource function in senior management decision-making, and, possibly, the degree to which multinational parent companies allow scope for autonomy in the industrial relations and human resource policies of subsidiary plants. It is common for multinational companies to impose corporate human resource policies on subsidiaries, which override any possibility of strategic choice at local level. Cases also exist, however, in which local management can use the leeway granted to them in developing human resource policies to agree partnership arrangements which are otherwise unknown in the parent company and are possibly even discordant with prevailing corporate human resource policies.

- The postures and policies of unions are an important influence on industrial relations innovation, including their level of support for the wider partnership strategy of the ICTU. SIPTU, which is supportive of partnership at leadership level, figures in a number of significant cases of new arrangements. The affiliation of the IBOA to ICTU in the aftermath of the 1992 banking strike is clearly an important factor in that union's willingness to explore partnership arrangements with the main banking groups. The posture or degree of engagement of local officials with plant-level arrangements can be important influences. Positive and active union officials can support moves to introduce industrial relations innovation. Inactive union officials can allow local innovations to develop through "benign neglect". The postures of shop stewards are clearly an important influence on industrial relations innovation. Usually it is they who act as the key union representatives in new industrial relations arrangements.

- Good pre-existing relations between plant management, shop stewards and local union officials, possibly born out of the handling of crisis, or out of earlier joint change initiatives, may also contribute to a high trust environment in which partnership can appear to develop "organically" out of strong bargaining relationships of a more conventional type.

The managements and unions involved in partnership arrangements of all the types considered above typically report that such arrangements are either essential for industrial relations, human resource and commercial performance, or play an important role in enhancing performance. Among the benefits reported by managements are a high level of ongoing flexibility in day-to-day work, a high degree of receptivity to changes in production processes or products, a high level of flexibility, low levels of absenteeism, commitment to the job and the company, and knowledge of the commercial and competitive circumstances of the firm. Unions and shop stewards point to such benefits as the securing of a meaningful role in company decision-making, the possibility of influencing some of the parameters of competitive strategy, particularly employment security and company policy on wage levels and trends. Also important are enhanced union security and the possibility of contributing to higher levels of work satisfaction on the part of union members.

CONCLUSION

We have outlined three broad ways in which HRM policies interface with trade unions at firm and workplace level: firstly, as a set of policies which include the aim of providing an organisational context for employees designed to remove the need for employees to join a trade union; Secondly, as a set of policies which operate alongside the traditional collective bargaining system, and thirdly, as a set of policies which are integrated with existing collective bargaining arrangements and, in its mature form, accommodates unions as social partners in the operation of the firm. In order to understand the possible future trajectories of HRM, trade unions and industrial relations, the logic of each model requires some elaboration.

The consequence of successful union substitution strategies on a large scale is the decline of trade unions and the replacement of collective bargaining with individual bargaining. Paradoxically, the expansion of the non-union sector could undermine the rationale for union substitution policies with possible adverse consequences for those employees who lack sufficient market power to bargain individually with their employer. A progressively larger non-union sector could also undermine the conditions essential to centralised wage agreements as trade unions might no longer have a large enough constituency to warrant government and employers seeking centralised wage agreements. In short, HR practices, including wages and conditions of employment, would respond more closely to market forces rather than to established collective bargaining arrangements or wider macroeconomic or social considerations.

The second and predominant relationship between HRM policies and trade unions can be described as "dualism", where new initiatives in HRM coexist, often uneasily, with the established collective bargaining system rather than heralding a new order in the organisation. HRM policies which impinge on established collective bargaining traditions, such as policies in the areas of pay and work organisation are strongly resisted by unions, while HRM policies which do not appear to effect existing arrangements (e.g. communications, recruitment practices) cause less resistance. It is a moot point whether such an arrangement can remain stable. The development of an individualist orientation in management/employee interactions is regarded by many as one of the most critical developments in employee relations (Kochan et al., 1986; Guest, 1987; McLoughlin and Gourlay, 1992; Bacon and Storey, 1993). The focus of many human resource practices is on developing a closer relationship between the organisation/management and the employee through direct communication; between performance and pay through contingent reward systems; and between organisation loyalty/commitment and career progression through rigorous appraisal of the individual employee. The consequent individualisation of the employment relationship is generally inimical to employees acting collectively. Gunnigle et al. (1997b), for example, report a negative relationship between almost every measure of individualism and collectivism in 53 newly established companies in Ireland. The trend appeared to indicate a decline in collectivism and conversely a pronounced shift in favour of more individualist management styles in industrial relations.

The third discernible relationship between HRM and trade unions is based on some form of joint co-operation between management and the unions. Rather than marginalising or tolerating the union, the collective bargaining system becomes the basis for a new relationship between management and unions. Co-operative bargaining is feasible where some basis for mutual gains can be identified, even though both parties may have different goals or interests. In the Irish context, social partnership type agreements between unions, employers and government since 1987 would appear to offer propitious conditions for the development of partnership at the firm level. However, the evidence indicates such arrangements are as yet limited to a small number of companies. The present national wage agreement, Partnership 2000, includes a more comprehensive reference to social partnership at firm level than previous agreements. Both the Irish Business and Employers Confederation (IBEC) and ICTU have agreed to encourage the development of appropriate initiatives at enterprise level. However, the agreement did not attempt to "impose any single structure or model of partnership" and recognised the need to "tailor the approach to fit different employment settings" *(Partnership 2000: 63)*. The agreement lists a number of topics appropriate for discussion which range from employee co-operation with change including new forms of work organisation to forms of financial involvement. Not surprisingly, perhaps, the ICTU and IBEC appear to differ on what are considered appropriate initiatives. While ICTU interprets partnership at firm level as allowing workers a say in corporate decisions such as future business and investment strategies and a share in company profits, IBEC, in contrast, prefer more direct forms of participation such as team-working, quality initiatives and employee involvement programmes. These disagreements indicate that the future and type(s) of social partnership at firm level will depend on a continual process of negotiation and compromise between capital and labour.

References

Bacon, N. and Storey, J. (1993): "Individualisation of the Employment Relationship and the Implications for Trade Unions", *Employee Relations* 15(1): 5–17.

Belman, D. (1992): Unions, The Quality of Labour Relations and Firm Performance, in Mishel, L. and Voos, P., (eds.) *Unions and Economic Competitiveness*, New York: Economic Policy Institute.

Blyton, P. and Turnbull, P. (1994): *The Dynamic of Employee Relations*, London: Macmillan.

Cutcher-Gershenfeld, J. and Verma, A. (1994): "Joint Governance in North American Workplaces: A Glimpse of the Future or the End of an Era", *International Journal of Human Resource Management*, 5(3): 547–80.

Flood, P. and Toner, B. (1997): "Large Non-union Companies: How do they Avoid a Catch 22", *British Journal of Industrial Relations*, 35(2): 257–77.

Foulkes, F. (1980): *Personnel Policies in Large Non-union Companies*, Englewood Cliffs, NJ: Prentice Hall.

Freeman, R. and Medoff, J. (1984): *What Do Unions Do?*, New York: Basic Books.

Guest, D. (1987): "Human Resource Management and Industrial Relations", *Journal of Management Studies*, 24(5): 503–521.

Guest, D. and Hoque, K. (1996): "Human Resource Management and the New Industrial Relations", in Beardwell, I. (ed.), *Contemporary Industrial Relations: A Critical Analysis*, Oxford: Oxford University Press.

Gunnigle, P., Flood, P., Morley, M. and Turner, T. (1994): *Continuity and Change in Irish Employee Relations*, Dublin: Oak Tree Press in association with the Graduate School of Business, University College Dublin.

Gunnigle, P. (1995): "Collectivism and the Management of Industrial Relations in Greenfield Sites", *Human Resource Management Journal*, 5(3): 24–40.

Gunnigle, P., Morley, M., Clifford, N. and Turner, T. (1997a): *Human Resource Management in Irish Organisations*, Dublin: Oak Tree Press.

Gunnigle, P., Morley, M. and Turner, T. (1997b): "Challenging Collectivist Traditions: Individualism and the Management of Industrial Relations in Greenfield Sites". *Economic and Social Review*, 28(2): 105–34.

Hourihan, F. (1996): "Non Union Policies on the Increase Among New Overseas Firms", Dublin: *Industrial Relations News*, 4: 17–23.

Huselid, M. (1995): "The Impact of Human Resource Management Practices on Turnover, Productivity and Corporate Financial Performance", *Academy of Management Journal*, 38: 635–72.

Ichniowski, C., Kohan, T.A., Levine, D., Olson, C. and Strauss, G. (1996): "What Works at Work: Overview and Assessment", *Industrial Relations*, 35(3): 299–333.

Industrial Relations News (1995): "SmithKline Beecham — Watershed Agreement Ends Dual Pay System, Involves Major Savings", *Industrial Relations News*, 7: 14–16.

Industrial Relations News (1995): "Bausch and Lomb Votes Illustrate Different Routes to Change", Dublin: *Industrial Relations News*, 19: 12–14.

Industrial Relations News (1997): "SIFA and SIPTU's Partnership Deal Allows for 10 per cent Above National Terms, Full Flexibility", Dublin: *Industrial Relations News* 3: 18–19.

Kochan, T., Katz, H. and McKersie, R. (1986): *The Transformation of American Industrial Relations*, New York: Basic Books.

Kohan, T.A., and Osterman, P. (1994): *The Mutual Gains Enterprise: Forging a Winning Partnership Among Labour, Management and Government*, Boston Mass.: Harvard Business School Press.

McLoughlin, I. and Gourlay, S. (1992): "Enterprise Without Unions: The Management of Employee Relations in Non-union Firms", *Journal of Management Studies*, 29(5): 669–91.

National Economic and Social Council (1995): *New Production, Organisation and Industrial Relations: An Annotated Bibliography*, Dublin: NESC, unpublished.

Organisation for Economic Co-operation and Development (1996): *Ireland: Local Partnerships and Social Innovation*, Paris: OECD.

Partnership 2000 for Inclusion, Employment and Competitiveness (1996): Dublin: Government Publications.

Pfeffer, J. (1994): *Competitive Advantage Through People*, Boston, Mass.: Harvard Business School Press.

Regini, M. (1995): *Uncertain Boundaries: The Social and Political Construction of European Economies*, Cambridge: Cambridge University Press.

Roche, W.K. and Turner, T. (1997): "The Diffusion of the Commitment Model in the Republic of Ireland", *Review of Employment Topics*, 5(1): 108–51.

Roche, W.K. and Kohan, T.A. (1996): *Strategies for Extending Social Partnership to Enterprise and Workplace Levels in Ireland*, unpublished report prepared for the National Economic and Social Council, Dublin: NESC.

Roche, W.K. and Turner, T. (1994): Testing Alternative Models of Human Resource Policy Effects on Trade Union Recognition in the Republic of Ireland, *International Journal of Human Resource Management*, 5(3): 721–53.

Services Industrial and Professional Trade Union (1995): *World Class Manufacturing: A Survey of Industrial Relations Implications of WCM and Related Developments*, Dublin: SIPTU Research Department, unpublished.

Services Industrial and Professional Trade Union (1993): "Human Resource Management", in Discussion Papers Series C, 5 February, Dublin: SIPTU Research Department, unpublished.

Smith, P. and Morton, G. (1993): Union Exclusion and the De-collectivisation of Industrial Relations in Great Britain, *British Journal of Industrial Relations*, 31(1): 97–114.

Storey, J. (ed.) (1989): *New Perspectives on Human Resource Management*, London: Routledge.

Storey, J. (1992): *Developments in the Management of Human Resources*, Oxford: Basil Blackwell.

Sweeney, P. and Mulcahy, G. (1997): "Aughinish Alumina Case Study", in *Partnership: Myth or Reality*, Dublin: Industrial Relations News, 1997.

Toner, B. (1987): *Union or Non-union? Contemporary Employee Relations Strategies in the Republic of Ireland*, London: London University, unpublished PhD. thesis.

Toner, B. (1985): The Unionisation and Productivity Debate: An Employee Opinion Survey in Ireland, *British Journal of Industrial Relations*, 22: 451–3.

Turner, T., D'Art, D. and Gunnigle, P. (1997): "US Multi-nationals: Changing the Framework of Irish Industrial Relations?", *Industrial Relations Journal*, 28(2): 92–102.

Verma, A. and Cutcher-Gershenfeld, J. (1993): "Joint Governance in the Workplace: Beyond Union — Management Co-operation and Worker Participation", in Kaufman, B.E. and Kliener, M.M. (eds.), *Employee Representation: Alternatives and Future Directions*, Madison, WI: Industrial Relations Research Association.

4

RECRUITMENT AND SELECTION PRACTICES

Noreen Heraty and *Michael Morley*

INTRODUCTION

Recruitment and selection lie at the heart of how businesses procure the human resources required to maintain a sustainable competitive advantage over rivals (Raghuram and Arvey, 1996; Aaker, 1989; Jackson et al., 1989; Walker, 1992) and hence staffing positions in organisations may well represent one of the most important human resources management functions (Judge and Ferris, 1994). Plumbley (1985) suggests that the profitability and even the survival of an enterprise usually depends upon the calibre of the workforce, while Pettigrew et al. (1988) indicate that human resources represent a critical means of achieving competitiveness. The terms recruitment and selection refer to complimentary processes in human resource planning. Recruitment is concerned with identifying requirements for new staff, and procuring a pool of appropriate applicants for these vacant job positions. The selection process is essentially concerned with assessing these applicants and engaging those that are deemed most suitable for employment. As such, the focus of recruitment and selection is on matching the capabilities and inclinations of prospective candidates against the demands and rewards inherent in a given job (Montgomery, 1996; Plumbley, 1985; Herriot, 1989). It has been argued that the recruitment and selection decisions are the most important of all decisions that managers have to make since they are a prerequisite to the development of an effective workforce, while the costs of ineffectual commercial viability can often be attributed to decades of ineffective recruitment and selection methods (Terpstra, 1996; Plumbley, 1985; Smith and Robertson, 1986; Lewis, 1984). Many companies address all aspects of managing the workforce through human resource planning, directly linking human resource actions to strategic business issues or priorities (Bechet and Walker, 1995).

In this chapter we review contemporary thinking on recruitment and selection in organisations and, drawing upon data from a 1995 survey[1], we explore the nature of current recruitment and selection practices in Ireland. In relation to recruitment, policy decisions are examined, recruitment methods are reviewed, and the influence of ownership, size, unionisation and sector on the methods chosen is presented. In terms of selection, the techniques employed are identified and the situations in which they are most likely to be utilised are highlighted.

THE CHANGING CONTEXT OF RECRUITMENT AND SELECTION DECISIONS

Much of the recent literature on personnel management has emphasised the necessity for the recruitment and selection of employees that are committed to the goals of the organisation. Recent waves of organisational restructuring have dramatically changed and, in many cases, destroyed existing employment relationships. As traditional autocratic structures flatten and organi-

---

[1] This chapter draws upon data generated by the 1995 Cranfield/University of Limerick survey of human resource management practices in Ireland. The sample frame used for the survey was the *Business and Finance Top 2000 Trading and Non-trading Bodies* in the Republic of Ireland. Organisations are ranked according to the level of turnover, financial institutions by the size of their assets, and non-trading bodies by the number of their employees. If one excludes organisations employing less than 50 employees, the size distribution of establishments in the sample is similar to the size distribution in the relevant population. A similar procedure was followed in 1992 and, where appropriate, comparisons are drawn between both rounds of the survey to highlight differences and/or similarities.

sations utilise multi-disciplinary teams to remain competitive, the need for strategic and transparent systems becomes paramount (Worren and Koestner, 1996; Raghuram and Arvey, 1996; O'Reilly et al, 1991; Hackman, 1986). Heraty et al. (1997) suggest that, increasingly, many organisations are being transformed from structures that are built on functions and jobs, to those where focused, self-directed work teams, made up of empowered individuals with diverse backgrounds, are replacing traditional specialised workers. Burack and Singh (1995) propose that firms need adaptable people who can adjust to rapidly changing customer needs and operational structures while Pfeffer (1994) argues that employees, and the way they work, comprise the crucial difference between successful and unsuccessful organisations. He argues that as technology increases and product life cycles shorten, the major source of competitive advantage will be the individual worker. Krauthamer and Dorfman (1996: 49) further develop this view of the prevailing business environment and highlight that

> With the sweeping changes in today's business climate and the rise of reengineering to meet the needs of organisations in the area of downsizing or cost diminution, (search) firms must be equipped to recruit individuals who can operate in a non-structured or "virtual" organisation. . . . Even in today's technically advanced business environment, the human factor will always be instrumental to the success of an organisation.

Furthermore, Terpstra (1996: 16) indicates that, as companies downsize, "de-layer" and try to boost productivity with fewer people, those that remain are being asked to assume more tasks, roles and responsibilities. He proposes that, as this trend continues, companies will be asking fewer employees to know more, do more, change more and interact more and thus interest is increasingly focused on identifying the recruiting sources that are most likely to yield high quality employees and the selection methods that best predict future job performance. Arguments such as these have led Ripley and Ripley (1994) to suggest that the critical organisational concern today is the hiring or promoting of the best qualified people while still meeting all regulatory requirements.

A study commissioned by the IPD's Recruitment Forum (Kilibarda and Fonda, 1997) highlighted a number of common failings in the recruitment and selection process. Included among these failing were:

- no obvious link with HR strategy, resourcing strategy and broader business and organisational goals;

- use of referencing for shortlisting;

- unclear use of structured interview design and application;

- increasing use of invalid prediction methods;

- lack of widespread monitoring and lack of remedial action in those organisations that did monitor recruitment;

- lack of validation of situation specific selection procedures.

These results are suggestive of an inability or unwillingness to appreciate the strategic imperative of effective recruitment and selection practices. Smith and Robertson (1993) argue for greater precision in recruitment and selection and caution that a company can be dragged to its knees by the weight of ineffective staff which decades of ineffectual selection methods have allowed to accumulate. Kilibarda and Fonda (1997) note that the problem of inefficiency may be as a result of a difficulty in distinguishing good practice from common practice. Should this be the case then the problem may lie less with the processes utilised and more with the traditional perception of what constitutes effective and valid recruitment and selection practices.

The traditional perspective on recruitment and selection assumed a rational framework where the largely objective qualifications of the individual were matched to the requirements of the job (Judge and Ferris, 1995). The assumptions of the rational model imply that those making the decisions have real knowledge about the job, real knowledge about the applicants' job-relevant qualifications, can objectively compare these qualifications with the job demands and select the applicant with the best match. However, more recently, there is growing evidence to suggest that the notion of "fit" as it relates to suitability has assumed heightened significance in organisational settings. Chatman (1989) defines "fit" as the degree to which the goals and values of the applicant match those of individuals considered successful in the organisation. Montgomery (1996: 94) further highlights this notion of fit as the key to job success:

> Think back in your career and ask yourself, of all the people you know who failed in a job and were terminated, how many of them failed because they lacked the right educational degree, the right job experience, or the right industry background? In all likelihood, most of them failed because of inadequate interpersonal skills, an inability to communicate, or because they just didn't fit in with the culture; in other words — bad chemistry!

More specifically, Ferris et al. (1991) identify the "organisational chameleon" as a corporate creature who embodies the perfect fit in terms of organisational demands for values, beliefs, attitudes and so forth, while Bowen et al. (1991) advocate that an organisational analysis be carried out prior to making staffing decisions to identify the dominant values, social skills, and personality traits required of potential job applicants. Such an approach challenges the rational model of recruitment and selection and brings into focus the "form versus substance" issue. According to Ferris and King (1991), the core of this problem is associated with the difficulties involved in distinguishing candidates who are truly qualified (i.e. substance) from those who simply construct images of qualifications and competence (i.e. form). This problem is compounded in a situation where candidates actively seek to alter and manage images of competence, with the result that the decision-maker is attempting to hit a moving, rather than a stationary, target (Judge and Ferris, 1994).

In an attempt to explain why the rational model has limited application in the current business environment, Worren and Koestner (1996) posit three particular arguments:

1. In an increasingly competitive environment the content of jobs may change quickly over time, because of shifts in corporate strategies or technological innovations. Stable person/job match is unlikely in such unpredictable organisational environments.

2. The increasing use of self-managed teams makes it difficult to view individual jobs as the key unit of analysis. Team members may be given the responsibility of allocating tasks between members and engage in collective problem-solving efforts that can be more meaningfully understood at the group level of analysis.

3. Research has documented that person/job match may not be sufficient to achieve high job satisfaction, commitment and job performance among employees. It is necessary also that employees hold values that are congruent with those of the organisation.

Adkins et al. (1994) conclude that this requirement for "fit" encapsulates the congruence of the personality traits, beliefs, and values of the employee with the culture, strategic needs, norms and values of the organisation and thus reinforces the necessity for greater empirical evaluation of the mechanisms employed to measure such characteristics.

THE PROCESS OF RECRUITMENT

Anderson and Shackleton (1986) indicate that the quality of new recruits depends upon an organisation's recruitment practices, and that the relative effectiveness of the selection phase is inherently dependent upon the calibre of candidates attracted. Indeed Smith, Gregg and Andrews (1989) argue that the more effectively the recruitment stage is carried out the less important the actual selection process becomes. When an organisation makes the decision to fill an existing vacancy through recruitment, the first stage in the process involves conducting a comprehensive job analysis. This may already have been conducted through the human resource planning process, particularly where recruitment is a relatively frequent occurrence. Once a job analysis has been conducted, the organisation has a clear indication of the particular requirements of the job, where that job fits into the overall organisation structure, and can then begin the process of recruitment to attract suitable candidates for the particular vacancy.

Farnham and Pimlott (1995) suggest that one result of effective recruitment and selection is reduced labour turnover and good employee morale. Recruiting ineffectively is costly, since poor recruits may perform badly and/or leave their employment, thus requiring further recruitment. However, Wood (1985), in a cross national study of recruitment practices, suggests that, in reality, recruitment practices involve little or no attempt to validate practices. Personnel managers tend to rely on feedback from line managers and probationary periods and disciplinary procedures to weed out mistakes. Firms with high quit rates live with them and tend to build them into their recruitment practices — they do not analyse the constitution of their labour turnover.

A number of recent studies have suggested that some recruitment methods are more effective than others in terms of the value of the employees recruited. Cook (1993) indicates that while advertising is usual for job vacancies, applicants are sometimes recruited by word of mouth, through existing employees. Besides being cheaper, the "grapevine" finds employees who stay longer (low voluntary turnover) and who are less likely to be dismissed (low involuntary turnover) (Breach and Mann, 1984; Kirnan et al., 1989). People recruited by word of mouth stay longer because they have a clearer idea of what the job really involves. DeWitte (1989) reviewed five studies in which average labour turnover of those recruited by advertising was 51 per cent. The labour turnover for spontaneous applicants was 37 per cent and turnover for applicants recommended by existing employees was 30 per cent. One hypothesis proposed to account for this was the *"better information"* hypothesis. It was argued that people who were suggested by other employees were better and more realistically informed about the job than those who applied through newspapers and agencies. Thus, they were in a better position to assess their own suitability. Better informed candidates are likely to have a more realistic view of the job, culture of the organisation and job prospects. Terpstra (1996) argues that recruitment sources are significantly linked to differences in employee performance, turnover, satisfaction and organisational commitment. In a survey of 201 large US companies, Terpstra asked respondents to rate the effectiveness of nine recruitment sources in yielding high-quality, high-performing employees. The three top ranked sources were employee referrals, college recruiting and executive search firms. However, Terpstra cautions that, while these general results are useful, there is a need for greater internal analysis of the relative quality of recruits yielded by different sources.

RECRUITMENT PRACTICES IN IRELAND

The decision to expand the current workforce is inherently linked to the organisation's market performance. Of those organisations that responded to the Cranfield/University of Limerick survey in 1995, 67 per cent indicated that demand for their products/services had increased over the last three years. Furthermore, when asked to assess their overall performance in terms of gross revenue, 35 per cent indicated that performance was well in excess of costs, or sufficient to make a small profit (29 per cent). Taking these two results into account, it is not therefore surprising that organisations are more likely to have expanded their workforce, rather than reduced it, in the intervening time period (see Table 4.1).

TABLE 4.1: CHANGE OF MORE THAN 5% IN WORKFORCE SIZE IN PAST THREE YEARS

Increased %	Decreased %	Same %
50	25	25

n=256

Source: Cranfield/University of Limerick Study, 1995.

While one quarter (25 per cent) of organisations surveyed indicated no change in organisation size, half of those surveyed indicated that they had, in fact, increased the size of their workforce over the past three years, which can, perhaps be attributed to the general upsurge being witnessed in the Irish economy over recent years. However, one in four of the organisations surveyed (25 per cent) reported that their workforce had decreased by more than 5 per cent in the same period suggesting perhaps that the general boom in the economy is not being experienced by all organisation types. Where downsizing was necessary, a combination of voluntary redundancy, natural wastage, early retirement and a recruitment freeze were the typical mechanisms employed.

Policy Decisions on Recruitment and Selection

Increasingly, the management literature has suggested a growing tendency towards decentralisation and a concomitant shift towards greater devolvement of responsibility to line management. Nowhere has this been more evident than in the human resource literature (Lawler, 1986; Storey, 1992; Dobbs, 1993), which proposes that a transition is occurring where line managers are increasingly being awarded responsibility for policy decisions in a range of human resource activity areas. It has further been suggested that, as organisations become more strategic in the management of their human resources, we are likely to witness greater line involvement in a range of activities traditionally held to be the sole preserve of the specialist HR function (Carroll, 1991; Kamoche, 1994; Storey, 1995). It becomes interesting, therefore, to determine whether this is being witnessed at the organisational level in the Irish context.

In order to understand the dynamics of the recruitment and selection process, respondents to the survey were first asked to indicate whether they had an explicit policy in relation to recruitment and selection. The results are quite positive since a total of 55 per cent of respondents reported that they had a written policy in relation to recruitment and selection, 33 per cent had an unwritten policy, and just 11 per cent had no policy at all. A further key area of interest here is a consideration of where decisions on such policy determination are taken. Table 4.2 presents some interesting comparisons (between the CUL 1995 and 1992 data) on policy determination in the areas of recruitment and workforce adjustments generally.

TABLE 4.2: LOCATION OF POLICY DETERMINATION

		Recruitment (%)	Workforce Adjustment (%)
International HQ	1995	7	30
	1992	4	16
National HQ	1995	39	37
	1992	37	38
Subsidiary	1995	10	18
	1992	10	13
Establishment	1995	44	23
	1992	42	32
Number	1995	165	148
	1992	164	147

Source: Cranfield/University of Limerick Study, 1992 and 1995.

The results above do not reveal any particular change, since 1992, in the location of policy decisions on recruitment. Decision-making tends to be primarily centred at national headquarter or establishment level, with some increase recorded at international headquarter level. Interestingly, the only level that appears to have lost some responsibility for recruitment decisions appears to be that of the subsidiary. However, when one explores where policy decisions in relation to workforce adjustment are taken, a number of interesting changes can be detected. Here, international headquarters appear to have considerably tightened their control over policies in this area over the last three years — policy decisions in relation to adjustments to the workforce are now almost twice as likely to be taken at international headquarter level than was the case in 1992 (30 per cent as against 16 per cent respectively). This increase in decision making power at international headquarter level appears to be to the cost of the establishment level which has suffered a decrease of 9 per cent in the same period. Taken together, the results on recruitment and workforce adjustment appear to suggest that, while organisations are largely free to establish specific policies in relation to their own recruitment needs, such decisions can be taken only within the broader ambit of policies relating to workforce adjustment, which are typically determined at either national or international headquarter level.

If we take the decentralisation debate a step lower, it becomes necessary to look within the organisation to determine who has ultimate responsibility for developing policies in relation to recruitment and selection. Figure 4.1 outlines where primary responsibility for policy decisions on recruitment and selection lies.

FIGURE 4.1: RESPONSIBILITY FOR RECRUITMENT
AND SELECTION (%)

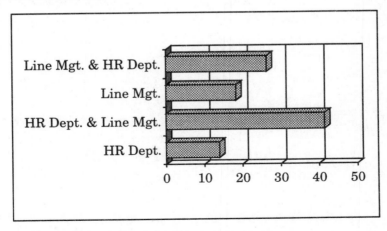

Source: Cranfield/University of Limerick Study, 1995.

The data here suggest that, for the most part, recruitment and selection is completed through a combination of the specialist HR function and line management involvement. It is interesting to note, however, that just 18 per cent of respondents indicated that, in their organisation, line management is solely responsible for recruitment and selection policy decisions. This represents a decrease on the comparable figure for 1992 which was 25 per cent. However, the overall results do not indicate a general decrease in line involvement. When further comparisons are made with the 1992 results, one notes that there has been a concomitant increase in joint responsibility between HR and line management — an increase from 32 per cent in 1992 to 41 per cent in 1995.

When the data are tested for variations linked with ownership, it would appear that, while the greater proportion of responding organisations report some increase in line responsibility for recruitment, Irish-owned organisations are the least likely to report such an increase. Thus while 23 per cent of Irish-owned organisations suggest that line management responsibility for recruitment has increased over the last three years, the comparable figures for EU-owned organisations is 52 per cent, for UK-owned organisations is 37 per cent and for US-owned organisations 34 per cent. Furthermore, larger organisations are more likely to report increased line responsibility in this area (39 per cent) than are their smaller counterparts (22 per cent), while union status does not appear to have any impact on line involvement in recruitment decisions.

From the data presented here, it could be argued that line management responsibility in areas traditionally held to be the domain of HR/Personnel specialists is becoming more pervasive. This is particularly true of larger, and non Irish-owned organisations. However there is no evidence of complete devolvement to line managers and, given that the level of reported line management involvement, from an overall perspective, is not significantly different than it was three years ago, one can only suggest that the specialist HR function retains considerable input in, and responsibility for, recruitment and selection policy-making.

Recruitment Methods Utilised

Prior to a discussion of the various recruitment methods utilised by Irish-based organisations, it is useful to determine whether such organisations have actively introduced new strategies in relation to recruitment generally. In the survey respondents were asked to identify specific measures that had been introduced in order to aid them in the recruitment process, or in the retention of employees (see Table 4.3).

TABLE 4.3: MECHANISMS INTRODUCED FOR THE RECRUITMENT/ RETENTION OF EMPLOYEES

	%
Relaxed qualification requirements	6
Recruiting abroad	24
Retraining	63
Increased pay	35
Relocation	3
Marketing image	19
Other	3

n=261

Source: Cranfield/University of Limerick Study, 1995.

While a variety of strategies are utilised by organisations to facilitate recruitment/retention, retraining is the most popular initiative (63 per cent). A total of 35 per cent of organisations felt it necessary to increase their pay/benefits package, while a further 24 per cent are actively seeking candidates from abroad. Very few organisations opted for either relocation and/or relaxed qualifications as a means of filling existing vacancies.

Various organisation characteristics are found to have some influence on the strategies employed by responding organisations. In terms of organisation size, larger organisations are more likely

to adopt a greater range of strategies than are their smaller counterparts. This is particularly so in terms of the use of those
strategies that require substantial resources, such as improving
the market image of the organisation, relocation, or increased pay
(Table 4.4).

TABLE 4.4: SIZE AS A DETERMINANT OF THE PRACTICES
INTRODUCED TO AID RECRUITMENT/RETENTION OF WORKERS (%)

	Relaxed Qualifi- cations	Recruit Abroad	Re- training	Increase Pay	Marketing Image
1–199	47	29	44	38	32
Over 200	53	71	57	62	68
	n=15	n=62	n=161	n=172	n=47

Source: Cranfield/University of Limerick Study, 1995.

Organisation ownership is also found to have some influence on
the choice of strategy adopted, with US-owned organisations
emerging as the most likely to use increased pay or improve the
organisation's marketing image in order to aid in the recruit-
ment/retention of employees. Retraining appeared to be the strategy most favoured by Irish-owned organisations (57 per cent)
which may be linked to a general policy decision to build and
maintain a strong internal labour market.

Turning to the process of recruitment, the most immediate
decision facing recruiters is whether to recruit internally from
those already employed by the organisation, or to source from the
external labour market. The decision to access the internal labour
market, (and here we perceive that an internal labour market exists to the degree that vacancies are filled from within the organisation), brings with it a number of distinct advantages. It is a cost
effective approach, both in terms of eliminating the need for external advertising/sourcing and also in terms of reducing the in-
duction or settling in period. It is also considered to be good per-

sonnel practice for, not only may it be viewed as a positive motivator by current employees, but the quality of the internal labour market is continuously upgraded and maintained through high quality recruitment, selection, promotion, career development and multiskilling. However, Cappelli (1995: 569) suggests that a number of infrastructural developments such as the proliferation of "headhunter" or placement firms, temporary agencies for part-time and contingent work and the growth of subcontracting, make it easier for organisations to rely on the outside labour market for securing skills. He further argues that demands for greater product/service innovation can often result in companies hiring skills from outside the organisation and dropping employees with the obsolete skills to avoid carrying the associated costs:

> Particularly in the service industry, where competencies reside more clearly with individual employees as opposed to within an organisational system (e.g. software development, accounting or legal services), rearranging competencies more clearly requires rearranging employees. And markets may change before an employer can develop these skills among its own employees.

An examination of the data relating to recruitment practices indicates that a broad spectrum of recruitment methods are being utilised to fill managerial vacancies (see Table 4.5).

Again, in Table 4.5, the results point to a combination of recruitment methods being used by responding organisations to fill managerial positions. Utilising the internal labour market for recruitment purposes appears to be the most popular recruitment method at all managerial levels. However, some variation is evident between the different managerial levels where, for example, middle and junior management vacancies are more likely to be filled internally than are senior management positions. Concomitantly, organisations report a greater tendency to utilise consultants for senior positions (52 per cent) than for middle management (38 per cent) or junior management (37 per cent) positions. These results are unsurprising. Organisations have always displayed a preference for "growing" their own managerial expertise which is facilitated by an increased investment in management development programmes and management trainee schemes. However, the growing internationalisation of organisations and the heavy recent emphasis on effective top management team dynamics has focused increasing interest on the necessity for innovative, multi-experienced, dynamic senior management and so it is not altogether unexpected that organisations are unwilling to limit themselves to filling senior vacancies from within their organisation.

TABLE 4.5: USUAL METHOD OF FILLING MANAGERIAL VACANCIES (%)

	Senior Management	Middle Management	Junior Management
Internally	57	75	77
Recruitment consultant	52	38	22
National newspaper	47	49	37
Professional magazine	12	13	5
International newspaper	12	7	2
Word of mouth	7	10	14

n=261

Source: Cranfield/University of Limerick Study, 1995.

Perhaps the most commonly recognised recruitment method is the advertisement, at local or national level. Plumbley (1985) suggests that where advertising judgements are based on reliable and relevant factors, and where they are effectively communicated, external advertising serves as a powerful recruitment tool. In the current survey, advertising at national level is common across all managerial grades, while targeted advertising at international level or in specialised magazines, although not that usual, is limited to more senior positions.

In relation to explaining variations in staffing practices, country of origin is essentially used as a proxy variable to assess the impact of managerial values. This is based on the rationale that managerial preferences in HRM policy areas will closely reflect underlying managerial values associated with country of origin of the organisation (Gunnigle et al., 1997). A positive correlation is found to exist between the frequency with which particular recruitment methods are used and the country of origin of the responding organisations. The most significant difference occurs between Irish-owned organisations and their US and EU counterparts, where, across managerial categories, Irish-owned organisations are seen to utilise their internal labour market to a lesser degree than do the foreign-owned companies surveyed (see Figure 4.2).

FIGURE 4.2: OWNERSHIP AS A DETERMINANT OF THE USE OF INTERNAL LABOUR MARKET

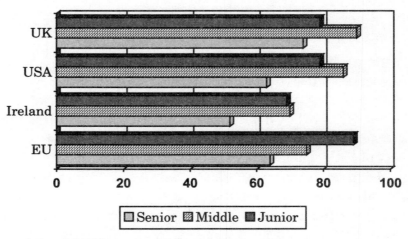

Source: Cranfield/University of Limerick Study, 1995.

Data relating to the use of recruitment consultants reflect a similar trend (see Figure 4.3). US-owned organisations are more likely to use consultants in the recruitment process for all managerial grades, than are their European counterparts. Irish-owned companies, on the other hand, are the least likely to use a recruitment consultant, relying to a greater extent on external advertising, particularly in national newspapers. Higgins (1992) suggests that Irish-owned organisations discount the need for consultants except in cases where they wish to recruit from overseas or where they intend operating abroad.

FIGURE 4.3: OWNERSHIP AS A DETERMINANT OF THE USE OF A RECRUITMENT CONSULTANT

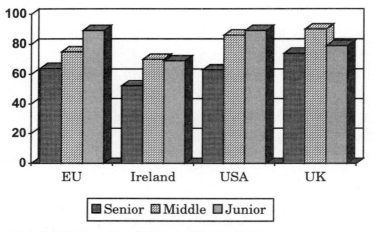

Source: Cranfield/University of Limerick Study, 1995

These results are broadly consistent with the contention that multinational organisations operating in Ireland practice strong elements of HRM, one example of which is the development of internal labour markets through such techniques as progressive career planning, management development, and extensive communication and information sharing (See Gunnigle, 1992; Murray, 1984). However, Capelli (1995: 573) asserts that, in the US, increased competition, declining union organising, changed public policy in relation to employment classification and organisation downsizing have resulted in evidence that US companies are moving away from the notion of maintaining internal labour markets:

The assertion here is simply that there has been a trend or shift towards employment practices based on criteria associated with markets outside the firm, and away from arrangements based on other criteria that typically reflect the internal interests of the firm. No doubt there is a continuum between "pure" internalised arrangements and complete market determination along which employers are moving, and the argument here is that, on average, practices are shifting along that continuum. The evidence is for the private sector.

Organisation size has figured prominently as an important explanatory factor impacting on variation in patterns of HRM, with several studies pointing to the existence of a positive relationship between organisation size and the level of HR policy sophistication. When the data is analysed for organisation size variations, a number of distinctions between the recruitment practices of larger and smaller organisations do emerge. Table 4.6 provides a comparison of organisation size with three particular recruitment strategies.

TABLE 4.6: SIZE AS A DETERMINANT OF RECRUITMENT METHOD UTILISED (%)

		Internally	Recruitment Consultant	National Newspaper
50–199	Senior	54	51	42
	Middle	72	33	46
	Junior	70	19	30
200+	Senior	60	52	53
	Middle	78	43	52
	Junior	82	25	42

n=261

Source: Cranfield/University of Limerick Study, 1995.

Larger organisations have a greater tendency to recruit internally, across all managerial grades, than do their smaller coun-

terparts. This is not altogether unexpected since large organisations, by virtue of their size, have access to a larger pool of potentially suitable candidates. Price (1997) suggests that the existence
of structured internal labour markets are inherently linked with
organisation size since internal labour markets is characterised
by series of career ladders that are associated with vertical mobility. Smaller organisations utilise recruitment consultants with
the same frequency as larger organisations when recruiting for
senior management posts, but marginally less so for lower managerial grades. Walton and Lawrence (1990) suggest that recruitment agencies are popular with smaller organisations, particularly where the personnel function is under-resourced and agencies are used to relieve the personnel department of an administrative burden. The picture in relation to national newspaper advertising suggests that both large and small organisations are
more likely to advertise externally for more senior positions, than
they are for junior management posts, but this trend is a little
more evident in smaller concerns.

When the data are tested for variation associated with union
presence, some differences again emerge (see Table 4.7).

TABLE 4.7: UNIONISATION AS A DETERMINANT OF RECRUITMENT
METHOD UTILISED (%)

		Internally	**Recruitment Consultant**	**National Newspaper**
Union	Senior	56	55	50
	Middle	76	38	49
	Junior	79	23	38
Non-union	Senior	64	42	36
	Middle	70	40	48
	Junior	64	16	30

n=261

Source: Cranfield/University of Limerick Study, 1995.

In relation to internal recruitment, it appears that unionised organisations are typically more likely to recruit internally than are their non-union counterparts. Again, these results are not that unusual since union agreements often require that vacancies be advertised internally, while the existence of a structured internal labour market is also a particular feature of many unionised environments. It is interesting to note, however, that, in a unionised environment, recruitment to senior management positions is less likely to be from within the organisation than is the case in non-unionised organisations (56 per cent as against 64 per cent respectively). The trend evidenced in the 1995 data differs from that revealed in the 1992 survey when it was found that non-union respondents used current employees to fill vacancies at managerial and professional/technical levels to a greater degree than those that did recognise a trade union. Recent employee relations literature presents evidence that foreign-owned multinationals (which are increasingly non-unionised) are exerting considerable influence on the practices of more established firms (which are more likely to be unionised), and this strong focus on internal recruitment, by unionised organisations, might be a reflection of this.

Location in either the public or private sector is seen as a particularly important factor impacting on variations in HRM. The survey data reveal a number of particular differences between the public and private sector with respect to their use of internal or external labour markets (see Table 4.8). Private sector respondents are far more likely to utilise the internal labour market for all managerial categories, than are their public sector counterparts. This is somewhat surprising since, traditionally, the public sector has been characterised by its heavy reliance on internal recruitment. In the current survey, just 39 per cent of respondents indicate that they recruit senior management posts internally — the corresponding figure for private sector organisations is 63 per cent. Interestingly, the use of recruitment consultants is also more likely in the private sector than in the public sector where, across all managerial levels, private sector organisations are almost three times more likely than public sector organisations to employ the services of consultants. These results point then to a combination of research methods being adopted, particularly in private sector organisations, and especially where the vacancy to be filled is a senior management one. Thus with reference to the use of consultants, one can turn again to Capelli's (1995) assertion that, in the private sector, there is evidence of some move away from internal labour markets. When it comes to advertising at national level, it emerges that public sector organisations are the more frequent users of this particular recruitment strategy, across all managerial grades.

TABLE 4.8: SECTOR AS A DETERMINANT OF RECRUITMENT METHOD UTILISED (%)

		Internally	Recruitment Consultant	National Newspaper
Private	Senior	63	61	41
	Middle	79	46	48
	Junior	80	26	35
Public	Senior	39	22	68
	Middle	63	15	54
	Junior	66	9	42

n=261

Source: Cranfield/University of Limerick Study, 1995.

From a broad perspective it would appear that all organisations are making greater use of their internal labour markets when targeting prospective candidates to fill managerial vacancies. Higgins (1992) suggests that the filling of vacancies from current employees may increase employee commitment by giving staff an incentive to perform well and may serve to preserve the organisation culture where those recruited to new positions within the organisation are already familiar with the beliefs, attitudes and norms expected by the organisation. However, as indicated at the start of this chapter, recruitment is merely the first stage of a highly critical organisational process and the strategies employed by the organisation at the selection stage have a pivotal role to play in ensuring that the organisation remains competitive.

THE SELECTION DECISION

While the calibre of candidates is determined by the value of the recruitment process, the selection decision remains a difficult one. Dale (1995: 159) argues that:

> most mistakes are caused by the fact that managers generally give little thought to the critical nature of the decisions. Employers are surprised and disappointed when an appointment fails, and often the person appointed is blamed rather than recognising the weaknesses in the process and methodology . . . even the soundest of techniques and best practice (in selection) contain scope for error. Some of this is due to the methods themselves, but the main source is the frailty of the human decision makers.

Selection tools available to organisations can be characterised along a continuum that ranges from the more *traditional* methods of interviews, application forms and references, through to the more *sophisticated* techniques that encapsulate biographical data, aptitude tests, assessment centres, work samples, psychological testing, and so forth. Each method of selection has its advantages and disadvantages and comparing their rival claims involves comparing each method's merit and psychometric properties. The degree to which a selection technique is perceived as effective and perhaps sophisticated is determined by its reliability and validity. Reliability is generally synonymous with consistency, while validity refers to what is being measured, and the extent to which those desirable attributes are being correctly measured (Anastasi, 1982; Muchinski, 1986). It is suggested that a good selection method should meet the following requirements: be practical to utilise; be sensitive in that it can distinguish between candidates; be reliable in that it consistently comes up with the same answer; and valid, in that it measures what it is supposed to measure — that the inferences that it makes about a person are correct.

In a comparison of personnel selection practices in seven European countries, Schuler, Frier and Kauffmann (1993) explored the utilisation of a range of established selection methods. They reported a general trend towards structured interviews in all countries and, while the general validity and acceptability of methods such as work samples, group exercises and assessment centres was widely recognised, reported usage of these methods was infrequent. Clear differences in the frequency of the use of several selection methods did emerge from the study which also reported the very high take-up of references and assessment centres in both the UK and Germany; the high, almost exclusive, frequency of graphology in France; and the limited use of testing and biographical inventories amongst all respondents.

In his study of recruitment and selection practices in the US, Terpstra (1996) found that approximately 25 per cent of respondent organisations conducted validation studies on their selection methods. Furthermore, in a rating of various selection methods, those perceived to be above average in their ability to predict employees' job performance included work samples, references/recommendations, unstructured interviews, structured interviews and assessment centres.

Storey (1992) suggests that developments in the realm of selection lend some support to those who propound the HRM thesis, where a key feature has been the increase in testing designed explicitly to assess behavioural and attitudinal characteristics. He further indicates that the extent to which these more sophisticated and systematic approaches can be, and are, deployed, depends to a large degree on sectoral circumstances and on the wider employment-management policies being pursued.

SELECTION PRACTICES IN IRELAND

The data generated by the survey in 1992 indicated that relatively little use was being made, by Irish organisations, of what are considered the more "sophisticated" selection techniques i.e. those with the highest levels of validity and reliability. The picture emerging from the 1995 data confirms that finding, with the application form, the interview and reference checks continuing to remain the most commonly used selection methods in Ireland (see Table 4.9).

TABLE 4.9: MAIN SELECTION METHODS USED (%)

	Every Appoint-ment	Most Appoint-ments	Some Appoint-ments	Few Appoint-ments	Not used	N=
Interview panel	41	28	18	6	7	235
One-to-one interview	37	14	23	14	12	217
Application forms	59	20	12	3	6	241
Aptitude tests	6	13	37	15	29	201
Psycho-metric tests	4	9	27	11	49	199
Assessment centre	2	2	9	8	79	181
Graphology	0.6	0.6	4	1	94	169
References	70	22	5	1	2	230

Source: Cranfield/University of Limerick Study, 1995.

Arguably few HR decision tools have been as widely studied or as heavily criticised as the interview. Among the common criticisms are that the decision is often made within the first five minutes of the encounter with the remainder of the interview spent confirming that decision; interviewers seldom change their opinion gained from the earlier application form or CV; negative information typically has a greater impact on the outcome than does positive and often the behaviour of the interviewer betrays his/her decision. Furthermore it has been calculated that the structured

interview can only give a prediction of 0.6 (against a perfect prediction of 1.0), while the unstructured interview is in the 0.3
range (Smith et al, 1989). Despite this, the interview continues to
enjoy considerable popularity across all organisations. However,
the data presented here might indicate a reduction in the traditional reliance on the interview. McMahon (1988) found that over
90 per cent of job categories in Ireland were filled with the assistance of an interview. In the present survey, however, just 41 per
cent of respondents indicated that they make use of an interview
panel for every position, while just 37 per cent suggested that a
one-to-one interview was used for every appointment Over the
years considerable research concerning both the validity and reliability of the selection interview have been undertaken, often with
conflicting results (Judge and Ferris, 1994; Anderson, 1992;
Hunter and Hunter, 1984; Wiesner and Cronshaw, 1988). Papa-
dopoulou et al. (1996) suggest that any evaluation of the interview
is complicated by the fact that it is a complex social event characterised by a dynamic relationship between interviewer and inter-
viewee where their perceptions of each other, and their role in the
interview, can affect either or both the interview processes and
the outcomes. Rynes (1993) notes that the interview is a two-way
selection decision where decisions are made by both candidates
and their prospective employers and can thus be viewed as a recruitment device whereby expectations are set regarding the prospective future employment relationship (Herriot and Rothwell,
1983) and a psychological contract can be negotiated (Herriot,
1989). Anderson and Shackleton (1993) suggest that, in terms of
validity and reliability, the overall efficiency of selection interview
decisions has, in fact, been much maligned and that the operation
of panel interviews or successive interviews can obviate many of
the inherent problems associated with interviewing and can facilitate greater validity and reliability in the final decision analysis.
However rigorous the process, interviewing remains essentially
subjective and thus the interviewer needs to ensure that, as far as
possible, errors or biases are eliminated from the process.

The reliability and validity of application forms, as a discrete selection tool, have similarly been tested, and it is widely held that they are open to misinterpretation, particularly where applicants portray a false persona (Muchinsky, 1986). In the present survey, more than half of those who responded indicated that they utilise the application form for all appointments (59 per cent). Guest (1983) cautions that, in this age of increasing numbers of applicants per vacancy, pre-selection devices are becoming more and more of a necessity, hence the importance of designing application forms in an analytical manner.

References again feature as a popular tool in the selection process, despite that fact that their predictive ability is in the region of 0.13 (against a perfect prediction of 1.0). Here 70 per cent of respondents make use of reference checks for all appointments which suggests continuing support for references as a key feature of the selection decision. In 1992, the Cranfield/University of Limerick study found that 88 per cent of respondents used references as a selection device while Robertson and Makin (1986), in their UK study of best selection techniques, found that over 67 per cent of employers surveyed used references for all vacancies. As with many of the more popular and "traditional" selection tools, the validity and reliability of references has been questioned, particularly with respect to their unstructured and often ambivalent nature, and it has been shown that referees who "like" a candidate tend to write longer and more complimentary references (Reilly and Chao, 1982; Dobson, 1989).

Many commentators have supported the use of assessment centres (which typically have a prediction rate of 0.6) and psychometric testing (with a prediction range of between 0.3 and 0.6) as consistently more valid behaviour predictors which are ideally suited as a pre-selection device (see, for example, Muchinsky, 1986; Hunter and Hunter, 1984; Smith, Gregg and Andrews, 1989; Terpstra, 1996). The use of these more sophisticated techniques has been reported to be low both in Ireland (McMahon, 1988) and in the UK (Robertson and Makin, 1986). However, there is evidence to suggest that testing, in particular, is becoming more widespread in the US (Anderson and Shackleton, 1986). Again, the figures presented in the table above suggest that these more sophisticated techniques are not used to any great extent in Ireland at present.

Further analysis of the data reveals a number of interesting variations with respect to selection techniques used by particular organisation types. Thus, while panel interviews are popular across all organisations irrespective of ownership, unionised organisations are twice as likely to use panel interviews for all appointments than are non-union companies (45 per cent as against 21 per cent respectively). Larger organisations are also more likely to use panel interviews for all appointments (45 per cent) than are smaller concerns (35 per cent). More disparate results are evident when one analyses the use made of one-to-one interviews. Here, it appears that US-owned organisations are more than twice as likely to use this interview form than Irish-owned organisations. Thus 58 per cent of US-owned companies utilise the one-to-one interview for every appointment, while just 26 per cent of Irish-owned organisations use this interview type. The comparable figure for EU-owned organisations is 29 per cent. Again, as is the case with panel interview utilisation, unionised organisations indicate a far greater propensity to make use of the one-to-one interview than do non unionised companies (61 per cent and 31 per cent respectively). However, smaller organisations record a slightly higher utilisation of this interview form than do their larger counterparts (41 per cent as against 34 per cent). Taken together, the data reported here suggest that the interview retains a central role in the selection decision. However, it is possible that organisations are, in fact, utilising both the panel interview and the one-to-one interview as a means of determining suitability, rather than relying solely on one meeting with job candidates. This can be seen to be a positive approach to selection since there is a greater likelihood that many of the inherent problems of interviewing will be obviated by having more individuals involved, and a greater number of stages in the process.

The use of application forms was earlier reported to be popular in Irish-based organisations. When their utilisation was analysed against various organisational characteristics, a number of pertinent differences emerge, particularly with respect to organisation ownership. The results revealed that Irish-owned organisations are, in fact, the least likely of all organisations surveyed to use application forms for all appointments. Thus while just 50 per cent of Irish-owned organisations use application forms for all positions, the corresponding utilisation for EU-owned companies is 60 per cent, for US-owned organisations is 74 per cent and for non-EU responding organisations is highest at 80 per cent. Here again, the data are suggesting some change has occurred since 1992 when the use of application forms was found to be almost as high among Irish-owned organisations as it was in foreign-owned companies. In 1992 87 per cent of Irish-owned respondents regularly utilised the application form, 91 per cent of EU and non-EU-owned companies and 98 per cent of US-owned organisations did likewise. In the 1995 data, organisation size does not appear to have any impact on level of usage, but unionised organisations are found to use application forms more frequently than do the non-unionised companies surveyed (62 per cent as against 51 per cent respectively).

Turning to the use of references as a selection tool, one can again detect a number of differences emerging with respect to various organisation types. Here again one might be surprised to note that Irish-owned organisations report the lowest frequency of usage of the reference check than do any of their foreign-owned counterparts. In fact, US-owned organisations indicate the highest level of usage (83 per cent) of the reference for all appointments, followed by other non EU-owned companies (73 per cent), and UK-owned concerns (73 per cent). The corresponding figure for Irish-owned organisations is 59 per cent. Interestingly, just four organisations indicated that they do not use reference checks at all — all four are Irish-owned companies. When these results are compared with those reported in 1992, it would appear that Irish-owned organisations are more likely to have reduced their reliance on the reference check than are their counterparts (use of references in 1992 for Irish-owned companies was 88 per cent, for EU-owned firms was 93 per cent, and for US-owned organisations was 98 per cent). In the present study the use of references is reported to be marginally higher in larger organisations as compared with smaller companies (76 per cent and 68 per cent respectively), but union status does not appear to be a determining factor.

Turning to the use of what were described earlier as more "sophisticated" selection techniques it would appear that Irish-owned organisations display a lesser tendency to utilise such selection techniques than do non Irish-owned organisations. A total of 36 per cent of Irish-owned companies do not utilise aptitude tests at all while the comparable figure for US-owned companies is 27 per cent, and for EU-owned companies is 22 per cent. When the data are compared with the 1992 survey results, however, it emerges that Irish-owned companies may, in fact, have increased their utilisation of aptitude tests since, in 1992, just 31 per cent of Irish-owned organisations reported that they used aptitude tests on a regular basis. As expected, larger-owned companies report a slightly greater propensity to use aptitude tests, while union status does not appear to have any discernible impact on aptitude testing.

The use of psychometric testing is reportedly low in most organisations surveyed, but again, it appears that Irish-owned organisations are the least likely to use this selection technique. Here, 58 per cent of Irish-owned organisations do not use psychometric tests while the comparator for US-owned organisations is 44 per cent, for EU firms is 43 per cent and for non-EU companies is 46 per cent. The data here supports the earlier findings in 1992 where Irish-owned organisations were far less likely to use psychometric testing than were their foreign-owned counterparts (just 14 per cent of Irish-owned companies used psychometric tests in 1992 compared with 37 per cent of US companies, 46 per cent of UK organisations and 46 per cent of non-EU-owned organisations). However, even though the use of psychometric testing is not that popular, the data here suggest that its use is becoming more widespread than was the case in 1992. While union status does not appear to affect the decision to utilise psychometric tests, their use tends to be more widespread in larger organisations (42 per cent of large organisations do not use such tests while the comparative figure for small organisations is 61 per cent).

The reported use of assessment centres as a selection device was reported low in the 1992 survey, and this appears to have continued in the intervening three years to 1995. Just 13 per cent of Irish-owned organisations report that they use assessment centres and, while this figure shows an increase on the 1992 figure of 4 per cent, assessment centres do not appear to be given serious consideration when making the selection decision. EU-owned organisations report a higher increased use of assessment centres than do any other ownership category which again is consistent with data reported in 1992, but this usage tends to be targeted at specific appointments rather than as a systematic assessment mechanism. This is not altogether unsurprising since the costs associated with assessment centres can often limit their application to certain job categories. No significant differences emerge with respect to union status or organisation size.

It would appear, then, that the traditional selection methods continue to be popular among most of the organisations surveyed but the data do suggest that organisations are slightly more disposed towards varying the selection techniques available to them, than was the case in 1992. For most organisations this is inherently linked to the job category involved and so it could be argued that sophisticated selection techniques are used on a piecemeal, incremental basis, rather than as the norm for all job vacancies.

CONCLUSION

This chapter has sought to examine the nature of recruitment and selection practices in Ireland using data generated by the 1995 Cranfield/University of Limerick Study. Where possible, comparisons have been made with data collected by the Cranfield/University of Limerick survey in 1992 in an effort to explore possible changes in recruitment and selection practices in the intervening three year period. Overall, the picture emerging with respect to the way in which organisations approach the recruitment and selection process is relatively unsurprising. Ireland has experienced an economic boom in the past few years and this upsurge in economic activity has resulted in more organisations expanding their workforce numbers to meet demands in their respective product/service markets. Interestingly, since 1993, the unprecedented growth in the Irish economy has resulted in the creation of mainly full-time jobs which may be related to the general expansion of manufacturing employment and the current "boom" being experienced in the building and construction industry.

A number of interesting findings emerged from the survey data that are worth summarising here. In general, policies in relation to recruitment and selection tend to be determined at either national headquarter level or at the level of the establishment. However, it would appear that broader or more strategic policies concerned with workforce adjustment are more likely to be decided at either the international headquarter or national headquarter level, than at local level. This represents a significant change since 1992 when such policies were twice as likely to be determined at local rather than at international headquarter level, suggesting, perhaps, that headquarters are reclaiming more strategic policy decisions while concomitantly devolving responsibility for some of the more procedural personnel activities, such as recruitment and selection. At the organisational level, responsibility for policy decisions in relation to recruitment and selection continues to be shared jointly by the specialist HR function and line management. Here, most organisational types surveyed indicate some increase in line involvement, but this tends to be more prevalent in larger organisations, and in non-Irish-owned companies. However, the devolvement thesis that advances the view that line management will become the primary "owners" of many personnel activities, including recruitment and selection, does not appear to be supported here.

A number of strategies have been adopted in an effort to facilitate the recruitment process. In particular, many organisations, particularly those that are Irish-owned, are investing heavily in retraining as a means of aiding their recruitment drive, while others have improved their pay/benefits package, targeted international recruits or sought to improve their corporate image. In terms of the recruitment process itself, a variety of internal and external recruitment methods continue to enjoy popularity. From an overall perspective, however, there is evidence to suggest that all organisations surveyed are making greater use of their internal labour markets for the purpose of filling managerial vacancies. This is particularly true for junior and middle management vacancies, whereas consultants are more likely to be utilised to fill senior management positions. Larger organisations continue to report a greater propensity to utilise their internal labour market, than do their smaller counterparts, while Irish-owned organisations are found to be less likely to make use of their internal markets than the foreign-owned organisations surveyed. This may be a reflection both of the loose nature of the external labour market where Irish companies have little difficulty finding suitable external candidates, and of the close association of HRM practices, particularly progressive internal career development, with foreign multinational organisations. The evidence overall does not support the trend away from internal labour markets as depicted in the US by Capelli (1995).

The results affirm the continuing popularity of the traditionally used selection techniques such as the interview, the application form and the reference, despite their reported lack of reliability and validity, while only a small number of organisations report their use of more sophisticated selection tools such as assessment centres and psychological testing. One can argue that this has been a pragmatic response to the oversupply that has characterised the Irish labour market in recent years where, in general terms, most organisations have found it relatively easy to attract candidates. The data do, however, indicate that organisations are demonstrating a greater propensity to vary the types of selection tools used depending on the vacancy being filled and so are likely to make greater use of some of the more "sophisticated" selection techniques for critical job positions. This does not, however, represent a deliberate, organisation-wide, strategic selection strategy.

Overall, the evidence presented in this chapter suggests that, while recruitment and selection practices remain largely unchanged since the early 1990s, there is some evidence to suggest that organisations are gradually becoming more strategic in their approach to workforce management. The increasing importance being placed on having a well-developed, flexible workforce will create a need for mobile internal labour markets, which may result in increased internal recruitment in Irish organisations. Finally, it is proposed that some of the more sophisticated selection techniques may witness increased usage in the future, since, where the labour market begins to exhibit tighter properties and growing shortages of particular skills begin to emerge, more sophisticated hiring practices that can identify the range of skills and capabilities required by organisations, will become critically important. Some evidence of this tightening has already begun to appear with skill shortages and poaching being experienced in the computer software and financial services sectors. As industries become more skill intensive, it is estimated that the demand for knowledge-based workers with the capacity to be creative and innovative will continue to escalate.

References

Aaker, D. (1989): "Managing Assets and Skills: The Key to Sustainable Competitive Advantage", *California Management Review*, Winter, 91–106.

Adkins, C., Russell, C. and Werbel, J. (1994): "Judgements of Fit in the Selection Process: The Role of Work Value Congruence", *Personnel Psychology*, Autumn, 47(3): 605–623.

Anastasi, A., (1982); *Psychological Testing*, London: Macmillan.

Anderson, N. (1992): "Eight Decades of Employment Interview Research: A Retrospective Meta-Review and Prospective Commentary", *The European Work and Organisational Psychologist*, 2: 1–32

Anderson, N and Shackleton, V. (1993): *Successful Selection Interviewing*, Oxford: Blackwell.

Anderson, N. and Shackleton, V. (1986): "Recruitment and Selection: A Review of Developments in the 1980s", *Personnel Review*, 15(4): 19–25.

Bechet, T. and Walker, J. (1995): "Aligning Staffing with Business Strategy", *Human Resource Planning*, 16(2): 1–16.

Bowen, D., Ledford, G. and Nathan, B. (1991): "Hiring for the Organisation, not the Job", *Academy of Management Executive*, 5: 35–51.

Breaugh, J. and Mann, R. (1984): "Recruiting Source Effects: A Test of Two Alternative Explanations", *Journal of Occupational Psychology*, 57: 261–67.

Burack, E. and Singh, R. (1995): "The New Employment Relations Compact", *Human Resource Planning*, 18(1): 12–20.

Cappelli, P. (1995): "Rethinking Employment", *British Journal of Industrial Relations*, 33(4): 563–602.

Carroll, S.J. (1991): "The New HRM Roles, Responsibilities and Structures", in Schuler, R.S. (ed.) *Managing Human Resources in the Information Age*, Washington D.C.: Bureau of National Affairs, 204–26.

Chatman, J. (1989): "Improving Interactional Organisational Research: A Model of Person–Organisation Fit", *Academy of Management Review*, 14: 333–49.

Cook, M. (1993): *Personnel Selection and Productivity* second edition, Chichester: John Wiley.

Dale, M. (1995): *Successful Recruitment and Selection: A Practical Guide for Managers*, London: Kogan Page.

DeWitte, K. (1989): "Recruitment and Advertising", in Herriot, P., *Recruitment and Selection in Organisations*, Chichester: John Wiley.

Dobbs, J. (1993): "The Empowerment Environment", *Training and Development*, February.

Dobson, P. (1989): "Reference Reports" in Herriot, P. (ed.), *Assessment and Selection in Organisations*, Chichester: John Wiley.

Farnham, D. and Pimlott, J. (1995): *Understanding Industrial Relations*, third edition, London: Cassells.

Ferris, G. and King, T. (1991): "Politics in Human Resources Decisions: A Walk on the Dark Side", *Organisational Dynamics*, 20: 59–71.

Ferris, G, King, T., Judge, T. and Kacmar, K. (1991): "The Management of Shared Meaning in Organisations: Opportunism in the Reflection of Attitudes, Beliefs and Values", in Giacalone, R. and Rosenfeld, P. (eds.), *Applied*

Impression Management: How Image-Making Affects Managerial Decisions, Newbury Park, CA: Sage Publications.

Guest, D. (1983): "Personnel Management Strategies, Procedures and Techniques" in Guest, D. and Kenny, J. (eds.), *A Textbook of Techniques and Strategies in Personnel Management*, London: IPM.

Gunnigle, P. (1992): "Human Resource Management in Ireland", *Employee Relations*, 14(5): 5–22.

Gunnigle, P., Morley, M., Clifford, N. and Turner, T. (eds.) (1997): *Human Resource Management in Irish Organisations: Practice in Perspective*, Dublin: Oak Tree Press.

Hackman, R. (1986): "The Psychology of Self Management in Organisations", in Pallack, M., and Perloff, R. (eds.), *Psychology and Work: Productivity, Change and Employment*, American Psychological Association Master Lectures, 89–136.

Heraty, N., Gunnigle, P. and Clifford, N. (1997): "Recruitment and Selection in Ireland", in Gunnigle, P., Morley, M., Clifford, N. and Turner, T. (eds.), *Human Resource Management in Irish Organisations: Practice in Perspective*, Dublin: Oak Tree Press.

Herriot, P. (1989): *Recruitment in the '90s*, London: Institute of Personnel Management.

Herriot, P. and Rothwell, C. (1983): "Organisational Choice and Decision Theory — Effects of Employer's Literature and Selection Interview", *Journal of Occupational Psychology*, 56: 7–31.

Higgins, C. (1992): "Executive Search — An Essential Requirement for the 1990s", *Industrial Relations News*, 38, October,16–19.

Hunter, J.E. and Hunter, R.F. (1984): "Validity and Utility of Alternative Predictors of Job Performance", *Psychological Bulletin*, 96: 72–98

Jackson, S., Schuler, R. and Rivero, J. (1989): "Organisational Characteristics as Predictors of Personnel Practices", *Personnel Psychology*, 42(4): 727–785.

Judge, T. and Ferris, G. (1994): "The Elusive Criterion of Fit in Human Resources Staffing Decisions", *Human Resource Planning*,15(4):47–66.

Kamoche, K. (1994): "A Critique and a Proposed Reformulation of strategic Human Resource Management", *Human Resource Management Journal* 4(4): 29–43.

Kilibarda, P. and Fonda, N. (1997): "Random Selection", *People Management*, December, 36–39.

Kirnan, J.P., Farley, J. and Geisinger, K. (1989): "The Relationship between Recruiting Sources, Applicant Quality and Hire Performance: An analysis by Sex, Ethnicity and Age", *Personnel Psychology*, 42: 293–308.

Krauthamer, G. and Dorfman, T. (1996): "Quality in an American Consultancy Organisation. Executive Search: How it Works, Why it Works and the Impact of the Quality Movement", in Smith, M. and Sutherland, V. (eds.), *Professional Issues in Selection and Assessment*, Chichester: John Wiley.

Lawler, E. (1986): *High Involvement Management: Participating Strategies for Organisational Performance*, London: Jossey-Bass.

Lewis, C. (1984): "What's New in Selection?", *Personnel Management*, January, 14–16.

McMahon, G. (1988): "Personnel Selection in Ireland: Scientific Prediction or Crystal Ball Gazing?", *IPM News*, 3(3): 20–23.

Montgomery, C. (1996): Organisation Fit is Key to Job Success, *HRMagazine*, January, 41(1): 94–97.

Muchinski, P. (1986): "Personnel Selection Methods" in Cooper, C. and Robertson, I.T. (eds.), *International Review of Industrial and Organisational Psychology*, New York: John Wiley.

Murray, S. (1984): *Employee Relations in Irish Private Sector Manufacturing Industry*, Dublin: Industrial Development Authority.

O'Reilly, C., Chatman, J. and Caldwell, D., (1991): "People and Organisational Culture: A Profile Comparison Approach to Assessing Person-Organisation Fit", *Academy of Management Journal*, 34: 487–516.

Pettigrew, P., Hendry, C., and Sparrow, P. (1988): *Linking Strategic Change, Competitive Performance and Human Resource Management: Results of a UK-based Empirical Study*, Coventry: University of Warwick.

Pfeffer, J. (1994): *Competitive Advantage Through People. Unleashing the Power of the Workforce*, Boston, Mass.: Harvard Business School Press.

Plumbley, P. (1985): *Recruitment and Selection*, London: Institute of Personnel Management.

Price, J. (1997): "Handbook of Organisational Measurement", *International Journal of Manpower*, 18(4,5,6): 404–410.

Raghuram, S. and Arvey, R. (1996): "Business Strategy Links with Staffing and Training Practices", *Human Resource Planning*, 17(3): 55–73.

Reilly, R., and Chao, G. (1982): "Validity and Fairness of Some Alternative Selection Procedures", *Personnel Psychology*, 35: 1–62.

Ripley, R. and Ripley, M. (1994): "CREAM: Criteria Related Employability Assessment Method: A Systematic Model for Employee Selection", *Management Decision*, 32(9): 27–36.

Robertson, I.T., and Makin, P. (1986): "Management Selection in Britain: A Survey and Critique", *Journal of Occupational Psychology*, 59: 45–57.

Rynes, S.L. (1993): "Who's Selecting Whom? Effects of Selection Practices on Applicants' Attitudes and Behaviour", in Schmitt, N. and Borman, W. (eds.), *Personnel Selection in Organisations*, San Francisco, CA: Jossey-Bass.

Schuler, H., Frier, D. and Kauffmann, H. (1993): *Personalauswahl im Europäischen Vergleich*, Göttingen: Hogrefe.

Smith, M. and Robertson, I.T. (1993): *The Theory and Practice of Systematic Staff Selection*, London: Macmillan.

Smith, M. and Sutherland, V. (1996) (eds.): *International Review of Professional Issues in Selection and Assessment*, Chichester: John Wiley.

Smith, M., Gregg, M. and Andrews, D. (1989): *Selection and Assessment — A New Appraisal*, London: Pitman.

Sparrow, P. and Hiltrop, J. (1994): *European Human Resource Management in Transition*, London: Prentice Hall.

Storey, J. (1995): *Human Resource Management: A Critical Text*, London: Routledge.

Storey, J. (1992): *Developments in the Management of Human Resources*, Oxford: Blackwell.

Terpstra, D. (1996): "The Search for Effective Methods (Employee Recruitment and Selection)", *HR Focus*, 17(5): 16–18.

Walker, J. (1992): *Human Resource Strategy*, New York: McGraw-Hill.

Walton, R. and Lawrence, P. (1990): *Human Resource Management — Trends and Challenges*, Boston, Mass.:Harvard Business School Press.

Wiesner, W.H. and Cronshaw, S.F. (1988): "A Meta-analytic Investigation of the Impact of Interview Format and Degree of Structure on the Validity of the Employment Interview", *Journal of Occupational Psychology*, 61: 275–90.

Wood, S. (1985): "Recruitment Systems and the Recession", *British Journal of Industrial Relations*, 23(4): 103–120.

Worren, N. and Koestner, R. (1996): "Seeking Innovating Team Players: Contextual Determinants of Preferred Applicant Attributes", *The International Journal of Human Resource Management*, 7(2): 521–33.

5

MANAGING HUMAN RESOURCE DEVELOPMENT

James Walsh

Small states must rely heavily on the quality of their strategic thinking to counter their vulnerability to international influences. Without superior strategic thinking, they will be buffeted rudderless, like a cork on a wave — J.J. Lee, 1989; *Ireland: Politics and Society: 1912–1985*, p. 631.

INTRODUCTION

This chapter focuses on how human resource development can contribute to the effectiveness of the organisation. The chapter focuses on the role of management development within the context of more broad-based employee development and begins with an overview of the argument in favour of investment in human resource development as one of the fundamental means of achieving and sustaining competitive advantage. The current situation in relation to both employee development and management development in Ireland is then outlined. Some of the critical elements in successful human resource development models are identified. A brief assessment of the future role of human resource development concludes the chapter.

WHY MANAGING EMPLOYEE DEVELOPMENT IS IMPORTANT

A number of trends have combined to ensure that employee development has become a focus of attention in recent years. These include research which has centred on the crucial role of firm-specific resources in the attainment of and sustaining of competitive advantage (Hamel and Prahalad, 1996; Pfeffer, 1994; Quinn, 1992; Barney, 1991). This strand of research in management contends that, as other sources of advantage become more imitable and more available to more competitors, then it is in the domain of intangible asset development that the greatest return in benefiting from assets can be realised. Of all the resources of the firm, this view maintains, it is the thinking capacity of the organisation — the creative human resource — which has most potential for delivering to the organisation that rarity which others cannot or will find difficult to copy (Flood et al., 1996; Garratt, 1996). Thus, in markets characterised by increasing rates of change and competition, moving beyond what Porter (1996) and others have termed "factor advantage" to higher value-added activities offers a route to firms seeking significant differentiation strategies. Porter has, of course, criticised Ireland in this regard, as having moved too slowly to build longer term and more indigenously focused strategies of differentiated industrial development:

> A development strategy based solely on foreign multinationals may doom a nation to remaining a factor-driven economy. . . . The growth of indigenous companies is a much slower, and in many ways riskier, process than attracting foreign multinationals. Yet if it succeeds, the result can be the means to move beyond factor-driven advantage, as Japan and Korea have demonstrated. Indigenous firms view the nation as the home base. They energise the process of creating advanced and specialised factors . . . they upgrade competitive advantages beyond basic factors. Provided government does not interfere, they eventually develop global strategies that make competitive advantage more sustainable and upgrade it further. Eventually as the

nation develops, factor cost-sensitive activities are shifted abroad, raising national productivity.

Foreign multinationals should be only *one component* of a developing nation's economic strategy, and an evolving component. At some stage in the development process, the focus should shift to indigenous companies. In Singapore and Ireland, my view is that the shift has been too little and too late. Neither nation has truly committed to the slow process of developing a broader base of indigenous firms (1990: 679).

It is an intriguing prospect, therefore, to consider whether recent record growth rates in the Irish economy have resulted in any significant shift in emphasis of Ireland's historic approach to economic development, and whether we have seen sufficient use of our human capital resources in the direction commentators like Porter recommend. It is also an interesting question to consider to what should our investment in *managerial* development be applied? Is it to efficiency improvement in the ranks of management within existing public sector organisations and indigenous and foreign-owned business? Or is it to the generation and implementation of new strategies [or entrepreneurial ideas] — which is, for Barney (1991), the pre-eminent resource available to organisations and the lack of which was for Fanning (1986) the ultimate "black-hole" in the Irish economy.

Not all commentators, however, characterise human resource development (HRD) as the development of *creative* resources, as the resource base view ultimately does. The more traditional and established route in the management discipline is to consider the activities of the organisation as requiring of sets of skills and abilities and to consider, in turn, employee development as the process whereby the strategic and operational direction necessary to link jobs more effectively to skilled employees can be accomplished. This interpretation has led to a useful, if sometimes overdone, emphasis on the costs of employee development — a feature of analysis which the resource base view of the firm seeks to supplant. Thus, the utility-based view of employee development suggests that employee training should be considered only where direct linkages to the actual work activities of the organisation can be identified, and then as costs to be minimised at every possible turn. Recent evidence in international HRD suggests that this is in fact what is happening (Karr, 1990).

In the resource base scenario, by contrast, employees are seen as one of the critical resources of the organisation (along with other resources such as brand names, physical assets, reputation and so on). An investment approach to the deployment of these assets is viewed as a more appropriate interpretation of current value and future potential. It is worth noting that attempts have been made for quite some time by some researchers to bring human assets onto the balance sheet (Flamholtz, 1974) but it is perhaps as much the "ethics" of considering the potential effects on human beings of conducting "net present value" or IRR analyses on one's stock of human capital more than any reluctance on the part of the senior management of the firm that represents the ultimate obstacle in this respect.

THE CONTRIBUTION OF EMPLOYEE DEVELOPMENT TO COMPETITIVE ADVANTAGE

As we have established, recent interest has centred on the internal resources of the organisation, especially the human resource, as representing the best source of potentially unique, non-substitutable and expensively-formed advantage (see Flood, 1996: pp 3–30 for a detailed explanation). Other researchers have also sought evidence to support the link between employees and competitive success. Pfeffer (1994) studied the companies which had consistently returned the highest returns on capital in the United States in the period 1974–94. His analysis suggest that it is companies which, among other characteristics, treat their employees as assets and as partners in their business which topped the list — among them Southwest Airlines, Nordstrom and Hewlett-Packard.

Another view of the importance of employee development is to consider how workforce knowledge can contribute to overall firm potential. Hamel and Prahalad (1995) stress the value of "core competencies" as being bundles of skills and abilities which can be harnessed and exploited by organisations. Clearly, a skilled and talented workforce is likely to provide much of what is "core" to "competence" in this definition. Tyson (1995: 97) in his study of 30 large, UK-based firms, established that employee and especially management development, was one of the "strongest levers which were pulled to make the organisations change". In the broad European context, Sparrow and Hiltrop (1994) in a comprehensive review of employee training and development (ETD) practices, conclude that ETD activities are going to be at the heart of HRM strategies being adopted by many European companies. They see the ETD process as representing the capacity of the organisation to manage transition successfully — from national to international and increasingly global competition, and from more traditional to knowledge-intensive competitive arenas:

> ETD centres around the efforts made by organisations to increase the ability of individuals and groups to perform, and the management of planned learning experiences that facilitate the acquisition of job or organisational-related knowledge and skills. The success of European organisations will in large part be determined by their ability to train and develop their employees to meet the challenges of business integration and change (Sparrow and Hiltrop, 1994: 423).

Finally, while most of the work on human resource strategy has taken the large enterprise as its unit of analysis, there has been some work both in Ireland and in the UK which has examined the impact of staffing development issues generally in the small and medium-sized enterprise (Walsh, 1995a; Hendry et al., 1995). A particularly eloquent defence of the importance of employees in the SME is given by Hendry and his co-authors, and the description could equally be applied to many larger organisations:

> If small-medium firms are important, why in turn should we study the people within them? A simple answer is that people are the actors through whom strategy unfolds, as a

result of which firms succeed or fail. However, a more complete answer needs to recognise the diverse roles people play in representing the history and interests of a firm, in providing specific knowledge and expertise, and in contributing to both internal and external communications. . . . People act, among other things, as owners, as entrepreneurs, as sources of skill and expertise, as collaborators, as participants in network and learning activities, and as agents of their own careers, all of which have a particular flavour in the small-medium firm setting (Hendry, et al., 1995: 10).

ELEMENTS IN EFFECTIVE EMPLOYEE DEVELOPMENT

In this section, we look at the components of effective employee development strategies and sketch the process by which employee development is managed. Most human resource development plans are considered as beginning with an assessment of the overall or corporate objectives to be achieved and a consideration of how the human resource management strategy contributes to the realisation of these goals. The training and development strategy is then articulated and a thorough diagnosis of training and developmental needs undertaken. Following this, the appropriate training/development programme is implemented and results — both from an individual participant's perspective and from the organisational view — are then evaluated. Ultimately, the purpose of much of this highly linear approach to employee development is to conduct what is termed "gap analysis". This approach centres on the notion that, given the rate of change in the internal and external firm environments and the rate at which domain knowledge is increasing and workforce obsolescence is likely as a result to be accelerating, there is the potential for a gap to exist between overall existing skill levels and required abilities. Figure 5.1 shows the typical sequence of the approach adopted:

FIGURE 5.1: TRADITIONAL/LINEAR APPROACHES TO HUMAN
RESOURCE DEVELOPMENT

The detail of each of these steps cannot be considered here and
the reader is referred to Beardwell and Holden (1997) or Garavan,
et al. (1995) for further in-depth consideration of the training and
development process.

However, despite the appeal of normative frameworks such as
the one outlined above, the question remains as to how much employee development activity actually follows such an integrated
pattern in the real politick of organisational life. For example,
Holden and Livian (1992) and Holden (1991) found that 41 per
cent of personnel departments in the UK Price Waterhouse/
Cranfield Survey (PW/C) of Human Resource Management did not
know how much money was being spent on training and 38 per
cent did not know the average number of days allocated per person in the organisation. Heraty and Morley (1997) report that 25
per cent of their 261 respondents in the PW/C survey — which
was a survey of HR practices in companies in Ireland employing
more than 50 employees — do not carry out systematic training
needs analysis, leading the authors to the conclusion that "in such
circumstances, it is difficult to envisage how employee development can make a strategic contribution to effective organisational
functioning" (p.137).

A further interesting finding from the PW/C survey of Irish organisations is that the proportion of firms responding that they did not know how many days' training were received by employee category ranged from 32 per cent in relation to management (the lowest "don't know" score reported) to 51 per cent in relation to manual employees, the highest "don't know" response. Given that survey questionnaires were mailed to either the personnel manager or the chief executive in this study, and allowing for the usual difficulties in determining who actually completes these instruments, these results are quite revealing about the state of employee development in Ireland.

MANAGEMENT DEVELOPMENT IN IRELAND

The history of management development in Ireland can be characterised as not benefiting from detailed empirical analysis, at least until recently. A 1984 survey of 15 private companies by FÁS (then known as AnCO) showed that only 25 per cent of them considered themselves fully committed to management training and development. A more intensive attempt at assessing the national situation in relation to management development was *the Report of the Advisory Committee on Management Training* (1988). Commissioned by the Department of Labour, the advisory committee found that 20 per cent of the firms they surveyed could not tell or did not know what they spent on management development and that average spend for half the top companies was £5,000 per company per annum on *all* management development activities. From this analysis followed the somewhat predictable, if none the less merited, recommendation that an enhanced commitment to management development was warranted among Irish companies, especially for smaller, indigenously-owned enterprises which were considered to do hardly any management training at all. A further recommendation, that the existing separate provision for managerial training, then provided by the Irish Management Institute and the Institute for Public Administration, be merged has not been followed through — even though public sector employee training is often similar to that in private sector organisations and commitment to HRD appears well spread throughout the public sector (Linehan and Walsh, 1996).

The Price Waterhouse/Cranfield Surveys of 1992 and 1995, conducted in Ireland by a research team from the University of Limerick, did collect data on training and development but did not focus specifically in depth on management development (see Gunnigle, et al., 1997 for the detailed analysis of the most recent survey). These developments were followed by the undertaking in 1996 of a large-scale survey of management development in Ireland by a research team based at University College, Cork. The survey used a postal questionnaire mailed to the Business & Finance Top 1000 companies and 500 firms employing from 1–50 and 51–100 employees respectively (Walsh et al., 1998). The survey reports a 23 per cent response rate across all three firm size categories and is the first such detailed research project of its kind in Ireland focusing in depth on management development. Initial findings reveal that most respondent firms do not have a written management development strategy document (69 per cent) even though 83 per cent of firms participating in the study reported that their most senior human resources/personnel manager was a member of their top management team. An average spend on management development activities of 2 per cent of payroll was reported and days of workforce training received ranged from 3 for the board of directors to 6 for senior management and 9 for middle management and 1st level supervisors. Three other aspects of the survey can be highlighted here. These are: (i) the importance of management development; (ii) frequency of use of formal career planning activities and (iii) the importance of management development for the future growth of the organisation.

Importance of Management Development

First, in terms of the perceived importance of management development strategy for corporate objectives, a majority of firms reported that they saw their management development activities as contributing either significantly or contributing somewhat to the achievement of corporate/organisational objectives (See Table 5.1).

At least a quarter of firms responding rated the contribution as significant in relation to each of the corporate objectives listed, with particular emphasis on the contribution of management development to cost reduction, continuous product improvement and improved customer satisfaction. Interestingly, almost a third of respondents considered that their management development strategy did not contribute to organisational objectives in relation to new product development, a finding which has implications for the notion of the "intelligent enterprise" where most if not all developmental activity centres on increasing the ability of the wider organisation to deliver creative responses to competition and market opportunity (Quinn, 1992, Walsh and Linehan, 1997a).

TABLE 5.1: PERCEIVED CONTRIBUTION OF MANAGEMENT DEVELOPMENT STRATEGY TO CORPORATE/ORGANISATIONAL OBJECTIVES (%)

Objective	Contributes Significantly	Contributes Somewhat	Does not Contribute	Don't Know
Increased market share	25	61	14	55 n=268
Cost reduction	38	52	10	34 n=268
Continuous process improvement	41	49	10	37 n=286
New product development	26	43	31	60 n=263
Improved customer satisfaction	44	49	7	33 n=290

Source: Walsh et al. (forthcoming, 1998).

Frequency of Use of Career Planning Activities

Second, respondents — who were the HR manager or most senior manager responsible for HR — were also asked about the frequency of their use of career planning activities for managers. These results are shown in Table 5.2 below. The results reveal that 6 in 10 respondents seldom or do not use succession planning in their managerial career planning activities and only 16 per cent of firms always or often use planned managerial job rotation for managerial career planning. These results suggest that managers are likely to maintain functional career paths in most Irish organisations and even within this approach, a majority of firms do not use succession career planning.

Highest use is made of project/team work (66 per cent of respondents reporting they always or often use this approach) and in individual manager development (68 per cent of respondent firms reporting that they always or often utilised this technique). Perhaps the most interesting result shown in this table, however, is that only 2 per cent of firms said that they always use international experience programmes to develop their managers' careers and only 19 per cent reported often using this approach. In an era of increasing global pressures on business and given the uniquely open nature of the Irish economy, this finding suggests that organisations based in Ireland are over-emphasising a domestically-oriented approach to career planning by not including overseas experience for management career development.

TABLE 5.2: FREQUENCY OF USE OF CAREER PLANNING ACTIVITIES FOR MANAGEMENT (%)

	Always	Often	Seldom	Don't use	Don't know
Succession planning	12	28	29	31	39 n=284
Planned managerial job rotation	2	14	28	56	52 n=271
Project/team work	14	52	20	14	26 n=297
Individual manager development	14	54	23	9	17 n=306
International experience programmes	2	19	35	44	62 n=261

Source: Walsh et al. (forthcoming, 1998).

Importance of Management Development for the Future

Finally, survey respondents were asked to consider how important they considered management development activity to be in relation to a number of organisational imperatives in the medium-term. This question allows some assessment of where management development emphasis is likely to be placed by organisations in the future (see Table 5.3 below). Results show that, with the significant exception of international management, all the areas listed were considered important, with strategic management and teamwork scoring particularly highly. The evidence that a quarter of responding firms do not consider that the area of international management will require an emphasis in their management development activities serves only to support the result shown in Table 5.2 and to add to the controversy as to how prepared organisations in Ireland are in terms of dealing with the increasingly global nature of international trade (Walsh and Linehan, 1997b).

TABLE 5.3: PERCEIVED IMPORTANCE OF MANAGEMENT DEVELOPMENT FOR ORGANISATIONAL IMPERATIVES IN THE NEXT 3–5 YEARS (%)

	Very Important	Important	Somewhat Important	Not at all Important
Strategic management	12	28	29	31
International management	2	14	28	56
Team work	14	52	20	14
New product development	14	54	23	9
Creativity	2	19	35	44

Source: Walsh et al. (forthcoming, 1998).

ELEMENTS IN EFFECTIVE EMPLOYEE DEVELOPMENT STRATEGIES

We can now turn to a consideration of some of the key elements in effective employee and management development strategies. Perhaps the most important question to be considered in relation to employee development is *purpose*, i.e. for what is the employee or management development exercise being undertaken? Is it for individual development, for organisational development, or for some combination of both? The distinction between training and development is also important, the standard difference being understood as training being appropriate for skill acquisition, while development is seen as a longer-term, more holistic approach to competency and conceptual enhancement (McBeath, 1990; Harrison, 1988). The second issue of major concern is *context* — an understanding of the culture and climate where the development is taking place. Larger organisations may have significant input from corporate headquarters relating to design and delivery of development programmes, which may militate against local initiatives and differentiated development strategies. More importantly, some sectors have inherent technology cycle influences which can permeate developmental and general HRM approaches (Iansiti and West, 1997). Motorola, as an example of a firm in the fast-moving software business, are known for their "five day goal" — where five days of training per year per employee are aimed for and usually achieved. By contrast, evidence suggests, smaller and owner-managed firms in Ireland tend not to place as much emphasis on employee development as their larger counterparts, a characteristic also shared by firms in traditional industries (Walsh, 1995b; Walsh and Anderson, 1997).

Third, the question of *relevance* needs to be considered in relation to employee and management development. Many managers will be aware of the "We have some cash in the budget, let's find a training course" approach, which at best can be characterised an haphazard and has no doubt helped generate major credibility problems for the training function in many organisations. Relevance, both to the manager and the organisation, is clearly a *sine qua non* of strategic employee development activity and can be improved through careful needs analysis and professional delivery of work-related projects where the employee/manager is involved in the design and resolution of the activity (Marchington and Wilkinson, 1996; Mumford, 1988). The fourth cardinal consideration in effective employee development is *time*. There is now sufficient evidence to suggest that knowledge-based competition is likely to continue to represent the defining characteristic of many markets into the foreseeable future. Where human resource costs can be the single highest cost of the firm, efficient management of human capital becomes a necessity, not a luxury. Given the recent emphasis in the strategy field on creativity as the ultimate firm-specific resource (Porter, 1997; Barney, 1991), maximising human creative potential has shifted from being a luxury firms thought they could ill-afford to being the very reason they can stay in business. The empirical evidence in relation to the time being committed by Irish organisations to human resource development in general, and to creative thinking in particular, is not encouraging, however. Both the Price Waterhouse/Cranfield study at the University of Limerick and the UCC Management Development project confirm that fewer than 10 days per year training are received by managers with the overwhelming majority of firms reporting fewer than five days training per capita for managers along with other employee categories such as technical and clerical staff. When we consider that an average working year of 45 weeks is the equivalent of 225 days; then five days of development equate to approximately two per cent of time at work. It is difficult to determine whether such an investment is sufficient to keep up with the extensive changes and cognitive development required in an knowledge-intensive era — and there are other means of development centred on individual motivation and proclivities — but such an amount does appear to err on the side of caution.

A fifth element in effective employee development is the amount of *resources*, both human and financial, devoted to it. Average spend by organisations in Ireland on employee development and management education appears to be in the region of two per cent of payroll (Heraty and Morley, 1997; Walsh, et al., forthcoming). Innovative responses by organisations to whether and how much time employees devote to creative thinking seems to be few and far between in the research literature, with the time-honoured exceptions in the case of companies such as 3M, where 15 per cent of time may be so spent. We are clearly in an era where creativity matters, however, and giving HR development the scale and scope it requires and deserves is one way of obtaining the commitment effective development demands (See Box 5.1).

The sixth element in any developmental process is *evaluation*. This step, often omitted from training efforts, comprises the twin components of individual evaluation — in what ways has development effected the employee — and organisational evaluation — how does the organisation benefit from the development undertaken? Again, as is the case with many of these elements, managers will realise that apart from often quite sanitised course satisfaction surveys, little is typically done about such evaluations in practice. This is to be regretted, as the techniques of cost-benefit analysis in training and development and the linking of training needs analysis to programme design and delivery have improved considerably in recent years (Truelove, 1992; McBeath, 1990; Baird, et al., 1983).

A seventh and potentially significant requirement in effective employee development is the notion of *continued commitment* — a need to move beyond the fads which have bedevilled so much activity in this area. Progressive organisations and reflective managerial practitioners are realising that building development into the entire human resource process is a vital element in ensuring the survival of organisations (McCall, 1997; Ulrich, 1996; Prahalad and Hamel, 1990). We are beginning to see the first signs of that in the take-up by Irish organisations of their own development programmes rather than relying on the often more generic courses offered by the universities and some consultants. In 1995–7, for example, some 50 unique projects were funded in Ireland by a budget allocated at c. £20 million under the ADAPT initiative of

the European Union, a programme designed to fund human resource development across all sectors of the economy. Organisations participating included Dairygold and Golden Vale in the food
sector, ICTU and SIPTU among trade union organisations, Guin-
ness and Waterford Crystal among publicly-traded private sector
enterprises and Macnas, the Galway-based cultural group. The
1997–9 ADAPT round of funding has attracted in the region of
150 applications from diverse organisations around the country,
all of whom are required to design and deliver bespoke and insti-
tutionally relevant human resource development programmes.

In conclusion, recent research is suggesting that organisational
focus on human resource development can be seen as following an
evolutionary tendency, i.e. a trendline followed by successful organisations which reveals movement from little or no investment
by firms in training to higher levels and deeper processes of human capital integration (Probst and Buchel, 1997: 147). This approach, which stresses the learning partnership idea, seeks to ensure that investment in human capital development is not left
simply or exclusively to formal training programmes, but becomes
a fundamental piece of organisational life, through "making
learning natural" (Sattelberger, 1991). Such a link between HRD
and the generation of more deep-seated and longer-lasting organisational routines represents a welcome deepening and broadening of the traditional role accorded employee development strategies. It is in this more systemic and revolutionary guise, as a critical part of the process by which "competent enquiry" (Argyris and
Schon, 1996) is generated in understanding and resolving the
complexities of organisational life, that we can reasonably expect
to discern the future for the strategic management of employee
development.

BOX 5.1: MANAGEMENT DEVELOPMENT AT DAIRYGOLD

Dairygold is a large agribusiness which employs some 3,000 staff, focused on food processing and dairy operations and headquartered in the heart of the Golden Vale in Mitchelstown, Co. Cork. In the period 1995–1997, the organisation was successful in obtaining funding assistance from the ADAPT programme of the EU to support HRD activities in the organisation. An internal project team comprising the Group HR Manager, Training Manager, Training Officer and one of the divisional personnel mangers, was formed and this group, along with a number of external consultants, designed a management development programme for senior managers across the company. The programme design was innovative and included presentations to senior management about the goals of the programme, individual interviews with those participating in order to determine training needs and "buzz" sessions with groups of mangers to elicit developmental needs across the various business units.

In an action learning format, 44 mostly senior managers, in two cohorts of 22, met in five week-long sessions once a month over a six-month period and also travelled overseas for a week to visit leading European industrial companies. A learning log system was used as an integrating mechanism throughout the programme and managers were encouraged to diary their learning and reflections on how the material covered in the class sessions was relevant at work and vice versa. Project teams of six/seven participants, which grouped together managers from different backgrounds and divisions of the business, focused on live issues of importance to Dairygold. Upon completion of the programme, the project teams made presentations to senior management on how relevant changes to organisational structure, culture and management should proceed. Participant reaction to the developmental aspect of the programme was uniformly positive, possibly reflecting the care taken to be inclusive at the design stage and the action-centred nature of the programme overall. The project format was considered to be another positive aspect of the programme and has resulted in a number of initiatives by managers themselves based on the recommendations of the teams involved.

Source: O'Gorman, 1997.

References

Argyris, C. and Schon, D.A. (1996): *Organisational Learning II: Theory, Method and Practice*, Reading, Mass.: Addison-Wesley.

Barney, J. (1991): "Firm Resources and Sustained Competitive Advantage", *Journal of Management*, 17: 99–120.

Beardwell, I. and Holden, L. (1997): *Human Resource Management: A Contemporary Perspective*, second edition, London: Pitman Publishing.

Beer, M., Eisenstat, R.A. and Biggadike, R. (1996): "Developing an Organisation Capable of Strategy Implementation and Reformulation: A Preliminary Test" in Moingeon, B. and Edmondson, A. (eds.) *Organisational Learning and Competitive Advantage*, 165–184, London: Sage.

Committee on Management Training in Ireland, Report of (1988): Chaired by P. Galvin, Dublin: The Stationery Office.

Fanning, C. (1986): *Renewing a Local Economy: the Entrepreneurial Response to Crisis*, Cork: Cork University Press.

Flood, P., Gannon, M.J., and Paauwe, J. (1996): *Managing Without Traditional Methods: International Innovations in Human Resource Management*, Wokingham: Addison-Wesley.

Garavan, T., Costine, P. and Heraty, N. (1995): *Training and Development in Ireland: Context, Policy and Practice*, Dublin: Oak Tree Press.

Garratt, B. (1996): *Developing Strategic Thought*, London: McGraw-Hill.

Gunnigle, P., Morley, M., Clifford, N, Turner, T. with Heraty, N. and Crowley, M. (1997): *Human Resource Management in Irish Organisations: Practice in Perspective*, Dublin: Oak Tree Press.

Hamel, G. and Prahalad, C.K. (1996): *Competing for the Future*, Boston, Mass.: Harvard Business School Press

Prahalad, C.K. and Hamel, G. (1990): "The Core Competence of the Corporation", *Harvard Business Review*, May–June, 79–91.

Harrison, R. (1988): *Training and Development*, London: IPM.

Hendry. C., Arthur, M.B. and Jones, A.M. (1995): *Strategy Through People: Adaptation and Learning in the Small-Medium Enterprise*, London: Routledge.

Heraty, N. and Morley, M. (1997): "Training and Development", in Gunnigle, P., Morley, M., Clifford, N., Turner, T. with Heraty, N. and Crowley, M., *Human Resource Management in Irish Organisations: Practice in Perspective*, 127–155, Dublin: Oak Tree Press.

Holden, L. (1991): "European Trends in Training and Development", *International Journal of Human Resource Management*, 2(2): 113–131.

Holden, L. and Livian, Y. (1992): "Does Strategic Training Policy Exist?: Some Evidence from Ten European Countries", *Personnel Review*, 21(1): 12–23.

Iansiti, M., and West, J. (1997): "Technology Integration: Turning Great Research into Great Products", *Harvard Business Review*, 75(3): 69–79.

Karr, A.R. (1990): "Work Skills Panel Urges Major Changes in School Education, Job Organisation", *The Wall Street Journal*, 19 June, A4 — quoted in Flood, P., Gannon, M.J. and Paauwe, J. (eds.), *Managing Without Traditional Methods: International Innovations in Human Resource Management*, 12, Wokingham: Addison-Wesley.

Lee, J.J. (1989): *Ireland 1912–1985: Politics and Society*, Cambridge: Cambridge University Press.

Linehan, M. and Walsh, J.S. (1996): "Working for Change: Service Quality and Customer Responsiveness in the Irish Local Authority Context", in Montanheiro, L., Rebelo, E., Owen, G. and Rebelo, E. (eds.), *Public and Private Sector Partnerships Working for Change*, 329–339, Sheffield: PAVIC Publications.

Marchington, M. and Wilkinson, A. (1996): *Core Personnel and Development*, London: IPD.

McBeath, G. (1990): *Practical Management Development: Strategies for Management Resourcing and Development in the 1990s*, Oxford: Basil Blackwell.

McCall, Jr., M.W. (1997): *High Flyers: Developing the Next Generation of Leaders*, Boston, Mass.: Harvard Business School Press.

Monks, K., and Walsh, J.S. (1997): "Interunit Linkages and Interunit Learning: The Role of Strategic Human Resource Management in the Multinational Enterprise", in *Proceedings of the 12th Workshop on Strategic Human Resource Management*, Turku, Finland, 24–25 March.

Mumford, A. (1988): *Developing the Top Manager*, Aldershot: Gower.

O'Gorman, P. (1997): Presentation to the *Annual Conference of the Irish Institute of Training and Development*, Shannon, March.

Pfeffer, J. (1994): *Competitive Advantage through People*. Boston, Mass.: Harvard Business School Press.

Porter, M.E. (1996): "What is Strategy?", *Harvard Business Review*, Nov–Dec, 61–78.

Porter, M.E. (1990): *The Competitive Advantage of Nations*, London: Macmillan.

Probst, G. and Buchel, B. (1997): *Organisational Learning: The Competitive Advantage of the Future*, London: Prentice Hall.

Quinn, J.B. (1992): *Intelligent Enterprise: A Knowledge and Service-based Paradigm for Industry*, New York: Free Press.

Sattelberger, T. (1991): *Der Lernende Organisation*, Wiesbaden: Gabler.

Sparrow, P. and Hiltrop, J-M. (1994): *European Human Resource Management in Transition*, London: Prentice Hall.

Truelove, S. (1992): *Handbook of Training and Development*, Oxford: Blackwell.

Tyson, S. (1995): *Human Resource Strategy: Towards a General Theory of Human Resource Management*, London: Pitman.

Uhlrich, D. (1996): *Human Resource Champions*, Cambridge, Mass.: Harvard Business School Press.

Walsh, J.S. (1995a): "The Process of Small Firm Internationalisation in Ireland: An Exploration of Human Resource Issue", in *Academy of Entrepreneurship Journal*, 1(1): 65–81.

Walsh, J.S. (1995b): "Education, Training and the Growth of the Owner-Managed Firm", in *Enterprise and the Irish Economy*, Burke, A. (ed.), 219–246, Dublin: Oak Tree Press.

Walsh, J.S. and Anderson, P.H. (1997): "Human Resources Issues in Hi-Tech Small Firm Employment Growth: A Comparison of Indigenous and Foreign-Owned Firms in Ireland", in Oakey, R. and Mukhtar, S-M. (eds.) *New Technology-Based Firms in the 1990s*, London: Paul Chapman Publishing, 189–196.

Walsh, J.S. and Linehan, M. (1997a): *Strategic Change in Employment Relations: The Case of Waterford Crystal*, mimeo, commissioned by the Labour Relations Commission, Dublin.

Walsh, J.S. and Linehan, M. (1997b): *Negotiating Change: The Case of the 1994 Rationalisation Programme at Beamish & Crawford*, mimeo, commissioned by the Labour Relations Commission, Dublin.

Walsh, J.S., Linehan, M. and Anderson, P.H. (1998): *Management Development in Ireland: A Critical Appraisal*, in press.

6

EMPLOYMENT EQUALITY: RHETORIC AND REALITY IN IRISH ORGANISATIONS

Kathy Monks

This chapter explores the human resource (HR) strategies involved in the promotion of employment equality. In writing this chapter, the aim is to redress to some extent the imbalance in the human resource management (HRM) literature which has for the most part tended to ignore the diversity of employees. This may seem at first sight strange, given that both the "hard" and the "soft" versions of HRM (Storey, 1989) place value on human resources, but employment equality has been neatly categorised as a "gender" issue within the mainstream literature and as a consequence has often been ignored elsewhere. Yet workforce diversity is increasing, and HR strategies need to be capable of catering for the different types of individuals that seek employment.

In exploring the issue of employment equality, this chapter concentrates on the position of women. This particular perspective is taken for two reasons. First, employment equality for women has been the focus of attention for at least twenty years with the Employment Equality Act of 1977 a major milestone in its provision of at least the legal acceptance of employment equality within Ireland. It is therefore possible to look back and consider the impact of this Act on women's employment. Second, organisations are changing rapidly and there is evidence that there are moves away from "command and control" approaches to managing organisations to ones which focus on "individual and team empowerment" (Partling, 1993). These new types of organisations require qualities such as teambuilding, consensus, facilitation and communications. Such skills have been characterised as "female" qualities, and it therefore necessary to explore whether the barriers that women face in work organisations can be overcome sufficiently for them to make use of these types of skills. In addition, organisations are now much leaner and need to utilise fully all their workforce; it simply does not make economic sense for the half that is female to be simply ignored. In considering the HR strategies that may be utilised in equalising employment opportunity, it should be noted, however, that such strategies cannot be viewed simply as measures which ensure that an organisation abides by the law. Davidson and Burke (1994: 5), in considering the issue of women in management, point to the competitive advantages that may accrue from policies and practices that support the career aspirations of women: the attraction and retention of the best talent, optimisation of potential and productivity, attraction and retention of clients and better quality of management. In addition, many employment equality issues may also be beneficial for men.

This chapter begins by considering the current position in relation to women's employment within Irish organisations and the legal framework which governs the employment of men and women. The obstacles to progression for women are then considered and the HR strategies used to promote employment equality are reviewed. The chapter concentrates on drawing together the available Irish research.

THE POSITION OF WOMEN IN THE LABOUR MARKET

A recent report from the Employment Equality Agency (Durkan et al., 1995) provides a comprehensive picture of the employment of women. The report charts the trend in female participation in the labour force and shows that this grew from 25.7 per cent in 1971 to 34.2 per cent in 1993 with the growth in the number of married women in the labour force rising from just 13.6 per cent in the early 1970s to 45.3 per cent in 1993. In addition, in 1994 women accounted for 36.4 per cent of the total employed labour force. There has also been a sustained increase in female participation rates and the report indicates an annual growth rate of 1.5 per cent over the period 1987 to 1993. In particular, participation rates for married women have continued to rise from 23.4 per cent in 1987 to 31.3 per cent in 1993, a growth of 34 per cent. These activity levels contrast with those of males which have seen a gradual decline of 0.7 per cent per annum since 1987.

Employment Trends

While labour force participation by women has seen a steady increase, has there been any change in the types of jobs undertaken by women? The EEA report (Durkan et al., 1995) again provides a valuable overview of the situation. This shows that female representation is highest in the categories of clerical worker (78 per cent), shop assistants and bar staff (60 per cent), textile and clothing workers (58 per cent), service workers (58 per cent) and professional and technical workers (51 per cent). The report points out that these rankings have not changed since 1987.

Women make up a considerable proportion of those employed within the Civil Service but they are mainly concentrated in the lower grades. A report from the Department of Finance (1991/ 1992) identifies the percentage of women in each general service grade in the civil service in the period 1987 to 1992. During this time very few women managed to advance to the senior positions: there were no secretaries and only 5 per cent of assistant secretaries and 12 per cent of principals were women. There had been little change in the position over the five-year period and women still predominate in the clerical officer and clerical assistant grades. Women are still missing from the top positions in local authorities and the Garda Síochána (Durkan, 1995) and in universities are very poorly represented at senior academic or administrative levels (Egan, 1994).

The Legal Framework

The original legislation underpinning the provision of employment equality consists of the Employment Equality Act (1977) and the Anti-Discrimination (Pay) Act (1974). The Employment Equality Act makes it unlawful for an employer to discriminate either directly or indirectly on the grounds of sex or marital status in areas such as recruitment, selection, training, promotion and dismissal. The Anti-Discrimination (Pay) Act "confers an entitlement to equal pay on men and women who are working in the same employment or for an associated employer, engaged on like work and working in the same place i.e. city, town or locality" (Employment Equality Agency [EEA]). The legislation has created an awareness of the rights of women workers to equal treatment and over the years the EEA and equality officers have dealt with a variety of cases brought under these two Acts: these cases have gradually extended the range of employment equality issues. There is evidence that there has been a gradual narrowing of the differences between male and female rates of pay in manufacturing industry but figures for other industries are not easily available (Durkan et al., 1995). However, it is difficult to judge the extent to which legislation on its own merely prevents direct discrimination rather than actively promoting equality. Many organisations may decide to comply with the equality laws simply to avoid prosecution and can arrange that their policies and procedures fit precisely the legal requirements. Thus, there has been a steady decrease in the number of cases of discriminatory recruitment advertisements recorded by the EEA: this dropped from 78 in 1989 to 15 in 1992 (EEA, 1992). Whether this indicates a desire on the part of employers to discriminate less or to comply more with legal requirements is difficult to gauge.

More recent legislation expands the range of issues under the heading of employment equality. Thus the Maternity Protection Act of 1994 provides employment protection over a range of issues and the Adoptive Leave Act (1995) stipulates a minimum of ten consecutive weeks of adoptive leave. In both these acts, provision is made for fathers, albeit in specific circumstances. This reflects the growing trend to see employment equality as an important issue for both men and women. New equality legislation, in the form of an Employment Equality Bill and an Equal Status Bill, has been drafted, but both bills have been ruled as unconstitutional by the Supreme Court (June, 1997) and await modifications.

Barriers to Progression

There is a good deal of evidence from international research that women face barriers to progression within organisations that are not faced by their male counterparts (e.g. Davidson and Cooper, 1992; White et al., 1992). These barriers are often referred to as "the glass ceiling". Parker and Fagenson (1994: 15) report on a study carried out in the USA (Morrison, 1992) in which interviews with top managers indicated that there are six major organisational barriers that constitute the glass ceiling:

> These include a lonely and non-supportive work environment, treating differences as weaknesses, excluding people from group activities because of their differences, and failure to help individuals prepare for management, to balance work/personal issues, and to develop organisational awareness or savvy.

In addition, women are often forced to adopt the male role model, are often not taken seriously, find they have to be better than their male colleagues in order to obtain promotion and still carry primary responsibility for child and dependent care and for the household (e.g. Alban-Metcalfe and West, 1991).

The available Irish data indicates that the difficulties facing women in progressing their careers do not differ greatly from those identified in the international research. A study of accountants (Barker and Monks, 1994; 1995) found that women could make it to the top of their profession, but that this was frequently at substantial cost to their personal lives. They had to work very long hours and had sometimes to forgo long-term relationships, yet without the benefit of the support networks, focused on golf

and rugby, which had been established by their male counterparts. These networks have been described by Mahon (1991: 36)
in her study of Irish civil servants as "informal settings where
men from different grades can meet, exchange ideas and display
their talents, again facilitating their visibility and subsequently
the visibility factor". Mahon categorises these networks as exclu-
sionary practices and a form of indirect discrimination. McCauley
and Looney (1996), in a study of Irish women engineers, found
little evidence of direct discrimination, but that women were often
given different types of work — more routine, less visible and
more monotonous — than their male colleagues; this type of work
was less likely to lead to career progression. Following a Report
on a Survey of Equal Opportunities in the Public Sector in Ireland
(Department of Equality and Law Reform, 1994) which showed
that no senior management posts and only 7 per cent of management positions were held by women within the Health Boards, a
study of women in the Midland and Mid-Western Health Boards
(O'Connor, 1995) was commissioned. The study indicated that the
barriers to women's promotion lay "at the level of organisational
procedures and culture" and that "within the Administrative sector women were competing within what was still, especially at
senior level, a male world" (O'Connor: ix). Yet despite these barriers, it is possible to note positive changes in women's employment
over the last decade. Thus, reports in the 1980s (McCarthy, 1986;
Wickham and Murray, 1987) painted a very gloomy picture of the
barriers to work encountered by women. While many barriers still
remain, some have been, if not actually broken down, successfully
bypassed.

HR STRATEGIES TO PROMOTE EMPLOYMENT EQUALITY

There are a variety of strategies which have been adopted to promote employment equality. These can be divided into two categories. In the first category are strategies which offer flexibility in
working arrangements or provide support such as childcare facilities and special leave policies. While most of these strategies were

originally intended to support working women, they are what the EEA calls "family friendly" (Fisher, 1996) and are intended to achieve a better balance between work and non-work activities for both men and women. The second category encompasses strategies which are intended to promote equal opportunity. Thus, there is an attempt to ensure that policies underpinning the recruitment, selection, training and promotion of staff are designed so that they neither discriminate against individuals nor hinder their advancement. In addition, specific measures may be adopted to promote equal opportunity. For example, some organisations have embraced positive action programmes, adopted sexual harassment policies, provided special training programmes and developed mentoring schemes (see Box 6.1)

BOX 6.1: MENTORING IN AER RIANTA

In 1992 women held only 14 per cent of the management positions within Aer Rianta and most of these were at the lower management levels. In 1993 a Mentoring Programme was launched as part of an Action Programme for women managers and involved 18 women managers who were mentored by senior managers, all of whom were male. Participation in the scheme was voluntary and the objective was to "provide a protected relationship in which learning and experimentation can occur, potential skills can be developed, and in which results can be measured in terms of competencies gained rather than curricular territory covered". Individual training needs analyses were carried out for each of the women and provided the basis for the identification of their personal objectives for the mentoring programme. In addition, separate half day training programmes for mentors and mentees were facilitated by an outside consultant. A review of the programme ten months later revealed that the women had more realistic expectations of their careers; they had learned the political skills of organisational life faster than if they had not been involved in the mentoring process; they had matured and had increased in self-confidence. Two years after the programme started, four of the women had been promoted and many of the others were recognised as candidates for future promotions.

Family Friendly Policies

There are now a range of measures which can be introduced within organisations under the heading of "family friendly" policies. The first set can be described as "flexible work practices" and include part-time work, job sharing, career breaks, flexi-time and flexi-place (the term now used to include all types of homeworking arrangements from traditional low-skilled outworking to sophisticated computer-based teleworking). Part-time work has been criticised as it is often badly paid and is clearly identified with low-status, insecure jobs with unsocial hours. However, recent legislation has remedied to some extent these elements. Other flexible work arrangements, such as job sharing, offer more security and opportunities for training and promotion, although job sharing is often confined to particular types of positions within organisations. Job sharing can operate on a split day, split week or week on, week off basis and it is estimated that approximately 5,300 people in the private sector and 8,000 in the public sector are involved (Fynes et al., 1996). Flexi-time is well established in many organisations but more complex arrangements for flexible working time, such as term time working, compressed working weeks or annual hour arrangements are less common. However, some of the Irish banks have recently introduced packages which enable employees to choose from a wide range of flexible work arrangements (see Box 6.2).

Childcare and Special Leave Arrangements

Various reports (McKenna, 1988, 1992; EEA, 1990; *Working Group on Childcare Facilities for Working Parents,* 1994) have indicated the low level of publicly funded childcare facilities in Ireland. In response, some organisations have established crèche facilities, but few have provided the after school or holiday care required by older children. Arrangements to support carers have also made slow progress except where specifically covered by legislation. Thus, while maternity and adoptive leave are well established, parental and paternity leave, although agreed, await implementation. Compassionate and emergency leave are allowed by some companies, but little attention has been paid to the care of elderly dependents. Yet Ireland's population is aging and more elderly people will require the long-term care which has traditionally been carried out by women. Career breaks are offered to at least some employees by about 10 per cent of private sector and 82 per cent of public sector organisations in Ireland (Fynes et al., 1996).

Box 6.2: AIB Choices

In 1996 Allied Irish Bank introduced *AIB Choices,* a set of flexible working options, in recognition of the growing need for employees to have more control over their time in order to manage their differing priorities. Four different types of employment arrangements are available under this scheme: Job Sharing, Personalised Hours, New Career Breaks and Special Short-Term Breaks.

- **Job Sharing** involves two staff members sharing one full-time post and equally dividing the responsibilities, duties, hours of work and individual benefits between them.

- **Personalised Hours** enables staff to vary their hours to suit their own individual needs by choosing any combination of between 14.5 and 31.5 hours to work each week.

- The **New Career Break** is a continuous leave of absence for a minimum period of 6 months and maximum period of 5 years

- The **Special Short-Term Break** is a leave of absence from three months to one year and is available as a *Short-Term Responsibility Break* to enable staff to spend time with their family at particular times of need such as illness, when children are starting school etc.; a *Caring Leave Break* to enable staff to take time off to care for elderly, sick or disabled relatives; or a *Family Short-Term Break* to enable staff to spend extended periods of time with their families.

Benefits and Costs

There are mixed views on the benefit of family friendly policies. They are perceived by some commentators as having many business benefits: the recruitment and retention of high quality employees, more motivated and productive staff who are less stressed and less prone to absenteeism and sickness, and an increased sense of trust and co-operation within the work organisation (Fisher, 1996). However, a study by Fynes et al. (1996) of 319 Irish firms indicated that some of these policies are not greeted with any great enthusiasm by Irish employers. For example, 75 per cent of private sector companies in the sample population in the study saw no advantages in job sharing arrangements, although their public sector counterparts were less disillusioned. The main difficulties mentioned were the problem of ensuring continuity and the costs involved. In addition, there was little support for career breaks. As a result, both job sharing and career break schemes were tolerated because they were seen as a way of "responding to employee preferences" (p. 210), rather than for any economic benefits.

In addition to the drawbacks identified by employers, one of the side effects of some family friendly policies is that are frequently perceived as designed and designated for women alone, although there has been some take-up by men. For example, in the study by Fynes et al., almost two thirds of career breaks were taken by women. Several problems can then arise: the policies are seen as "women only" and therefore excluding of men; the policies become mechanisms for sidelining women into certain types of jobs with limited promotion and training opportunities; men feel discriminated against because they feel unable to participate in such schemes and perceive them as fostering the development of women. These measures cannot, therefore, be introduced without some thought being given to their appropriateness within a particular organisational context: the age profile, needs and wishes of employees need to be considered carefully and a process of consultation undertaken before their introduction. Some of these measures are expensive, others require little more than the adaptation of existing policies or practices, but all need to be considered in the light of both current and projected staffing requirements and of the changing needs and expectations of employees and of the balance they wish to strike between work and non-work activities.

Equal Opportunities Policies and Positive Action

There is general agreement that certain conditions must be fulfilled if equal opportunities policies are to be translated successfully into equal opportunities practices. The EEA (EEA, 1991: 11) suggests that the four principal steps in implementing an equal opportunity policy are complete when it is agreed that there is a need for change, when the objectives are decided, when decisions are made on how success will be measured and when the individuals who will take responsibility for the necessary positive action are identified. In considering these matters, a distinction has to be made between positive action and positive discrimination. The EEA defines positive action as "a policy driven action or set of actions designed to achieve real equality of opportunity, particularly for members of a group or category who have hitherto suffered either directly or indirectly from less favourable treatment" (EEA, 1991: 13). In contrast, positive discrimination, which may include a quota system or involve discrimination in the selection process, although widely accepted in the USA, could be seen in Ireland "to contravene equality legislation" (EEA, 1991: 13). A positive action programme consists of four phases: commitment by the organisation; analysis of the workforce; employment practices and barriers; an action plan; and monitoring and evaluation (Department of Equality and Law Reform, 1993: 10).

Many Irish organisations have undertaken equal opportunities programmes. A government report, *The Development of Equal Opportunities* (1992), identifies the equality initiatives taken by government departments. These range from, at a basic level, the adoption of an equal opportunity policy (e.g. An Bord Tráchtála) to an integrated set of measures including the appointment of a manager, equal opportunities development, and the incorporation of career development, personal development, assertiveness training and equal opportunities into all training programmes (Aer Rianta). Within higher education, a Higher Education Equality Unit has been established and several conferences have taken place (*Equal Opportunities Policies in Third Level Institutions,* 1995). The promotion of equal opportunities initiatives has been much more pronounced in the public than the private sector in Ireland and this trend appears to be common throughout Europe (Hegewisch and Mayne, 1994). However, many of the larger institutions such as the banks have actively promoted equal opportunities policies for a long number of years (see Box 6.3).

BOX 6.3: EQUAL OPPORTUNITIES IN BANK OF IRELAND

Bank of Ireland has an ongoing programme of long-term cultural change devoted to the issue of equal opportunities. The objective of the programme is "to ensure that the diverse characteristics and contributions of all employees are valued and maximised to ensure the highest quality of service to customers". A Diversity Strategy has been developed which provides the focus for the implementation of initiatives. This strategy consists of four main elements: awareness raising and education; integration into all business initiatives; line management accountability for the implementation of the strategy and supporting initiatives; and monitoring and measurement. Specific actions include:

- The appointment of an Equal Opportunities Manager (1985);

- Work/life support initiatives for employees at all levels include 1 week's paid paternity leave, career breaks, job sharing, reduced hours/part-time working and unpaid career and parental leave (3 months to 1 year);

- Customer related initiatives to ensure that female customers perceive themselves as equally valued as male customers;

- The opening of a crèche (1991);

- Equal Opportunities Survey (1993) of 10,000 employees with communication of results through facilitated feedback sessions supported by a video;

- Equal Opportunities Steering Groups (1994–1996) established to address survey findings;

- Equality Review Group established (1996), chaired by the Chief Executive, with quarterly meetings to review progress;

- Diversity workshops, commencing with senior management teams;

- Positive action training initiatives to address under-representation of women in management;

- Circulation of "Equality Action" newsletter to all employees;

- Equal opportunities included in annual individual management goals;

- Ongoing review and revision of people-related policies e.g. staff benefits, recruitment, harassment etc.

Employment equality policies need to permeate all organisational policies which incorporate a "people" element. Thus, policies on recruitment, selection, training and development, appraisal, remuneration etc. need to be examined in the light of an equal opportunities philosophy. Equal opportunities policies also need to be allied to the flexible work practices already discussed which acknowledge the demands of family responsibilities. However, it is at this juncture that conflict may occur between an organisation's commitment to equal opportunities and its ability to deliver these commitments in full. A study of one British organisation which employed part-time workers as part of its commitment to equal opportunities found that such measures simply raised the expectations of part-time staff (Skinner, 1996). The part-timers felt that they should enjoy the same opportunities in training, development, job experience and promotion as their full-time colleagues, but the reality of their experience was very different:

they were often too removed from the important organisational issues to be in the running for promotion or development. Thus, there was a conflict between the expectations of employment equality and the reality.

Sexual Harassment Policies

There has been a steady rise in the number of sexual harassment cases reported to the EEA and there is certainly a greater awareness in all organisations of the need for appropriate policies. In 1994 the Department of Equality and Law Reform launched a code of practice, *Measures to Protect the Dignity of Women and Men at Work* which provides a guide for both employers and employees on duties and responsibilities in this area. In addition, many organisations have also published their own guidelines, in some cases extending the concept to include sectarian and racial harassment, victimisation and bullying (e.g. Bank of Ireland).

DISCUSSION

This chapter has considered the issue of employment equality in Ireland and has explored the range of strategies which can be used to encourage equal opportunities. This analysis has focused on the employment of women and has revealed that there are now a range of options available to and utilised by Irish employers to support women's employment. However, in the case of "family friendly" policies, there is the problem that such policies merely reinforce the status quo by simply making it easier for women to manage both their work and domestic responsibilities rather than ensuring that those responsibilities are shared more equally between men and women. There is also no reason to suppose that the introduction of employment equality measures on their own will result in dramatic changes within organisations: societal attitudes towards the role of women need to change in tandem.

In discussing these issues, the emphasis has been placed on the HR strategies required to engender equal opportunities and the position of women in relation to these issues. In taking this approach, there is a danger of making the assumption that equal opportunities is the responsibility of the HR department, that equal opportunities is an issue of interest only to women, and that the adoption of policies and procedures will result in equal opportunity. These issues are further clouded by the fact that more organisations are now adopting *human resource* rather than *personnel* strategies in their approach towards employees. Much debate has raged over the meaning and significance of these two, by now, value-laden terms (see Legge, 1995). But there is general agreement that companies adopting a HRM perspective are more likely to take a unitarist stance and to make extensive use of individualised contracts with a focus on business needs and performance (Storey, 1992). But as Woodhall (1996: 336), in an analysis of human resource management and women in the UK, points out:

> A unitarist philosophy underpins HRM whereby employee interests are held to be identical to those of employers, but equal opportunities rests on the foundation of pluralism, starting from the premise that employees have independent rights and interests which may very well be infringed by employers.

In addition, under a HRM philosophy, responsibility for human resource issues is pushed down to line managers. Yet, line managers are mainly male and, given recent downsizing and delayering strategies, are already overburdened and therefore unlikely to muster enthusiasm for additional tasks in the shape of employment equality responsibilities

An alternative approach is to rethink equal opportunity by focusing instead on the issue of diversity so that differences between individuals, whether they are ones of race, religion, age, sexual orientation, gender etc., become seen as a source of strength, rather than weakness, to organisations. Liff and Wajcman (1996: 84), both based in Warwick Business School in the UK, see a compatibility between diversity approaches and HRM. They suggest that:

> An approach based on diversity appears to fit much more
> comfortably with this [HRM] style . . . since it recognises
> differences within the workforce and sees it as the respon-
> sibility of the individual to grasp opportunities assisted by
> an empowering organisation.

The concept of diversity focuses on differences between individuals — and places value on those differences — while traditional
equality measures have suggested "sameness" and may require
women to minimise differences between themselves and their
male colleagues in order to make themselves eligible for certain
types of jobs and occupations. Yet, Woodhall (1996: 334) points out
that the enthusiasm for diversity management "was born in a
climate of male backlash in the 1980s, and the irritation of US
businesses with federal contract compliance conditions in respect
of equal opportunities". Such an enthusiasm may have a short
shelf-life and may not transfer easily to an Irish culture which has
traditionally been slow to accept any deviance from what was considered to be the norm. However, the increasing internationalisation of Irish firms may open up a wider need for and acceptance of
diversity within the organisation: cross-cultural encounters with
their resultant communication difficulties and misunderstandings
may lead to an acceptance of the requirement to gain a wider understanding of differences which underpin human behaviour and
of the prejudices which colour the way interactions take place.

Whatever the approach adopted towards ensuring employment
equality, there will undoubtedly be a need to take account of the
fact that individuals may not necessarily wish to be treated as if
they were all exactly the same. Recent research (Sparrow, 1996)
on changes in the psychological contract in the banking sector in
the UK has suggested that traditional ways of categorising employees, such as those based on age, sex, service or grade, can only
partially explain different attitudes to work. Sparrow's research
suggests that employee expectations are increasingly fragmented
and not easily categorised and that HRM tools and techniques
which are designed to operate throughout the organisation will
become "blunt and ineffective" and that the solution is "to create a

series of layered and individualised career contracts". The challenge is to develop HR strategies which enable this to take place in an organisational culture which supports and values the various choices that individuals make.

References

Alban-Metcalfe, B. and West, M. (1991): "Women Managers" in J. Cozens and M. West (eds.), *Women at Work. Psychological and Organisational Perspectives*, Milton Keynes: Open University Press.

Barker, P. and Monks, K. (1994): *Career Progression of Chartered Accountants, Report to the Institute of Chartered Accountants in Ireland*, Dublin: Dublin City University Business School.

Barker, P. and Monks, K. (1995): "Women in Accounting: Career Progression", *The Irish Accounting Review*, 2(1): 1–25.

Davidson, M. and Burke, R. (1994): *Women in Management. Current Research Issues*, London: Paul Chapman.

Davidson, M. J. and Cooper, C.L. (1992): *Shattering the Glass Ceiling — the Woman Manager*, London: Paul Chapman.

Department of Equality and Law Reform (1993): *Report on a Survey of Equal Opportunities in the Public Sector*, Dublin: Department of Equality and Law Reform.

Department of Finance (1991/92): *Development of Equal Opportunities, Second Coordinated Report*, October 1988 — February 1992, Dublin: Stationery Office.

Durkan, J., Donohue, A., Donnelly, M. and Durkan, J. (1995): *Women in the Labour Force*, Dublin: Employment Equality Agency.

EEA (1990): *Childcare in Ireland: Challenge and Opportunity*, Dublin: EEA.

EEA (1991): *A Model Equal Opportunities Policy*, Dublin: EEA.

Egan, O. (1994): "Overview of Equal Opportunities in Third Level Education in Ireland", in *Equality of Opportunity in Third Level Education in Ireland*, Cork: National Unit on Equal Opportunities at Third Level.

Equal Opportunities Policies in Third Level Institutions (1995) Proceedings of Conference in Tallaght RTC, 28 April.

FÁS (1992, 1993): *Positive Action Programme for Women*, Dublin: FÁS.

Fisher, H. (1996): *Introducing Family-Friendly Initiatives in the Workplace*, Dublin: EEA.

Fynes, B., Morrissey, T., Roche, W., Whelan, B. and Williams, J. (1996): *Flexible Working Lives*. Dublin: Oak Tree Press.

Hegewisch, A. and Mayne, L. (1994): "Equal Opportunities Policies in Europe" in Brewster, C. and Hegewisch, A. (eds.) *Policy and Practice in European Human Resource Management*, Routledge: London and New York.

Legge, K. (1995): *Human Resource Management, Rhetoric and Realities*, Basingstoke: Macmillan.

Liff, S. and Wajcman, J. (1996): "'Sameness' and 'Difference' Revisited: Which Way Forward for Equal Opportunities Initiatives?", *Journal of Management Studies*, 33(1): 79–94.

McCarthy, E. (1986): *Transitions to Equal Opportunity at Work: Problems and Possibilities*, Dublin: EEA.

McCauley, L. and Looney, L. (1996): "Women in Engineering", *The Engineer's Journal*, 4(3): 24–29.

McKenna, A. (1988): *Childcare and Equal Opportunities*, Dublin: Employment Equality Agency.

Mahon, E. (1991): *Motherhood, Work and Equal Opportunity*, First Report of the Third Joint Committee on Women's Rights, Dublin: Stationery Office.

Morrison, A.M. (1992): *The Leaders: Guidelines on Leadership Diversity in America*, San Francisco: Jossey-Bass.

O'Connor, P. (1995): *Barriers to Women's Promotion in the Midland and Mid-Western Health Boards*, Longford: Midland and Mid-Western Health Boards.

Parker, B. and Fagenson, E. (1994): "An Introductory Overview of Women in Corporate Management", in Davidson, M. and Burke, R. (eds.) *Women in Management, Current Research Issues*, London: Paul Chapman.

Partling, S. (1992): "We Only Discriminate on Ability", in *Equality and Europe, Positive Strategies for Recruiting and Retaining Europe's Women Managers*, UK: Emery Associates.

Skinner, D. (1996): "When Organisational Commitment to Equal Opportunities is not Enough: the Experiences and Expectations of Part-time Staff and their Managers", paper presented to the Open University Conference, HRM — the Inside Story, April 1–2, Milton Keynes: UK.

Sparrow, P. (1996): "Transitions in the Psychological contract in the UK Banking Sector: Implications for HRM", *Human Resource Management Journal*, 6(4): 1–26.

Storey, J. (1992): *Developments in the Management of Human Resources*, Oxford: Blackwell.

White, B., Cox, C. and Cooper, C. (1992): *Women's Career Development*, Oxford: Blackwell.

Wickham, J. and Murray, P. (1987): *Women in the Electronics Industry*, Dublin: EEA.

Woodhall, J. (1996): "Human Resource Management and Women: the Vision of the Gender-blind?", in Towers, B. (ed.) *The Handbook of Human Resource Management*, Oxford: Blackwell.

Working Group on Childcare Facilities for Working Parents (1994): Report to the Minister for Equality and Law Reform, Dublin: Stationery Office.

7

MANAGING HUMAN RESOURCE ISSUES IN A QUALITY CONTEXT

Kathy Monks, Finian Buckley and *Anne Sinnott*

Quality has become a key issue for companies seeking competitive advantage and recent research indicates that a focus on the human resource (HR) implications of these initiatives may be critical to their long-term success (Powell, 1995). This chapter considers the implications for both the HR function and for HR practices of the changes which have occurred within organisations involved in the implementation of quality initiatives. The chapter begins by briefly tracking the development of the quality movement within Ireland before considering some of the debates within the quality literature. The role played by the HR function and the changes to HR practices required in quality-focused organisations are then considered. Finally, the role played by communications strategies in providing the conduit for the successful introduction and maintenance of a quality programme is described.

TOWARDS TOTAL QUALITY MANAGEMENT

Quality Systems

A number of quality management systems have been developed in Ireland, the UK and elsewhere in an attempt to provide an objective basis for assessing a company's ability to ensure the conformance of goods and services to specification. The principles of quality systems can readily be found in such documents as British

Standard 5750, Allied Quality Assurance Publications, ISO 9000, the European Quality Award System, the Deming prize criteria, the Malcolm Baldrige Award system in the US and many variants created by specific organisations. The most widely recognised system is the International Standards Organisation, ISO standard 9000 series, which sets out a method by which a management system, incorporating a range of activities associated with quality, can be implemented in an organisation to ensure that all the specified performance requirements and needs of the customer are fully met (Oakland, 1989). Ireland is one of 87 countries in the International Organisation for Standardisation and is represented by the National Standards Authority of Ireland (NSAI).

Excellence Ireland

Many companies in Ireland have found that the process of applying for ISO accreditation becomes much easier if they have first succeeded in acquiring the quality mark (*Q Mark*) awarded by Excellence Ireland (formerly the Irish Quality Association (IQA)). Excellence Ireland is a voluntary non-profit-making organisation funded mainly by membership subscriptions. Its support comes from the many companies who recognise that quality is at the heart of the matter when it comes to survival and expansion (O'Neill, 1991). Excellence Ireland's quality mark scheme for Irish industry was first launched in 1982 and a special quality mark for the service industry was introduced in 1989.

Excellence Ireland works closely with the European Foundation for Quality Management (EFQM) which was formed in 1988 by some of Europe's leading businesses to promote best practices and thereby increase the competitiveness of European industry. The EFQM model has been adopted by Excellence Ireland as the Irish Business Excellence Model (IBEM). This model can be used by organisations to assess how well they are handling key areas of activities in a business and the quality of their business results. It is described as "a strategic management tool which provides a powerful framework for continuously improving performance and overall competitiveness both for the individual organisation and Irish industry in general" (IQA, 1997). There is general agreement that quality standards can provide considerable benefits to their holders, both in terms of potential savings and improvements to employee morale (Smith, 1992; Murphy, 1993).

Total Quality Management

While quality standards are useful tools in enabling organisations to both chart and benchmark their progress, they are not an end in themselves and managing quality effectively involves much more than just meeting specifications. Thus, many companies are engaged in the implementation of total quality management (TQM), a system "designed as an integrated, customer-focused approach to improve the quality of an organisation's processes, products and services" (Waldman, 1994: 31). While notions of the exact nature of TQM vary, there is general agreement that it will involve factors such as top management commitment to quality, a focus on continuous improvement, employee involvement in quality efforts, concern with customer satisfaction, process orientation; in effect, the development of a quality culture permeating every element of organisational life (Waldman, 1994; Wilkinson and Witcher, 1991; Hill and Wilkinson, 1996). In addition, organisations will introduce changed working arrangements with a focus on teamworking, leadership, employee involvement and communications, and see themselves on a path of continuous improvement rather than as simply involved in completing the tasks required to meeting specific standards (see Box 7.1 for an example of an Irish organisation involved in TQM).

While there is a great deal of enthusiasm within the management literature for TQM, there are also tensions within the quality movement. Thus the "conformance to specification" mentality embedded in quality systems sits uneasily with the focus on teambuilding and empowerment philosophies conducive to TQM. Indeed, many commentators would argue that quality initiatives have led to work intensification, increased surveillance and increased managerial control, often through individualising accountability, albeit under the banner of involvement and empowerment (e.g. Sewell and Wilkinson, 1992; McArdle et al., 1995; Delbridge et al., 1992). In addition, Rosenthal et al. (1997: 483) point to the "manipulation of meaning" which may occur within such initiatives:

> Those concerned with the manipulation of meaning suggest that, in structuring meaning, corporations manage to influence how their employees think about and interpret "reality". Structuring may take place either via ideologies or discursive practices, following different theoretical perspectives, and the effect is to create norms and meanings that are congruent with corporate interests.

Yet, while some commentators would support the "manipulation of meaning" (e.g. Tuckman, 1995), a study carried out by Rosenthal et al. (1997) in a major British supermarket found "no support for the view that, if a company's objectives in improving service quality are realised, they are achieved through some combination of sham empowerment, work intensification and increased surveillance" (p. 497). Instead, this study found an unanticipated consequence of the rhetoric of the quality discourse used in this particular quality initiative: its use by staff to "bring managers in line with *their* expectations" (p. 496). Thus, as Rosenthal et al, point out, "the discourse of quality and customer service may be a double-edged sword which can be used as much by employees to "reconstitute" management, as by management to "reconstitute" employees" (p. 397).

TQM and HRM

The tensions and debates within the quality literature mirror those ongoing among HRM researchers. For example, there has been much discussion about "hard" and "soft" versions of HRM (Storey, 1989; Legge, 1995). The "hard" model (Storey, 1989) focuses on the resources, including human resources, required to push forward business objectives and gain competitive advantage.

In contrast, the "soft" version of HRM focuses on employees as assets and suggests that competitive advantage may be gained through employees' commitment and the quality of their contribution to organisational effort (Guest, 1987). In addition, many of the criticisms leveled at HRM correspond closely to those focused on TQM: its failure to provide a "moderating influence on managerialism" or act as a "catalyst for genuine innovation in workplace relationships" (Hart, 1993); its attempts to redefine the meaning of work for employees (Keenoy and Anthony, 1992). Certainly it is difficult to disentangle TQM from HRM and some writers view the two movements as intertwined (e.g. Legge, 1995; Wilmott, 1993).

The Impact of TQM in Ireland

While Irish studies which focus specifically on the impact of quality initiatives are scarce, it is possible to understand at least some aspects of the relationship between quality and HR issues by examining research which has considered the changes wrought by moves to new forms of work organisation (see Jacobson, 1995, for an extensive annotated bibliography). Quality is frequently seen as a driving force of these changes and there is an acceptance by both management (O'Connor, 1995; Cogan, 1995; Donnelly, 1995) and unions (SIPTU, 1993; ICTU, 1993) of the need to rethink traditional ways of managing in the context of these developments. Thus, there is evidence from case studies of Irish organisations that the changes brought about by moves to new forms of work organisation have implications for the types of HR practices traditionally adopted by such organisations. A study by Morley (1995), which explored in particular the introduction of teams within an Irish manufacturing plant, indicated that employees experienced enhanced work variety and autonomy. Another case history (Kromkowski and Murphy, 1996: 272) considered that the introduction of a total quality programme "released the repressed energy and tacit knowledge of the workforce" with considerable benefits to the organisation. However, while employees may be gaining greater satisfaction from their jobs, evidence from a survey of 402 employees in nine manufacturing firms (Turner and Morley, 1995) suggests that they are working harder as a result of organisational changes. Other research has indicated that TQM may be associated with more intensive work systems and closer monitoring of performance (Geary, 1994) and this finding mirrors international research (Preece and Wood, 1995; McArdle et al., 1995; Sewell and Wilkinson, 1992). These changed work arrangements frequently raise fundamental questions about how employees are managed, about the role that the HR function should play in this new type of organisation and about the types of HR practices, in particular the specific communications strategies, that are most suitable in these new environments.

HRM AND QUALITY

The Role of the HR Department

The debate on the role that the human resource function may play in the implementation of quality initiatives is part of the larger debate on the nature of personnel/human resource management (see Legge, 1995: 7). For example, quality is one of the elements comprising Guest's (1987) model of human resource management with the emphasis on the quality of staff, performance and public image based on human resource policies. The elements that often surround the introduction of quality initiatives — teamworking, communications and a focus on commitment — are seen as some of the aspects of "soft" HRM (Storey, 1989) already discussed. The involvement of the HR department in the formulation stages of quality initiatives requires participation in strategic decision making which is also seen as important in differentiating between personnel and human resource management (Storey, 1992; Guest, 1987; Hendry and Pettigrew, 1986).

Evidence from a variety of studies carried out in the UK suggests that the level of involvement by the HR function in quality programmes can vary considerably. For example, TQM has been seen as providing an opportunity for the HR function to play a more strategic role within the organisation (Giles and Williams, 1991). However, case studies of 15 companies involved in quality programmes (Wilkinson and Marchington, 1995: 41–42) identified four roles that practitioners may play in the implementation of quality programmes. They describe these as "Change Agent" (strategic/high profile), "Hidden Persuader" (strategic/low profile), "Internal Contractor" (operational level/high profile) and "Facilitator" "operational level/low profile). This wide range of roles is supported by other research. For example, Cowling and Newman (1995) in a study of two banks found that their HR departments did not emerge with enhanced status following the implementation of quality programmes. Within the debate about the precise role that the HR function should play, there are commentators who argue that there is no need for a centralised staff function within corporate headquarters in total quality organisations: HRM becomes integrated into the core processes of the organisation and "the entire HRM function shifts to the ownership of the line manager" (Flood, Gannon and Paauwe, 1996: 26).

There is some Irish evidence on the role played by the HRM function in major organisational changes, including quality initiatives. In the first place, there are indications that some, but certainly not all, HR departments are involved in these major changes. Case studies of 11 manufacturing companies (Foley and Gunnigle, 1993) revealed that in only three cases was there major involvement of the HR department. Research in the Irish food industry (Bin Othmann, 1996) highlighted the fact that HR departments are not including themselves, or are not being included, in the strategic aspects of organisational development. Rather the function remains tied to its traditional zone of responsibility, typically, recruitment and selection, appraisal and training roles.

A survey of 249 *Q Mark* companies (Monks, Buckley and Sinnott, 1997) obtained responses from 133 companies, 52 of which had a human resource department. The survey found that less than half of the HR departments were very involved in the various stages of the implementation of quality initiatives, and about

15 per cent had no involvement at all. Where the HR department is involved, there is evidence that this may result a variety of outcomes. In about half of the companies with specialised HR departments there was a perception that the introduction of quality initiatives had increased personnel's involvement in strategic decision-making. There was involvement in a greater range of activities and a more business-oriented approach to HR management. A decentralisation of personnel activity to line managers was also reported in half the companies and the emergence of a consultancy role for the personnel department in advising line managers had emerged. The data suggested that involvement in quality initiatives may be a double-edged sword for the HR function. It may lead to increased participation in strategic decision-making, but there is always the difficulty that if more HR activities are delegated to line management that this will relegate the HR department to an advisory role, with perhaps less need seen for a well-staffed HR function. However, the majority of respondents considered that the quality programme had had a positive impact on the HR function and they also reported that the utilisation of quality principles had been extended to the HR function, although in only 39 per cent of firms had this been carried out to any great extent.

Changes to HR Practices

There are many suggestions from commentators as to the sort of HR practices that TQM requires, although in contrast there is little hard evidence on either the sorts of practices that work most effectively or what practices are actually being tried. Most commentators agree that there is a need for additional training, a focus on teamworking, greater emphasis on employee involvement in decision making, and more intensive communications. Communications strategies are certainly seen as a key factor and are discussed in more detail below. However, in general there is little attention given to creating new HR practices which might constructively maintain such initiatives. Wilkinson and Wilmott

(1995: 3) point out that there are tensions within the definition of quality when applied to the method of organising work:

> For quality management gurus, "quality" does not neces-sarily mean the attainment of exceptionally high standards with regard to employees' terms and conditions of work. In-stead, it means the development of "uniform and depend-able" work practices that are congruent with delivering products or services at low cost with a quality suited to the market (Deming, 1986).

Thus, suggestions that remuneration or appraisal schemes should be revised to reward for productivity improvements achieved as a result of quality initiatives have been spurned by many of the quality gurus such as Deming and Crosby. Yet reward systems may need to be restructured with the introduction of quality measures to reflect the move to team-based working; how this is to be accomplished is perhaps less clear (Drummond and Chell, 1992; Hackman and Wageman, 1995). The current enthusiasm for performance-related pay, with its individual approach, is unlikely to provide the solution and a performance management system focused on group level appraisal and rewards may be more effec-tive (Waldman, 1994; *Personnel Review*, 1994). While there is some evidence that selection and appraisal systems have been changed as a result of the introduction of quality systems, in many cases these could be seen simply as attempts to replace the traditional ways of monitoring employees, rather than new ap-proaches to these issues (Sewell and Wilkinson, 1992; Townley, 1989). In addition, while the findings of an international study of quality systems (Kochan et al., 1995) suggest that "to influence the adoption of innovative human resource and total quality practices, human resource managers could benefit from a partnership with unions" (p. 220), there is little evidence that this actually happens in practice to any great extent (Wilkinson et al., 1992).

Research in Ireland broadly confirms findings reported in other countries. In the study of *Q Mark* companies (Monks, Buckley and Sinnott, 1997) it was found that the techniques used in recruit-ment and selection, training and development and performance appraisal had intensified, although few companies had revised their reward systems. However, it was not possible to gauge the extent to which this was an attempt to intensify work in the ways reported in other research. In addition, it was found that the unions are for the most part bypassed in the development, maintenance and evaluation of quality programmes and only involved in some cases in the implementation. Yet, the Irish unions have actively signalled an interest in, and enthusiasm for, involvement in quality programmes (ICTU, 1993; SIPTU, 1993).

The Role of Organisational Communications

Verification of the importance of a focus on communication is provided by Morris, Meister and Hunt (1994) in their study of why many quality initiatives fail. Their findings indicated that without first conducting an objective internal communication audit many quality initiatives, despite the original objectives, are doomed to falter. Klein (1996) gives some insight as to why this may occur by highlighting that differential levels and degrees of communication are required with employees at the different phases of organisational change. To navigate smoothly through the different phases of a change programme, employee communication must be assessed and met. Sims (1994) asserts that it is a fundamental function of the HR department to ensure that such effective and efficient communication is supported within the organisation.

In an Irish context, an analysis of communications strategies as part of a survey of the *Q Mark* companies (Buckley, Monks and Sinnott, 1996) found positive changes to all aspects of communication within participating organisations. There was clear evidence of employees perceiving that upward and downward communication had become more democratic and balanced. Lateral communication (with co-workers) had also developed significantly, presumably aided by practices such as teamworking and improved employee participation systems. Overall, the communication climate had improved with employees feeling more freedom to get involved in problem-solving and solution planning. There was a clear sense of a closer bond between management and employees with the improved relational aspect of communications leading to a stronger sense of common purpose.

While these results from an Irish population appear very positive, Rhodes (1997) warns that organisational change experiences may be subject to overly positive interpretations and labels. Such a culture of positive interpretation of change-based practices may hide, indeed suppress, a darker interpretation. In the Buckley et al. (1996) study, while the stated tangible output objectives of the quality initiative had been reached, this was not true for employee expectations regarding communications. In all aspects of communication (upward, downward, lateral and empathic-collaborative) there was an expectation that there would be a significant improvement in the future. So while significant positive increments in communication processes were recorded as a result of the quality initiatives, employee expectations had not been totally fulfilled. This echoes Klein's (1996) warning of having a clear sense of the communication needs and wants of employees at all phases of the change process. In addition, there is the issue of who is to manage employee expectations for increased communications. Research in the UK (Storey, 1992) has indicated that most communications programmes delivered within organisations undergoing change were conducted by outside experts or internal public relations specialists. This raises issues for the HR department which, in its traditional role at least, was seen as primarily responsible for organisational communications and as the department potentially most capable of understanding the purpose, nature and outcomes of communications processes.

CONCLUSION

The ideas which first drove manufacturing industry to emulate the Japanese in their concern with quality have now permeated all areas of organisational life and all types of organisation in both the public and private sector within Ireland. Yet many issues surrounding the implementation of quality initiatives remain unresolved. Thus the question remains for many organisations of how to maintain an enthusiasm for, and an interest in, such initiatives on the part of all their members once the initial excitement has worn off. Also, organisations embarking on such programmes must face the fact that there is a great deal of evidence that quality programmes, in common with change programmes in general, have a high failure rate (Morris et al., 1994). Many of the issues that remain unresolved are interlinked with questions that are also central to understanding the nature and operation of HRM. Hackman and Wageman (1995: 5) suggest that "TQM, by philosophy and design, skirts four features of work systems that are fundamental to organisational behaviour and performance". These are the design of work, the allocation of gains, opportunities for learning, and distribution of authority. While each of these issues has a quality dimension, each also raises fundamental questions for HRM policies and practices. For example, what types of rewards systems are appropriate in a quality culture? How can learning at individual, team, and organisational levels be enhanced to promote the focus on continuous improvement critical to TQM? Can empowerment philosophies be incorporated into the authority structures which predominate in most organisations? These types of questions create challenges for the HR function in both developing its own role within the organisation and in developing a set of HR practices which can meet an often conflicting set of demands and needs.

BOX 7.1: TOTAL QUALITY MANAGEMENT IN AMDAHL IRELAND

Amdahl is a major supplier of large-scale mainframe computers, UNIX system software and servers, data storage subsystems, data communications products, applications development software and a variety of educational and consulting services.

Amdahl products and services are sold in over 30 countries with annual sales of $1.7 billion. Amdahl Ireland was established in 1978 to provide a total support service for the Corporation's European customer base. The company is committed to Total Quality Management (TQM) and has a reputation for high quality products and services.

TQM at Amdahl Ireland focuses on individuals and work-groups who create quality processes and produce quality output, either product or service. It is continuously meeting agreed customer requirements at the optimum cost, by releasing the potential of all employees.

At the core of its TQM philosophy is the fundamental understanding by each employee of the cornerstones of quality, a clear insight of customer requirements, and a continuous improvement ethos in everything the company does.

Clarity of direction is achieved through communication of its company vision mission, operating principles, goals and strategies, while cross-functional teams equipped with problem solving tools and techniques provide the flexibility to achieve significant business performance improvement.

TQM has been a fundamental part of Amdahl Ireland's management and behaviour for the last nine years, in good times and bad. The first three years saw a significant investment on grappling with the concepts and some personalisation of the widely-held theories and practices to suit the Amdahl environment. The second three years capitalised on that early investment and saw Amdahl grow to 700 people and a very successful and profitable operation.

During the last three years, Amdahl experienced a significant downturn in mainframe requirements worldwide.

Being a TQM company is not an end in itself and will not protect against the rigours of the external environment. Nevertheless, the full utilisation of TQM practices in the subsequent downsizing of operations proved essential and facilitated the unpleasant task significantly.

Amdahl has changed its focus to provide a much broader, solutions-based service to its customers. IT solves IT problems.

In turn, over the last two years Amdahl Ireland has also refocused its skill sets and expanded its core business activities to reflect these corporate changes. This has resulted in the establishment of an Information Technology Centre in Dublin.

> The integration of total quality practices was and continues to be a major asset, particularly as it related to the speed in which Amdahl refocused; from organising effective meetings with new customers, to developing project and delivery plans. Today, the company is expanding rapidly in this area and delivering quality products and services with TQM as a key enabler.

Source: *Sunday Business Post* May 28 1995: 17. Used with permission of *The Sunday Business Post*.

References

Bin Othman, R. (1996): "Strategic HRM: Evidence from the Irish Food Industry", *Personnel Review*, 25(1): 40–58.

Buckley, F., Monks, K. and Sinnott, A. (1996): "Communication Enhancement: A Process Dividend for the Organisation and the HRM Department?" *Dublin City University Business School Research Paper Series*, 18, Dublin: Dublin City University.

Cogan, J. (1995): "The Management of Change: the Pfizer Case Study", in Gunnigle, P. and Roche, W. (eds.).

Cowling, A. and Newman, K. (1995): "Banking on People. TQM, Service Quality and Human Resources", *Personnel Review*, 24(7): 25–40.

Delbridge, R. and Turnbull, P. (1992): "Human Resource Maximisation: the Management of Labour Under Just-in-Time Manufacturing Systems", in Blyton, P. and Turnbull, P. (eds.) *Reassessing Human Resource Management*, London: Sage.

Deming, W. (1986): *Out of the Crisis*, Cambridge: Cambridge University Press.

Donnelly, S. (1995): "World Class Manufacturing: Implications For Work Practices And Employment", in Gunnigle, P. and Roche, W. (eds.).

Drummond, H. and Chell, E. (1992): "Should Organisations Pay For Quality?", *Personnel Review*, 21(4): 3–11.

Foley, K. and Gunnigle, P. (1993): "The Personnel/Human Resource Function And Workplace Employee Relations", in Gunnigle, P., Flood, P., Morley, M. and Turner, T., *Continuity and Change in Irish Employee Relations*, Dublin: Oak Tree Press.

Flood, P., Gannon, M. and Paauwe, J. (1996): *Managing Without Traditional Methods: International Innovations in Human Resource Management*, Wokingham: Addison-Wesley.

Garvin, D.A. (1988): *Managing Quality: The Strategic Competitive Edge*, New York: Free Press.

Geary, J. (1994): "New Forms Of Work Organisation: Implications For Employers, Trade Unions and Employees", Working Paper, 9, Dublin: Graduate School of Business, University College Dublin.

Giles, E. and Williams, R. (1991): "Can The Personnel Department Survive Quality Management?", *Personnel Management*, April: 29–33.

Guest, D. (1987): "Human Resource Management and Industrial Relations", *Journal of Management Studies*, 24(5): 503–521.

Gunnigle, P. and Roche, W. (eds.) (1995): *New Challenges to Irish Industrial Relations*, Dublin: Oak Tree Press.

Hackman, J.R. and Wageman, R. (1995): "Total Quality Management: Empirical, Conceptual and Practical Issues", *Administrative Science Quarterly*, 40: 309–342.

Hart, T. (1993): "Human Resource Management — time to Exorcise the Militant Tendency", *Employee Relations*, 15(3): 29–36.

Hendry, C. and Pettigrew, A. (1986): "The Practice of Strategic Human Resource Management", *Personnel Review*, 15(5): 3–8.

Hill, S. and Wilkinson, A. (1996): "In Search of TQM", *Employee Relations*, 17(4): 1–24.

ICTU (Irish Congress of Trade Unions) (1993): New Forms of Work Organisation: Options for Unions, Dublin: ICTU.

Irish Quality Association (1997): *In Pursuit of Excellence*, Dublin: IQA.

Jacobson, D. (1995): "New Production, Organisation and Industrial Relations In Ireland: An Annotated Bibliography", *Dublin City University Research Paper Series*, 9, Dublin: Dublin City University Business School.

Juran, H. (1988): *Juran on Planning for Quality*, New York: Free Press.

Keenoy, T., and Anthony, P. (1992): "HRM: Metaphor, Meaning and Morality", in Blyton, P. and Turnbull, P. (eds.) *Reassessing Human Resource Management*, London: Sage.

Klein, S.M. (1996): "A Management Communication Strategy for Change", *Journal of Organisational Change Management*, 9(2): 32–42.

Kochan, T., Hoffer Gittell, J. and Lautsch, B. (1995): "Total Quality Management and Human Resource Systems: An International Comparison", *International Journal of Human Resource Management*, 6, May: 200–222.

Kromkowski, J. and Murphy, E. (1996): "Managing Without Quality Boundaries", in Flood, P., Gannon, M., and Paauwe, J. (eds.).

Legge, K. (1995): *Human Resource Management Rhetoric and Realities*. London: Macmillan.

Lowry, J. (1994): "Management Adapts to Standards", *The Sunday Business Post*, January 2: 17.

Mc Ardle, L., Rowlinson, M., Procter, S., Hassard, J. and Forrester, P. (1995): "Total Quality Management and Participation. Employee Empowerment or the Enhancement of Exploitation?", in Wilkinson, A. and Willmott, H. (eds.), *Making Quality Critical*, London: Routledge.

Monks, K., Buckley, F. and Sinnott, A. (1997): "Human Resource Management in a Quality Context: Some Irish Evidence", *Employee Relations*, 19(3): 193–207.

Morley, M., (1995): "Current Themes In Organisational Design and Work Restructuring", in Gunnigle, P. and Roche, W. (eds.).

Morris, R.E., Meister, G. and Hunt, T. (1994): "Quality Initiatives Fail More Often than Not", *Human Resource Professional*, 75: 23–27.

Murphy, J.A. (1993): *Service Quality in Practice*, Dublin: Gill and Macmillan.

Oakland, J.S. (1989): *Total Quality Management*, first edition, London: Heinemann.

O'Connor, E. (1995): "World Class Manufacturing in a Semi-State Environment: The Case of Bord na Mona" in Gunnigle, P. and Roche, W. (eds.).

O'Neill, P.A. (1991): "IQA", *Sunday Independent*, November 24: 13L.

Personnel Review, (1994): "The Role of Rewards on a Journey to Excellence", Personnel Review, 23(2): 3–5.

Powell, T. (1995): "Total Quality Management As Competitive Advantage: A Review And Empirical Study", *Strategic Management Journal*, 16: 15–37.

Preece, D. and Wood, M. (1995): "Quality Measurements: Who is Doing the Sums and for What Purpose?", *Human Resource Management Journal*, 5(3): 41–55.

Rhodes, C. (1997): "The Legitimisation of Learning in Organisational Change", *Journal of Organisational Change Management*, 10(1): 10–21.

Rosenthal, P., Hill, S. and Peccei, R. (1997): "Checking Out Service: Evaluating Excellence, HRM and TQM in Retailing", *Work, Employment & Society*, 11(3): 481–503.

Sewell, G. and Wilkinson, B. (1992): "Empowerment or Emasculation: Shopfloor Surveillance in a Total Quality Organisation", in Blyton, P. and P. Turnbull (eds.) *Reassessing Human Resource Management*, London: Sage.

Sims, R.R. (1994): "Human Resource Management's Role in Clarifying the New Psychological Contract", *Human Resource Management*, 33(3): 373–382.

SIPTU (Services Industrial Professional and Technical Union) (1993): "Total Quality: The Implications for Competitiveness and Positive Trade Unionism: The SIPTU Position", Dublin: SIPTU.

Smith, P. (1992): "AMEV Insurance Gains ISO 9002" Quality News, 14(2): 4–5.

Storey, J. (1992): *Developments in the Management of Human Resources.* Oxford: Blackwell.

Townley, B. (1989): "Selection and Appraisal: Reconstituting Social Relations", in J. Storey (ed.) *New Perspectives on Human Resource Management*, London: Routledge.

Turner, T. and Morley, M. (1995): *Industrial Relations and the New Order*, Dublin: Oak Tree Press.

Waldman, D. (1994): "Designing Performance Management Systems for Total Quality Implementation", *Journal of Organisational Change*, 7(2): 31–44.

Wilkinson, A. and Marchington, M. (1995): "TQM: Instant Pudding for the Personnel Function", *Human Resource Management Journal*, 5(1): 33–49.

Wilkinson, A. and Witcher, B. (1991): "Fitness for Use? Barriers to Full TQM in the UK", *Management Decision*, 29(8): 46–51.

Wilkinson, A. and Wilmott, H. (1995): "Introduction", in Wilkinson, A. and H. Willmott, (eds.) *Making Quality Critical*, London: Routledge.

Wilkinson, A., Marchington, M., Goodman, J. and Ackers, P. (1992): "Total Quality Management and Employee Involvement", *Human Resource Management Journal*, 2(4): 1–20.

Wilmott, H. (1993): "Strength is Ignorance; Slavery is Freedom: Managing Culture in Modern Organisations", *Journal of Management Studies*, 30(4): 515–552.

Wood, S. and Peccei, R. (1995): "Does Total Quality Management Make a Difference to Employee Attitudes?" *Employee Relations*, 17(3): 51–62.

8

REWARD SYSTEMS AND REWARD STRATEGIES

Pauline Grace and *Anne Coughlan*

INTRODUCTION

While people may gain a host of rewards from worklife — from promotion and recognition to job satisfaction — pay remains the common currency of exchange at work. It is pay that propels people to take up employment. Pay is conducive to quantification, comparison and bargaining (Brown and Walsh, 1994). Pay also provides the vent to most employees' dissatisfaction.

Without derogating the role of intrinsic reward, this chapter will focus on extrinsic rewards. The chapter will commence with a review of the alternative reward systems. Fixed rate pay forms the point of departure, the commentary then moving to variable reward systems. The second section reports on the incidence of the different reward systems in Irish organisations. Following from this the essentials of reward strategy will be considered. The role of implementation, and the role of evaluation, as key components of an organisation's reward strategy, will receive attention. Reference will be made to research evidence on the nature of reward strategy in Irish companies. The penultimate section reviews contemporary debate on rewards in the context of human resource strategy, assessing in particular the relationship between commitment-oriented human resource management and reward strategy. A look at current pay trends and the factors driving them will conclude the chapter.

ALTERNATIVE REWARD SYSTEMS

Fixed Pay and Salary Systems

Notwithstanding a thriving body of literature on performance and contingency pay, fixed or job-based pay endures as the dominant system of pay. (A 1996 EU-wide study put the figure at 94 per cent (EFILWC Study, 1997)). Typically, fixed pay is the rate or salary for the job or grade, derived from a simple time rate, or as a result of work study, such as measured day work, or derived from job evaluation. The actual money amount set can be determined from market rates, from ranges set for grades, or through collective bargaining. Under such a system the level of effort expended by the employee and the quality of the output is controlled by supervision, custom and practice or norms of professional practice.

A complaint commonly voiced in relation to fixed pay is that it lacks discrimination across poor to excellent performers (Smith, 1989). Critics argue that fixed rate systems trade equality of all, at the expense of equity for all. Pursuing the goal of paying each employee according to his or her contribution is however fraught with practical problems. Stymieing the quest to pay "each according to contribution" is the difficulty of articulating in sufficient and exact terms the desired performance levels for each employee. Furthermore, if the prescriptive literature is to be obeyed, this task is never-ending, reflecting the ongoing re-definition and re-specification of requisite performance. Scrambling through this first hurdle, a second proves equally gruelling. That is, management must now adjudicate employees against these standards — and do so systematically and objectively. Faced with this dual challenge, equity can become a rather elusive ideal.

Fixed pay systems need not be anathema to a high-performance culture. Those defending job-based pay contend that the concept of a given job, which is derived through job evaluation, automatically factors in notions of skill requirements and expected performance level, as well as the basic enumeration of duties (Barrett and Doverspike, 1989). Furthermore, various non-pecuniary tools for managing performance are available to managers. Flagging performance levels can be rallied by actively attending to recruitment and selection, training, supervision and performance management techniques. As Lockyer indicates, time, rate and grade systems encapsulate much of what a successful payments system should be: "They are simple and cheap to operate and are easily understood by all" (1996: 291).

The ease of administering fixed rate pay is frequently complicated by various additional payments. For example, the ubiquitous use of overtime bewilders many commentators (Brown and Walsh, 1994). Persistent and injudicious use of overtime may create the feeling amongst workers that such additional payments are theirs by right. Other payments, on top of basic wages, that may, through custom, take on the hue of entitlement include length of service payments and gratuities or seasonal bonuses. The non-pay component of the remuneration package is increasing in significance (Brown and Walsh, 1994). Benefits assume the form of company cars, sporting facilities, subsidised canteens, personal accident payments, and pensions. Underpinning these aspects of reward may be attempts to reaffirm employee positions of status, to shroud the real value of a pay package, or to tie employees to the organisation.

Job Evaluation

Job evaluation allows the determination of the level or range of base pay for the different jobs within an organisation. Traditionally, job evaluation has been conducted through either the non-analytical comparison of jobs in their entirety, or by analytically breaking jobs down into component parts. In the later form these parts typically refer to the skills, responsibility, effort and working conditions that the organisation is prepared to compensate for. The analytical method then awards either points or a weighting, the sum of which determines where the job is placed in the infrastructure of jobs. The purpose is to establish the relative worth and pay of each job, in a manner "that is broadly acceptable to the employees concerned" (Brown and Walsh, 1994: 445). Increasingly the case is made that job evaluation is failing to keep pace with the accelerated rate of change and fluidity within jobs (Armstrong and Baron, 1995: 614). Critics claim that the production of detailed job descriptions, as an antecedent to job evaluation, inhibits flexibility. Further rigidity can be created if employees are reluctant to undertake responsibilities that are associated with jobs at a higher level. It has also been contended that job evaluation encourages a preoccupation among employees with getting "regraded" or promoted rather than improving performance in their existing positions (Gunnigle et al., 1997a). This combined with efforts by managers to get employees to take on extra tasks can result in wage spirals, and grading drift. Commentators have also pointed out the inconsistency of evaluating the job as a single unit whilst allocating work responsibilities on the basis of the work-unit.

Brown and Walsh (1994) hint that changing technological imperatives and individualised career paths could prompt the demise of traditional job evaluation. It has been contended that "competence-based" job evaluation holds promise as a possible successor (Armstrong and Baron, 1995). Competence- or skill-based job evaluation focuses on the person who performs the job. Unlike traditional job evaluation which centres on the job grade or title, the emphasis is on the job incumbent's competence and ability to perform (Gunnigle et al., 1997a). This method is considered more suitable for an organisation that is striving for flexibility, multiskilling, individual and team autonomy, and knowledge work.

Another recent modification in the area of job evaluation is the concept of "broadbanding". Broadbanding involves holding on to some form of grading system while significantly reducing the numbers of grades or salary bands. This compression of job grades is deemed fitting with the trend towards flatter de-layered organisational structures. According to the literature, broadbanded structures increase the discretion that managers have in setting internal pay differentials (Torrington and Hall, 1998). It allows organisations to reward on the basis of performance or skills acquisition, whilst retaining some of the order of traditional job structures. However, as the IBEC survey (1998) results to be presented below indicate, the number of firms in Ireland engaged in such revisions is, at this time, limited.

VARIABLE ELEMENTS OF PAY

Output or Production-related Bonus Systems

Output or production-related systems attempt to establish a formal relationship between pay and output or exertion. These systems assume that employees can vary output according to the effort put in, and that this can be related to earnings in a comprehensible fashion. The logic is that employees, confident of the linkages from effort through to reward, and inspired by the prospect of greater financial gain, will engage in greater effort.

In practice, the simplicity and putative motivational impact of output bonuses are lessened for several reasons. First, the system requires some mechanism to ascertain apposite performance levels. This commonly results in the deployment of rate-fixing or work study, for example measured day work. Second, beliefs about fairness condition individuals to expect that employees of like skills and contribution should earn similar pay. Third, putting an employee on a system that is 100 per cent variable is a rare practice. A fixed element is generally included to provide the security of some minimum level of fallback pay. This payment also mitigates, to some extent, unproductive spells that arise through no fault of the worker, such as machine breakdown or disrupted supply of raw materials. Output or production-related systems are further complicated by evidence suggesting that workers adjust their effort and pace to coincide with group norms, showing a rather more sluggish response to the effort-pay link. In addition, by exaggerating the extent to which individuals respond to financial incentive, production bonuses may distract attention from the value of other sources of motivation, including the satisfaction derived from work itself.

Variable systems inject an element of unpredictability into planning for payroll and production. Unsophisticated systems can encourage myopic behaviour, as individuals channel energies into the achievement of elected goals to the detriment of other dimensions of the job. Attempts to overcome this problem through the introduction of multi-faceted measures serve to complicate the system and make it administratively more onerous on line managers and those charged with overseeing its operation. Where production or output-based pay is used, no consensus emerges on the best way to link pay to effort. Numerous trajectories exist, as indicated by Brown and Walsh (1994: 454–455):

> Payment by results systems come in numerous varieties, with pay linked to physical output in linear and non-linear, progressive and regressive, lagged, cushioned, periodically contracted, and sometimes curious other ways. At best they offer a means of maintaining effort that is cheap to manage and popular with employees; at worst they provide the surest methods imaginable of disrupting industrial relations.

Lockyer (1996) alludes to ways in which output or production-related systems can complicate industrial relations. First, such incentives may give rise to protracted negotiation when changes are sought which will affect earnings such as new work practices, or alterations in the level of output. The issue of internal relativities also surfaces as workers paid according to results struggle to keep pace with rises that fixed rate workers might obtain. Finally, in times of skill shortages output-based systems can inflate payroll costs as workers strive to retain average earnings in the face of new work methods and patterns (Lockyer, 1996).

Teamwork Pay Systems

In such systems, payments are shared among all members of an established team. The choice of a group incentive plan may provide a way to reconcile the need for group co-operation, the intricacies and interdependence of jobs, and the reality of group performance norms, with the incentive effect of clear goals, and pronounced links between performance and pay (Milkovich and Wig-dor, 1991). Interest in team-based pay partly stems from the bid to circumvent the dysfunctions of individual systems, in particu-lar the absence of a unifying purpose. Enthusiasts of team-based pay refer to intensified worker involvement, greater sharing of resources, and the synergies of group problem solving. Research evidence endorsing these effects is scarce. Where these outcomes are apparent, it is unclear whether success is due to circum-stances within the work context or the actual performance plan itself (Milkovich and Wigdor, 1991).

Although there are signs of team working taking hold (Turner and Morley, 1995), evidence of the adoption of teamwork pay is thin on the ground. That managers are deliberately deferring any links to pay until team working is well established remains unclear.

Profit-sharing Systems

Profit-sharing is a system where the employees receive, in addi-tion to their normal remuneration, a variable element of income directly linked to profits. The profits can be distributed in several ways, but the most common are as follows: provision of immediate or deferred benefits to workers; payment in cash, shares or other securities; or additions made to investment funds designated for employees benefit (MSF, 1998). Traditionally used to support a paternalistic employment ethos (Mahoney, 1992), profit-sharing also accommodates budgeting objectives, as payroll expenditure fluctuates in tandem with profit levels.

Employee Share Ownership Systems

Employee share ownership is another type of financial participa-tion. Systems characteristically are implemented in one of three ways. First, company shares can be set aside to be offered to em-ployees at preferential rates. Second, employees may be afforded options to buy company shares on favourable conditions after a specified length of time. Third, organisations can avail of Em-ployee Share Ownership Plans (ESOPs). In this arrangement shares are held in a specially dedicated trust on the employees behalf (MSF, 1998). Fiscal changes that followed on from the national agreement, *Partnership 2000*, have further facilitated the spread of financial participation. In particular the 1997 Finance Act introduced changes that increased the attractiveness of Approved Profit-Sharing Systems (APSS) for employees. It simultaneously assists, by way of tax relief, companies and employees who wish to set up an Employee Share Ownership Plan (ESOP). (Since the 1998 Finance Act, tax relief is available on newly issued shares purchased by employees up to a value of £10,000. Also the minimum holding period has been reduced to three years). Within the Irish public sector, ESOPs are being developed as a component of comprehensive programmes to elevate performance in commercial semi-state companies. This strategy is being pursued by Aer Lingus, ESB and Telecom Éireann (MSF, 1998). Adoption of this genre of reward has also been widespread in the UK since tax relief was introduced in 1978 for approved profit-sharing systems. Interestingly estimates suggest that up to one third of the systems in the UK are in fact types of executive share option systems (IDS 1994). Thus the promised link between reward and company output is limited by a sharper link between reward and position.

Gain-sharing Systems

Gain sharing generally refers to the rewarding of employees for improvements either in productivity levels or in cost containment. Usually the reward will relate to organisational gains made on a specific measure, or in excess of a set target. The distribution of gains or savings made has found particular application in team-based operations.

Skill- or Competence-based Pay Systems

Skill-based payment systems tie pay to the number, type and depth of skills which employees acquire and use. Competence-based pay is a system whereby an individual's pay and grade is related to the achievement of defined levels of competence. It necessitates competence-based job evaluations. These evaluations assess the work of the job incumbent in terms of the competencies required to perform effectively in different roles and at graduated levels in the organisation. In recent times the acquisition and recording of skills appears to be increasingly job-related and frequently accompanies a quest for flexibility. To bolster the appeal of such initiatives to employees, some companies seek to synchronise skill accumulation with more widely recognised qualifications.

From the employer's perspective this type of reward system appears appropriate where an organisation is experiencing growth and requires the rapid acquisition of new skills. To satisfy employees' hunger for skills and competencies (which now have a direct bearing on their pay), the training department must be well resourced and capable of responding quickly to employee requests for training. Close links must also be established between HR and the line to ensure that the skills being disseminated remain relevant to the company's present operations and future direction.

According to research carried out by the Income Data Services (1996), companies with competence-based pay may have difficulties ensuring the consistent application and rating of competencies, in addition to the problem of identifying well defined competencies and associated performance standards. Other difficulties include raising expectations through the promise of paying for improved competence and then only being able to deliver moderate rewards. "Topping out" may also occur. This is when employees arrive at the top of the designated structure of recognised skills. Thus having reached a plateau in skill development they are no longer explicitly remunerated for learning in the workplace. Conversely, companies could end up paying for staff with qualifications they do not need, resulting in escalating pay and training costs for no tangible improvement in company performance.

Performance-/Merit-related Pay Systems

The concept of performance pay is not new, but it is useful to distinguish performance-related pay (PRP) from conventional performance-based systems such as payment by results. Although, Lockyer (1996: 292) wryly comments that it is "easy to argue that performance-related pay is the designer version of piece-work for white-collar and managerial staffs", there are differences beyond the type of employee involved. PRP is based primarily on a formal appraisal or assessment of employees' behaviour. Its link with physical output is less acute.

Performance-/merit-related pay is typically administered in either of two ways. The payment can be made either as a once-off bonus or it can be paid as a permanent increase in the basic wage or salary. Companies who distribute payments in the form of a permanent increase are thought to experience higher levels of worker commitment (Wood 1996). Questions of employee effort and performance invariably crop up in any treatment of pay. Payment for performance at an individual level is a topic to be taken up in Chapter 9 by Gerard McMahon. However, it is apposite that brief mention is now made to a key debate enveloping the measurement of work performance. It was noted earlier that pay is amenable to quantification, comparison and bargaining. Behavioural norms, conditioning and the contortions of perception will always conspire to make this an inexact process. However, the difficulty of fixing a correct price to an individual's remuneration is insignificant in comparison to the conundrum of attempting to pay individuals according to their contribution. Making the link between pay and performance explicit is too often a vague and vacillating venture: vague in the sense that it entails a campaign of conjecture, reductionism and generalisation; vacillating to the extent that the act of articulation makes a reality of a behaviour and simultaneously delimits it. Moreover, if to measure an activity is to simultaneously create that activity, then this construction of norms is inevitably expedited when a price is attached to these measured actions. Intuition and evidence suggests that this orientation towards rewarded tasks is often accompanied by a neglect of other tasks (Thompson, 1992).

RESEARCH EVIDENCE ON THE INCIDENCE OF REWARD SYSTEMS

This section, while concentrating on evidence from a survey conducted by the Irish Business and Employers Confederation (IBEC) in 1997, will also make reference to the Cranfield/University of Limerick (CUL) survey (1995) and a recent UK study carried out by the Institute of Personnel and Development (IPD, 1998). The focus of the IBEC study is variable reward systems[1]. Respondents thus supplied information on variable components which exist in addition to the organisation's fixed pay structure. Both the IBEC and CUL surveys looked primarily at firms employing fifty or more employees[2].

Table 8.1 provides details of the percentage of companies in the IBEC survey with various reward systems. (The total number of systems does not add up to 100 per cent as a number of companies have more than one system).

Overall individual performance-/merit-related systems are the most common (with 57 per cent of companies reporting this type of system). The next most popular system is company performance-related pay (applicable in 37 per cent of companies). Other

---

[1] In the survey questionnaire administered by the Survey and Business Information Unit of IBEC, the terms "system" and "scheme" were used interchangeably. Throughout this chapter consistent use will be made of the single term "system".

[2] In the Irish Business and Employers Confederation (IBEC) survey, questionnaires were sent to a random sample of manufacturing and services companies employing more than 50 employees, and for the Chemical/Pharmaceutical sector and the Electronics sector, questionnaires were also sent to companies with less than 50 employees. The sample frame used for the 1995 Cranfield/University of Limerick (CUL) Study in Ireland was the *Business and Finance Top 2000 Trading and Non-trading Bodies* in the Republic of Ireland. Organisations are ranked according to level of turnover, financial institutions by the size of their assets, and non-trading bodies by the number of their employees.

high incidence systems include output-/production-related systems (30 per cent), commission (25 per cent) and profit-sharing (19 per cent). The newer forms of reward/payment systems, such as skill-based pay, competency pay, teamwork pay and gain sharing are much less common than the other systems, which had generally been in existence longer. Some ten per cent of respondents had none of the designated variable pay systems.

TABLE 8.1: INCIDENCE OF REWARD SYSTEMS

Type of System	Percentage of Companies
Output-/Production-related Bonus	30%
Commission	25%
Profit-sharing	19%
Performance-/Merit-related — Individual	57%
Performance-related — Company	37%
Teamwork Pay	6%
Skill-based Pay	6%
Competency Pay	3%
Gain Sharing	3%
Broad Banding	2%

Source: IBEC Survey of Reward Systems (1998).

In terms of sectoral differences, some 92 per cent of organisations in the banking/insurance and finance sector had an individual performance-/merit-related system, as had approximately two-thirds of the food/drink/tobacco, chemical/pharmaceutical and healthcare, and the electronics sectors (Table 8.2). Other manufacturing and other services had the lowest incidence of this type of system, at 36 per cent and 47 per cent respectively. Output-/production-related bonus systems were highest in the other manufacturing sector at 49 per cent and commission was most common in the banking/insurance/finance sector, at 40 per cent.

TABLE 8.2: TYPE OF REWARD SYSTEM BY MAIN ACTIVITY OF COMPANIES

Type of System	Main Activity						
	Food / Drink / Tobacco	Chemical / Pharm. / Healthcare	Electronics	Banking / Insurance / Finance	Other Manufacturing	Other Services	Total
Output/Production-related Bonus	26%	20%	12%	19%	49%	16%	89
Commission	28%	21%	18%	40%	23%	32%	74
Profit-sharing	22%	16%	21%	32%	18%	11%	57
Performance-/Merit-related — Individual	65%	69%	67%	92%	36%	47%	173
Performance-related — Company	39%	34%	45%	40%	32%	42%	110
Teamwork Pay	4%	3%	9%	4%	9%	-	17
Skill-based Pay	2%	11%	6%	4%	5%	5%	18
Competency Pay	4%	1%	3%	8%	3%	11%	10
Gain Sharing	2%	3%	3%	-	3%	5%	8
Broad Banding	9%	3%	-	-	-	-	7
Total No. of Companies. (100%)	46	75	33	26	102	19	301

Source: IBEC Survey of Reward Systems (1998).

There was a fairly even spread of profit-sharing systems across a number of sectors, however, the lowest incidence was recorded in the other services sector (11 per cent), and the highest incidence in the banking/insurance/finance sector (32 per cent).

The highest incidence of team-based pay was in the electronics and other manufacturing sectors. The highest incidence of skill-based pay was in the chemical/pharmaceutical and health-care sector and the highest incidence of competency pay was in the other services sector. There was little difference between the sectors in terms of the incidence of gain sharing systems, with the exception of the banking/insurance/finance sector, which did not report this type of system.

Eligibility for Reward

While 25 per cent of respondent companies operated reward systems for individual categories of employee *only* (e.g. management only, manual workers or sales staff), three-quarters stated they had systems for more than one category of employee (Table 8.3). In addition 75 per cent or more of these companies with systems stated that *all* employees in their companies were covered by a system, indicating a fairly high density of coverage in these companies. (The unexpected exception was managerial staff, where all managerial employees were covered in only two-thirds of companies. A possible explanation for this is that only senior management are covered in some companies by a particular system).

Individual performance-/merit-related systems are the most widespread of variable systems for all employees, with the exception of manual grades and sales staff. Close to one-third of companies have this variety of system for skilled/technical/professional and clerical, and over half (53 per cent) have this system for managerial/supervisory categories. Company performance-related systems are the next most common systems for skilled/technical/professional, clerical and sales staff. Between 13 per cent and 18 per cent of organisations have profit-sharing for all grades of employee.

TABLE 8.3: CATEGORY OF EMPLOYEE COVERED BY A SYSTEM — BY TYPE OF REWARD SYSTEM

Type of System	Manual	Skilled/ Technical/ Professional	Clerical	Sales Staff	Managerial/ Supervisory
Output-/Production-related Bonus	29%	12%	5%	5%	8%
Commission	–	1%	–	41%	3%
Profit-sharing	13%	14%	14%	17%	18%
Performance-/Merit-related — Individual	10%	35%	33%	30%	53%
Performance-related — Company	10%	16%	16%	19%	34%
Teamwork Pay	4%	3%	1%	2%	1%
Skill-based Pay	2%	4%	3%	1%	1%
Competency Pay	1%	2%	2%	2%	2%
Gain Sharing	3%	2%	2%	2%	2%
Broadbanding	1%	1%	1%	1%	2%
Total No. of Companies with Systems	62%	64%	58%	77%	79%
Total No. of Companies *	269	269	299	176	301

* The percentages shown in the columns are calculated out of the total number of companies who employed these categories — for example, not all companies in the survey employed sales staff.

Source: IBEC Survey of Reward Systems (1998).

Companies would also appear to favour different systems for the different categories of employee, such as the output-/production-related bonus system for manual workers (with 29 per cent of companies choosing this option), and a commission system for sales staff (with 41 per cent of companies using this type of system). Some 53 per cent of companies have individual perform-ance-/merit-related pay systems for managerial/supervisory grades, and 34 per cent have company performance-related pay systems for this same group.

A study of 1,138 companies carried out in the UK in 1997 (IPD, 1998), also found individual performance-related pay to be the most popular type of variable reward system, followed by profit-related pay (Table 8.4). The incidence of team-based pay and skill-/competency-based pay trailed the other systems quite considera-bly. In this study the incidence of systems for management and non-management grades were very similar, with the exception of individual performance-related pay, where there were distinct differences between management and non-management employ-ees.

TABLE 8.4: UK EVIDENCE OF SYSTEMS

Type of System	Management	Non-Management
Individual Performance-related Pay	40%	25%
Team-based Pay	8%	8%
Skill-/Competency-based Pay	6%	11%
Profit-related Pay	35%	34%

Source: "IPD 1998 Performance Pay Survey".

Table 8.5 provides comparisons across the Irish CUL survey (1995) and the IBEC survey (1998). Results from both surveys show a fairly consistent application of systems. In terms of profit-sharing systems the results show a marginally higher incidence in the IBEC study, which is to be expected given that the survey was carried out two years later.

TABLE 8.5: CATEGORY OF EMPLOYEE COVERED BY A SYSTEM — BY TYPE OF SYSTEM

Type of System	Manual		Skilled/Technical/Professional[1]		Clerical		Managerial/Supervisory	
	IBEC	CUL	IBEC	CUL	IBEC	CUL	IBEC	CUL
Profit-sharing	13%	10%	14%	13%	14%	13%	18%	19%
Share Option	–	10%	–	14%	–	12%	–	23%
Performance-/Merit-related — Individual[2]	10%	15%	35%	45%	33%	37%	53%	51%
Performance-related — Company[2]	10%		16%		16%		34%	

Source: IBEC Survey of Reward Systems (1998) and "Human Resource Management in Irish Organisations"/CUL survey (1995).

Notes: [1] The CUL Survey does not explicitly include "skilled" employees in this category.
[2] The table from which the CUL survey data were taken did not distinguish between merit-related/individual and company performance-related pay.

Trends in the Uptake of Reward Systems

According to the IBEC study (1998), the majority of reward systems identified had been in existence for more than three years (Table 8.6). More companies had initiated company performance-related systems in the last three years (31 per cent) than individual performance-/merit-related systems (19 per cent). In relation to the systems showing lower incidence such as teamwork pay, gain sharing, skill-based pay and broadbanding, between a quarter and three-quarters of these systems were introduced within the last three years. In addition, between one per cent and six per cent of companies were currently considering introducing one or other of these systems, (the most popular of which was company performance-related systems (6 per cent), followed by profit-sharing, competency pay, gain sharing and individual performance-/merit-related systems (4 per cent)).

TABLE 8.6: INTRODUCTION OF REWARD SYSTEMS — TIMING

Type of System	More than 3 Years Ago	Within Last 3 Years	Currently Under Consideration
Output-/Production-related Bonus	85%	10%	2%
Commission	81%	11%	1%
Profit-sharing	65%	25%	4%
Performance-/Merit-related — Individual	77%	19%	4%
Teamwork Pay	45%	40%	3%
Performance-related — Company	68%	31%	6%
Skill-based Pay	53%	24%	3%
Competency Pay	50%	20%	4%
Gain Sharing	75%	25%	4%
Broadbanding	25%	75%	–

Source: IBEC Survey of Reward Systems (1998).

Research in the UK parallels the pattern of uptake of these various "non-traditional" reward systems (Table 8.7). The IPD study (1998) shows an increase in the use of all systems with over half of the companies surveyed introducing individual performance-related pay within the last five years. The other types of systems have also grown, although from a smaller base, with approximately half having been inaugurated within the last two years.

TABLE 8.7: LENGTH OF TIME REWARD SYSTEMS IN OPERATION (UK)

Type of System	0–2 years	3–5 years	5+ years
Individual Performance-related Pay	21%	38%	41%
Team-based Pay	45%	33%	22%
Skill-/Competency-based Pay	50%	23%	27%
Profit-related Pay	45%	45%	10%

Source: "IPD 1998 Performance Pay Survey".

Costs of Reward Systems

Companies in the IBEC study (1998) were asked to provide information on both the initial cost of introducing the various systems, and the current cost of the systems (Table 8.8). They were also invited to present these costs as a percentage of payroll. More data was provided by respondents for the current operating cost, than for the initial cost of introducing the systems.

The more "traditional" systems such as output-/production-related bonus systems and commission systems, tended to have higher average set-up and current costs, than the newer systems. (Average costs of 8.5 per cent and 12.6 per cent, set-up and running costs respectively, were shown for output-/production-related bonus systems, and 4.3 per cent and 7.2 per cent for commission systems). In terms of current costs, profit-sharing and performance-related systems had the next highest average costs, at 5.4 per cent and 4.1 per cent to 4.4 per cent respectively.

TABLE 8.8: APPROXIMATE INITIAL COST OF INTRODUCING REWARD SYSTEMS/CURRENT COSTS — AS A PER CENT OF PAYROLL

Reward/payment System	Set-up Cost			Current Cost		
	No. (%) of Companies with Systems who Provided Information	Mean Cost %	Median Cost %	No. (%) of Companies with Systems who Provided Information	Mean Cost %	Median Cost %
Output-/Production-related Bonus	44 (49%)	8.5	5.0	52 (58%)	12.6	8.0
Commission	26 (35%)	4.3	1.0	32 (43%)	7.2	3.0
Profit-sharing	14 (25%)	3.0	2.7	29 (51%)	5.4	4.6
Performance-/Merit-related — Individual	76 (44%)	3.3	2.2	98 (57%)	4.1	3.5
Teamwork Pay	6 (35%)	1.0	1.0	10 (59%)	3.0	2.2
Performance-related — Company	51 (46%)	2.7	2.0	65 (59%)	4.4	3.0
Skill-based Pay	5 (28%)	3.8	0.0	7 (39%)	3.8	2.0
Competency Pay	4 (40%)	0.0	0.0	5 (50%)	3.6	1.0
Gain Sharing	5 (62%)	0.8	0.0	5 (62%)	1.2	0.0
Broadbanding	3 (43%)	4.0	—	2 (29%)	0.0	—

Source: IBEC Survey of Reward Systems (1998).

The UK IPD survey (1998) furnishes some interesting information about the size of variable rewards made to different categories of employee. The figures (see Table 8.9) show mean and median values expressed as a percentage of base pay in the last 12 months. The survey results indicate a mean value of around 10 per cent across all organisations, while the median value is around 4 per cent. This difference, according to the survey, might indicate that whilst a minority are in receipt of substantial awards, the majority of employees are receiving significantly smaller rewards. Again, according to the results, the awards are slightly higher for senior managers.

REWARDS STRATEGY

The aim of this section is to examine the key principles that underpin the development of rewards strategy. Issues of congruence between reward systems and human resource strategy more generally will be considered, as will the pivotal role of "process".

The Contingencies of Reward Strategy

There is no one best reward system. There are rather a range of systems, their suitability being largely contingent on a number of factors. There is a body of knowledge offering managers guidance in determining a payment system that is consistent with the particular circumstances of the organisation. As Figure 8.1 illustrates, it is possible to identify reward types that complement contextual factors. Reflecting the essence of the contingency approach to reward, Figure 8.1 portrays the various situational factors which render one system more appropriate than another. Lupton and Gowler (1969) did much early work in identifying the different scenarios of "best fit". Contextual factors which impinge upon the appropriateness of a reward system include the production technology, profile of the workforce, characteristics of the labour market, and the extent and nature of competition. Furthermore, it has been argued that within one organisation several systems might be used simultaneously for strategic reasons (Mahoney, 1992).

TABLE 8.9: AVERAGE AND MEDIAN AWARDS, EXPRESSED AS A PER CENT OF BASE PAY

Type of System	Senior Managers		Middle Managers		Junior Managers/Senior Supervisors		Non-Managers	
	Mean	*Median*	*Mean*	*Median*	*Mean*	*Median*	*Mean*	*Median*
Individual Performance-related Pay	11%	5%	9%	4%	9%	4%	9%	4%
Team-based Pay	11%	8%	10%	5%	7%	5%	10%	7%
Skill-/Competency-based Pay	9%	4%	10%	5%	10%	4%	10%	5%
Profit-related Pay	11%	6%	11%	6%	10%	7%	10%	6%

Source: "IPD 1998 Performance Pay Survey".

FIGURE 8.1: REWARD SYSTEMS AND CONTEXTS

Basis for Pay Method	Method	Measure	Technology Work Method	Product Strategy
Job	Hourly rate salary grade	Standardised procedures	Taylorist systems	Mass production, stable technologies and work systems
Performance input	Skill-based pay	Qualifications, competency	Teamwork, variable technology and work flows	Variable production and technology, flexible organisations
	PRP	Behavioural, attitudes, etc.	Teamwork, individual work, where quality, effort, manner are important	High time cost in appraisal; management vulnerable to pressures to reduce costs
Performance output	PRP	Targets, quantifiable measures		
	Piecework	Need to identify work	Batch, short assembly lines, independent operations	Limited supervision, but time to set and monitor rates

Source: Adapted from Lockyer, 1996.

The Role of Process in Reward Strategy

Bowey and Thorpe (1988: 23) argue that when time is a limited resource effort should not be consumed in the identification of an elusive "best" pay system. Rather attention should shift to *process* issues. Management should be concerned with

> achieving a match between the payment system and the expectations, motivations, patterns of interrelationships, past history and understandings of the people in the systems.

Behavioural issues should thus prevail. Bowey and Thorpe believe that this strategy can best be adopted by including employees from the early stages. The advantages are threefold. Management learns of the contextual factors from the job incumbents. The social and behavioural environment will become clearer. Finally, the act of involving employees should help foster their understanding and support.

In addition before management attempts to sell a system to the employees, it is critical that line managers or those charged with the implementation of the system, are taken on board (Kessler, 1994). Many consider these processes worthy of greater thought than the actual reward system infrastructure itself. Indeed it might well be through the process that the actual objectives are achieved. This is particularly pertinent if the thinking revolves around the symbolic aspects of pay; the messages it transmits on issues such as control, participation, and the culture being engendered. Finally, managers should be most cautious when tackling existing reward systems as extant imperfections often appear trivial in comparison to the trauma of dismantling and redesigning a system.

Factors in the Commercial Environment

Notwithstanding this theme which promotes the role of process, it remains that the payment system and rate of pay does convey signals to stakeholders. Companies may be concerned with remunerating at a level that is competitive enough to attract and retain what it considers to be high calibre employees. In this respect, Irish firms are forced to reckon with the global context, labour mobility, and the concomitant competition for skills. The extent to which premium incentives are required vary according to sector and the type of skill in question (Roche and Geary, 1997). Alternatively the organisation may be constrained in terms of the financial package it can make available and may innovate to contrive rewards deemed competitive with other employers in the labour market. Increasingly managers are cognisant of the absolute cost of remuneration, especially where payroll costs represent a significant proportion of total costs (Roche and Gunnigle, 1995).

Payment systems are also influenced by wider constraints which encourage the adoption of certain payment practices. Pay rates may be regulated by bargaining units, industry norms and national agreements. The state is concerned with the level of pay (wage spirals), the living standards of people and the effect of pay on inflation. Morley and Gunnigle (1997: 159) state that

> overall, in the Irish context, economic and managerial factors coupled with the strength of the trade union movement have shaped the development of pay bargaining carried out at all levels.

In this regard, both the IBEC (1998) survey and the CUL (1995) survey indicate that for manual grades pay is more likely to be determined at national level (through collective bargaining), while at the other end of the hierarchy, management pay tends to be more "individualised". The contextual factors that must be taken into account, from internal considerations, to environmental factors through to generic principles are summarised in Figure 8.2 (Lockyer, 1996).

FIGURE 8.2: THE TRADITIONAL CONTEXTS OF PAY

Factors Internal to Organisation	Environmental Factors	General Principles
Need to control labour costs	Relationship to market rates	Easy and cost-effective administration
Equity between jobs of equal worth	National/tripartite agreements	Easy to operate
Rewarding the good employee	Legislation, equal pay and value provisions	Easy to understand
Personnel management policies, and employee opportunities for progression	Macroeconomic and fiscal policy	Perceived as fair
Technological and organisational constraints	Trade union policies and industry practices	Solves problems and achieves aims
Product cycle and changes	Product markets and competition	
Purchasing power and consequent standard of living Visible and potent communicator of management's aims, values and priorities		

Source: Adapted from Lockyer, 1996.

DEVELOPING AND IMPLEMENTING A REWARD STRATEGY

Reward Strategy

An organisation's reward strategy should support the overall business and financial strategy. Thus the reward strategy must be consistent with the key goals of the organisation. It is also suggested that the strategy be flexible enough to respond to new challenges and opportunities. Armstrong (1996) warns of the danger of a strategy that promises too much but comes up short in terms of delivery. His advice is also to keep it simple, concentrate on no more than one or two issues critical to the organisation at any one time, thus enabling organisations to focus their resources in areas that will bring about the maximum added value, and ensure that it is realistic and practical.

Research Findings: Objectives of Reward Systems and the Attainment of Objectives

In the IBEC study (1998), a broad and general question was first posed to ascertain the overall objective(s) for introducing the various systems. The main responses to this question were as follows: to reward employees (24 per cent), to increase productivity, quality, efficiency and flexibility (23 per cent), to provide an incentive and to create a more focused, committed and motivated workforce (16 per cent), to improve/maintain competitiveness in the marketplace and to achieve company goals and objectives (10 per cent), to increase an awareness between individual effort, business performance and financial reward, and to foster a sense of participation/partnership involvement in company performance (10 per cent).

Apart from the main objective mentioned above, companies were presented with a list of six objectives (as follows) and asked to rank them in order of importance:

- To retain and recruit staff.

- Part of reorganisation/restructuring.

- To facilitate new forms of working.

- Increasing the link to company performance.

- To foster a more participative structure.

- Parent company policy.

The objective most frequently quoted (either as the main objective or the 2nd or 3rd objective) was the need to "increase the link to business performance" (Figure 8.3). The next most often quoted objective was the need "to foster a more participative structure", followed by the need "to retain and recruit staff". The least quoted objective was that the various reward/payment systems were introduced as "part of re-organisation/rationalisation /re-structuring".

FIGURE 8.3: FIRST/SECOND/THIRD OBJECTIVES — ALL REWARD SYSTEMS (%)

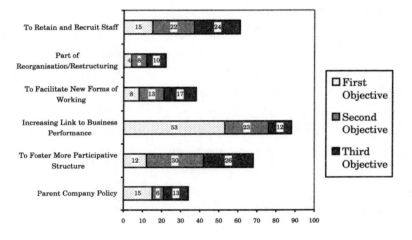

Source: IBEC Survey of Reward Systems (1998).

Where companies identified and ranked their three main objectives in introducing the various reward systems, they were asked to rank their perceptions of the company's level of success in attaining these objectives. Figure 8.4 provides information on the perceived level of success in achieving objectives, for all systems. Overall it is noticeable from Figure 8.4, that only a very small number of companies stated that they were "unsuccessful" in terms of achieving their objectives. Approximately two-thirds of respondents stated that the outcomes had either "exceeded their expectations" or were "successful". However, the figure does show that while there is a high level of success, there is also a certain level of dissatisfaction with the systems in that the remaining third of companies stated that they found that their objectives to be only either "moderately successful" or "unsuccessful".

FIGURE 8.4: LEVEL OF SUCCESS IN TERMS OF ACHIEVING OBJECTIVES — ALL REWARD SYSTEMS (%)

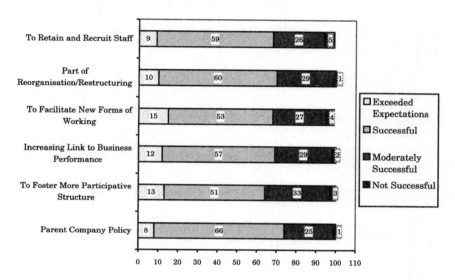

Source: IBEC Survey of Reward Systems (1998).

The UK-based IPD survey (1998) portrays respondents' perceptions of the success of the specific reward systems. The perceived effect of individual performance-related pay (IPRP) provides an interesting illustration (Table 8.10). Nearly three-quarters (74 per cent) of respondents noted a positive impact on employee performance. There was also a widespread perception (69 per cent) amongst respondents that the use of individual performance-based pay sends clear signals indicating the priority given to organisational performance. Forty-three per cent of respondents, however, felt that IPRP had either a harmful effect (14 per cent), or no effect (29 per cent), on the sense of fairness employees feel in relation to reward. Less than half (41 per cent) of those involved noted any improvement in either employee commitment or the ease with which change is facilitated. Confirming the fears of the literature on IPRP, 72 per cent of respondents remarked a deterioration or no change in the quality of team working as a result of IPRP. Finally, it is worth noting that 84 per cent of respondents stated that IPRP had no impact on the trade union's role in pay issues; only 14 per cent per cent recorded a diminution in trade union influence.

TABLE 8.10: THE EFFECTS OF INDIVIDUAL PERFORMANCE-RELATED PAY (IPRP)

"What effect do you think your system of IPRP has had on the following?"	Improves	No Change	Worsens
Employee Performance	74%	26%	0
Delivering a clear message about the importance of organisational performance	69%	27%	4%
Rewarding employees in a way they think is fair	57%	29%	14%
Your ability to identify and get rid of poor performers	52%	46%	2%
Facilitating change in your organisation	41%	54%	5%
Employee commitment/loyalty	41%	53%	6%
Employee willingness to stay with your organisation	35%	60%	5%
Encouraging employees to suggest improvements and innovations	28%	68%	5%
Effective teamworking	28%	59%	13%
Curbing trade union influence on pay decisions	14%	84%	3%

Source: "IPD 1998 Performance Pay Survey".

Just under one in five respondents in the IBEC survey (1998) stated that they had met with difficulties when implementing the various systems. Examples of the difficulties encountered with alternative reward systems are provided below in Figure 8.5.

FIGURE 8.5: DIFFICULTIES ENCOUNTERED WHEN IMPLEMENTING REWARD SYSTEMS

Type of System	Difficulty Encountered
Output/Production-related Bonus	• Measuring output accurately • Setting/maintaining accurate standards/targets • Getting agreement from unions • Resistance to change/Breaking traditional methods of assessments • Defining criteria • Manipulation by employees of criteria/information
Commission	• Resistance to change
Profit-sharing	• Move away from the "traditional" approach
Performance-/Merit-related Pay — Individual	• Defining measurement criteria • Getting accurate market data • Some staff against PRP — don't like the uncertainty • Time consuming to carry out • Difficult to negotiate • Establishing targets for performance • Relativity, with certain grades • Tendency for reviewers to give equal increase to most personnel • Subjectivity of appraisal — no guidelines
Teamwork	• Changing from individual to team pay • Breaking link with overtime

Performance-related Pay — Company	• Definition of Profit — Group or Individual company contribution • Time consuming to carry out • Maintaining confidentiality on company financial details • Staff unhappy that all staff get same bonus regardless of performance • Staff not happy with grades
Competency Pay	• Assessment Process — credibility of assessors • Relativity
Gain Sharing	• Staff expecting a bonus each year, although it is only payable if company reaches its profit targets • Difficulties in adjusting payment formula having implemented the system
Broadbanding	• Scepticism

Source: IBEC Survey of Reward Systems (1998).

MONITORING AND EVALUATION OF REWARD SYSTEMS

Monitoring and evaluation are key steps in the implementation of any successful reward strategy. According to Armstrong (1996), an evaluation or audit of the reward system should consist of:

- An analysis of each component of the reward system to assess its effectiveness, the extent to which it is adding value and its relevance to the present and future needs of the organisation;

- An assessment of opinions about the reward system by its key users and those who are affected by it. This may be conducted by means of interviews or through attitude surveys and/or focus groups;

- A diagnosis of strengths and weaknesses leading to an assessment of what needs to be done and why.

Armstrong (1996) recommends continuous monitoring through such audits. He also states the necessity to analyse data on up-gradings, the effectiveness of performance management processes, the cost of systems and the impact on results. Perhaps most importantly he cautions that no reward innovation should take place unless a cost-benefit analysis has forecast that it will add value. The monitoring and evaluation processes should establish the magnitude to which the forecasted gains have been obtained and review the costs against the prediction.

Research Findings: Monitoring and Evaluation of Reward Systems

In the IBEC survey (1998), one hundred and seventy four companies (64 per cent) stated that they had a system in place for monitoring and evaluating their reward/payment systems. Of these 174 companies with systems, 88 (51 per cent) were formal systems; 83 (48 per cent) were informal systems; and one company had both an informal and formal system. Examples of monitoring systems given include:

- Annual appraisals of individual performance.
- The monitoring and review of targets/goals/results on a regular basis.
- Committee monitoring of systems.
- Computerised monitoring of systems.
- Recording of daily/weekly/monthly production costs.
- Participation in pay surveys/ regular comparability studies with other companies.
- The linking of reward systems to quantitative measurement.
- Setting key objectives, linked to overall company profit.
- Performance communicated to employees on a regular basis.
- Setting of definite objectives for individuals.

Strategies used by survey respondents appeared to have the following common components:

- Setting of clear objectives/targets/goals.

- Communication of objectives.

- Monitoring/recording and reviewing of objectives.

- Measuring outcomes (including "benchmarking").

- Feedback on performance.

- Communication of company information to staff.

- Linking reward to performance.

HUMAN RESOURCE MANAGEMENT AND REWARDS SYSTEMS: CURRENT DEBATES AND TRENDS

Commitment-oriented Human Resource Management and Reward Systems

The High Commitment Model (HCM) of Human Resource Management seeks to develop techniques to elicit the motivation and commitment of employees. HCM is synonymous with practices such as teamworking, employee involvement and functional flexibility. The identification of a reward system to partner high commitment practices (HCP) is, however, a matter of contention (Wood, 1996). It is not uncommon to find individual performance-related pay (PRP) linked with HCM (Storey, 1992). This linkage is not however to be taken as a necessary endorsement of PRP, with several writers expressing doubts about the efficacy of PRP as a commitment eliciting device (Kessler and Purcell, 1991; Storey and Sisson, 1993). Interest in other methods of contingent pay is now gaining momentum. Advocates of skill-based pay, profit-sharing and teamwork pay variously claim that these systems better foster the notion of the learning, committed and co-operative workforce.

Indeed the question has been raised as to whether HCM and contingency pay are really compatible concepts. In light of studies which explore the link between pay and motivation, the two concepts might actually be at cross purposes. That is, if management institute performance-related pay are they not undermining intrinsic motivation, autonomy and commitment? A body of thought contends that HCM is best achieved through levers other than reward management. In this perspective, fixed-rate pay systems are not indicative of low commitment, as managers deliberately eschew performance-related payment systems. This debate is addressed by Wood (1996) as he surmises possible reasons for the lack of association between HCM and the use of performance or contingent pay systems in the UK. On the basis of research into manufacturing plants in the UK, Wood (1996: 53) concludes that:

> there is no systematic association between the use of HCM and the use of performance or contingent pay systems, such as merit pay and profit-sharing systems.

However, it is worth noting that the IBEC study reports that use of both individual performance-/merit-related pay and company performance-related pay is lowest in the other manufacturing and other services sector. It is conceivable that the sector and type of business activity has more bearing on the payment strategy than management approach (HCM or otherwise).

Finally, other tenets of HRM are visible in the shift from collective pay systems to methods focused on the individual. The use of performance-related pay, as a strand within HRM, is illustrative of this point. PRP may be grasped by management as an opportunity to increase the proportion of payroll within their discretion. Examples exist of the introduction of performance-related payment systems coinciding with the phasing out of established collective bargaining arrangements (Lockyer, 1996; IBEC, 1998). Based on a study of Irish greenfield sites, Gunnigle et al. (1997b: 123) report that the diffusion of PRP systems is indicative of employers' wish "to individualise the employment relationship and exclude union penetration". It is not uncommon for PRP to oper-

ate in unionised organisations. However, such a modus operandi
may mask management's objectives (Thompson, 1992).

The Changing Context of Reward Systems

In 1989 Mahoney (1992: 345) postulated that " . . . it is unlikely
that any single pay contingency will replace job-based pay as a
dominant form of compensation." This prediction at a time when
much activity was occurring in pay circles proved to be well
grounded. Studies suggest, however, that experimentation is
taking place in relation to the variable adjuncts to fixed pay or
salary; additions such as performance-related pay, profit-sharing
and, to a lesser extent, teamwork pay (CUL, 1995; IBEC, 1998;
IPD, 1998). At the outset, the ready adoption of new tools or techniques by management might not surprise the observer. Management is frequently accused of faddism. Human resource management is particularly vulnerable, being described by Braham
(1982: xi) as the "market place for every peddler of far-fetched
ideas". However, the periodic ratification of new payment techniques and tools is not without rudiments of rationale. Huczynski
(1993) believes that unless a payment system is reviewed and revised, it can give rise to certain employee expectations. These may
become formidable constraints which act to delimit the flexibility
and scope of the organisation. As Brown and Walsh (1994: 451)
observe

> With growing familiarity, employees come to treat as an
> entitlement that which they once perceived as a reward . . .
> Minor loopholes become normal pathways.

To overcome the contempt that accompanies familiarity payment
systems require continuous review. Moreover, today's business
environment has to a large extent made organisational change
inevitable. Some of the current commercial trends forcing managers to review or appraise their reward systems are as follows:

- The impact of new technologies which have reshaped jobs (e.g.
  evident in more flexible working practices);

- Adjustments in the composition of skills (e.g. broader range of competencies required) and in the types of people needed;

- Rapidly emerging technologies and a growing services sector which have created a demand for a certain type of labour with, in some cases, consequent skill shortages;

- The potential competitive advantage employees bring to a company;

- De-layering/introduction of flatter organisations with less emphasis on hierarchy and greater priority afforded to role flexibility;

- The heightened importance of cost management and realising "value for money".

If simplicity, cost effectiveness, ready comprehensibility and ease of administration are the *sine qua non* of a successful reward strategy, it follows that many of the newer systems barely warrant consideration. However, wider issues such as competition, flexibility and mobility are demanding that managers re-evaluate their reward strategy (see Figure 8.6). Thus the onus is on managers to weed out obsolete reward systems whilst affording employees adequate time to become familiar with, and develop trust in, the new system. Time is a necessary (though not sufficient) prerequisite on which such trust is built. Research hints that ample "bedding down" time can confer respectability on even the more controversial of reward systems (Dowling and Richardson, 1997).

FIGURE 8.6: THE CHANGING LANDSCAPE OF PAY

Traditional Pay Issues		Current Pay Issues
Fixed pay	⇒	Variable pay
Jobs organised along functional lines	⇒	Jobs organised along customer or market lines
Efficient and error-free work styles	⇒	Reasonable "risk" taking/entrepreneurial spirit encouraged
Specialisation/fixed job descriptions	⇒	Flexible roles
Loyalty equals security	⇒	Job security is based on results achieved and contribution made to the success of the company
Jobs for Life/long-term career	⇒	Greater mobility/turnover/contract employees
Reward for length of service	⇒	Reward for individual/group contribution
Market Rate for Job/Narrow grades	⇒	Market worth of individual/ broad pay bands
Demarcation/role rigidity	⇒	Teamwork/role flexibility
Aspirational incentive/Bonus systems	⇒	Integration of reward systems with business strategy/Performance management systems
Hierarchical structures	⇒	Flatter organisations/partnership
Financial rewards	⇒	Financial + non-financial rewards
Rigid administration system	⇒	Value for money

CONCLUSION

This chapter began with an examination and assessment of the different reward systems. This discussion provided the background for a review of empirical work which reported the usage of the different systems. The survey findings (IBEC, 1998) indicated experimentation in the area of contingent reward systems. Findings suggest a growth in the use of performance-related pay, both individual and company-wide, and in the use of profit-sharing.

The most significant uptake was in the area of individual performance-related pay. The use of newer systems such as team-based pay, skill-based pay or competence-based pay was marginal. Indications are that use of the variable elements of reward is assuming an auxiliary role, with fixed pay remaining the dominant reward system. It is likely that future developments will follow this paradigm: variable pay operating in conjunction with, rather than as a replacement for, basic salary.

Following from this review of the incidence of systems, fundamental themes which inform the choice, design and operation of reward systems were discussed. The specifics of the organisation, its goals, workforce, technology and the nature of its competition, all influence the suitability of the different reward systems. Survey findings (IBEC, 1998) suggest that an element of this contingent approach might be occurring, with sectoral patterns emerging across the choice of payment systems applied. According to this research, employee grade or category also appears to be a factor in determining appropriate pay systems. This chapter also considered the argument that the contingency approach is not sufficient in itself to guide the design of rewards strategy. Rather managers should look to issues of process. They should concern themselves with communicating the purpose and essence of the reward system, with involving staff and bringing on board those charged with implementation, and most critically with building credibility and trust.

The reasons why managers might use pay as a strategic tool were considered. It is important to note nonetheless that levers other than pay exist for improving performance. Excessive tinkering with reward systems can distract from these other management tools. Reward systems can never substitute for effective management. If anything, it might be argued that the newer forms of reward systems demand even greater and more refined management skills than more traditional or familiar systems.

References

Armstrong, M. and Baron, A. (1995): *The Job Evaluation Handbook*, London: Institute of Personnel and Development.

Armstrong, M. (1996): *Employee Reward*, London: Institute of Personnel and Development.

Barrett, G.V. and Doverspike, D. (1989): "Another Defence of Point-factor Job Evaluation", *Personnel*, March: 33(6).

Bowey, A. and Thorpe, R. (1988): "Payment Systems and Performance Improvement: Design and Implementation", *Employment Relations*, 10(4).

Braham, J. (1982): *Practical Manpower Planning*, London: Institute of Personnel Management.

Brown, W. and Walsh, J. (1994): "Managing Pay in Britain" in Sisson, K. (ed.) *Personnel Management, a Comprehensive Guide to Theory and Practice in Britain*, London: Blackwell.

Cranfield/University of Limerick (CUL) study cited in Morley, M. and Gunnigle, P. (1997): "Compensation and Benefits", in Gunnigle, P., Morley, M., Clifford, C., Turner, T., Heraty, N., Crowley, M., in *Human Resource Management in Irish Organisations: Practice in Perspective*, Dublin: Oak Tree Press.

Dowling, B. and Richardson, R. (1997): "Evaluating Performance-related Pay for Managers in the National Health Service", *The International Journal of Human Resource Management*, 8(3).

European Foundation for the Improvement of Living and Working Conditions (EFILWC) (1997): *New Forms of Work Organisation: Can Europe Realise its Potential?*, Dublin: EFILWC.

Gunnigle, P., Heraty, N. and Morley, M. (1997a): *Personnel and Human Resource Management: Theory and Practice in Ireland*, Dublin: Gill and Macmillan.

Gunnigle, P., Turner, T. and D'Art, D. (1997b): "Counterpoising Collectivism: Performance Related Pay and Industrial Relations in Greenfield Sites", Paper presented to the fifth IIRA European Regional Industrial Relations Congress, Dublin, August.

Huczynski, A.A. (1993): "Explaining the Succession of Management Fads", *The International Journal of Human Resource Management*, 4(2).

Incomes Data Services (IDS) (1994): *Employee Share Ownership Plans*, Study No. 568, London: IDS.

Incomes Data Services (IDS) (1996): Management Pay Review: *Pay for Competency Research File*, August, London: IDS.

Institute of Personnel and Development (IPD) (1998): *IPD 1998 Performance Pay Survey*, London: Institute of Personnel and Development.

Irish Business and Employers Confederation (IBEC) (1998): *Survey of Reward/Payment Schemes: 1998*, Dublin: IBEC.

Kessler, I. (1994) "Performance Pay", in Sisson, K. (ed.) *Personnel Management, a Comprehensive Guide to Theory and Practice in Britain*, UK: Blackwell.

Kessler, I. and Purcell, J. (1991): *Performance Related Pay, Theory and Practice*, Oxford: Templeton College.

Lockyer, C. (1996): "Human Resource Management and Flexibility in Pay: New Solutions or Old Problems?" in Towers, B. (ed.), *Human Resource Management in Action, The Handbook of Human Resource Management*, second edition, London: Blackwell.

Lupton, T. and Gowler, D. (1969): *Selecting a Wage Payment System*, London: Kogan Page.

Mahoney, T.A. (1993): "Multiple Pay Contingencies: Strategic Design of Compensation" in Salaman, G. (ed.), *Human Resource Strategies*, London: Open University/Sage Publications.

Manufacturing, Science and Finance (MSF) (1998): *Understanding Partnership at the Workplace — an MSF Guide to Profit-Sharing, ESOPs and Equity Participation in Association with Farrell Grant Sparks, Chartered Accountants and Business Consultants*, Dublin: MSF.

Milkovich, G. and Widgor, A. (1991): *Pay for Performance: Evaluating Performance Appraisal and Merit Pay*, National Research Council, Washington DC.: National Academy Press.

Millward, N. and Stevens, M. (1986): *British Workplace Industrial Relations: 1980–1984*, Aldershot: Gower.

Morley, M. and Gunnigle, P. (1997): *Compensation and Benefits, in Gunnigle, P., Morley, M., Clifford, C., Turner, T., Heraty, N., Crowley, M., in Human Resource Management in Irish Organisations: Practice in Perspective*, Dublin: Oak Tree Press.

Roche, W.K. and Geary, J.F. (1997): "Multinationals and Industrial Relations Practices", in Murphy, T. and Roche, W. (eds.), *Irish Industrial Relations in Practice*, second edition, Dublin: Oak Tree Press.

Roche, W.K. and Gunnigle P. (1995) in Gunnigle, P. and Roche, W.K. (eds.): *New Challenges to Irish Industrial Relations*, Dublin: Oak Tree Press in association with the Labour Relations Commission.

Smith, I.G. (1989): *Incentive Schemes: People and Profits*, London: Croner Publications.

Storey, J. (1992): *Developments in the Management of Human Resources*, Oxford: Blackwell.

Storey, J. and Sisson, K. (1993): *Managing Human Resource and Industrial Relations*, Buckingham: Open University Press.

Thompson, M. (1992): *Pay and Performance: The Employer Experience*, IMS Report No. 218, Falmer, Brighton: Institute of Manpower Studies.

Torrington, D. and Hall, L. (1998): *Human Resource Management*, fourth edition, London: Prentice Hall.

Turner, T. and Morley, M. (1995): *Industrial Relations and the New Order: Case Studies in Conflict and Co-operation*, Dublin: Oak Tree Press.

Wood, S. (1996): "High Commitment Management and Payment Systems", *Journal of Management Studies*, 33(1).

9

MANAGING REWARD SYSTEMS FOR EFFECTIVE PERFORMANCE

Gerard McMahon

In recent times the practice of linking pay to performance has become increasingly popular, particularly in the form of merit or performance-related pay (PRP). This is a system of awarding individual payments to employees, linked to some form of performance appraisal. It is one of the most dynamic issues in human resource management, and arguably the most topical component of contemporary reward management. Merit or performance-related pay schemes are widespread in the developed world, and are especially popular in the United States, France, Italy and Switzerland (Hegewisch, 1991: 29–37). They are the most commonly used pay incentive amongst organisations operating in the Republic of Ireland and are particularly prevalent in the private sector, amongst managerial and professional staff categories (Gunnigle et al. 1994: 58–81), with increasing evidence of their application to the public sector and to all categories of staff.

WHY PRP?

The prime objective of PRP is to convert the remuneration package from an indiscriminate machine to a more finely-tuned mechanism, which is responsive to the needs of the organisation and its workforce. In reality, it is frequently used to support a performance-oriented culture. PRP's rising popularity can be attributed to attempts to change organisational cultures in the direction

of commercial, customer, quality or performance considerations
(see Box 9.1 and Box 9.2). It is seen as central to efforts to adapt
to the competitive economic environment. In effect, since the early
1980s, the resurgent market forces philosophy has been extended
downward — from macroeconomic imperatives, to pay for the individual employee at the workplace — whilst the concept of value
for money has gained increased currency. At the heart of this pay
revolution is frustration with the productivity bargaining practices of the 1960s, the measured day work practices of the 1970s,
and reservations about the "organisation behaviourist" opposition
to the "money motivates" thesis (Biddle and Evenden, 1989: 42).
In effect, PRP constitutes an assault on national "going rates" and
complex grading systems for staff that reward inertia and length
of service before performance. In their place, the "internal labour
market" has grown in importance, driven by the premise that employers should seek the commitment and loyalty of employees, by
rewarding them according to their individual and — ultimately —
company performance.

According to the data presented by Gunnigle et al. (1994: 58–
80), there has been a significant swing toward merit or
performance-related payment schemes in Ireland in recent years.
The take-up of such schemes is especially correlated with company ownership — with American-owned companies far more
likely to employ such pay incentives than others, (especially Irish
indigenous companies) (Gunnigle et al., 1997: 135). However, it is
evident that this development is spreading, via the application of
such systems, to large sections of the Irish public sector (see, for
example, Box 9.2). Likewise, in recent years, there has been a
steady increase in the proportion of the UK's public companies
adopting such payment systems. For example, in 1979 only 8 per
cent of the largest companies had an annual bonus scheme for
their top executives. Almost 15 years later, practically all of these
companies had such a scheme (Income Data Services, 1993: 1).

The most common types of reward systems in use are: merit
pay, individual bonuses, team bonuses, company-wide schemes,
share schemes, incentive gifts and skill- and competency-based

pay. There is even evidence of some organisations linking pay to levels of customer satisfaction (e.g. IBM, Rank Xerox) (Littlefield, 1996: 7). Detailed evaluations of these options can be found in Armstrong (1996: 195–320), Wright (1991: 82–112) and Gunnigle et al. (1997: 118–142). According to the latter, there is also increasing evidence of interest in the use of non-monetary benefits to promote achievement of the strategic aims of the organisation.

Effectively, organisations now want to link company objectives and the individual's and/or the team's work objectives, while differentiating between the high and low performers. This is well reflected in the instance of the Educational Building Society, where incremental pay scales have now been replaced by a (potentially) more expensive PRP system — on the grounds that it will ultimately lead to increased business and, therefore, increased profits — which should more than offset the higher wage costs. Ideally, then, with PRP employers regain control over wage costs and employees take control of their earnings potential.

EFFECTIVE PRP SYSTEMS

The main principles associated with merit pay, or PRP schemes targeted at the individual, are as follows:

1. Strong performance planning process, with established plans, goals and targets. Focused effort to where it is wanted, via such plans, goals and targets.

2. Pay for performance via a link that offers the biggest rewards to the biggest contributors. Consequently, pay is for contributions rather than availability (i.e. the bigger the contribution the bigger the reward).

3. Accountable managers, as they are made responsible for PRP implementation, and consequently for the impact of their assessments.

4. Accountable workers, as PRP reflects the trend from collectivism to individualism, with pay determined by performance rather than peer group pressure.

Getting the PRP scheme right requires considerable care and forethought. This entails:

- Having an understanding of the purpose and implications of the scheme. Accordingly, careful planning, managing, assessing and rewarding of *overall* performance, together with the deployment of adequate time, effort and financial resources to facilitate same, is important.

- Management commitment to the scheme, and workers trusting them in the introduction, implementation and delivery of rewards from it. If workers see PRP as a facade, they will lose confidence in it, and it will be practically impossible to regain this confidence.

- Having a balanced reward package. That is, the different parts of the pay package should address different objectives (i.e. to attract, motivate and retain staff). Consequently, these objectives and the associated remuneration practices, need to be kept in balance. A balance also needs to be struck between rewards for individual and group/team efforts, if divisiveness and low morale are to be avoided. This is particularly important where team working is central to the achievement of high and enduring performance levels. The operation of more than one PRP system to facilitate different reward strategies, therefore, tends to be characteristic of a good overall pay plan (i.e. an amalgam of group and individual bonus payments).

- Having a purpose-built scheme. The scheme should reflect the corporate culture, as opposed to being an inappropriate "off the shelf" purchase, which is reputed to work well elsewhere.

The Institute of Personnel and Development (IPM, 1990: 4) has identified four key characteristics of successful PRP schemes. First there is the crucial matter of defining and deciding how to measure the appropriate "performance criteria". These criteria should reflect a linkage of corporate and individual goals, which accommodate not just the quantitative but also the (more problematic) qualitative aspects of same. Indeed, in many jobs the requisite knowledge, skills and competencies to perform will be readily identifiable, but it may be difficult to assess how they actually translate into performance. This will be most apparent with managerial jobs, where many of the tasks are amorphous and not directly observable. Related to this is the obligation on management to be seen to differentiate fairly between workers at varying performance levels.

Second, there is the associated issue of job definition, so that all employees understand the nature and level of their interdependency with others in the organisation in achieving objectives and work targets. This has major implications for the aforementioned search for an appropriate balance between the individual's and the team's performance and pay rewards.

Third, the incentive pay-out levels should be commensurate with the direction and amount of effort required from employees. For example, according to Lawler (1990: 20), a pay change of 10 to 15 per cent is probably required to significantly increase motivation whilst (Armstrong, 1996: 241) supports this contention, arguing that a pay increase of 3 to 5 per cent is not sufficient to improve performance. The cost implications of these findings are self-evident, and are often enough to dissuade employers from taking the PRP road.

Finally, the organisation must ensure that the scheme is properly communicated to staff, and that appropriate training is made available to support it. In this regard it is evident that employees are more likely to trust the scheme if they participate in its design and development. The importance of regular reviews to facilitate modifications to the scheme must also be acknowledged.

DOES PRP WORK?

There is no evidence that PRP schemes are more likely to be found in high performance organisations. Indeed, some researchers even contend that the pay and productivity link itself is rather tenuous (Brewster, 1992: 116). According to Hendry et al. (1997: 20) there has been a preoccupation with defining measures that could be attached to individual rewards, with too little consideration of their connection to organisational performance. Research on the capacity of PRP to motivate employees yields mixed but, on the whole, mildly negative conclusions (*People Management*, 1995: 40). Evidence based on attitude surveys conducted both before and after their introduction, reveals a patchy success rate. According to the Institute of Personnel and Development (IPM, 1990: 3) such schemes can be divisive, and in instances have demotivated ten workers for every one motivated. This appears to be an expensive way to demotivate one's staff! A survey conducted by the British Inland Revenue Staff Federation discovered that about 80 per cent of members felt that PRP had not improved the quantity or quality of their work (*Special Correspondent*, 1992: 55). Furthermore, two-thirds felt that their work priorities or effectiveness in dealing with the public had not improved as a result of the scheme. Indeed, it is notable that PRP schemes, though designed to challenge collective bargaining, (through the growth of individualism and the demise of group loyalties) have in instances, when badly managed, actually served to increase trade union strength (Brewster, 1992: 114).

Despite the apparent logic of performance pay, there is no established correlation between its use and organisational success (Wright, 1991: 85). Furthermore, despite its reputed growing popularity, a recent British earnings survey discovered that as many as 80 per cent of the country's workers still receive no form of incentive payment whatsoever (Brewster, 1992: 116). Where such payments are available they amount, on average, to — a hardly motivational — 4.1 per cent of earnings. It is also contended that PRP is both costly and inflationary, serving merely to top-up the general "cost of living" pay increase received by most workers (Brewster, 1992: 116).

MAIN RESERVATIONS ABOUT PRP

The main reservations being expressed about merit or performance pay may be classified under three headings: ineffective or bad appraisal systems, the neglect of other reward and change considerations and the morale or industrial relations implications.

Ineffective Appraisal Systems

For the PRP scheme to work satisfactorily, the performance of staff must first be assessed or appraised. However, there is an inherent conflict if the appraisal system is also expected to develop staff. As the appraiser attempts to play the (almost incompatible) roles of judge and counsellor, there is the prospect of appraisees becoming defensive about both their actual performance and potential shortcomings. The temptation to blame others or "the system", and to ensure that modest targets are set for the coming review period (which will constitute the basis for future rewards) is often irresistible. One review of the Irish Civil Service system (see Box 9.2), agrees that the

> twofold objective is perceived to create difficulties for the appraiser who must discharge two conflicting roles . . . and problems for the appraisee who may be less than forthright about job-related problems in order to safeguard promotion prospects (Irish Business and Employers Confederation, 1994: 5).

Indeed, one recent British survey of 1,000 workers in a building society, a local authority and a food retail company, clearly identified significant levels of staff discontent with the lack of line management skills in appraisal and merit pay (Institute of Manpower Studies, 1994: 4). In the aforementioned study of the British Inland Revenue's scheme, it was revealed that four-fifths of those with responsibility for conducting PRP appraisal type interviews, believed that a quota was in operation for the distribution of merit payments, and a third thought favouritism was influential in box markings (appraisal ratings), while more than half felt that the system was demotivating for staff. Related to this, in the Irish context, research on the Greencore Group's PRP scheme revealed that their primary difficulty was the lack of objectivity in the measurement of performance (Kelly, 1996). On the same theme, there is also convincing evidence that ratings used to make decisions on pay and promotion are more lenient than ratings used for feedback and developmental purposes (McMahon and Gunnigle, 1994: 12).

Surveys of employees and personnel managers undertaken in the U.S. also reveal a distinct lack of enthusiasm about the ability of their formal appraisal systems to support effectively their PRP system (Milkovich and Wigdor, 1991: 106). A frequent criticism here, again, is the absence of an objective measurement system. For example, successive American studies report that less than one-third of organisations rate their appraisal systems as "effective" in tying pay to performance (Milkovich and Wigdor, 1991: 106). Many managers find it difficult to measure the performance of staff involved in, for example, administration, accounts and personnel work. Furthermore, how do you measure performance and grant rewards when an organisation is fortunate enough to be in a growing market and enjoying windfall profits? What works as an incentive will, therefore, also be influenced by where the organisation finds itself in the business cycle. There is also substantial evidence to show that many organisations have allowed the money or reward-driven approach to organisational performance management to dominate detrimentally other important human resource development-type policies (Bevan and Thompson, 1992: 6). This consideration has led Loctite (Ireland) Ltd. to avoid such schemes in favour of employee development initiatives, and for both the London Boroughs of Brent and Lewisham to discard their PRP schemes (Littlefield, 1996: 15).

The Neglect of Other Reward and Change Considerations

Beyond the inherent difficulties associated with PRP schemes, there are a host of other factors which affect performance at work and cannot be overlooked (e.g. job security and satisfaction, recognition, work environment, promotion, pay level equity). Undoubtedly, the evidence on the effects of pay for performance, pieced together from research, theory, clinical studies, and surveys of practice, suggest that, in certain circumstances, such pay plans can produce positive effects on individual job performance (Milkovich and Wigdor, 1991: 4). However, pay is a complex, multi-faceted factor, serving as both a tangible and intangible motivator, offering intrinsic and extrinsic rewards. It is difficult, therefore, to generalise on its applicability across a wide range of individual and organisational contexts. That is, the evidence is insufficient to determine conclusively how merit pay can enhance individual performance. As Herzberg (1968: 125) argues, whilst too little pay may irritate and demotivate, it does not follow that more and more money will produce increased satisfaction and motivation.

The value of some schemes has also been called into question for their neglect of longer-term considerations, innovations or investments with delayed paybacks. Performance pay tends to focus on short-term quantitative factors, rather than the potentially more consequential longer term qualitative ones. Complex long-term projects are often critical to an organisation's success and are likely to be what senior managers spend most of their time addressing. Related to this is the argument that many schemes are not flexible enough to adapt to the quickening pace of change in job demands. For example, staff who normally achieve a high merit rating may be unwilling to accept new responsibilities that could be difficult to achieve, and would therefore interfere with earnings potential. If staff perceive that their present duties give them a high profile for "merit" consideration, they are also less likely to co-operate in job changes that will take them into less prominent positions.

The Industrial Relations Dilemma

The industrial relations impact has also been shown to backfire, in instances providing trade unions with increased solidarity and issues upon which to negotiate. For example, the operation of a highly structured and tightly quantified rating scheme where "points mean money" is likely to provoke union opposition. According to the ICTU:

> the disadvantage with individual appraisal and merit pay
> is that the assessment is highly subjective and can lead to
> the "blue eyed boy/girl syndrome" . . . (it) can lead to secre-
> tiveness, resentment and infighting (Wall, 1992: 7–8).

Of course, given the in-built subjectivity of most rating schemes, together with the threat to the whole raison d'être of trade unions posed by PRP, this reaction is understandable. A consequence of such opposition may well be the significantly larger proportion of non-union organisations operating such schemes in Ireland (Gunnigle et al. 1994: 68). However, such practices are not entirely trouble free in the non-union sector either, as Intel's world-wide system of "ranking and rating" staff has left it facing court action in the United States over the allegation that it gives rise to defamation and discrimination on the grounds of age, race and physical handicap (Welch, 1997: 9). Trade union suspicion about the practice of PRP is well reflected in the view of the Manufacturing Science Finance Union that: "the pressure for (it) is coming from management not because it believes it will improve performance but in order to have "flexibility" and control." (MSF, 1994: 1).

PRP schemes have also been shown to interfere adversely with team spirit or morale (e.g. the British Petroleum case). If the scheme is based on a set percentage of the staff winning the (higher) bonus or merit award, teamwork may be replaced by staff competitiveness. This will also be reflected in staff who were previously prepared to work beyond their own work responsibilities, and to help other colleagues or departments. Now they have good reason to concentrate on their own narrow personal level of achievement. A consequence of this is the increasing evidence of a swing toward team-based pay in both Britain and the US (*Income Data Services*, 1994: 5; *Special Correspondent*, 1996: 5) Furthermore, managers with appraisal responsibility may lose the confidence and trust of some of their staff, as the process of determining merit awards creates divisions which did not previously exist. Indeed, the experience with some experiments in this area has led many practitioners to warn that alterations to reward schemes create more resistance than any other organisational change initiative, with the exception of closure. Revised pay structures, however desirable, are likely to be counterproductive if they antagonise the workforce and jeopardise existing staff/management relationships — hence the reluctance of large Japanese firms to abandon lifetime employment, seniority wages and large non-performance-related bonuses. This test of employee acceptability remains the most enduring lesson from pay research through the ages (White, 1985: 23).

THE WAY FORWARD

The potential benefits of PRP make it an initiative worthy of consideration in all organisational contexts. For example, at the Greencore Group, the majority of the managerial staff agree that PRP is successful in improving the Group's performance, and in providing the company with a useful tool for increasing productivity. In fact, three-quarters of Greencore's managers agree that PRP contributes to a general improvement in performance, with the increased interaction with one's supervisor and the greater focus on individual targets especially beneficial (Kelly, 1996: 1).

The success of PRP is largely dependent on the effectiveness of the appraisal process (McMahon and Gunnigle, 1994: 66) (see Box 9.1). Problems arising from poorly designed appraisal systems, inadequate interviewing skills, generous and consequently costly pay-related appraisals, are all having an adverse impact on PRP Even recent surveys of personnel professionals in both the United States and Britain reveal that less than 1 in 5 are satisfied with the effectiveness of their appraisal systems (McMahon and Gunnigle, 1994: 54). To get the best out of the PRP scheme then, it must be solidly supported by an appraisal system which enjoys the backing of those expected to work it.

The characteristics of such successful appraisal systems are set down below. Of particular relevance to the industrial relations climate, is the importance of consultation in the design and monitoring of the system, and the balanced and objective assessment of workers' performance (McMahon, 1997: 24).

- The system is actively supported by top management, both in their practice and resource allocations.

- The system's objectives are clear, compatible, attainable and acceptable.

- There is consultation with all affected parties in the design process.

- The system is job-related and fits with the corporate culture.

- An appropriately customised training programme is provided for appraisers and appraisees, with refresher and specialised programs available as required.

- The appraisal system used incorporates a preparatory and self-appraisal dimension.

- The appraisal interview involves a *joint* approach to goal setting and problem solving.

- Set goals and targets involve both a quantitative and a qualitative dimension.

- Performance is assessed inside an objective and balanced framework.

- The system is part of an ongoing feedback process which, if operated in conjunction with TQM, performance pay or a performance management system, maximises their complementariness and minimises their conflict.

- The system is characterised by efficiency, results and a people-focus, rather than bureaucracy and a paper or process-focus.

- The system is the subject of ongoing monitoring and evaluation.

All of these characteristics are addressed in detail in McMahon and Gunnigle (1994).

CONCLUSION

In conclusion, while it is to be expected that the incidence and extent of performance-related pay will increase, its impact on industrial relations and its capacity to improve organisational efficiency and morale remains questionable. The basic principle underpinning performance-related pay is unassailable — that it is equitable to reward people according to their contribution. Thereafter, as the recipes abound, the consensus is absent. Nevertheless, a key lesson emerging from experience to date is that successful implementation requires more than "off-the-shelf" schemes and appraisal systems. The belief that a company's success depends primarily on adopting a state-of-the-art pay system is now regarded as naïve. Motivation is a complex matter, and designing a pay system is fraught with difficulties. Consequently, the method and implications of introducing such performance management systems should be carefully considered in advance. No one type of payment system is preferable in all settings. The choice depends on an organisation's circumstances, value systems, the characteristics of the products or services it provides and of its workforce. For many organisations performance-related pay could well be the right answer, but it has to be planned and operated with great care, and the organisation must be flexible, adapting the scheme in the light of changed circumstances and staff feedback.

BOX 9.1: CASE STUDY: PERFORMANCE MANAGEMENT AT THE FIRST NATIONAL BUILDING SOCIETY

First National is Ireland's biggest and longest-established building society. It employs 750 people.

The 1990s heralded a new era in competition for the Society, as it became increasingly customer- and sales-focused. In order to help promote a culture of continuous improvement in performance, the company introduced a new performance management system in 1994. This initiative was sponsored by the Society's executive team, and an external consultancy firm was used to help design a system appropriate to the performance needs of the organisation. It was launched at a managers' conference, and extensive training was undertaken to introduce the system and help managers to operate it effectively.

Underpinning the initiative was the view that overall organisational performance is dependent on the individual performance of all staff. The new system focused on the link between the organisation's goals and the individual goals of all managers and staff. Corporate goals were broken down into specific targets and goals for each business unit, which in turn were broken down into individual targets for each person. In this way the performance management system provided a mechanism to break down the corporate goals into SMART (Specific, Measurable, Agreed, Realistic and Time related) individual goals which could be achieved. These goals were then agreed between the individual and his/her line manager. The individual's performance was then appraised against these goals.

An attitude survey conducted prior to the introduction of the performance management system had clearly identified the aspiration of managers and staff for a greater link between their own individual performance and their rewards. A team-based reward mechanism was introduced as part of the performance management initiative and all participants achieving their goals qualified for a merit payment, provided that the organisation itself met its corporate level goal as measured in pre-tax profit.

To date, the performance management system has proven successful, helping people to focus and improve their individual performance, thereby contributing positively to overall corporate performance (as measured by the organisation's results, individual results and staff feedback). It has evolved and been improved upon, in response to staff feedback.

First National has more recently introduced competencies (i.e. key knowledge, skills, attitudes) for managers and staff, and there is an increasing focus on "how" jobs are performed, as well as the work output. There is an argument that the integration of such competencies into the performance management system might provide further added-value.

First National is currently reviewing its options as to how best progress its performance management system to ensure its continuing relevance in a changing business environment.

Source: Karl O'Connor, Training & Development Manager, First National Building Society.

BOX 9.2: CASE STUDY: PERFORMANCE APPRAISAL IN THE IRISH
CIVIL SERVICE

Performance appraisal was first introduced to the Irish Civil
Service for executive grades in 1977. The attempt failed, to a large
degree, for a host of different reasons. Central to its failure, was a
lack of real commitment and clarification in the Government departments to the practice. This may be attributed, at least partially, to their lack of ownership and commitment to procedures devised and driven centrally by the Department of Finance. The
"permanent and pensionable" culture of the working environment
was also unlikely to be a fertile location for notions of change, development or objective setting. This culture, with little experience
of targets, or management systems based on personal responsibility
for results etc., together with an inability on the part of supervisors
to provide honest, critical feedback to staff about their performance,
did not augur well. With top management remaining broadly un-
committed, and a workforce guaranteed permanency, index-linked
salaries and a certain degree of guaranteed promotion based on
seniority, appraisal practices were always unlikely to be allowed to
upset traditional working methods and relationships.

The Strategic Management Initiative came to the fore in the
Service in 1994, with the purpose of improving effectiveness and
ensuring that employment practices in the Civil Service would reflect best practice elsewhere. This forced Government Departments to place renewed emphasis on "value for money", via strategic planning, objective setting and outputs, and by definition
specified those measures of performance and success which underpin key Departmental goals. The merit of the initiative effectively depends on the development of better management systems, increased accountability and a much greater emphasis on
individual performance. Allied to this development, in 1992, the
Department of Finance and the Public Service Executive Union
(P.S.E.U.) agreed both the principle and the mechanics of a man-
datory performance appraisal system, under Clause 2 of the Programme for Competitiveness and Work. Under this system a
novel form of performance-related pay was also conceived. This
provides for 25 per cent of Executive and 30 per cent of Higher
Executive Officers and Administrative Officer grades to avail of a
higher pay scale. To be eligible for transfer to this scale, an Officer must have been assessed under the appraisal system over a

two-year period, must have substantially achieved the objectives agreed in the course of the appraisal meetings and have co-operated with the implementation of training and development plans which have also been agreed in the course of the appraisal meetings. It is also intended that the appraisal documentation would be available to interview boards and Management Committees when promotions are being considered.

Whilst this latest initiative may well follow its predecessors to the scrapheap, it should be acknowledged that its success in securing the relevant trade union's agreement, in linking the performance of key executive grades to their pay (however tenuously) and promotion, constitutes a formidable achievement. It also provides a powerful incentive to keep the system working. However, whether the quality of the interactions serve to justify the system, via improved working relationships and effectiveness, remains to be seen.

References

Armstrong, M. (1996): *Employee Reward*, London: Institute of Personnel and Development.

Bevan, S. and Thompson, M. (1992): *Performance Management in the UK*, London: Institute of Personnel Management.

Biddle, D. and Evenden, R. (1989): *Human Aspects of Management*, London: Institute of Personnel Management.

Brewster, C. (1992): "Managing Industrial Relations", in Towers, B. (ed.) *A Handbook of Industrial Relations Practice*, 105–122, third edition, London: Kogan Page.

Gunnigle, P., Foley, K. and Morley, M. (1994): "A Review of Organisational Reward Practices", in *Continuity and Change in Irish Employee Relations*, Gunnigle, P., Flood, P., Morley, M. and Turner, T. (eds.), Dublin: Oak Tree Press.

Gunnigle, P. Heraty, N. and Morley, M. (1997): *Personnel & Human Resource Management: Theory and Practice in Ireland*, Dublin: Gill and Macmillan.

Hendry, C., Bradley, P. and Perkins, S. (1997) "Missed a Motivator?" in *People Management*, May, 20–25.

Herzberg, F. (1968): "One More Time: How Do You Motivate Employees?", in *Harvard Business Review*, Jan–Feb, 115–125.

Income Data Services, (1993): *Management Bonus Schemes*, Research File November, London.

Income Data Services, (1994): *Income Data Services Report*, September, London.

Institute of Manpower Studies, (1994): *Performance-Related Pay: The Employee Experience*, University of Sussex: IMS.

Institute of Personnel Management, (1990): "Performance-Related Pay", Factsheet 30, London: IPM.

Institute of Personnel Management, (1992): *Performance Management in the UK*, London: IPM

Irish Business and Employers Confederation, (1994): "Performance Appraisal in the Civil Service" in *Industrial Relations Data Bank*, October, 13(295): 5–6.

Kelly, A. (1996): *Performance Related Pay: What Makes A Successful Scheme?* A report prepared for Pat Lunny, Director of Human Resources, Greencore Group, Dublin City University Business School, October.

Lawler, E. (1990): *Strategic Pay*, San Francisco: Jossey-Bass.

Littlefield, D. (1996): "Electricity Firm Plugs into Customer Power", in *People Management*, June.

Littlefield, D. (1996): "Councils swap PRP for staff development", in *People Management*, September.

Manufacturing Science Finance Union (MSF) (1994): *A Negotiator's Guide to Performance-related Pay*, Dublin: MSF.

McMahon, G., (1997): "Revisiting and Revamping Your Performance Appraisal System", *IPD. News*, Dublin: Institute of Personnel and Development, May, 4(2).

McMahon, G. and Gunnigle, P. (1994): *Performance Appraisal: How To Get It Right*, Dublin: IPM/PPL.

Milkovich, G. and Wigdor, A. (1991): *Pay for Performance: Evaluating Performance Appraisal and Merit Pay*, National Research Council, Washington DC: National Academy Press.

People Management, (1995): "The Jury's Still Out on the PRP Trial", *People Management*, October.

Special Correspondent, (1992): "Problems with Performance-related Pay", in *Bargaining Report*, 113, London: Labour Research Department.

Special Correspondent (1996): "Pay 'less of a factor'", *People Management*, May.

Wall, T. (1992): "Union Involvement in Performance-related Pay", paper presented to the ICM Conference Recognition, Motivation and Award, February, Dublin.

Welch, J. (1997): "Intel Faces Fight over Termination Quotas" in *People Management*, June, 9.

White, M. (1985): "What's New in Pay?", *Personnel Management*, February, 20–24.

Wright, V. (1991): "Performance-related Pay", in *The Handbook of Performance Management*, Neale, F. (ed.), London: Institute of Personnel Management.

10

MANAGING WORK ORGANISATION: MOVING TOWARDS TASK PARTICIPATION

John Geary

Work and its re-organisation have become one of the most critical ingredients of human resource management. In its various new forms — teamworking, quality circles, employee involvement, and autonomous work groups — the structure of work has been identified as a key competitive lever in organisations' response to new competitive circumstances. Much too has been written of the significance of these initiatives for employees' working lives, their effects on organisational performance and their implications for employers and trade unions (see, for example, Fröhlich and Pekruhl, 1996; Ichniowski, 1996). Given the quantity of such material, this chapter concentrates on one aspect of work organisation, which is referred to here as task participation. The discussion draws from and builds on recent publications of the author (Geary, 1994; 1995) and jointly authored work (Edwards, Geary and Sisson, 1997).

The chapter is divided into four sections. It begins by defining the nature and theory of task participation (hereafter TP). It then looks at the diffusion of TP in Ireland and, where appropriate, comparisons are made with other countries. As to its effects the chapter draws on case study evidence. The discussion pays particular attention to the effects of TP on employees' working lives and its place in employee management relations. In assessing its significance for organisational performance the discussion draws predominantly from the recent EPOC survey of direct employee participation in Europe and American literature. The degree to which TP has or might be able to reshape employees' relationship with management is assessed. Finally, some attention is given to the role of public institutions in supporting the diffusion of TP in Ireland.

The chapter's argument is that first, TP, particularly in its advanced form, is not widely diffused in Ireland. Second, in contrast to much of the current debate which is divided between the optimists who look upon TP as constituting a transformation of employee relations and its critics, who often see it as another form of management control and exploitation, it is argued that it resides between these two positions and rests within more mundane and modest efforts to re-regulate the employment relationship (Edwards, Geary and Sisson, 1997). Finally, for TP to become more widely diffused in Ireland, it is argued that a number of specific support structures need to be put in place. Amongst the most pressing requirements are the adoption of workplace partnership arrangements between employers and trade unions, more investment in training and the establishment of "learning forums" to identify and to support the diffusion of "best practice".

NATURE AND THEORY OF TP

There is an obvious danger in equating TP with labels such as job rotation, job enlargement, quality circles, teamworking, problem-solving groups and TQM, and in particular, when some are referred to as *old* forms of work organisation and others *new*. It is better that TP is looked upon as a set of processes. It is also the case, of course, that there are numerous different definitions for teamwork and TQM in the literature and specific practices are rarely applied as they appear in textbooks. For this reason the term "task participation" is used and a broad definition offered.

Elsewhere TP has been defined as opportunities which management provides at workplace level for consultation with and/or delegation of responsibilities and authority for decision-making to its subordinates either as individuals or as groups of employees relating to the immediate work task, work organisation and/or working conditions (Geary, 1994; Geary and Sisson, 1994). With this conceptualisation, TP is rendered timeless. What may be new now is that management is increasingly adopting new work organisation strategies, with greater urgency than heretofore, and defining the terms of its implementation and operation. Having rejected many similar techniques in the past, employers are beginning to discuss the advantages of TP with renewed interest.

While this definition of TP lays stress on the role of managers — that they are increasingly defining the terms of TP — it must be understood that its ultimate shape, as it manifests itself on the shop-floor or in the office, will have evolved through continuous negotiation and definition: it does not have an automatic effect once implemented. Existing institutions, formal and informal rules of behaviour, modes of understanding and ways of managing will all have a bearing on the shape assumed by TP. It is not a question of managers having a free hand, to design TP as they please: it is an ongoing process evolving within a given arena of opportunities and constraints.

Therefore, with TP employees are granted more control over their immediate work situation and are invited to participate in decisions that relate to the organisation of work at the point of production. Thus, workers may influence the manner in which work is allocated, the scheduling of work and when to take breaks. They are also actively encouraged to seek solutions to problems and to make suggestions that will improve the organisation's efficiency. This, of course, means that workers are expected to adopt the ends of the enterprise as their own: workers' interests and those of their employer are seen to be inextricably linked. TP is used thus as a means of generating employee commitment, motivation and co-operation. It is an effort on management's part to gain employees' active consent and to persuade them to work diligently in furthering the interests of the organisation.

It is useful to think of task participation as having two key forms, one *consultative*, the other *delegative*. With consultative participation, employees are encouraged, and enabled, to make their views known. Management, however, retains the right to accept or reject employees' opinions as well as reserving the right to take action. An example of this form of participation might be quality circles, where employees, typically in small groups, meet on a regular basis to discuss solutions to work-related problems. Employees are not normally empowered to implement, however, only to recommend.

With delegative participation, responsibility for what has traditionally been an area of management decision-making is placed largely in employees' hands: participation is designed into peoples' jobs. Examples here may include semi-autonomous work groups and teamworking. In its most developed or purest sense, this form of participation refers to the granting of autonomy to workers by management so that they may become self-managing. The distinctive feature of this form of TP is that participation *extends into* new forms of work organisation: employees are entrusted to plan, conceive and execute the daily organisation of work.

This chapter looks at both forms of TP but gives more attention to delegative participation where employees have some active participation in defining the nature of work tasks and the manner in which they are to be carried out. Teamworking is often seen to constitute such an "advanced" form of participation, and will be looked at closely here.

The literature on TP can be broadly divided in two: on one side there are those who hold that TP heralds a new dawn in human resource management, that employers are determined to move away from old ways of organising work around Taylorist principles and that their intention is to create a distinctly new form of work organisation. In the management literature the effects of such initiatives were often seen to be improved trust and commitment by employees and a greater concern by employers to make work more enriching and rewarding. The most celebrated account of this transformation thesis is Walton's (1985) claim that there has been a shift from the management of control to the management of commitment.[1]

On the other hand, there is a critical literature that takes the more extreme proponents of transformation at their word and calls TP to task for not delivering on its promise. In contrast to the optimists' claim that TP will lead to greater employee empowerment and commitment, its critics claim that management's intentions are firmly based in intensifying management control: in this sense management's motives are the same as they have always been; all that has changed, is the means by which management hope to attain control. An example here is Rinehart et al.'s (1997) recent study of lean production systems in CAMI Automotive in Canada which dismisses many of the great claims made for lean production by its main protagonists, Womack et al. (1990). While there are elements of the new production system that are new, they are used for the sole purpose of extracting more from employees and regulating their efforts more closely. Few, if any, benefits are seen to accrue to workers themselves under this system of production.

As argued previously (Geary, 1995; Edwards, Geary and Sisson 1997), it is more appropriate to look upon "control" in less stark terms than is often articulated and implied in much of the previous work on new forms of work organisation. There are a number of reasons for this. First, control is not a one-dimensional issue. Management is not simply about controlling employees, it is also about tapping into and releasing employees' discretionary effort and creativities. It is well understood that a workforce which is engaged enthusiastically in its work is more likely to act in a constructive fashion, to identify solutions to problems at work than one that is policed closely and permitted little discretion. But in having an interest in releasing employees' creativity management remains caught between two opposing imperatives where attempts at regulating employees too tightly runs the risk of endangering the possibility of fostering employees creativity and commitment to management goals, while empowering employees runs the risk of reducing management control. Thus while management have an incentive in granting employees increased autonomy in their work, it is unlikely to cede full autonomy. It is for this reason that we must continue to talk about control, but not in the stark terms as conceived by some of TP's more extreme critics and proponents.

Second, there is the important distinction between "detailed" and "general" control, first made by Edwards (1986: 79–80). The former refers to who controls all the decisions about how immediate work tasks are to be carried out. The latter covers the broader issue of securing workers' commitment to the aims of the enterprise. With TP, management's motives reside more with enhancing general control than with maximising their detailed control over the labour process. The value of Edwards' distinction is twofold: first, it permits us to move away from the idea of control being a zero-sum phenomenon. That is, while detailed control does entail a zero-sum view, where management seek to acquire greater control over such aspects of work organisation as line speeds, work allocation or resource levels, then, if successful, it is to employees' loss. The concept of general control does not however entail such an assumption: an improvement in general control does not necessarily involve taking something from employees. What bears emphasis then is that control contains a number of elements which may be assembled in different combinations and with different consequences. The second benefit of this distinction is that it allows us to escape from the idea that employees' and employers' interests are totally opposed. Where management place more emphasis on improving general control and giving employees more discretion to manage work organisation, employees may feel more empowered, may enjoy their work more and welcome the prospect of increased employment security. They may thus have an interest in change, but that may have to be balanced against a series of new demands and obligations, like increased effort levels, a requirement to engage in "spontaneous involvement"[2] and foregoing working practices which might have been used as a bargaining item with management.

Third, there is the issue of worker expectations. Borrowing from the work of Collinson et al. (1998) we have argued that employees' interest in TP must not be measured against some measure of total freedom and autonomy in the workplace (Edwards, Geary and Sisson, 1997). Very often employees' expectations are more limited than that and may be quite specific in what they expect of TP. In this respect, Collinson et al. have spoken of the "disciplined worker thesis": the argument that in certain circumstances workers accept managerially defined disciplines as boundaries to the exercise of discretion within TP. Indeed, it may be that workers would look for and expect a tightening of managerial authority particularly where it establishes a more orderly and better managed work process. In such circumstances, workers may value and support a work system with clear performance standards and may be willing to make extra effort if there is a perceived value in doing so.

In summary, TP is likely to be introduced for a variety of reasons and workers are likely to respond in varying ways according to its perceived effects on different sets of interests. It is thus unlikely to have neat aims and results. TP is part of a continuing relationship between management and worker, and involves a re-regulation of work: a re-organisation of the conduct of work, which will have variable effects, and is not a self-contained activity (Edwards, Geary and Sisson, 1997). This re-regulation of work thus entails a re-organisation of the control of work in which more effort and higher performance levels may be expected of employees but in which there may also be an improved technical division of labour and in some cases greater levels of skill and autonomy. In terms of workers' response, such a re-regulation of work may lead to higher and more demanding effort levels, but this might be compensated for by more enjoyable work and a better managed work process. In proposing that TP leads to a re-regulation of work, in place of a simple exploitation or emancipation view, it is important to bear in mind that it may not have led to a dissolution of tensions around the control of work: specific aspects of the new organisation of work may be welcomed by employees, levels of co-operation between employees and employer may increase, and a more favourable view of management may be acquired, but whether this could lead to a high commitment response and a transformation in employees' trust in management is perhaps more doubtful. Much more likely is a pragmatic adjustment on the part of employees, where increased effort levels and "spontaneous involvement" are seen to be necessary in difficult economic circumstances.

SURVEY EVIDENCE OF TP

In this section the discussion begins by considering a number of issues in relation to method. Results from a number of surveys are then discussed and observed variations in the adoption of TP are explained.

A Note on Methodological Issues

First, TP is notoriously difficult to define and measure. It is not unusual in some surveys to see respondents being asked simply, do you have teamworking or quality circles, without seeking to add a more precise definition or description as to what might be meant by such terms. Understanding of what constitutes such popular labels, however, varies enormously. Second, if TP is difficult to define it becomes almost impossible to measure its diffusion. But it is not simply a matter of incidence. Knowing that a workplace has teamworking says little or nothing about its nature: whether for example, the team is a loose group of people who work together occasionally or formally-established and permanent unit; whether the team is semi-autonomous or under close management supervision and so on.

Third, there are the issues of response rates and quality of response. Expectations have tended to be set by the workplace industrial relations surveys in the UK and Australia (hereafter UKWIRS and AWIRS respectively), which are models in terms of representativity, comprehensiveness and response rates. In both cases, a national representative sample, stratified by workplace size has been used and a total of over 2,000 workplaces surveyed in face-to-face interviews. The response rates have been very high, 87 per cent for the first AWIRS (Callus et al., 1991) and 83 per

cent for the third UKWIRS (Millward et al., 1992). It is very difficult to get close to these response rates in surveys which, because
of pressure of resources, have usually had to rely on postal or
telephone surveys, which are less effective than the face-to-face
surveys.

An associated issue relates to the "quality of response". Where
the subject of study is the extent of workplace innovations, it is
certainly likely that, where such changes have been introduced,
their champions may be anxious and eager to have their efforts
recorded. Organisations not associated with such innovations,
however, may be less likely to agree to participate in a survey.
There is therefore the possibility of over-estimating the diffusion
of workplace change.

Fifth, there is the importance of a study's sampling frame.
Irish studies of industrial relations and human resource management practice have not been able to avail of a sampling frame
which lists all known workplaces in Ireland; most are leading or
large trading company listings and listings of non-trading organisations. Consider for example the recent Cranfield/University of
Limerick (CUL) study of HRM in Irish organisations (Gunnigle et
al., 1997) which drew its sample from the *Business and Finance
Top 2000 Trading and Non-trading Bodies* and whose coverage is
confined to companies. In such circumstances, it is not possible to
give precise estimates as to the incidence of a given practice. Only
one study has tried in recent years to overcome this handicap —
UCD Graduate School of Business study of *Irish Management
Practice in the Changing Marketplace*. This chapter will draw on
some preliminary results from this study. Many past studies, too,
have been confined to companies with 50 or more employees and
have rarely, if ever, examined smaller workplaces. Again, one
would obviously need to exercise extreme caution in making
statements as to the diffusion of TP when using such sampling
frames. It may be, for example, that large firms are most likely to
have present the conditions necessary for TP's introduction. In
such circumstances, its diffusion is likely to be considerably over-
stated.

Sixth, there is the durability of TP. Unfortunately, there is no Irish survey with a longitudinal or panel design which would allow one to assess the staying-power of TP. The CUL study that was repeated in 1995, three years after the original study, did not retain a panel sample, relying instead on drawing another cross-sectional sample. While the study does allow us to compare the diffusion of TP in two points in time, the omission of a panel sample is to be regretted, for unlike the UKWIRS and AWIRS which contain a panel sample, we are not only prevented from examining the survival rates of TP, but we are also denied the means of assessing whether any change that may occur is "within-unit" change or compositional change (i.e. it is not possible to say whether any overall change in the adoption of TP is to be accounted for by changes in the practices of continuing workplaces or whether compositional changes in the population of workplaces is more important).

Survey Evidence

In this section, a brief account is provided of the extent of TP in Ireland, concentrating in particular on three sources of evidence: the Cranfield/University of Limerick (CUL) surveys, the European Foundation's EPOC survey and interim findings from the recent UCD Graduate School of Business' study of *Irish Management Practice in the Changing Marketplace.*

The CUL Surveys

Before considering the findings of the CUL surveys (conducted in 1992 and 1995) it is important to bear in mind three features of the studies' research design which compel us to exercise caution in any interpretation of their findings.

First, the survey was limited to companies with 50 or more employees.[3] Second, no attempt was made either to stratify the sample (by size or sector) or to adjust the results by weighting factors so that the number of firms in each size or sector band might be matched to their profile in the survey population.[4] The accuracy of the estimates is therefore likely to be questionable and any meaningful comparison between small and large companies difficult to conduct. Finally, the unit of analysis was the company and not the workplace. In sum, because of the shortcomings of the sampling strategy pursued by the CUL research team, together with the low response rates achieved (23 per cent in 1992 and 21.5 per cent in 1995) their findings are of uncertain statistical generalisability and must be treated with some caution.

The CUL surveys examined a number of broad areas in HRM and of those, work organisation was least well covered. Only one specific question was asked: whether "major change" had been introduced in people's jobs which made them "more specific or flexible". The respondent was asked to reply in respect of four categories of staff — management, professional/technical, clerical and manual. The data reveal some significant changes in the last three years with people's work being made more flexible, especially amongst manual and clerical employees. Change was, however, found to be less apparent in Irish organisations than in foreign-owned enterprises and the absence of change was particularly marked amongst public sector organisations (Gunnigle et al., 1997: 122–125).

The results of the 1995 survey do not provide a composite measure of the total number of organisations that have or have not undertaken initiatives of this sort. Estimates are provided only in respect of the four occupational categories. Data are however available from the first survey which found that 47 per cent of companies had not pursued any changes in work structures for any of the four categories of staff in the three years preceding the survey. Only 15 per cent of companies responded that they had made jobs wider or more flexible for all categories of employee (Roche and Turner, 1996). Notwithstanding the increased incidence of new initiatives, as found in the 1995 CUL study, experimentation with new work structures in Ireland would seem to be confined as yet to a relatively modest number of organisations. To add further support to this view, quality circles were present in little over a quarter of organisations surveyed in 1995 and in only

15 per cent of cases had their use increased over the preceding three years.

In a secondary analysis of CUL (1992), Roche and Turner (1996) employed multivariate statistical techniques to examine the influence of a range of internal and external influences on the incidence of new forms of work organisation, as well as other elements of HRM. Three indicators of change were examined: whether jobs had been made more flexible, the presence of quality circles and the use of teambuilding training for managers. The latter was used as a proxy for the importance attached by an organisation to teamworking. Not surprisingly, exposure to international competition and the degree of priority given to integrating human resource policy with business strategy were amongst the factors found to be associated with new forms of work organisation. More unexpected perhaps was the absence of any relationship between the take-up of new work structures and the presence of trade unions and whether a firm operated in a "high technology" industry. As the authors point out, this might be due to factors such as the limited variability of product strategies and manufacturing processes in Irish high technology firms and secondly, the predominance of routine fabrication in this sector. That is, within these organisations employees are concentrated in low skilled positions and, in the absence of a variety of skilled occupations, the structure of the internal labour market is such that it is incapable of supporting sophisticated forms of work organisation.

Relative to other areas of HRM, innovation in the area of work organisation, (as well as payment systems), was low. The authors explain this in respect of inertial forces that exercise a significant drag on management initiatives that are directed towards the "wage-effort bargain". Those factors identified as being important are the low levels of trust which exist between employers and employees in both unionised and non-unionised workplaces in Ireland, the slowness with which Irish employers have invested in research and development, in new technologies and new manufacturing and service delivery systems as well as the challenges new work structures present to established industrial relations arrangements.

The European Foundation's EPOC Survey, 1996

The EPOC survey was designed to minimise many of the limitations of previous surveys of employee participation and new work structures. Critically, it was not just concerned with measuring incidence, but also took into account coverage, scope and the degree of autonomy allowed for under task participation. It was also a cross-national survey with the same instrument being used in ten European countries. In this section, the findings as they pertain to Ireland will be discussed, but some attention will be paid to comparisons with countries elsewhere in Europe.[5]

In the area of consultative participation, "temporary groups", such as project groups or task forces, were found in 36 per cent of firms and "permanent groups" like quality circles were used in 28 per cent of Irish enterprises. This compared with a ten-country average of 31 per cent and 30 per cent respectively. Delegative participation organised around team structures was found in 42 per cent of organisations. This is above the average score of 36 per cent in the study as a whole coming third behind Sweden (56 per cent) and the Netherlands (48 per cent). From these estimates it would seem that TP is practised in about a third of Irish workplaces.

When coverage is taken into account, that is whether TP involved more than 50 per cent of the largest occupational group, the figures for Ireland hold up comparatively well in comparison to most other European countries. They are (the average ten-country score is given in brackets): temporary group consultation 73 per cent (48%); permanent group consultation 71 per cent (48%) and group delegation (i.e. teamworking) 58 per cent (47%). Where TP is practised in Ireland well over half, and in some case nearly two-thirds, of enterprises involve more than half of the largest occupational group. There is some evidence for a "greenfield" effect: that is, newly established enterprises in Ire-

land would seem to be more likely to use TP than older established "brownfield" sites (Edwards, Geary and Sisson, 1997).

One of the most novel features of the EPOC survey was its attempt to measure the intensity of teamworking. Two indicators
were used: the first was the "scope" of teamworking which measured the number of rights of employees to make decisions on how
they performed their work without reference to immediate management in areas like scheduling and allocation of work. The second was the degree of autonomy permitted to employees to choose
their own team members and to decide which issues the group
might address. Where high levels of discretion are allowed to employees this form of teamworking would approximate closely with
what has often been referred to as "semi-autonomous work
groups". Of those Irish enterprises using teamworking only 17 per
cent were found to have a high level of intensity of group delegation; most (51 per cent) had a medium level and a third had a low
level of intensity.

In yet another attempt to distinguish between forms of teamworking the EPOC team made a distinction between two forms:
the first a "Scandinavian" model, the other, a "Toyota" or lean
production model. The former permits more autonomy to team
members, team members come from a variety of skill groupings
and there is considerable emphasis on training. The latter, in contrast, places strict limits on teams' autonomy and employees'
skills would be largely of a generalist or routine kind. The types of
group work are detailed below in Table 10.1.

The distinction between these two forms of teamworking
proved to be very illuminating in accounting for the different economic effects of teamworking. Organisations which used forms
which came close to the Scandinavian model were considerably
more likely to report improvements in organisational performance
along indicators like reductions in costs and through-put times,
improvements in quality and, most strikingly, in increases in total
output. They were also more likely to indicate a decrease in sickness and absenteeism levels and reductions in the number of employees and managers employed.

TABLE 10.1: TYPES OF GROUP WORK

Dimensions	Scandinavian	Toyota/Lean Production
Membership	Voluntary	Mandatory
Selection of group members	By the group	By management
Selection of group leader	By the group	By management
Qualifications	Mixed	Generalists
Reward	Skill dependent	Uniform (seniority)
Task	Complex	Simple
Technology	Independent of pace	Dependent on pace
Autonomy	Large	Narrow
Internal division of labour	Voluntary	Largely prescribed

Source: Edwards, Geary and Sisson (1997). Based on Fröhlich and Pekruhl (1996).

Thus, it would seem that where organisations grant employees autonomy to manage their own teamworking arrangements and where the organisation of work and technology is configured in a way which gives employees the scope to determine the pace of work and where skill sets are complex and mixed, the benefits to the organisation are considerably greater than where teamworking is organised around the so-called Toyota model where management control the organisation of work far more closely. The worrying aspect for Ireland is that, while teamworking is as widely diffused in Ireland as elsewhere in Europe, it is predominantly of a form that comes close to the Toyota model. Only 0.3 per cent of Irish companies have adopted the Scandinavian model, which compares with a ten-country average of 1.4 per cent and, not surprisingly, a high of 4.6 per cent in Sweden.

In summary, a considerable proportion of Irish employers would seem to be experimenting with TP, but a majority of enterprises continue to rely on more traditional forms of work organisation. More significantly, the number of Irish employers who have introduced forms of teamworking which concede control of the organisation of work to employees is small. To this extent, the EPOC findings would confirm earlier evidence that TP, particularly of an advanced form, is a minority practice in this country.

UCD Graduate Business School study of "Irish Management Practice in the Changing Marketplace", 1996–97

The UCD survey bears some close resemblance with the EPOC survey in that an attempt was made to measure the scope of teamworking, rather than just measuring its mere incidence.[6] Its sampling strategy was more rigorous than that of previous surveys conducted in Ireland. It is the first and only survey to have examined industrial relations and human resource management practices at the workplace level in Ireland. In this respect it is quite unlike other surveys of industrial relations previously conducted in Ireland, many of which have relied on "bootstrapped" or "convenience" samples from company listings of uncertain statistical generalisability. In the UCD study, in only 61 per cent of cases were the company and workplace synonymous. Thus in significant respects other surveys have failed to provide a complete analysis of developments at the workplace level. The study's methodology is explored in more detail in the endnotes below.[7]

Re-regulating the Irish Workplace: The Case of Teamworking

Teamworking was found to be present in 57 per cent of workplaces. Taken on its own, this finding would indicate that teamworking is quite widely practised in Ireland and, in comparison to most other countries where similar research has been conducted, Ireland would rank amongst those countries at the top of any "league table" that one might develop. It appears, however, that employers' experimentation with teamworking is a relatively recent phenomenon, with only 19 per cent of workplaces having introduced it three years or more ago. In the remaining cases, 21 per cent said they had introduced teams in the last year to three years, and 17 per cent in the last year. It would seem then that teams are only firmly embedded in a fifth of Irish workplaces; elsewhere, its introduction is too recent to make any firm claims as to durability or permanence. The fragility of teamworking was most apparent in small workplaces with 20 to 49 employees where 41 per cent had only introduced teams in the year prior to our study.

The most widely diffused form of teamworking, but only by a small margin, were those forms which brought people together from similar skill categories (52 per cent) and which included both management and non-managerial employees (52 per cent). Teams which contained employees with different skills were present in little under a half of workplaces (49 per cent) and teams which involved employees from similar functions or departments operated in 45 per cent of workplaces. Cross-functional or cross-departmental teams were the least frequent, existing in a little over a third of work sites (39 per cent).

In workplaces using teams, respondents were asked about how teams operated and, in particular, whether management or team members played the leading role in deciding on a range of issues. The results are listed in Table 10.2.

The Organisation of Work

One might normally associate the use of teamworking with managerial efforts to reorganise the structure of work and, as part of that, to grant employees autonomy to manage work allocation, scheduling and pace. In respect of the first of these two items, less than half of the workplaces surveyed permitted team members to play the leading role, and in only 53 per cent of cases was control over pace of work vested in team members. While it would seem that responsibility for the organisation of work has moved from management to teams in some workplaces, in the majority of cases control continues to reside with management.

TABLE 10.2: LEVELS OF AUTONOMY PERMITTED TO TEAM MEMBERS

	% of Workplaces Where Team Members Play the Leading Role
The Organisation of Work	
Allocation of work	41
Scheduling of work	47
Pace of work	53
Quality Management and Continuous Improvement	
Dealing with customers and suppliers outside this establishment	33
Addressing/resolving problems with employees from other teams	36
Responsibility for the quality of work	71
Making suggestions for improving work processes	90
Management of Attendance and Working Time	
Control of absence/attendance	32
Control of time-keeping	51
Control of Team Boundaries and Team Composition	
Selection of team members	15
Selection of team leader	24

Quality Management and Continuous Improvement

Working in teams is also seen to provide employees with a means for identifying problems and empowering them to make suggestions and resolve difficulties. The management of quality and the continuous improvement of work processes which was previously the preserve of quality engineers or supervisors is now assumed by employees under these new arrangements. There is considerable evidence to show that teams have been given significant levels of autonomy in this field, particularly in making suggestions for improving work processes (90 per cent), and responsibility for the quality of work (71 per cent), but the evidence would suggest that significantly less discretion is permitted to teams to deal with problems which are shared by, or arise between, a number of teams. In only a third of cases were employees said to be given control in this area. Similarly, in only a third of workplaces did teams exercise a significant say in dealings with external customers. In sum, the evidence here would accord with the already considerable evidence that teamworking does place new demands on employees, particularly around managerial expectations that employees are *required* to use their initiative to resolve workplace problems and improve quality, but that such involvement is confined to the immediate work task in most instances.

The Management of Attendance and Working Time

Arguably this and the items listed under the next head represent a critical litmus test of the level of autonomy management has been prepared to permit to employees with the introduction of teamworking. Where management are prepared to grant employees a say in defining and policing acceptable standards of time keeping and attendance this might be reasonably taken as a significant departure from traditional practice. Of course, much of this has resonance with notions of "self-discipline" or, perhaps its harsher side, peer surveillance and peer discipline. Interestingly, in over half of companies the management of timekeeping was enforced, or at least controlled by team members. Control of attendance rested with employees in about a third of workplaces. From this evidence the management of discipline around two key aspects of work — the time one comes to work and attendance at work — is vested in work teams in a surprisingly high number of workplaces.

Control of Team Boundaries and Team Composition

In contrast to the level of control exercised by teams over time keeping and attendance, employees were given very little discretion over the selection of team members and team leaders. In these two areas, control rested very firmly with management. In only 15 per cent of cases were employees allowed to select team members, and in a little under a quarter of workplaces were teams in a position to chose their own team leader.

Another finding that merits attention is that teamworking was associated with a reduction in the number of supervisors in 45 per cent of workplaces, an indication perhaps that employees were acquiring tasks and responsibilities once performed by their immediate superiors. That 47 per cent of respondents reported that there was no such reduction does illustrate, though, that in many Irish workplaces teams operate alongside traditional supervisory levels and, arguably, hierarchical relations. The continued presence of supervisors and the limited discretion permitted to team members in most instances would suggest that conventional forms of authority relations continue to persist in most Irish organisations, even where teamworking has been introduced.

A number of points can therefore be made: first, the levels of autonomy permitted to teams is tightly circumscribed; second, employers do not depend on participative structures alone to persuade workers to work hard, but rely also on the continued presence of a supervisor; and finally, the rules and understandings of the workplace are, in significant respects, being defined and policed by non-team members.

It would seem that the "new workplace order" contains many elements, some of which a priori might not have been expected, especially in regard to the management of attendance and time-keeping. Yet alongside this management would seem to exercise more control in other areas like work organisation where it might not have been anticipated. Are such findings contradictory? Not entirely. Empowerment and control are not self-contained categories, but this is to make a point familiar to most students of shop-floor employment relations: that is, employers have an interest in releasing employees' inventiveness and imagination as well as regulating them closely (cf. Cressey and MacInness 1980; Edwards, Geary and Sisson, 1997). It is not the case that full autonomy is being granted or ceded to employees. But this point has another significance: neither concept — control or empowerment — can be used to describe the nature of a given workplace; they are not mutually exclusive practices, but come together in a variety of ways.

The Introduction of Teamworking and the Role of Trade Unions

In those organisations, which had introduced teamworking, the largest occupational group was represented by a trade union for bargaining and/or consultation purposes in 45 per cent of workplaces. Respondents in these organisation were asked whether unions had been involved in the introduction of teamworking and, if so, why. Surprisingly, only 28 per cent of managers reported that unions were involved. The main reason reported for providing unions with a role was that management was required by existing agreements to consult with the trade union before making changes to working practices (81 per cent). The other reasons cited were: "they showed themselves to be reasonable and willing to co-operate" (63 per cent); "unions have a right to participate in all such changes" (56 per cent); "they were seen as being able to secure employees' acceptance" (44 per cent); and finally, "they had an expertise and knowledge to contribute" (37 per cent).

The question — in phrasing it "were trade unions involved in the introduction of teamworking" — allowed for a broad range of situations to be reported upon; ones where unions might have exerted considerable influence through joint regulation or detailed negotiations or where they have been merely consulted of management's wish to introduce teamworking. Nonetheless, the evidence paints a bleak picture of the position and level of influence exerted by unions at workplace level, at least as perceived by operations managers.

The Diffusion of Teamworking: Examining Potential Influences

This section will examine a range of possible factors identified in the academic literature as being likely influences on the adoption of teamworking arrangements in Irish workplaces. The statistical techniques used in this study are standard. Some complex multi-variate models are estimated, relying on various forms of regression analysis which are well known and for the purposes of this chapter will not be presented in any detailed way here.

The factors identified as being likely predictors of the presence of teamworking were:

- *Operating in international markets*: workplaces which produce goods or services for international markets are more likely to use teamworking

- *Competitive intensity*: workplaces which face intensive competition are more likely to use teamworking

- *Greenfield sites*: newly-established workplaces sites are more likely to use teamworking

- *Customisation*: workplaces which produce standardised goods or services are less likely to use teamworking

- *Workplace size*: large workplaces are more likely to use teamworking

- *Services sector*: workplaces located in the services sector are more likely to use teamworking

- *High-tech*: high-tech workplaces are more likely to use teamworking

- *Skilled employees*: workplaces where the largest occupational group is comprised of skilled or managerial employees are more likely to use teamworking

- *Financial services*: workplaces in the financial services industry are more likely to use teamworking

• *Nationality*: foreign-owned workplaces are more likely to use teamworking.

Three models that use different definitions or aspects of teamworking were estimated. The results for each will be reported in turn. For the purposes of brevity, the detailed statistical results are not reported here, but Table 10.3 below highlights the factors that are associated with teamworking. The first column refers to the presence or absence of teamworking; the second shows which variables are associated with intensive or advanced forms of team working and the final section of the table is subdivided in four to illustrate the four different components of teamworking and the conditions associated with each.

TABLE 10.3: EXAMINING POTENTIAL INFLUENCES ON THE INCIDENCE AND INTENSIVENESS OF TEAMWORKING

Model 1 = presence/absence of teamworking; Model 2 = intensiveness of teamworking; Model 3 = four aspects of team working: (1) work organisation; (2) management of attendance and working time; (3) quality management and continuous improvement; (4) control of team boundaries and team composition

Independent Variables	Model 1	Model 2	Model 3			
			(1)	(2)	(3)	(4)
Financial services	+***	+**	+**	+**	+***	−***
Prod/serv customisation	+***	+**	+*	+**		
High-tech industries		+***	+***	+***		
Services sector				+*		+***
Intense market comp.		−**		−*	−***	
Foreign ownership	−***				+*	
International markets	+***		+**			+*
Workforce size			+*		−**	
Skilled workforce						
Greenfield site						

Notes: + = positive coefficient; − = negative coefficient
* significant at 10% level; ** significant at 5% level; *** significant at 1% level

Model 1: The Presence of Teamworking

In the first model some of the ten variables identified above do
help to explain the presence of teamworking. In brief, teamworking was positively associated with financial services, prod-
uct/service customisation, with establishments operating in international markets and, surprisingly, Irish-owned workplaces.

Model 2: The Intensiveness of Teamworking

In contrast to the first model, which involved a straight-forward
examination of the factors associated with the presence or absence
of teamworking, the second model sought to examine the influences associated with the *intensiveness* of teamworking. It was
believed this would provide a more precise estimate of the incidence and shape of teamworking, particularly in respect of the
degree of autonomy enjoyed by teams in decision making. An in-
dex was constructed by expressing the number of times team
members played the leading role in decision-making as a proportion of the items listed in the questionnaire. The values of the in-
dex range from 0 where no item was decided upon by team members, to 11 where team members played the leading role on all issues. The analysis is confined to those establishments that had
introduced teamworking arrangements.

The model found that the intensiveness of teamworking was
positively associated with high-tech workplaces, establishments
operating in the financial services industry, the production of customised goods or services and workplaces encountering low levels
of competition.

Model 3: Dimensions of Teamworking

In Table 10.2 above teamworking was split into a number of constituent elements: the organisation of work; quality management
and continuous improvement; management of attendance and
working time; and control of team boundaries and team composition. Separate equations were estimated for each of these aspects
of teamworking. Several factors appear important. Most impres-

sive is the financial services sector, followed by high-tech industries, the services sector, low levels of market competition, customisation, and foreign ownership.

In brief, several conclusions can be made from these models' estimates. Most noteworthy is the importance of the financial services sector as a predictor of the existence of teamworking in its various forms: in all but one equation was the coefficient positive and significant. Other variables that produce consistently robust results, particularly in explaining teamworking of an advanced form are establishments which produce customised products or services, workplaces which are insulated from stiff international competition and establishments which operate in high-tech sectors. Contrary to expectations, factors such as nationality and workplace size register weak and inconclusive results. Perhaps most surprisingly, in none of the models is there evidence to support a greenfield site or skilled workforce effect. The significance of these results will be considered in some more detail below.

CASE STUDY EVIDENCE OF TP

In the case volume (Monks et al., 1998) which accompanies this text book, Tony Dobbins and I consider in some detail the case of a particular pharmaceutical company based in Munster that has introduced teamworking in recent years. The case illustrates that teamworking's introduction led neither to "exploitation" nor "empowerment", but rather to a re-regulation of labour. The discussion here will not comment on the details of this case study, but instead will extract and comment on its principal findings. The reader is invited, however, to read the paper in the accompanying volume. This section of the chapter will also consider the wider case study evidence to explore the conditions that might support the successful adoption of TP.

The Case of Munster Pharmaceuticals (MP)*

MP is a subsidiary of a large US MNC. Established as a greenfield facility in 1976, it quickly grew into a profitable and successful operation and currently employs over 300 people. For the first fifteen years it produced bulk pharmaceutical products. In recent years, local management has successfully acquired new product lines that are produced in smaller batches with higher margins. This repositioning of the plant's capabilities away from low cost, low value added product lines towards the development of flexible production processes to manufacture high value products was seen to be a prerequisite to maintaining the Irish subsidiary's future. To a large degree it has been a successful strategy: corporate headquarters have recently invested in new plant and technology and the workforce is due to expand by near a hundred employees. It has been a development which has however imposed a number of new demands on the Irish operation, most notably in the form of greater effort levels, new training requirements and the need to "empower" employees and reduce the cost of supervision.

A survey of employees' views of teamworking revealed a number of important findings. First, employees drew considerable satisfaction from working in teams, although attachment to the new arrangements varied, in some instances, significantly across occupational categories. In a very fundamental way the findings point to the importance of context in explaining this variation: a similar management programme was perceived in a different light and had had very different consequences in different parts of the company. Employee participation, for example, offered little new to craft employees, whereas junior administrative employees embraced the new initiative in spite of the increased effort and pressure levels.

Alongside TP, however, must be placed other developments in management's human resource strategy. With the introduction of

---

* I am grateful to Tony Dobbins for his help in collating the data for this case study.

teamworking management also tried to alter the structure and nature of supervision. To a large degree this was met with a positive response from employees. Supervision had perhaps been at its most repressive in the craft section and employees here reported a considerable relaxation in the closeness of supervision. So, for craft employees, this meant more to them than the "introduction" of teamworking. This showed itself in the level of trust that was reported to exist between management and employees.

This leads to the wider issue of workers' response to TP and its wider implications for management employee relations. Employees at MP generally welcomed the introduction of teamworking in spite of the increased effort levels, but there was little evidence of a shift in values towards higher management. The evidence here accords with the "disciplined worker model" of Collinson et al. (1998) where increased effort levels and closer supervision came together with greater levels of employee autonomy, and as a new system of work organisation was not only valued and accepted but was also seen to be necessary. Second, there is the issue of management's objectives. Here the evidence suggests that management's goals were quite limited, it wanted to introduce TP but it was to be a controlled form of participation. There were, therefore, definite limits to the extent to which employees were empowered to make decisions for themselves and their work group. Its introduction did however make some significant contributions to the organisation of work, to employees' day-to-day experience of work and to the performance of the company. It is within this context that TP must be seen: it is limited and controlled, but is neither transformative nor exploitative.

Linking the Case of Munster Pharmaceuticals to Other Sources of Evidence

The case of Munster Pharmaceuticals would suggest that a number of conditions need to be present to facilitate the implementation of TP. In exploring these in some detail reference will also be made to evidence from other case studies. First, employees enjoyed a high level of employment security. Where employees feel insecure in their jobs, there is considerable evidence to suggest that TP is unlikely to prosper (cf. Marchington et al., 1994; Edwards et al., 1997). Second, many of MP's employees worked with process technology, which has often been identified in the literature as being particularly appropriate to the development of teamworking. Conversely in labour intensive industries, where work is organised around an assembly line or is relatively routine it is difficult for concepts of empowerment to take root (Edwards et al., 1997).

Third, there is the issue of management choices and the strategies they pursue. There was a conscious and deliberate attempt at MP to reposition the competitive strategy of the company around the manufacture of small batch, high margin, and high quality goods. To support this strategy management made considerable investment in training and employee involvement. It also made some considerable efforts to restructure industrial relations at the plant. In combination these changes conveyed a reasonably coherent message to the workforce. In contrast, an earlier study of two American owned electronics plants in Ireland illustrated the problem of how a lack of consistency in management's actions sent competing messages to employees and undermined any support for TP (Geary, 1993). With its introduction management also introduced a policy of closely policing time-keeping and attendance. In the absence of a coherent view of change, managers' approach became increasingly piecemeal, and in the end they were forced to rely on traditional forms of workforce co-operation.

Fourth, there is the state of industrial relations. At MP, management had enjoyed good relations with the trade unions down through the years. The strategy of introducing TP with trade union involvement and co-operation through the Steering Committee achieved considerable success. Evidence from elsewhere would suggest that where management seek to bypass and marginalise trade unions in the introduction of TP or where its implementation is designed to reduce union influence then it is often difficult for TP to take root. That said, it is often difficult for unions to position themselves strategically in the face of changes in work organisation, particularly where such changes alter job boundaries and payment structures. These problems are especially acute in countries like Ireland, the UK and the US where trade union identity and organisation was traditionally formed around job territories and where the institutional security of employee representatives (shop stewards) was based on control of work organisation and day-to-day production. In such circumstances, it is not hard to see how TP might be seen as a threat to unions, especially when they are not involved in its introduction.

CONDITIONS SUPPORTING TP TO TAKE ROOT AND PROSPER

The next task is to build on the discussion of the previous sections and to draw on wider sources of evidence to understand why some organisations have adopted new forms of work organisation with more enthusiasm and with more success than others have. Attention is also given to identifying those conditions that are associated with TP and improved business performance. The discussion draws in particular from two sources: Edwards, Geary and Sisson (1997) and Ichniowski et al. (1996).

"Bundling" TP with Human Resource Management Practices

One of the most unequivocal findings to come from the literature is that if TP is to develop, be sustained over time and have a significant effect on business performance, it needs to be integrated with other elements of HRM practice. Amongst the most important of these practices are: investment in skills and training, the development of new internal labour market structures and perhaps, most importantly, a commitment to employment security. The problem as seen by many commentators, however, is that too few employers have been able to "bundle" human resource management practices in this way and that the HRM infrastructure supporting TP has tended to be inconsistent and contradictory (cf. Ichniowski et al., 1996; Kochan and Osterman, 1994; Pil and MacDuffie, 1996).

In a recent account of experiences in the US, for example, Peter Cappelli and colleagues document how the deliberate importation of product and labour market pressures within the enterprise has worked to undermine the trust and mutual commitment thought necessary to support workplace innovation (Cappelli et al., 1997). No longer buffered from the excesses of market forces, employees are required to take individual responsibility for their own training and development; payment systems have adopted an increasingly contingent design, and most significantly, the one-time commitment to employment security is no longer supported. This internalisation of market disciplines has led, Cappelli claims, to the formulation of a new psychological contract wherein the obligations and expectations of employee and employer alike have been redrawn with the effect of providing little incentive for employers to invest in, or for employees to be committed to, new workplace innovations. In such circumstances, where both parties display reduced commitment to one another, the sustainability of TP becomes inherently suspect.

The Nature of Competition

It is commonly assumed by commentators and practitioners alike that competition, and in particular international competition, is the spur for employers to introduce TP, along with other strategic initiatives in HRM. Where that competition is based on quality and innovation and where price is less a consideration the pressure to adapt existing work structures to empower employees would seem to be more pressing.

Recent evidence from the EPOC and UCD surveys would however suggest the position is much more complicated. In the former study, the need to improve quality, to reduce costs and lower through-put times were the dominant motive for the introduction of various forms of participation. Yet the overall incidence of employee participation and the incidence of its various forms in the countries surveyed hardly varied with the level of competition, which was an unexpected result. It was only in the case of the scope of participation that the picture was more in line with the expectations and even here the differences were marginal (Edwards, Geary and Sisson, 1997).

Employing multivariate statistical techniques to examine the influence of a range of factors on the incidence and intensiveness (i.e. the degree of autonomy enjoyed by team members) of teamworking the UCD survey's results also reveal a complex picture. Intense market competition was found not to be associated with the presence of teams, but rather the reverse; in two of the models in Table 10.3 above there was an inverse relationship between teamworking and market competition. But like the EPOC results, what seems to be crucial in explaining the incidence and intensiveness of teamworking is the degree to which firms compete on the basis of product/service customisation. The influence exerted by international markets is also remarkable. Here there are similarities with the findings of Osterman (1994) in the US where it was found that companies' experience of selling goods in international markets was a crucial factor in explaining the presence of new work structures. It would seem then that operating in international markets exposes employers to new ways of organising work and in facing common competitive pressures there may be a tendency for them to learn from each other or from common models of "best practice": a process referred to as "isomorphic mimicry" (DiMaggio and Powell, 1983). The relationship between teamworking and the absence of intense market competition is surprising. It may be that to develop new work structures employers require resources, space and time to experiment and invest. Intense exposure to international competition may deny management the opportunity to develop team working and the room to recoup the up-front costs that such an initiative requires.

"Greenfield" versus "Brownfield": The Opportunity to Start Anew

While piecemeal innovation seems to be the predominant message from much of the available evidence there are, it would seem, a small number of organisations who have been able to introduce TP in a coherent fashion together with complementary bundles of human resource management practices. In countries like Ireland, the US and the UK, for example, such strategic innovations seem to be associated in the main with foreign-owned companies establishing operations on "greenfield" sites (Locke et al., 1995; Roche and Geary, 1996; Sisson, 1995). The task of transforming work structures in older "brownfield" sites with more deeply embedded organisational cultures and industrial relations processes would seem to be significantly more problematic. Innovations are pursued more often than not in an incremental fashion and very often when the need for change has become incontrovertible (see, for example, Dobbins' study of Jaguar and Massey Ferguson in the UK, 1997). In contrast, a "greenfield" site provides management with a significant window of opportunity to contemplate, design and successfully introduce a new form of work organisation integrated with a comprehensive system of human resource practices.

This picture is complicated somewhat, however, by evidence from the recent UCD and EPOC surveys. The latter found that MNCs establishing operations on "greenfield" sites were equally divided between those not adopting and those practising TP. Interestingly, there were distinct country differences with MNCs in Germany, Italy, the Netherlands and Sweden using employee participation techniques to a greater extent than MNCs in other European countries. This might suggest that there are distinct country effects at work depending on the nature of a country's industrial relations regime and level of labour costs (Edwards, Geary and Sisson, 1997). The UCD survey found no evidence to suggest that there was a relationship between the existence of teams or the intensiveness of teamworking and whether a company was newly established or not.

Enterprise-based Partnership Arrangements

There is now a rich literature in industrial relations which sees "partnership" arrangements as a fundamental constituent or necessary accompaniment to the development of new business strategies based on flexible production and service delivery systems (Piore and Sabel, 1984; Kochan et al. 1984; Regini 1995). In many

European countries, the mechanism for providing employees with such a "voice" has been through works councils. In other countries, where such bodies have been absent and where management union relations have come from a tradition of adversarialism, there has been considerable support for the development of new forums to promote more consensual relations between management and trade unions. In Ireland, the recent establishment of a National Centre for Partnership, agreed to by the social partners under the terms of *Partnership 2000*, is evidence of this recent interest in workplace partnership. In the literature, a variety of terms have been used to call attention to these initiatives: "social partnership" arrangements, "jointness" in the management of change, "micro-concertation", "productivity coalitions", and "mutual gains" solutions.

Findings from the EPOC study suggest that while the incidence of TP was largely unaffected by the presence or absence of employee representatives, TP with wide scope was associated with strong forms of employee representative involvement. Furthermore the greater the level of involvement of employees representatives in the introduction of TP, the greater the economic benefits to the organisation (Edwards et al., 1997).

The reasons why the development of workplace arrangements may ease the introduction of TP and lead to economic benefits are complex and not easily understood, but perhaps one of the clearest presentations as to why this is the case has been that of Wolfgang Streeck (1995). For Streeck economic adjustment has required a fundamental transformation in the mechanisms of management union (employee) dialogue and interaction, even in countries which have made legislative provision for workplace consultation. Streeck observes that where such consultation takes place it is *more than* a mere consequence of a set of institutional constraints acting on management. In some countries like Germany and the Netherlands such structures were already in place in the form of workplace works councils. In other countries like Sweden and Italy where workplace representation is based on trade unions only, management have moved *voluntarily* to extend to unions consultation and co-determination rights. That they have done so, it should be stressed, is, in part at least, a reflection of unions' strength in both countries.

The thrust of Streeck's argument is that the move from mass production to "flexible specialisation" has unleashed a series of industrial relations and HRM imperatives. The background to this is well-recorded and well-known: new production strategies require a decentralisation in decision-making processes, the winning of employees' active consent and commitment, the creation of new structures to allow for employee involvement informed not by bureaucratic rules and procedures but by the articulation and communication of organisational objectives and economic imperatives. Here then is the crux of the argument: the old system of industrial relations rarely encountered such frequent and radical change within the workplace; workers' interests were precise and confined such that they could be addressed through representative structures at defined intervals at the top of the organisation. With new systems of production and service delivery, however, where change is ongoing and where issues relating to economic performance and efficiency are continuously being addressed at a local level, the issue of workers' interests comes immediately to the fore. For this reason, issues of economic performance and workers' concerns and interests must be addressed simultaneously and at all levels in the organisation. As a consequence, "consultation on production needs and representation of worker interests tend to be even less separable than in traditional work organisations. Where under a system of decentralised competence, major production decisions are made, not by "management", but by workers as part of their routine work assignments, *consultation between workers and management on how to increase efficiency becomes impossible to keep apart from negotiations on the mutual accommodation of interests* (emphasis in original)" (p. 331–2).

In summary, the full economic benefits of TP would seem more likely to accrue to employers when changes in work practices are combined with a comprehensive package of human resource policies and when management involve employees and their representatives in workplace partnership arrangements. Within the organisation a number of factors are identified as being crucial for TP to take root. Amongst the most important are: employment security, the type of technology or production systems in operation, prior expectations and experiences of workers, management strategies and choices, and finally, the shape and nature of industrial relations.

The final section of the chapter looks at the wider context of public institutions and public policy and its role in supporting or hindering the diffusion of TP.

Public Policy and the Future for New Forms of Work Organisation

The empirical evidence reviewed above points to the uneven, limited and fragile nature of TP in Ireland, particularly of an advanced kind. In the face of such a sober assessment the critical question then becomes whether the conditions thought necessary to support a wider diffusion of TP could be put in place or, for those support structures that do exist, how might they be better mobilised.

First there is the issue of workplace partnership. Recent evidence from the UCD National Survey would suggest that the development of strategic partnerships between employers and trade unions are poorly diffused in Ireland and confined to a small number of well-publicised companies (Roche and Geary, 1998). As we have seen, the formation of such "coalitions" is seen by many as a necessary precursor to the successful implementation of TP. The perceived advantages for developing such arrangements are many: the provision of a voice mechanism so that employees' support for workplace innovations might be fostered; improvements in the quality of decision-making; the provision of additional expertise and legitimacy for management's actions; the breaking free from an adversarial industrial relations culture; and the enfranchisement of the entire workforce, including those who may not have been, or who do not wish to become, trade union members. To this extent, the introduction of TP through and alongside such workplace partnership arrangements has come to be seen by many commentators to constitute a new model of good industrial relations (cf. Kochan and Osterman, 1994).

The import of many of the contributions to the academic and policy debate is that employee involvement at the level of the task or work organisation, separated from joint union- or employee-management partnership arrangements, is fundamentally a truncated or an impoverished form of employee participation and that, without such arrangements, TP is unlikely to be sustained or prosper.

While it might be easier to see such institutional innovations become more diffuse and more systemic in countries like Germany or the Netherlands, where works councils enjoy a long and established tradition, it is perhaps more difficult to envisage that they might become more widespread in countries like Ireland where industrial relations traditions are more adversarial in nature. But the example set by Sweden and, particularly Italy, are instructive, where, as Streeck (1995) has put it, against the institutional odds there was a renaissance in consultation arrangements. Two factors would appear to be at work here: first, and this is especially true in the case of Sweden, strong unions are difficult to avoid and management are more likely to use existing industrial relations institutions, particularly where unions reciprocate a willingness to work with management, than work against them. Second, the role of public institutions for nurturing the development of such arrangements cannot be doubted. It is to this issue the discussion now turns.

The establishment of the new National Centre for Partnership under *Partnership 2000* does represent a significant initiative in this area. Charged with acquiring data and information on why and, under what conditions, workplace innovations succeed and then providing support and guidance to ensuring that these lessons can be diffused to other organisations, the Centre is well positioned, at this juncture at least, to promote a wider diffusion of workplace partnership arrangements. If this were to happen then one important institutional structure would be in place to support the introduction of TP.

A second area of policy, which needs to be looked at in more depth, is the area of training. The evidence clearly demonstrates, the acquisition of technical, behavioural and analytical skills is a prerequisite for TP's effective implementation. In many instances investment in skills' training is difficult to justify or too expensive, especially for SMEs and for firms operating under the constraints of financial short-termism, where the benefits from training may be seen to be too uncertain or take too long to realise. This problem is compounded by companies reluctance to invest in training, lest their trained employees are poached by other employers. The effects of these processes are likely to become particularly acute as skill shortages become exposed in sectors where labour markets continue to tighten. Yet the evidence is overwhelming: without investment in training, changes in work organisation and TP are unlikely to prosper and diffuse.

Third, there is the issue of "learning forums" and the diffusion of "best practice". As stated in the introduction to this section, current initiatives around TP remain isolated. In order to identify "best practice", institutions and networks need to be established to collect and disseminate data to as wide an audience as possible. Without such support structures it is difficult to see how TP might be fostered and sustained. To date there have been a number of worthy initiatives, such as IPC's "New Work Organisation Programme", Forbairt's World Class Manufacturing programme and SIPTU's project on the Management of Change funded under the ADAPT programme. But, plainly, more needs to be done. In comparison to other countries where the resources available to, and influence exercised by, union and employer organisations (like Germany and Sweden) are of a different order, it is difficult to see how their counterparts in Ireland might be able to position themselves strategically to further the adoption of TP. Similarly, with the absence of an institution like Japan's Productivity Centre for Socio-Economic Development, the means by which lessons from past TP initiatives might be diffused are likely to remain ad hoc and informal.

The difficulties in supporting the diffusion of new work structures are perhaps most acute in the public services sector. To ensure that change will take hold will require considerable attention and energy than is perhaps evident under the current SMI programme. For here the problems assume a particular configuration and complexity: vertically-organised trade unions, strong vested identities and interests across occupational groups, management restrained by rigid pay and grading systems and by the mediated and more "muffled" character of "consumer market" pressures (see Roche, 1998).

Part of the problem in Ireland is that responsibility for innovation in industrial relations and work organisation remains fragmented and divided across a number of public agencies, like the LRC, IPC, and Forbairt (Roche and Kochan, 1996). The LRC, for example, has a long history and a high level of expertise in managing industrial relations and in proposing alternative and progressive models of new industrial relations (cf. LRC, 1996). On the other hand, it has little expertise in innovations in new production or service delivery systems or in new forms of work organisation. Some of the responsibilities and roles of the new National Centre for Partnership have and are being pursued by the LRC. Such replication and duplication of roles and lack of clarity of purpose lead to predictable problems: competition for scarce resources, a lack of strategic direction and focus in public agencies' actions, "institutional deadlock" and the unattractive, yet understandable, process of each body defending its "territory" and claiming success for each of its endeavours. Plainly, what is required is for such structural complexity to be reduced, for the social partners to take stock and move towards the formation of a single agency with responsibility for developing an expertise in industrial relations, human resource management and work organisation.

CONCLUSION

In summary, this chapter's arguments are: first, although Irish employers' interest in new forms of work organisation and in TP have increased in recent years, its practice, especially of an advanced form, remains relatively isolated.

Second, as to the intentions of management in introducing TP, the evidence would suggest that managerial motives are considerably more complex and variable than allowed for by optimists and pessimists. What stands out from the national and international evidence is that TP is more limited and controlled than the enthusiasts claim, but more constructive than the critics admit (Edwards, Geary and Sisson, 1997).

Third, with regard to TP's effects, the argument is that TP has middling and complex effects. The common tendency to see it as being either exploitative or transformative is to exaggerate its intentions and consequences; this chapter's claim is that it rests within a more mundane and modest effort to re-regulate labour. Nor is it simply a matter of seeing it as a zero-sum game. There are elements of TP which are of benefit to employees and may be welcomed, but there are also aspects which impose new demands and which may not be seen to be so advantageous. Employee responses and the ultimate shape of TP are influenced by, and are connected to, the way work is being re-organised. There is thus no one new, distinct, self-contained model: TP assumes different forms in different settings, and has variable effects. But where employees buy into TP and accept the need for a more disciplined work environment, co-operation between employees and employer may occur, but not necessarily of a form which leads to a transformation in employees' trust in management.

Finally, the prognosis for a wider diffusion of TP in Ireland is not very bright. There are significant transition costs associated with a move towards transforming work structures around the implementation of TP. For "Ireland Inc." to move towards a more participative work place — both at the level of the work task and management decision-making — will require not only some fundamental changes in the attitudes of employers and trade unions but also in the policy-emphasis of "supporting institutions". Such shifts are not likely to be easily secured.

Appendix

TABLE A.1: SAMPLE REPRESENTATIVENESS: POPULATION AND
SAMPLE DISTRIBUTIONS BY COMPANY SIZE AND SECTOR

Number of Employees	Population (%)	Target Sample (%)	Effective Sample (%)	Reweighted Sample (%)
20–49	54	20	12	38
50–99	21	30	22	20
100–249	15	30	32	20
250–499	5	10	17	10
500 plus	5	10	18	12
Sector				
Services	56	55	57	60
Manufacturing	44	45	43	40
Total	**4,062**	**815**	**273**	**435**

---

[1] In the wider literature, for a period in the 1980s and early 1990s, it became popular too to speak in optimistic terms of the eclipse of one mode of work organisation and the rise of another. The demise of Fordism and the rise of "flexible specialisation", particularly associated with the American writers Piore and Sabel (1984) and, in the UK, with Hirst and Zeitlin (1989) became an infuential canon of thought. In Germany there was the "end of the division of labour" and the rise of "new production concepts" (Kern and Schumann, 1984) and in France there was much made of the rise of neo- and/or post-Fordism associated with the so-called regulation school.

[2] The phrase is borrowed from Wolfgang Streeck who used it in a presentation at a seminar on "The End of the New Industrial Relations?", at the Graduate School of Business, University College Dublin, 27 August 1997.

[3] That this should have been the chosen size threshold is surprising given that the vast bulk of companies (61%) with more than 20 employees are in the 20–49 employee size category (this figure is derived from data supplied by Brendan Whelan of the ESRI in 1996). The authors' admission that the inclusion of smaller workplaces "might distort the findings of the survey"

would seem a disarmingly honest position to have adopted. With such a bias towards large organisations, any analysis of the data, but particularly of a multivariate kind, would find it very difficult to say with confidence the way in which workforce size might be associated with the presence or absence of TP.

[4] Despite the authors' claims (p.23–24), there would seem to be significant disparities between the achieved sample size and the overall distribution of firms in the population, in particular firms in the 50–100 size category.

[5] Although the EPOC study as a whole took the workplace as its unit of analysis, no population list of workplaces was available at the time the survey was conducted in Ireland. Thus, like the CUL study, it was forced to rely on company listings for its sampling frame; the statistical generalisability of its findings (at least in respect of Ireland) must, therefore, be in some doubt. The firm's general manager was invited to complete the questionnaire or to give it to a colleague who might have been better placed to answer the questions asked. The size threshold in the case of Ireland was firms with 25 employees. The study's findings were weighted to make adjustments for any distortions in the size and industrial sector of companies. In Ireland, the survey achieved a response rate of nearly 39 per cent, 382 organisations in all. All questions were asked in respect of an organisation's largest occupational group.

[6] A novel feature of the survey was its use of two sources of information: one questionnaire was sent to the most senior designated manager at workplace level who had responsibility for human resource management. This questionnaire addressed a broad range of issues in the HR/IR area. Where a specialist operations manager was present another questionnaire focusing on an array of issues was administered covering product technology, service delivery systems, manufacturing practices, customer relations and organisational performance. While the former instrument did contain a number of questions on work organisation, the latter asked a range of detailed questions on the practice of teamworking. For this chapter data from the operations manager questionnaire are used. The advantage of reporting on this data set is that it is derived from responses from an operations manager, who, it was felt, would be best placed to comment on the practice of teamworking and to have relied solely on a personnel manager or site manager, especially in larger organisations, might have risked losing a detailed insight into the day-to-day functioning of teams.

[7] The ESRI provided the sample list of 1,003 enterprises. Forty-five per cent of the companies were in the manufacturing sector and the remainder, 55 per cent, were in the services (transport, distribution, retail, financial) sectors. Nearly 20 per cent of the sampled companies employed between 20–49 employees and 10 per cent employed more than 500 persons. The sample listing was then scrutinised so that: first, companies outside the sample design — construction companies and non-commercial public sector organisations — would be identified and excluded; and second, that multi-site companies

might be isolated to enable a separate sampling plan to be designed. As indicated above, for approximately 61 per cent of firms the company and workplace were synonymous. The majority of the remaining companies operated in the services and retail sectors, such as bank branches and stores of supermarket chains. The sample for these multi-site companies included the headquarters, if appropriate, and at least one workplace. In some instances the headquarters and a workplace were synonymous and in other situations the headquarters was a distinct workplace. The number of sites selected was determined by the size of a company's workplace population and by applying a 1-in-10 sampling fraction. The number of workplaces selected was consistently rounded upwards, so that for example a company with 5–10 sites resulted in one sample workplace while a company with between 11–20 sites produced two sample sites. In total, the target sample was 153 workplaces from 52 multi-site companies.

The overall response rate was 35 per cent which is very good in comparison to most other surveys of this type where 20 per cent is the norm. There were some observable differences across workplace size and a definite pattern emerged. Small workplaces employing less than 50 employees had the lowest response rate of 25 per cent; workplaces of between 50 to 100 employees and more than 100 persons had a response rate of 32 per cent and 43 per cent respectively. The response for the workplaces of multi-site companies was 31 per cent.

The total effective sample of 273 workplaces and the reweighted sample (proportionate weighted) of 435 is somewhat biased towards larger workplaces (see Table 1 in the appendix). There are two reasons for this: first, as indicated above, the response rate from large workplaces was higher than for smaller workplaces and second, it will be recalled that two instruments were used in the field; one dedicated to HR/IR issues and answered by a HR specialist and another which addressed a broad array of issues in operations management and which the operations manager answered. Where two different managers managed these functions it was feasible to administer two separate questionnaires. In other cases (29% of workplaces) the same manager was responsible for both functional areas and here a third, composite questionnaire was designed to cover both IR/HRM and operational matters, but to reduce the demand made on this sole respondent some questions, including those on teamworking, were omitted. In most instances, as one might expect, these workplaces were small in size.

Naturally, this bias in the achieved sample was worrying, particularly as size might be seen to be an important determinant of teamworking. Two points can be made in reply to such a fear: one, as the data analysis below shows, size exercised little or no effect on the incidence or intensiveness of teamworking; and two, when the present sample was 'reweighted' to correct for the sample bias, size was found not to have any effect. It is therefore safe to say that the present sample's findings are not distorted by the bias towards larger firms. It should be noted that there is no bias in the sectoral distribution of workplaces. Finally, the data reported here refers to the incidence and penetration of teamworking as it applied to a workplace's largest occupational group.

This chapter is a slightly shortened version of a paper delivered under a different title "New Work Structures and the Diffusion of Team Working Arrangements in Ireland" for the 6th Annual John Lovett Memorial Lecture, University of Limerick, April 2nd, 1998. I am grateful to the Department of Enterprise, Trade and Employment for the financial assistance provided towards the survey fieldwork costs associated with the UCD National Survey of Irish Management Practice in the Changing Marketplace. I am also indebted to Teresa Brannick for advice and help on compiling the data used in this study.

References

Callus, R., Morehead, A., Cully, M. and Buchanan, J. (1991): *Industrial Relations at Work: The Australian Workplace Industrial Relations Survey*. Canberra: Australian Government Publishing Service.

Cappelli, P., Bassi, L., Katz, H., Knoke, D., Osterman, P. and Useem, M. (1997): *Change at Work*, Oxford: Oxford University Press.

Collinson, M., Edwards, P. and Rees, C. (1998): *Involving Employees in Total Quality Management*, London: Department of Trade and Industry.

Cressey, P. and MacInnes, J. (1980): "Voting for Ford", *Capital and Class*, 11, 5–33.

DiMaggio, P.J., and Powell, W.W. (1983): "The Iron Cage Revisited", *American Sociological Review*, 48(1): 147–60.

Dobbins, T. (1997): *Employment Security Policies and New Working Practices in Two Brownfield Manufacturing Plants*, unpublished MA thesis, Warwick University.

Dobbins, T. and Geary, J. (forthcoming) "What Works with Teams?: The Case of Munster Pharmaceuticals" in Monks, K., Roche, W.K. and Walsh, J. (eds.) *Cases in Strategic Human Resource Management*. Dublin: Oak Tree Press.

Edwards, P.K. (1986): *Conflict at Work*, Oxford: Blackwell.

Edwards, P., Geary, J.F. and Sisson, K. (1997): *Employee Involvement in the Workplace: Transformative, Exploitative, or Limited and Controlled?* Paper prepared for the Canadian Workplace Research Network Conference, "Industrial Relations in the New Workplace: Research, Practice and Policy", University of Laval, Quebec, Canada, September 18th–20th.

Fröhlich, D. and Pekruhl, Ulrich. (1996): *Direct Participation and Organisational Change, Fashionable but Misunderstood?* Luxembourg: Office for Official Publications of the European Communities.

Geary, J.F. (1993): "New Forms of Work Organisation and Employee In-volvement in Two Case Study Sites", *Economic and Industrial Democracy*, 14(4): 511–34.

Geary, J.F. (1994): "Task Participation" in Sisson, K. (ed.), *Personnel Management*. Oxford: Blackwell.

Geary, J.F. (1995): "Work Practices: the Structure of Work". In Edwards, P. (ed.), *Industrial Relations*. Oxford: Blackwell.

Geary, J.F. and Sisson, K. (1994): *Conceptualising Direct Participation in Organisational Change*. Luxembourg: Office for Official Publications of the European Communities.

Gunnigle, P., Morley, M., Clifford, N. and Turner, T. (1997): *Human Resource Management in Irish Organisations: Practice in Perspective*. Dublin: Oak Tree Press.

Ichniowski, C., Kochan, T., Levine, D., Olson, C. and Strauss, G. (1996): "What Works at Work?" *Industrial Relations*, 35(3): 299–333.

Kochan, T., Katz, H. and McKersie, R. (1984): *The Transformation of American Industrial Relations*, New York: Basic Books.

Kochan, T. and Osterman, P. (1994): *The Mutual Gains Enterprise: Forging a Winning Partnership among Labor, Management and Government*, Boston Mass.: Harvard Business School Press.

Locke, R., Kochan, T. and Piore, M. (eds.) (1995): *Employment Relations in a Changing World Economy*, Cambridge, Mass.: The MIT Press.

Labour Relations Commission (1996): *A Strategic Policy*, Dublin: Labour Relations Commission

Marchington, M., Wilkinson, A., Ackers, P. and Goodman, J. (1994): "Understanding the Meaning of Participation", *Human Relations*, 47(4): 867–94.

Millward, N., Stevens, M., Smart, D., and Hawes, W.R. (1992): *Workplace Industrial Relations in Transition*. The ED/ESRC/PSI/ACAS Surveys. Aldershot: Dartmouth.

Osterman, P. (1994): "How Common is Workplace Transformation and How Can We Explain Who Adopts it?", *Industrial and Labor Relations Review*, 47(1): 173–187

Pil, F.K. and MacDuffie, P. (1996): "The Adoption of High-Involvement Work Practices", *Industrial Relations*, 35(3): 423–455.

Piore, M. and Sabel, C. (1984): *The Second Industrial Divide*, New York: Basic Books.

Regini, M. (1995): *Uncertain Boundaries: The Social and Political Construction of European Economies*, Cambridge: Cambridge University Press.

Rinehart, J., Huxley, C. and Robertson, D. (1997): *Just Another Car Factory? Lean Production and its Discontents*, Ithaca, NY: Cornell University Press.

Roche, W.K. (1998): "Public Service Reform and Human Resource Management", *CEROP* Working Paper, 24, Graduate School of Business, University College Dublin.

Roche, W.K. and Geary, J.F. (1996): "Multinational Companies in Ireland: Adapting to or Diverging from National Industrial Relations Practices and Traditions?", *Irish Business and Administrative Research*, 17, 14–31.

Roche, W.K. and Geary, J.F. (1998): "Workplace Partnership and Employee Involvement in Irish Workplaces", *CEROP* Working Paper, 26, Graduate School of Business, University College Dublin, forthcoming.

Roche, W.K. and Kochan, T. (1996): "Strategies for Extending Social Partnership to Enterprise and Workplace Levels in Ireland", *Report prepared for the National Economic and Social Council*, July.

Roche, W.K. and Turner, T. (1996): "The Diffusion of the Commitment Model in Ireland", *CEROP* Working Paper, 17, Graduate School of Business, University College Dublin.

Sisson, K. (1995): "Change and Continuity in British Industrial Relations: 'Strategic Choice' or Muddling Through?" In Locke, R., Kochan, T., and Piore, M. (eds.) *Employment Relations in a Changing World Economy*, Cambridge, Mass.: The MIT Press.

Sisson, K. (ed.) (1997): *Towards New Forms of Work Organisation — Can Europe Realise its Innovative Potential? An Interim Report of the Results of the EPOC Questionnaire Survey of Direct Employee Participation in Europe*, Luxembourg: European Foundation/Office for the Official Publication of the European Communities.

Streeck, W. (1995): "Works Councils in Western Europe: From Consultation to Participation", in Rogers, J. and Streeck, W. (eds.) *Works Councils: Consultation, Representation and Co-operation in Industrial Relations*. Chicago: University of Chicago Press.

Walton, R.E. (1985): "From Control to Commitment in the Workplace", *Harvard Business Review*, 53(2): 77–84.

Womack, J., Jones, D., Daniel, T. and Roos, D. (1990): *The Machine that Changed the World*, New York: Rawson Associates.

11

MANAGING ORGANISATIONAL CHANGE

Paul McGrath and *Charles Geaney*

INTRODUCTION

Change has become a pressing reality for most organisations. While change has always been a feature of organisational life one can argue that the situation facing organisations today is substantially different from anything experienced in the past. The latter stages of the twentieth century, a period Reed (1996) refers to as "late modernity", are seeing organisations exposed to ever increasing levels of uncertainty and complexity. The globalisation of business, competition for an increasingly well-educated and mobile workforce, major advances in technology and an increasingly diverse and demanding customer base are examples of these trends. The growing literature on the information or knowledge society provides some interesting insights into these emerging trends. Stehr (1994: 10) sees the trend towards a knowledge society as signalling, "first and foremost a radical transformation in the structure of the economy". This is primarily manifest in terms of a shift away from an economy based on material inputs to one based primarily on symbolic or knowledge-based inputs which are now seen as the engine of much of the dynamics of economic activity. This new combination of factors of production is resulting in a new structure and organisation of economic activity which Stehr categorises into nine specific and interrelated changes:

1. *Diminishing role of primary materials*: Where an apparent collapse in primary commodity prices since the 1960s appear to have had little impact on the world's industrial economy, particularly on the growth in production and consumption.

2. *Changing manufacturing sector*: Increasingly, the technical means of production will shift from experienced-based or craft-based technologies towards knowledge-based technologies — the "scientification of skills". In a knowledge society there is a greater integration of scientific knowledge and technical expertise, linkages or interdependencies among economic sectors become increasingly important and more difficult to differentiate as the distinction between goods and services becomes increasingly ambivalent.

3. *Production against employment*: In knowledge economies the restoration of full-employment will become impossible. There will be an overall decline in the quantity of work available. Technology will have an increasing impact on the service and public sectors which will, in turn, be unable and unwilling to absorb employees displaced from the agrarian and manufacturing sectors.

4. *The social anatomy of work*: In a knowledge society there will be an increasing emphasis on intellectual labour and on knowledge and learning in shaping work and the ability to work. While there is general acceptance that the conditions of work have changed there is no agreement as to whether the management of intellectual labour represents a new paradigm of management or simply a more technologically sophisticated "intellectual assembly line" (Stehr, 1994: 148).

5. From *the employment society to the consumption society*: Consumption becomes increasingly independent from production and changes the specificity of social conflict.

6. *The emergence of the symbolic economy*: Symbolic commodities (knowledge) such as capital movements, exchange rates, credit flows, statistics, fashion regimes, computer programmes are

assuming an increasingly important role in the world economy increasing uncertainty and the rate of obsolescence.

7. *The eclipse of time, distance and place*: As commodities and services increasingly embody knowledge, the constraining nature of time, place and distance diminish allowing for many more locational configurations than was previously the case. This "irrelevance" of time and place is linked with technological advances and the qualities of the objects that need to be moved.

8. *New limits to growth*: The growing centrality of knowledge in the productive process has opened up a whole new set of limits to growth in the global economy.

9. *The fragility of the future*: The economy of knowledge societies will increasingly be subject to a rise in indeterminacy. The fragility of markets and the need of organisations to become more flexible are further compounded by the nature of technological developments by accelerating the malleability of specific contexts. Progress is no longer inevitable.

Clearly the management of change is now top of the managerial agenda and it is a competency around which many managers will make or break their careers. Glib statements from a number of influential management gurus that organisations must radically change (in a specific way) or cease to exist (Kanter, 1983; Peters, 1987 Hammer and Champy, 1992) have become accepted truisms as organisations frenetically busy themselves becoming more responsive, flexible, innovative and adaptive. Despite all this activity and the considerable volume of academic and professional literature on this issue, change management remains a contested and conceptually undeveloped topic. In addition, the slow trickle of literature evaluating planned change efforts consistently indicates that change efforts fail much more frequently than they succeed (Burnes, 1992: 151). Indeed, research into the success of business process re-engineering (BPR), the latest packaged approach to organisational change, is showing failure rates of up to ninety per cent (similar to those experienced with Total Quality Management programmes). We thus have a situation where change is a pressing managerial concern and yet, at both a theoretical and prescriptive level, we appear to have a very limited understanding of the change process and as to how this dynamic process can be managed.

This chapter will attempt to put a loose theoretical and prescriptive framework around the rather messy and complex topic of strategic or large-scale organisational change. The chapter will start with a brief historical overview and critique of the planned change literature. It will then go on to consider a range of practical issues in the areas of environmental responsiveness, diagnosis, transition management and evaluation. The chapter will conclude with a brief examination of the theoretical trends within the organisational change literature and offer some views as to the necessary role of the HR manager within this complex process.

THE PROCESS OF CHANGE

Planned change can be broadly defined as a form of social change involving the application of "systematic and appropriate knowledge of human affairs for the purposes of creating intelligent action and change" (Bennis et al., 1961: 4). Planned organisational change can thus be seen as a deliberate and conscious effort to bring about change in an organisation in response to experienced problems (Beckhard, 1969: 50). Attempts at conceptualising organisational change typically embody two core assumptions. First, most change agents in the planning, design and implementation of organisational change will hold some form of descriptive and normative model of change. Second, organisational change is typically assumed to be an objective phenomenon, a reality occurring outside the mind that is amenable to being directed by managerial action or, in the case of unplanned change, that can at least be proactively responded to in some constructive manner (see Legge, 1984; Wilson, 1992). While we propose working within these two core assumptions it is our intention to highlight their problematic and contested nature. We will return briefly to consider the second assumption when addressing problems around the evaluation of planned change. The first assumption will be considered in this section.

The debate as to how the process of planned organisational change ought to be conceptualised represents a subset of the wider debate within the planning and decision-making literature. An understanding of the long running and still unresolved dispute as to whether planning is a rational/bounded rational (Simon, 1960) or an incremental (Lindblom, 1959) process, or a mixture of both (Etzioni, 1975), is central to understanding the debates within the planned change literature. While there is a considerable volume of literature on theories of planned change, the field has remained theoretically unsophisticated, relying heavily on poor descriptive or programmed theories of change (Wilson, 1992) and a narrowly prescriptive shopping list of do's and don'ts (Pettigrew, 1985: 23).

Change presents itself in a variety of forms to organisations and is generally categorised as either radical or incremental in nature. Radical change programmes are essentially large-scale, organisation-wide transformations which represent a complete break from the past and are typically undertaken in a coercive manner. Such "discontinuous" changes are comprehensive in scale, affecting all aspects of the organisation, involving rapid and wholesale disengagement from the old ways and old ideas and replacing them with new and unique ones. The speed and scale of this kind of change, however, cannot be achieved solely through extensive changes to structures and systems. New forms of behaviour are required including a co-ordinated programme of smaller, more localised projects spread over a longer period of time, designed to establish and build on the central components of the overall programme. Incremental change, by contrast, begins by implementing change projects which are small scale, localised and designed to solve a particular problem or improve the performance of some designated unit of an organisation. This form of change is less dramatic and more evolutionary in nature and tends to result in localised improvement in performance which can merge in the longer-term to give rise to a more comprehensive change strategy.

At the risk of excessively simplifying matters, there are currently two main perspectives on the process of change. The dominant model is the rational-linear model which draws heavily on analytical rationality and "relies on the logic of problem solving, emphasising the phasing of diagnosis, identification of solutions, and implementation" (Buchanan and Boddy, 1992: 27). The traditional project management literature (IT and construction) would fall under this approach as would the highly participative organisational development (OD) approach. OD, to a large extent, represents Western textbook orthodoxy on the management of change (for example Cummings and Worley, 1993; Schermerhorn et al., 1997; Robbins, 1998) and remains the primary approach to organisational change taught in management departments and business schools of most Western universities (Dawson, 1994: 16; Buchanan and Boddy, 1992: 14). It represents a planned, participatory, "normative-reeducative" and long-term approach to improving an organisation's problem solving and renewal processes (French and Bell, 1990). It is typically initiated at the top, data based, consultancy-led and draws heavily on the value system and interventions from the behavioural sciences. OD adopts a simple, unidirectional, linear–rational view of the change process and suggests a "one best way" to manage change with an emphasis on gradual, participatory change aimed at lessening resistance and engendering commitment to the change programme among the workforce. While OD or the "truth, trust, love and collaborative approach to change" (Pettigrew, 1985 quoted in Buchanan and Body, 1992: 14) remains an ethically attractive approach to change its optimistic, idealised values about people and the nature of Western progress have gradually been displaced by a tougher, less optimistic and more pragmatic set of rationalities in the 1970s, 1980s and 1990s (Pettigrew, 1985: 27; Kumar, 1995). Two examples of rational–linear models taken from the OD literature are detailed in Table 11.1.

TABLE 11.1 RATIONAL–LINEAR MODELS OF CHANGE

Lippitt, Watson and Wesley's Phases of Planned Change (1958)	Kolb and Frohman's Process of Planned Change (1970)
Development of a Need for Change	Scouting
Establishment of a Change Relationship	Entry
Diagnosis	Diagnosis
Examination of Alternatives	Planning
Actual Change	Action
Generalisation and Stablisation of Change	Evaluation
Achieving a Terminal Relationship	Termination

Rational–linear models tend to provide neat conceptual models of the change process and simple prescriptive advice both of which tend to be of little use to managers and consultants in managing the complex realities of strategic change. Their prescriptive advice, in particular, while seemingly easy to follow (see Beckhard and Harris, 1987; Burnes, 1992) requires enormous time investment and the support of an experienced project team. In defence of these simplistic rational–linear models, Buchanan and Boddy (1992: 60), while acknowledging both their descriptive and prescriptive limitations, highlight the key symbolic or legitimating role played by these simplistic models as the change agent strives to build support, commitment and establish legitimacy for the change programme.

The second model of change is the contextual or processual approach which emerged from a general dissatisfaction with the rational–linear models which were typically considered to be "ahistorical, aprocessual, and acontextual" (Pettigrew, 1985: 23). The processual approach is broadly sociological in approach viewing change as a cumulative, emergent or incremental process involving a wide range of actors in a complex political, symbolic and ritualistic dynamic. It is a multidisciplinary approach relying heavily on in-depth longitudinal qualitative data and best typified by the work of Pettigrew (1985, 1987), Whipp et al., (1987), Johnson (1987), Clark et al., (1988), Pettigrew and Whipp, (1991) and Dawson (1994). The earlier and influential work by Quinn (1980) is frequently cited as processual in nature. In the Irish context ongoing work by Moore (1995) would broadly fall under this general category. While there are considerable differences between a number of the contextualist studies they all share a common concern with:

- An holistic approach to the issue

- The inner and outer context in which change occurs (a so-called "vertical level" of analysis)

- The content or substance of the change programme (e.g., technology, new working practices etc.) and

- An historical/temporal and non-linear change process (a so-called "horizontal level" of analysis).

As Dawson explains:

> it is the relationship between the content of a specific change strategy, the context in which the change takes place and the process by which it occurs which is the basic analytical framework adopted by the contextualist approach (1994: 23).

Two of the main difficulties encountered in trying to explain the processual approach to change are the depth of detail found in many of the preliminary studies and the evolving nature of the findings and underlying theory. This latter point is primarily a feature of the ongoing nature of the longitudinal qualitative research underlying most, if not all, of the studies. Pettigrew's (1985) detailed study of change at Imperial Chemical Industries (ICI) is a good case in point. A recent interesting and succinct contribution to the processual approach is the work of Dawson (1994). Figure 11.1 presents Dawson's processual framework for analysing and explaining the process of managing organisational transitions.

FIGURE 11.1: DAWSON'S PROCESSUAL FRAMEWORK OF
ORGANISATIONAL CHANGE

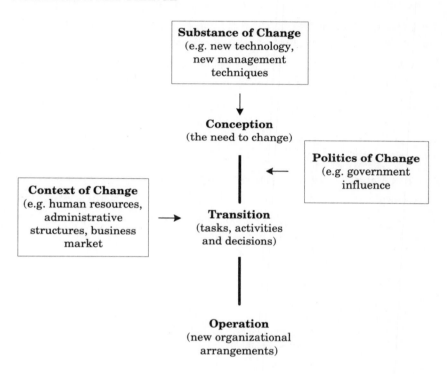

Source: Dawson, (1994: 44).

Dawson breaks the process of change down into three general time frames: conception of a need to change; process of organisational transition; and operation of new work practices and procedures. This simple, temporal and non-linear model provides a useful starting point for the conceptualisation and elaboration of the process of organisational change. The conception of a need to change focuses on the various internal and/or external pressures that cause organisations to change. The process of organisational transition is presented as complex, non-linear and political, involving a diversity of tasks, decisions and activities both within

and outside the organisation. Dawson stresses the non-linear nature of this stage referring to the work of Quinn (1980, 1989) and
his view that strategies are often implemented prior to formulation. The final stage, the operation of new work practices represents the period when the new changes in organisational arrangements and practices are no longer regarded as new, becoming part of the normal operating system. While the change process
continues, often overlapping and being overlapped by and evolving with other change programmes, the situation has stabilised
sufficiently to allow some form of evaluation of the change programme to be undertaken. Within this temporal framework, the
management of change is shaped by three groups of determinants.
The first, the substance of change, entails a strategic decision on
the type and scale of change to be introduced. The second, the
politics of change, concerns the internal and external political activity (consultation, negotiation and conflict management) that
occurs during the process of managing change. The third determinant, the context of change, refers to

> the past and present external and internal operating envi-
> ronments as well as the influence of future projections and
> expectations on current operating practice (Dawson, 1994:
> 42).

This framework with its three general timeframes and three categories of activities provides a conceptually useful device for analysing and explaining the main factors that shape outcomes at
different periods during the process of organisational change.

While the contextualist approach is slowly gaining credibility
in view of its ability to capture the detailed complexities of the
change process, it has been criticised at a number of levels. Contextual studies tend to improve our understanding of the complexities of the change process but typically have difficulty in developing this understanding into an agenda for action (Argyris,
1988; Buchanan and Boddy, 1992). In particular, the rich nature
of the data produced has tended to "mask, mystify and create barriers of interpretation to the non-academic practitioner who seeks

practical tools for action" (Dawson, 1994: 25). Questions have also been raised about the quality of the theoretical generalisations emerging from this approach given that the studies tend to be based on a very small number of case studies. While acknowledging the limitation and complexity of the contextualist approach, we propose using Dawson's (1994) processual framework of organisational change as a basic device to structure our consideration of three central in the management of change namely the context or why of change, managing the transition and evaluating change programmes.

In this section we have focused on the contextualist or processual approach to change. We wish to emphasise the viewpoint that planned organisational change is not a simple linear–rational issue as portrayed in much of the popular management literature but a complex, non-linear, emergent process where rationality and politics are closely intertwined and the management of meaning is of crucial importance (Pettigrew, 1985: 442). Effective change management requires the skilful and simultaneous management of the content, context and process of change. While there are still considerable debates and disputes as to how this complex challenge can best be achieved, the remainder of this chapter will attempt to offer some constructive advice based on cases of strategic change in a range of Irish companies and our own consulting experience. The next section will start this process exploring the context or the "why" of the change process focusing on organisational diagnosis.

THE CONTEXT OF CHANGE

Ongoing environmental assessment is vital for organisational survival and an essential feature of effective change management. This section will explore the issue of general environmental assessment (the external context) within the process of change and incorporate consideration of the internal context as part of this diagnostic dynamic.

Most academic texts on managing change tend to present organisations as simple open systems that must constantly adapt to their environment or cease to exist (French and Bell, 1990; Dyer, 1984). This open systems approach sees organisations as living organisms (Morgan, 1986: Ch. 3) composed of a set of interrelated subsystems that constantly interact with each other and with the external environment. Organisations are seen as having a natural equilibrium or steady state which is achieved and maintained when the internal subsystems are internally congruent and are in harmony with the external environment. The OD and contingency approaches to change embrace this open systems perspective in a highly deterministic manner. It is particularly in evidence in the value system and diagnostic models used within these approaches. This deterministic acceptance of open-systems theory tends to give rise to a general neglect of the socially constructed nature of both organisations and environments and the potential for autonomous action within organisations. In addition their excessive concern with subsystem harmony tends to present an unrealistically unitarist perspective on organisational functioning.

The contextualist approach to change also places a strong emphasis on the need to be open and responsive to both the internal and external environment but in a much less deterministic manner and with a less passive role for the organisation and its employees. It also place an emphasis on past experiences and future projections and expectations (Dawson, 1994). With the increasing turbulence of Western economies in recent years has come a recognition that organisations must understand and act upon environmental information if they are to compete effectively but also a realisation that traditional approaches to environmental analysis (industrial/organisational economics and professional business planning) are proving inadequate to the task. Pettigrew and Whipp (1993) found in their study that organisations which successfully understood and acted upon their environment tended to exhibit four identifiable features:

1. They did not view environmental assessment as an isolated technical activity but as a sequence of actions involving analysis, judgement and action across time.

2. They recognised that the assessment process is shaped equally by influences from the specific industry (the external context) and by the internal nature of the firm itself (the internal context).

3. They recognised that environmental assessment must not be a specialist activity but should occur across the different functions and levels of the organisation, each of which has a slightly different connection with and perspective upon the environment.

4. They accepted that the process of analysis, judgement and action is not a neat, rational one but is uncertain and contested requiring individual sensing and collective "sense-making" if it is to result in meaningful action.

A crucial feature of these organisations is that they are open to their environment, are receptive to changes within their environment and have a capacity to act upon and learn from the data generated over time — in effect they are becoming learning organisations.

The external or outer context of the contextual approach, outlined above, focuses on the firms' general and specific environment (competitors' strategies, demographic changes, government legislation, technological innovations, etc.). The internal or inner context focuses on the structure, politics and culture of the firm itself. It is this inner context which is the primary focus of the extensive literature on organisational diagnosis which is a central feature of the OD and contingency approaches. Again one finds an emphasis on open-systems theory with the various interconnected sub-systems, which make up the totality, open to and interacting with each other. A change which may occur in one part of the system will have a consequential impact on other parts of the system, resulting in some affect on overall performance. The open-systems approach to change is based on diagnosing problems in sub-systems, to determine how they should be changed in order to achieve desired improvements in the total system. The objective of this approach is to structure the interdependent functions of an organisation to establish a general alignment between the respective sub-systems to ensure that the goals of the business are collectively pursued. The emphasis is on achieving overall synergy, rather than optimising the performance of individual subsystems. While diagnostic models based on systems theory are intuitively attractive and generally useful they are limited in their ability to conceptualise the complex realities of organisational life. The application of systems theory to organisations generally has been criticised in that it does present a rather orderly, indeed unitarist image of organisational life and can easily lead to managerialism (see Thompson and McHugh, 1995; Morgan, 1985: 3).

While conceptually limited, organisational diagnostic models are fundamental to effective diagnosis and change. They provide a framework for generating diagnostic data and for arranging them into meaningful patterns so that appropriate change strategies can be developed and implemented. The diagnostic process generates a phenomenal amount of information and to plan for effective change this diagnostic data must be identified and organised into appropriate categories. The dynamic manner in which these categories interrelate must be examined and understood prior to application. In this way diagnostic models force managers to be explicit about desired outcomes and how intended changes will affect these outcomes. Unfortunately, at a practical level one is faced with a bewildering range of well known diagnostic models ranging from Lewin's simple technique of force-field to a range of systems-based consultancy and academic models. Examples include McKinsey's Seven S framework; Weisbord's Six Box Model, 1976; Nadler and Tushman's Congruence Model, 1980; Beer's Social Systems Model, 1980.

Most models include the general environmental system as a component and then typically organise around a list of internal subsystems. Figure 11.2 illustrates Beer's Social Systems Model.

FIGURE 11.2: A SOCIAL SYSTEMS MODEL OF ORGANISATIONS

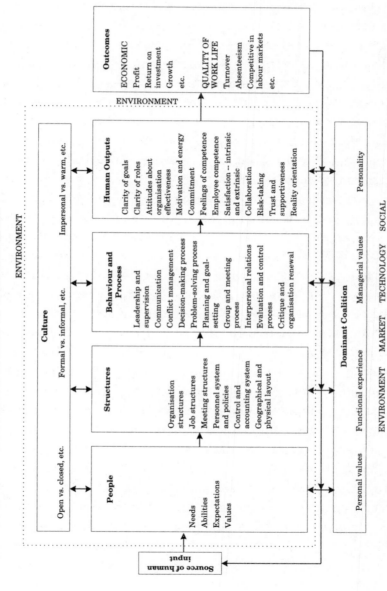

Source: Beer (1980) p38.

Based on systems theory, Beer's model identifies eight major organisational components which need to be congruent for an organisation to be effective. The model is useful in terms of its relative comprehensive nature, its dynamic character and its emphasis on the close interdependencies between each of the eight components. The model starts with the employees of the firm and the qualities they bring to the organisation and ends with their attitudes and psychological states (human outputs). Structures (controls, procedures, rewards) shape employee behaviour and the processes by which they interact. Structure and process together aid the development of a psychological contract between the employees and the organisation. Culture is developed through the interaction of people, structure, behaviour and process but, in turn influences these four components. The dominant coalition, the key decision-makers, influence and are influenced by the various components. Organisational outcomes are a function of the interaction of the previous six components and a reflection of the performance of the organisation in its market and social and technological environment. The loose nature of the model implies a highly contingent view of management (Beer, 1980: 37). A desired outcome must first be chosen and then management must set about deciding on one of many possible fit combinations between the various components of the system. As internal and external components are constantly changing management must regularly reconfigure the organisation bearing in mind issues of efficiency, effectiveness and health (Beer, 1980: 39).

Choice of diagnostic model is very much dictated by the type and nature of the organisation undergoing change. Guidelines are offered in the literature (Harrison, 1987; Burke, 1994) but tend to be rather simplistic and unhelpful. None of the models are perfect and some positively unworkable. Box 11.1 details a diagnostic process undertaken at the Mater Private Hospital.

BOX 11.1: DIAGNOSIS AT THE MATER PRIVATE HOSPITAL

The Mater Private Hospital (MPH) is a company within the Mater Misericordiae Hospital complex. It is wholly owned by the Sisters of Mercy. Two key staff appointments were important precursors to a major change programme currently being undertaken within MPH. November, 1996 saw the arrival of a new human resource manager and in January, 1997 a new managing director, an engineer by profession, was appointed. While MPH was and is successful and leading the field in certain areas of medical practice, the new MD clearly saw a need for major change and called in the assistance of a change consultant. At a series of meetings the MD outlined his views on the situation facing the hospital. The external environment was perceived as becoming more uncertain primarily due to changing customer needs and demands. While the technology in MPH was largely state-of-the-art, it was facing a range of technological investment decisions which would have a major impact on the nature and type of service it provided. In addition, increasing competition in the provision of medical health insurance within Ireland (the result of legislative moves within the European Union to deregulate the market) was causing problems for the hospital.

Focusing on the internal diagnosis of MPH, the MD saw a leading-edge, technologically sophisticated hospital. The staff were highly trained, open to technological change and extremely professional in outlook and behaviour. In striving for increased performance, quality and, in particular, ever-increasing levels of customer satisfaction the MD saw the need for new internal systems to provide improved managerial control and feedback on performance at both the technological and social level. There was a clear need for management to improve its co-ordination of organisational performance, heighten its leadership role and to adopt a more proactive role in motivating the employees. The existing reward system, a straightforward salary payment system, was seen as inadequate in motivating performance. The existing two-tier structure, while very organic, was highly dependent upon informal arrangements relying upon local staff anticipating and reacting to issues and taking necessary initiatives. Communications and decision-making, as a consequence, tended to take place on a rather ad hoc basis.

While the MD saw distinct advantages associated with this highly organic set of arrangements he also saw a need for more formal and clearly defined structural arrangements and systems including a more proactive approach to conflict management. What was needed was an organic and adaptable system with appropriate levels of autonomy, responsibility and accountability.

Following these early meetings it was agreed between the MD, the HR manager and the change consultant that a diagnostic workshop involving the top management group would be arranged and implemented. An open-systems diagnostic model to match the requirements of the organisation was developed by the consultant. The purpose of the model was to facilitate the organisation of the data to be gathered, to ensure that all relevant subsystems received attention and to focus the effort of the workshop participants. This process produced an overall diagnostic report. Following the workshop it was decided to establish a steering group which would handle the continued elaboration of the diagnostic process. Individual members of the steering group extended the process down throughout the rest of the organisation through the use of individual and group interviews. Use was also made of secondary data sources within MPH including financial and other numerical records and past reports and business plans. This phase of the diagnostic process continued for five months and ended with the production of a detailed report on overall organisational effectiveness within MPH and a clear, detailed set of recommendations for change. At the time of writing a change programme within the hospital had just been initiated.

Source: Authors.

MANAGING THE PROCESS OF ORGANISATIONAL TRANSITION

Based on an analysis of the context of change an organisation may decide to undertake a certain type and scale of change. In each case an understanding of the particular characteristics of certain types of change (e.g. the enabling and constraining potentiality of new technology) is an important prerequisite to the subsequent process of effectively managing the process. Organisational change tends to be represented as a three-phase process which takes the organisation from its present state with its current problems and moves it through a transition stage to achieve a desired future state as its ultimate goal. The central objective of any change programme is to establish a clearly defined future state with its component systems clearly aligned.

No single approach or structure can be recommended in managing the transition processes from the present organisational state to a desired new one. Each organisation must develop its own strategy to match its own unique needs, culture and business imperatives. The transition process itself tends to be complex and non-linear. In reality it is not possible to select a single issue and pursue it rationally to a conclusion. In most situations it is necessary to pursue a number of change goals simultaneously and the change goals themselves need to be continuously reviewed and altered and sometimes abandoned. Instead of one centralised, charismatic leader, it is necessary to rely on teams of collaborating individuals who hammer out the emerging details of a change process through bargaining and compromise. No matter how carefully leaders prepare for change and no matter how realistic and committed they are, there will always be factors outside their control that may have a profound impact on the success of the change process.

The literature on the implementation of change generally presents two alternative approaches regarding system-wide change and the need to motivate others: top down and bottom up (Lupton, 1986). Top-down change is essentially a unilateral approach where changes are implemented through the authority of the organisation's senior management. Assuming that people actually respond to such decisions in the manner expected by senior management, these changes can be implemented very rapidly. Bottom-up change is the opposite approach to autocratic top-down changes, where senior management empower the lower levels to identify and define problems and implement solutions. This approach to change is generally slower, but its potential advantage results in greater commitment to the change in question. Most interest at present tends to be focusing on a shared or jointly directed approach (Beer, 1980).

Turning to the issue of the conditions for successful change management a review of a cross-section of the literature would suggest that the following issues need to be addressed:

- Change in any organisation is not simply a matter of dictate from the top. In order to ensure success, management must become a role model for the lower levels, take the initiative and be seen to be actively participating in the change process. Effective change is unlikely to occur in organisations unless top management is actively committed, able and willing to exercise the necessary influence within the overall system.

- Slack resources, primarily in the form of additional human and financial resources, must be made available to facilitate the implementation of the change programme, if day-to-day operations are to be maintained at existing levels.

- The key stakeholders in the system must be identified and their active support enlisted in implementing the change.

- Committees, task forces and workshops tend to be effective mechanisms to expand political support and desired outcomes can be positively influenced through the co-options of selected members onto committees.

- Initial risk taking by those managing the change is vital. Highly visible public initiatives which require the commitment of resources, management time and energy, and which seek reciprocal action by lower levels, can help build the commitment to the change programme.

- Build on existing strengths and legitimate alternative viewpoints by creating forums to discuss issues and evaluate options.

- Early success is important and it is advisable to provide the necessary rewards to maintain momentum and commitment to the change programme.

- Continue to communicate the change vision to ensure both understanding and agreement. Maintain overall focus by stating the change goals in clear concrete terms and actively build consensus around them.

A specific issue that needs to receive special attention during diagnosis and during and after implementation is resistance to change. There are a number of reasons why employees (including managers) react differently to change — from passively resisting it, to aggressively undermining it, to indifference, to sincerely embracing it. Managers need to be aware of the four most common reasons why people resist change. These include a desire not to loose something of value, a misunderstanding of the change and its implications, a belief that the change does not make sense for the organisation and lastly a low tolerance of change. Kotter and Schlesinger's (1979) classic contribution on the issue of dealing with resistance remains one of the seminal works on this topic. Their six categories of strategies for dealing with resistance represent a continuum extending from education and communication, participation and involvement, facilitation and support, (more appropriate with slow, incremental change focusing on involvement and minimising resistance) to negotiation and agreement, to explicit and implicit coercion (more appropriate with rapid, clearly planned changes where resistance is to be overcome). Each approach has specific advantages and disadvantages and choice is guided by four situational factors namely the extent of resistance anticipated, the relative power of the initiator, the diagnostic abilities and energy of the initiator and the size of the stake involved. The best choice of approach is rarely obvious and a compromise strategy is a normal outcome.

The OD literature is particularly strong on the more democratic and collaborative strategies for dealing with resistance (see for example Beckhard and Harris, 1987; Cummings and Worley, 1993). Two good contributions on the use of more coercive or "backstage" strategies are Kanter (1983) and Buchanan and Boddy (1992).

By way of summary, successful change management can be aided by seeking a desired future state where the social system components display good overall alignment and possess the following broad characteristics:

- Structures, systems and processes become more organic, developing and fostering trust, ownership and goal congruence.

- Work environment becomes regenerative, providing involvement and potential for personal growth.

- Management/Staff relations are characterised by a climate of mutual trust and a collaborative approach to problem solving.

- The organisation is managed and staffed by personnel with the required technical and social skills to compete effectively.

Box 11.2 details a range of transition activities undertaken in International Office Furniture (IOF), an Irish subsidiary of a division of a US multinational.

BOX 11.2: MANAGING THE TRANSITION AT IOF

IOF began its manufacturing operations with the central objective of supplying the European market. Within 12 months of commencement of the Irish operations a decision was made to sell off the firm's US parent. A decision was also made to retain the Irish subsidiary with the intention of operating independently by developing the European market. A recruitment embargo was imposed on the Irish subsidiary and at the time it was estimated that the firm was operating at around 50 per cent of its staffing requirement. As a consequence, if the organisation was going to develop and function effectively, a complete redesign based on total flexibility was required.

An in-depth diagnosis of both technical and social systems was launched. A project group composed of a diagonal slice across the entire organisation was established to carry out in-depth interviews, design and analyse questionnaires and implement diagnostic workshops on the social component of the organisation. A separate group was established to evaluate the existing production system and recommend alternative designs.

An intensive diagnostic period lasting approximately four months covering the entire organisation culminated in the production of a wide range of evaluative data from which a number of design decision could be made. The thirty-six members of staff involved in administering the process to date were then brought together in a two day intensive workshop to address issues and recommend a change plan. Two groups were formed which separately addressed the social and technical issues raised in the diagnosis. When each group had made its recommendations the groups were alternated to critically re-examine the conclusions reached and suggest appropriate modifications. As a third stage in the workshop process subgroups were established to combine technical and social components and make recommendations consistent with an organic team based system which would exhibit total flexibility.

Implementation of the change plan involved the establishment of teams around six core processes identified during the socio-technical analysis. Team boundaries were specified allowing a high level of autonomous operation. Each team had its own management structure which included a team leader, a production controller, a quality controller, a trainer and a financial controller. These roles rotated on a regular basis to support ownership of all team issues and flexible behaviour. Teams were restricted to a maximum size of 15 members and were to be self-controlling and accountable for performance within the boundary. At the beginning of each shift a meeting of all staff was held where team leaders delivered a factual account of performance and identified specific problems to be addressed by the incoming shift. Staff members with an input to problems identified were expected to meet on a cross-team, cross-functional basis to address the issue and implement a solution. The autonomous structure with supporting roles allowed performance within each team to be measured on a value-added basis thereby supporting an overall improved managerial orientation and greater accountability.

The logic of the team design encouraged the development of a strong managerial ethos within each team. The role behaviour of team members supported and drove new attitudes and thinking. A team/skills-based rewards system was designed to support the overall structure. The existing supervisor and middle-manager grade moved from the traditional, mechanistic and centralised approach to a more organic approach of facilitating cross-boundary operations and as an expert support within team boundaries as required.

> This move from a mechanistic to a more commitment-based system now required that all aspects of team life be managed within the team boundary including problem-solving, decision-making, conflict management, etc. An intensive training and development programme was implemented to provide each team with the necessary skills and knowledge to carry out all functions.
>
> The change programme was evaluated on a range of different levels which included team performance and flexibility, performance at the level of the organisation and satisfaction and performance at the level of the individual. Independent performance evaluation overall was carried out by the financial controller based in head office in the US. Other than a continuing high level of absenteeism, performance within IOF was estimated to have improved by 64 per cent over a 12-month period.

Source: Authors.

EVALUATING THE CHANGE PROCESS

The evaluation of planned change is one of the least researched and discussed topics in the field. It tends to get a brief mention in most texts, typically as the penultimate stage in the linear/rational change process (prior to termination). Most authors agree that it is essential to assess the actual impact of change on those involved and see it as vital that the initial planning of the change should determine in advance how success or failure should be measured (Dyer, 1984). However, beyond these simple platitudes there is little detail as to how, if at all, this can be achieved. Tichy (1983: 363) suggests that most of the change programmes undertaken over the past two decades, involving billions of dollars, had virtually no systematic monitoring or evaluation. He goes on to outline a number of technical (e.g. the measurement of culture change, its impact on the bottom line and relating these back to specific actions of the change programme), political (e.g. over-advocacy of a programme resulting in managers and consultants having a vested interest in hiding poor results) and cultural forces (national cultural biases against evaluation and monitoring and subsequent adjustment to the "grand strategy") which act against the development of systematic evaluation. These forces, allied with the current Western management preoccupation with the "quick fix", management myopia about the realities of change and the need to learn from our mistakes represent considerable impediments to the insightful evaluation of change.

Cummings and Worley (1993) identify two types of change evaluation programmes. The first type is evaluation to guide the actual implementation and the second assesses the overall impact of the change programme. Our concern here is with both forms. Following the basic model of the processual approach to change outlined above, evaluation needs to focus systematically on the internal and external context, on the actual transition and on the outcomes of the change programme. The issue of contextual assessment has already been adequately addressed. As the change programme progresses the accuracy of the initial diagnosis needs to be checked. During the transition, assessment should highlight and evaluate the underlying implicit assumptions made during diagnosis, planning and implementation about the organisation and its employees. Faulty assumptions must be corrected. The effectiveness of specific interventions (e.g. job redesign, team building) must also be assessed as the organisation proceeds through the transition. Finally, hard data needs to be gathered on the overall, bottom-line impact of the change programme. Its impact on productivity, quality, worker attitudes, absenteeism, turnover, etc., relative to the cost of the programme, need to be established. Box 11.3 provides an overview of a change evaluation programme undertaken at Bord na Móna during its experimental introduction of autonomous work groups.

BOX 11.3: EVALUATING CHANGE AT BORD NA MÓNA

Bord na Móna is a commercial semi-state company with four operating divisions all focused around the development and exploitation of natural peat resources. In 1988, in the face of major changes in its business environment and a seriously declining financial performance, the company initiated a wide range of radical changes. A key component of the change strategy concerned the introduction, on an experimental basis, of new work systems (employee enterprise units, autonomous working groups and autonomous enterprise units). These experimental work systems were introduced following extensive management and union negotiations. The design of these new work systems was developed around team structures, job enrichment, employee empowerment and self-regulation and reward for results. A key aim was the successful optimisation of the social and technical work systems in the organisation. By 1991 41 groups or units were in operation involving around 570 employees (out of a total workforce of 2,100 permanent employees).

A joint management/union monitoring group was established to evaluate the new work systems. As part of the ongoing evaluation process it was decided to have an independent assessment of the more qualitative dimensions of the work group innovations. A researcher from the Social Science Research Centre, University College Dublin was recruited for this purpose. This particular project was supervised by a committee composed of representatives from management, the unions and the external research body. The purpose of the study was to gather relevant qualitative information and knowledge about the workings of the system which would, in turn, aid organisational learning and future planning. Ten work groups were randomly selected for investigation. In-depth semi-structured interviews were undertaken with all group leaders and a random sample of 48 non-core group members (permanent and seasonal employees) within these ten groups between December, 1990 and April, 1991. A range of qualitative issues were examined including levels of entrepreneurial behaviour, flexibility and adaptability, teamwork, innovation, attitude change and general effectiveness. A synthesis report of the study was subsequently published in December, 1991.

While the study identified a number of minor design problems in connection with the operation and design of the work group innovations, the findings were predominantly positive. In particular, it was found that employee work motivation increased substantially. While this was partially attributable to an increase in monetary rewards associated with the new reward system, the study results clearly indicated that participants, particularly core members, were now being provided with conditions for high job satisfaction and quality of work life. This extensive qualitative data complemented a substantial amount of quantitative data on a range of operational and performance measures already available within the company.

Overall, the review of the new work systems indicated a wide range of positive qualitative and quantitative outcomes associated with the change programme at both the individual and organisational level. It was acknowledged, however, that the period in which the evaluation was carried out coincided with a period of excellent weather resulting in extremely favourable harvesting. The new work system is now established within the company and its extension is being considered. The system continues to be under continuous review and development.

Source: Faughnan (1991); Magee (1992); O'Connor (1995).

While the evaluation of a change programme seems an intuitively simple task it does face considerable problems. Apart from the forces acting against the need for accurate evaluation outlined above there are considerable methodological problems in rigorously analysing the impact of a specific intervention while trying to control for other ongoing activities and change programmes. It can be very time consuming given that the outcomes may take some time to materialise and one may need to consider first, second and third order changes. It can also be a very costly business particularly if external evaluators/researchers are involved. The frequent involvement of external consultants in the change process can add a further level of complexity to this issue. Alvesson (1993) provides an interesting discussion on the high level of ambiguity that accompanies any attempted evaluation of the work results of knowledge-intensive firms. He suggests that there are currently no reliable criteria for evaluating knowledge-intensive work involving experts in conditions of high uncertainty and considers that consumers of expert services often have little understanding of or insight into the quality of these external services. He adds a further complication in terms of the placebo effect of this type of work. He explains

> To separate out any consequences of "expert knowledge" from the placebo effect in, for example, management consulting is not just empirically very complicated but also theoretically misleading. The belief and expectations of the client are a necessary, indeed a crucial component of success (1993: 1006).

This latter point brings us back to a point raised at the start of this chapter concerning the dominant assumption that organisational change is typically assumed to be an objective phenomenon, a reality occurring outside the mind, amenable to being directed by managerial action and thus positivistically and objectively evaluated. As doubts about the tenability of this position within organisational studies continue to mount consideration needs to be given to the design of a more interpretative form of evaluation (see Legge, 1984).

MANAGING CHANGE AND THE HR FUNCTION

The role of the personnel/human resource (P/HR) professional in the management of organisational change is an under-researched issue. Surprisingly this is a topic that is rarely given specific consideration in most personnel/human resource texts (Torrington and Hall, 1991; Storey and Sissons, 1993; Legge, 1995; Towers, 1996; Gunnigle and Flood, 1990; French, 1994). Irish personnel/human resource texts are unusual in this regard in that they do normally raise the issue of managing change. There is an extensive critical and descriptive literature on the nature of contemporary changes facing organisations today (Galbraith, 1967; Toffler, 1980; Huber, 1982; Atkinson, 1984; Piore and Sabel, 1984; Pollert, 1991; Davidow and Malone, 1992; Clegg, 1992; Drucker, 1993;

Handy, 1994;). While a wide range of interpretations have been put forward as to the nature and direction of these contemporary changes, a significant and commonly shared point among the majority of these works is that

> something is going on: economic, ecological, personal, social and cultural uncertainties are being experienced on an unprecedented scale. Institutional frameworks and individual cognitions are being stretched to, and perhaps beyond, the limits of their capabilities (Blackler et al., 1993: 857).

It is also clear that if these changes are to be effected successfully then the human resources of these organisations must become the central focus of concern (Senge, 1990; Nonaka, 1994; Blackler, 1995). From this perspective one would expect the P/HR function to play a central role in the management of change but the limited research evidence available would not support this case.

Moore (1995), drawing on research by Fombrun (1986), Schuler and Jackson, (1987) and her own qualitative research, stresses the need for integrating the industrial relations and personnel management functions into the overall strategic change process of the organisation. In her view, the traditional role of the industrial relations practitioner in particular, has been to deal with the effects of strategic change without having any substantive input into planning and implementation issues. (p. 59). The ability of the P/HR function to become more involved in strategic change is tied up with the general role of this function within the organisation. Foley and Gunnigle (1994) found a tentatively favourable situation for the P/HR function in certain types of Irish companies (primarily unionised, foreign-owned companies) with

> a trend towards higher strategic integration of the personnel/human resource function, a move towards greater board level participation and a potentially greater impact on the strategic direction of the organisation (1994: 50).

While these changes would appear to indicate an increasing "change-maker/architect" role for the P/HR function, Foley and

Gunnigle's research into the specialist activities and core future objectives of this function does not show any indication of ownership of the strategic change process or even a direct concern with the strategic change process (1994: 51). Clearly further research is needed on this topic.

CURRENT TRENDS IN THE LITERATURE ON THE MANAGEMENT OF CHANGE AND THE STATE OF RESEARCH ON MANAGING CHANGE IN IRELAND

We wish to conclude this chapter with a tentative consideration of the current direction of the literature on managing change and a brief synopsis of the state of research on this topic in Ireland. It is rather difficult to draw any firm conclusions about the current state of play or indeed current direction of the literature on planned organisational change. The field continues to grow rapidly but in a relatively diverse and uncoordinated manner. At a conceptual level there is a healthy level of debate with new and interesting contributions from areas such as complexity theory (Stacey, 1995), chaos theory (Wheatly, 1992) and postmodernism (Dibella, 1992). These debates can be seen as a microcosm of the healthy theoretical ferment ongoing within organisational studies generally. At a more pragmatic level, one clear trend in evidence in the organisation behaviour (OB) literature on change is a shift away from the strongly behavioural and consensual approach to change typified by the traditional OD literature towards an approach with a more managerial, contingent and strategic orientation. Indeed, one could argue that the relatively recent concern with strategic change is providing a useful and desirable focal point for the successful merging of the OB and strategic management literatures. It is to be expected that these two areas will continue to experience an increasing level of integration in considerations about the management of organisational change. Within the strategic change literature, a further encouraging trend is the apparent merging of the rational–linear and processual perspectives on change at both a methodological and theoretical level (see Johnson, 1987: 60; Buchanan and Boddy, 1992,

Ch. 3) with the attendant favourable increase in conceptual depth allied to understandable perscriptive advice for managers and practitioners. However, as things stand at present Pettigrew's cautionary advice to "beware of the myth of the singular theory of social or organisational change" (1985: 1) still holds true.

On the research front in Ireland one is struck by the low level of significant research focusing directly on organisational change and its management. While much management and organisational research is ultimately concerned with issues of change, the number of contributions dealing directly with the process and management (diagnosis, implementation and evaluation) of organisational change is low. A number of reasons can be put forward for this relatively low level of research activity into such an important topic. First, change management has become such a diverse and multidisciplinary topic that it frequently falls between established academic disciplines and as such is avoided as a topic of investigation. Second, quality research into managing change typically involves a significant investment in time and money both of which are typically in short supply. Finally, there appears to be a general unwillingness among both indigenous and foreign-owned companies in Ireland to allow research access and/or publication of their change experiences. One can only hope that this culture of secrecy will change as organisations realise that they have much to learn from each other's experiences.

Despite the problems associated with undertaking research into organisational change there have been a number of interesting Irish contributions on the topic a sample of which is detailed below. Coughlan (1994) and Rashford and Coughlan (1994) have undertaken work on the nature of the change process with a particular focus on intervention methods and styles. Leavy (1991, 1994, 1997), through a range of Irish case studies, has examined the process of strategic and/or transformational change with a particular emphasis on the role of leadership. Mapstone (1994) is examining the complex dynamic of change within the Royal Irish Regiment with a particular focus on the unique and historical inner and outer context of change in that case. McHugh (1996,

1998) has examined behavioural issues in the implementation of strategic change concentrating on stress. Finally, Hill (1993) has carried out some work on implementation, measurement and evaluation issues primarily within the context of TQM in an educational environment.

CONCLUSIONS

To conclude, this chapter has presented a brief overview of a number of important themes and issues around the topic of managing organisational change. The content of the chapter was loosely structured around a contextualist or processual model stressing the view that planned organisational change is not a simple rational–linear issue but a complex, political, non-linear and emergent process. Buchanan and Boddy (1992: 27) talk about successful change requiring the blending of the logic of problem-solving, the logic of establishing ownership of the change in those directly affected and the logic of establishing legitimacy of the behaviour of the change agent. This complex reality is frequently ignored in much of the literature on the planned organisational change. Finally, it is clear that the level of research into this issue in an Irish context is inadequate and that the field would benefit considerably from a coherent and integrated national research agenda.

References

Alvesson, M. (1993): "Organizations as Rhetoric: Knowledge-Intensive Firms and the Struggle with Ambiguity", *Journal of Management Studies*, 30(6): 997–1015.

Anthony, P.D. (1990): "The Paradox of Management Culture or He Who Leads is Lost", *Personnel Review*, 19: 3–8.

Argyris, C. (1988): "Review Essay: First- and Second-order Errors in Managing Strategic Change: The Role of Organizational Defensive Routines" in Pettigrew, A.M. (ed.), *The Management of Strategic Change*, Oxford: Blackwell.

Atkinson, J. (1985): "Manpower Strategies for Flexible Organizations" *Personnel Management*, August.

Beckhard, R. (1969): *Organization Development. Strategies and Models*, Reading, Mass.: Addison-Wesley.

Beckhard, R. and Harris, R. (1987): *Organizational Transitions: Managing Complex Change*, Reading, Mass.: Addison-Wesley.

Beer, M. (1980): *Organizational Change and Development — A Systems View*, Santa Monica, CA: Goodyear.

Bennis, W.G., Benne, K.D. and Chin, R. (1961): *The Planning of Change*, New York: Rinehart and Winston.

Blackler, F., Reed, M. and Whitaker, A. (1993): "Editorial Introduction: Knowledge Workers and Contemporary Organizations", *Journal of Management Studies*, 30(6): 851–862.

Blackler, F., (1995): "Knowledge, Knowledge Work and Organizations: An Overview and Interpretation", *Organization Studies*, 16(6): 1021–1046.

Buchanan, D. and Boddy, D. (1992): *The Expertise of the Change Agent. Public Performance and Backstage Activity*, London: Prentice Hall.

Burke, W. (1994): *Organization Development: A Process of Learning and Changing*, Reading, Mass.: Addison-Wesley.

Burnes, B. (1992): *Managing Change*, London: Pitman.

Clark, J., McLoughlin, I., Rose, H. and King, R. (1988): *The Process of Technological Change: New Technology and Social Choice in the Workplace*, Cambridge: Cambridge University Press.

Clegg, S. (1990): *Modern Organizations: Organization Studies in a Postmodern World*, Sage: London.

Coughlan, D. (1994) "Research as a Process of Change: Action Science in Organisations", *Irish Business and Administrative Research*, 15: 119–130.

Cummings, T. and Worley, C (1993): *Organization Development and Change*, St. Paul, MN: West.

Davidow, W.H. and Malone, M.S. (1992): *The Virtual Corporation*, New York: Harper.

Dawson, P. (1994): *Organizational Change: A Processual Approach*, London: Paul Chapman.

Dibella, A. (1992) "Planned Change in an Organized Anarchy: Support for a Postmodern Perspective", *Journal of Organizational Change Management*, 5(3): 55–65.

Drucker, P. (1993): *Post-Capitalist Society*. Oxford: Butterworth-Heinemann.

Dyer, W.G. (1984): *Strategies for Managing Change*, Reading, Mass.: Addison-Wesley.

Etzioni, A. (1975): *A Comparative Analysis of Complex Organizations*, New York: Free Press.

Faughnan, P. (1991): *The Dynamics of Work Group Operation in Bord Na Móna*, Synthesis Report, Social Science Research Centre, University College Dublin, July.

Foley, K. and Gunnigle, P. (1994): "The Personnel/Human Resource Function and Employee Relations" in Gunnigle, P., Flood, P., Morley M. and Turner, T. (eds.), *Continuity and Change in Irish Employee Relations*, Dublin: Oak Tree Press.

Fombrun, C. (1986): "Environmental Trends Create New Pressures on Human Resources" in Rynes, S.L. and Milkovich, G.T. (eds.), *Current Issues in Human Resource Management*, Plano, TX: Business Publications Inc.

French, W. (1994): *Human Resource Management*, Boston, Mass.: Houghton Mifflin.

French, W. and Bell, C. (1990): *Organization Development. Behavioral Science Interventions for Organizational Improvement*, Englewood Cliffs, NJ: Prentice Hall.

Galbraith, J. (1967): *The New Industrial State*, Boston, Mass.: Houghton Mifflin.

Gunnigle, P. and Flood, P. (1990): *Personnel Management in Ireland. Practice, Trends and Developments*, Dublin: Gill and Macmillan.

Hammer M. and Champy J. (1993): *Reengineering the Corporation; A Manifesto for Business Revolution*, New York: Harper Business.

Handy, C. (1994): *The Empty Raincoat*, London: Hutchinson.

Harrison, M.I. (1887): *Diagnosing Organizations. Methods, Models, and Processes*, Newbury Park, CA: Sage.

Hill, F.M. (1993): "An Evaluative Study of the Attitudinal and Performance-Related Outcomes of Quality Circle Participation", *International Journal of Quality and Reliability Management*, 10(4): 28–47.

Huber, G.P. (1984): "The Nature and Design of Post-Industrial Organizations", *Management Science*, 30(8), August.

Johnson, G. (1987): *Strategic Change and the Management Process*, Oxford: Basil Blackwell.

Kanter, R.M. (1983): *The Change Masters: Corporate Entrepreneurs at Work*, London: George Allen & Unwin.

Kolb, D. and Frohman, A. (1970): "An Organization Development Approach to Consulting", *Sloan Management Review*, 12(1): 51–65.

Kotter, J. and Schlesinger, L. (1979): "Choosing Strategies for Change", *Harvard Business Review*, March/April: 106–114.

Kumar, K. (1995): *From Post-Industrial to Post-Modern Society*, Oxford: Blackwell.

Lawrence, P. and Lorsch, J. (1967): *Organization and Environment*, Cambridge, Mass.: Harvard University Press.

Leavy, B. (1991) "A Process Study of Strategic Change and Industry Evolution: The Case of the Irish Dairy Industry", *British Journal of Management*, 2: 187–204.

Leavy, B. and Wilson, D. (1994): *Strategy and Leadership*, London: Routledge.

Leavy, B. (1997): "Strategic Renewal: Is Disruptive Revolution Unavoidable?" *Strategic Change*, 6(5): 283–298.

Legge, K. (1984): *Evaluating Planned Organizational Change*, London: Academic Press.

Legge, K. (1995): *Human Resource Management. Rhetorics and Realities*, Basingstoke: Macmillan.

Lewin, K. (1947): "Frontiers in Group Dynamics", *Human Relations*, 1: 5–42.

Lindblom, C.E. (1959): "The Science of Muddling Through", *Public Administration Review*, 19: 91–99.

Lippitt, R. Watson, J. and Wesley, B. (1958): *The Dynamics of Planned Change*. New York: Harcourt Brace and World.

Lupton, T. (1986): "'Top-Down' or 'Bottom up' Management" in Mayon-White, B. (ed.) *Planning and Managing Change*, London: Harper and Row.

McHugh, M. (1996): "Managing the Stress of Strategic Change," *Journal of Strategic Change*, 5(3): 141–150.

McHugh, M. (1998): "Strategic Change in Government Agencies Influenced by Apollo and Zeus — Two 'Gods of Management'", *Public Policy and Administration*, 13(1).

McKinsey's Seven S Framework, @ McKinsey Corporation.

Magee, C. (1992): "Self-Managed Work Teams: The Bord na Móna Experience", paper presented at the Recognition, Motivation, Reward Conference, Dublin, 18–19 February.

Mapstone, R. (1994): "Confronting Organizational Change: A Northern Ireland Case Study", *Irish Business and Administrative Research*, 15: 131–145.

Moore, S. (1995): "Strategy Formulation and Implementation in a Context of Change" in Gunnigle, P. and Roche, W.K. (eds.), *New Challenges to Irish Industrial Relations*, Dublin: Oak Tree Press.

Morgan, G. (1986): *Images of Organization*, London: Sage.

Nadler, D. and Tushman, M. (1980): "A Model for Diagnosing Organizational Behaviour", *Organizational Dynamics*, Autumn: 35–51.

Nonaka, I. (1994): "A Dynamic Theory of Organizational Knowledge Creation" *Organization Science*, 5(1): 14–37.

O'Connor, E. (1995): "World Class Manufacturing in a Semi-State Environment: The Case of Bord na Móna" in Gunnigle, P. and Roche, W.K. (eds.), *New Challenges to Irish Industrial Relations*, Dublin: Oak Tree Press.

Peters, T. (1987): *Thriving on Chaos*, Basingstoke: Macmillan.

Pettigrew, A. (1985): *The Awakening Giant: Continuity and Change in Imperial Chemical Industries*, Oxford: Basil Blackwell.

Pettigrew, A. (1987): "Context and Action in the Transformation of the Firm", *Journal of Management Studies*, 24: 648–670.

Pettigrew, A. and Whipp, R. (1991): *Managing Change for Competitive Success*, Oxford: Basil Blackwell.

Pettigrew, A. and Whipp, R. (1993): "Understanding the Environment" in Mabey, C. and Mayon-White, B. (eds.), *Managing Change*, London: Paul Chapman.

Piore, M. and Sabel, C. (1984): *The Second Industrial Divide*, New York: Basic Books.

Pollert, A. (1991): *Farewell to Flexibility?*, Oxford: Blackwell.

Quinn, J.B. (1980): *Strategies for Change: Logical Incrementalism*, Homewood, IL.: Irwin.

Quinn, J.B. (1989): "Managing Strategic Change", in Asch, D. and Bowman, C. (eds.), *Readings in Strategic Management*, London, Macmillan.

Rashford, N.S. and Coughlan, D. (1994): *The Dynamics of Organizational Levels: A Change Framework for Managers and Consultants*, Reading, Mass.: Addison-Wesley

Reed, M. (1996): "Expert Power and Control in Late Modernity: An Empirical Review and Theoretical Synthesis" *Organization Studies*, 17(4): 573–597.

Robbins, S. (1998): *Organizational Behaviour: Concepts, Controversies, Applications*, NJ: Prentice Hall.

Schermerhorn, J., Hunt, J. and Osborn, R. (1997): *Organizational Behaviour*, New York: Wiley.

Schuler, R. and Jackson, S. (1987): "Organizational Strategy and Organizational Level as Determinants of HRM Practice", *Human Resource Planning*, 10(3): 125–141.

Senge, P. (1990): *The Fifth Discipline. The Art and Practice of the Learning Organization*, New York: Doubleday.

Simon, H. (1960): *The New Science of Management Decision*, Englewood Cliffs, N.J.: Prentice Hall.

Stacey, R. (1995): "The Science of Complexity: An Alternative Perspective for Strategic Change Processes", *Strategic Management Journal*, 16: 477–495.

Stehr, N. (1994): *Knowledge Societies*, London: Sage.

Storey, J. and Sisson, K. (1993): *Managing Human Resources and Industrial Relations*, Buckingham: Open University Press.

Thompson, P. and McHugh, D. (1995): *Work Organizations. A Critical Introduction*, London: Macmillan.

Tichy, N. (1983): *Managing Strategic Change: Technical, Political and Cultural Dynamics*, New York: Wiley

Toffler, A. (1980): *The Third Wave*, New York: Marrow.

Torrington, D. and Hall, L. (1991): *Personnel Management: A New Approach*, Hemel Hempstead: Prentice Hall.

Towers, B. (1996): *The Handbook of Human Resource Management*, Oxford: Blackwell.

Weisbord, M. (1976): "Organizational Diagnosis: Six Places to Look for Trouble with or Without a Theory", *Group and Organizational Studies*, 1, December, 430–447

Whipp, R., Rosenfeld, R. and Pettigrew, A. (1987): "Understanding Strategic Change Processes: Some Preliminary British Findings", in Pettigrew, A. (ed.) *The Management of Strategic Change*, Oxford: Basil Blackwell

Wilson, D. (1992): *A Strategy of Change. Concepts and Controversies in the Management of Change*, London: Routledge.

Wheatley, M. (1992): *Leadership and the New Science: Learning about Organization from an Orderly Universe*, San Francisco, CA: Berrett-Koehler Publishers.

12

INTERNATIONAL HRM: RECENT DEVELOPMENTS IN IRISH MULTINATIONALS

Hugh Scullion and *Noelle Donnelly*

INTRODUCTION

The aim of this chapter is to explore the field of International HRM (IHRM) in the context of the internationalisation of Irish business. IHRM may be defined as

> the human resource management issues and problems arising from the internationalisation of business, and the human resource management strategies, policies and practices which firms pursue in response to the internationalisation process (Scullion, 1995: 352).

Reviews of the literature have suggested that international HRM is more complex than domestic HRM and that the complexities of operating in different countries and employing different national categories of workers are the main factors that differentiate domestic and international HRM, rather than any major differences between the HRM functions performed (Dowling, Schuler and Welch, 1994).

Brewster and Scullion (1997) identify a number of reasons why an understanding of IHRM is of growing importance at present. First, recent years have seen rapid increases in global activity and global competition, which has resulted in an increase in the number and influence of multinationals companies (MNCs) (Young and Hamill, 1992). Second, the effective management of human resources internationally is increasingly being acknowledged as a key source of competitive advantage in international business (Edwards, Ferner and Sisson, 1996). Third, it is increasingly recognised that the effective implementation of international business strategies will depend on the ability of companies to develop appropriate human resource strategies for the recruitment and development of their "international managers" (Bartlett and Ghoshal, 1992). Fourth, there is growing evidence to suggest that the human and financial costs of failure overseas are more severe than in domestic business and that many companies underestimate the complex nature of the HRM problems involved in international operations (Tung, 1984). Fifth, the advent of the Single European Market and the rapid growth of Irish direct investment abroad mean that IHRM issues are increasingly important concerns for a far wider range of companies than the traditional giant MNCs, particularly amongst the growing number of smaller and medium-sized enterprises (SMEs) who have significantly internationalised their operations in recent years (Scullion, 1995).

International HRM in an Irish context is particularly pertinent for several reasons. First, recent research suggests the emergence of a growing number of Irish-owned MNCs (Donnelly, 1996). Given the current economic climate of steady growth, low inflation and interest rates, Irish companies are reported to be increasingly internationalising, primarily through overseas acquisitional activities (Chapman Flood, 1993). Second, Irish MNCs, while large in national terms, are small to medium-sized when compared with other European and North American MNCs. Despite evidence suggesting that SMEs are becoming increasingly "internationalised" the internationalisation of small to medium-sized MNCs is an area previously neglected (UN, 1993). Indeed research suggests that SMEs expanding overseas often face such HRM constraints as a lack of managerial capability and limited foreign experience (UN, 1993). Third, many Irish MNCs are relatively new to the international scene. With the exception of a few companies, such as CRH plc and the Jefferson Smurfit Group, who pioneered the route to internationalisation in the 1970s, the majority of Irish

MNCs have only begun to diversify into overseas markets since the early 1980s (see Box 12.1). As Forster and Johnsen (1996) highlight, a further under-researched area is the management of expatriates within *newly* internationalised companies. Lastly, much of the previous research to date has focused on large MNCs from large advanced economies, while little is known of small to medium-sized MNCs from small and/or "late industrialised" economies, such as Ireland.

Within Irish-based research there is virtually no previous research on the IHRM policies and practices of indigenous companies. Indeed, the majority of Irish-based research hitherto has either centred on the role of HRM in foreign-owned MNCs (Gunnigle, 1992; Monks, 1996); or, alternatively, on issues of convergence between the HRM practices of foreign and domestic companies (Kelly and Brannick, 1985; Enderwick, 1986; Roche and Geary, 1997). Moreover, Dineen and Garavan (1994) argue that the growth in HRM research is indeed largely the result of a growth in the number of foreign-owned MNCs within the Irish economy. In an attempt to redress this imbalance, this chapter will focus on outlining some empirical findings concerning the IHRM practices of Irish companies. First, we seek to locate IHRM in an Irish context by considering the internationalisation strategies of Irish businesses.

INTERNATIONAL HRM IN AN IRISH CONTEXT

As the internationalisation of Irish business gains momentum, IHRM has become firmly on the agendas of a growing number of Irish companies. Evidence suggests that the number of Irish-owned enterprises investing overseas has been increasing, particularly since the mid-1980s (OECD, 1994). Research conducted by the United Nations in the early 1990s identified seventeen indigenous small to medium-sized transnationals[1] within Ireland

---

[1] In this case, SMEs were defined to be any enterprise with a home base (head office or parent firm) in a developed country, that operates at least one affiliate in another country and whose employment level in its home country is fewer than 500 people.

(UN, 1993). More recent research, into the approach of Irish companies to industrial relations, identified a conservative estimate of twenty indigenous MNCs (Donnelly, 1996).[2] As Table 12.1 highlights, Irish MNCs are predominately located within what Lynch & Roche (1995) define to be "traditional" and "resource-based" sectors of Irish industry. The sectoral location of these Irish MNCs would, at first sight, seem to support O'Malley's (1985) "late industrialisation" thesis. The basic premise of this thesis is that, as a result of Ireland's late industrialisation, "barriers to entry for latecomers" have constrained and shaped the internationalisation of indigenous industry. O'Malley (1992: 36) argues that barriers to entry have resulted in the "clustering" of Irish international companies into either sectors involving the processing of local produce or sectors with "non-traded activities" which afforded a "significant degree of natural protection against distant competitors". Large in domestic terms but small in international terms, Irish International firms are either "the survivors of many years of intensifying competition or else they are relatively young companies which were established in a competitive environment" (O'Malley, 1992: 45).

TABLE 12.1: IRISH-OWNED MNCS BY SECTOR, SIZE AND EUROPEAN SITES, 1994

Name	Main Activity	Group Employment	Location of Other European Sites
CRH	Building materials	14,000	UK, Belgium, Germany, Spain, Netherlands
Kerry Group	Dairy & food	9,500	UK, Germany
Avonmore Foods	Dairy & food	6,348	UK, Belgium, Germany, Hungary

---

[2] This figure excludes those companies whose overseas operations are located outside of Europe. Irish international companies were identified as *wholly Irish-owned firms* (i.e. over 50 per cent shareholding within Ireland) *employing 1,000 or more employees world-wide and with at least two operating sites within Europe* — one of which could be within Ireland itself.

Waterford Foods	Dairy & food	3,224	UK
Golden Vale	Dairy & food	2,250	UK, Denmark, Netherlands, France
Greencore	Dairy & food	1,840	UK, Belgium
Glen Dimplex	Electrical appliances	4,800	UK, Belgium, Germany
Fyffes	Exporter of food produce	3,000	UK, France, Germany, Netherlands, Spain, Eastern Europe
An Bord Bainne	Exporter of dairy produce	2,300	UK, Belgium
Allied Irish Banks	Financial services	16,000	UK
Bank of Ireland	Financial services	12,000	UK, Eastern Europe
Waterford Wedgewood	Household goods	9,000	UK, France, Eastern Europe
Fitzwilton	Industrial holding	5,000	UK
James Crean	Industrial holding	2,185	UK, Netherlands
IWP International	Industrial holding	1,828	UK, Netherlands
Unidare	Industrial holding	1,413	n/a
Jefferson Smurfit Group	Print and packaging	34,500	UK, Belgium, France, Germany, Italy, Netherlands, Spain
Independent Newspapers	Print and publishing	9,000	UK, France
Clondalkin Group	Print and packaging	2,340	UK, Netherlands, Switzerland
Aer Lingus	Transport	5,556	UK, Belgium, Spain
	Total = 20	146,084	

Source: Donnelly (1996).

Internationalisation Strategies of Irish Companies

While the number of Irish companies internationalising are reported to be increasing, evidence suggests that the pace of overseas business expansion amongst Irish companies is also accelerating. As Figure 12.1 indicates, the acquisitional activity levels of Irish companies have been rapidly increasing since 1990, reaching record levels in 1996. Most of the acquisitional activities of Irish companies were found to be located in overseas markets. In 1996 sixty percent of completed acquisitions by Irish companies were *outside* domestic markets, of which the United Kingdom accounted for the largest proportion, followed by the United States and other European countries (Chapman Flood, 1996). The recent acceleration in internationalisation is widely attributed to an increase in the purchasing power of indigenous companies, the ready availability of significant venture capital, and the ability to extract a quick return on acquisitions (*The Sunday Business Post*, December, 1996).

FIGURE 12.1: ACQUISITION ACTIVITY OF IRISH COMPANIES, 1988–96

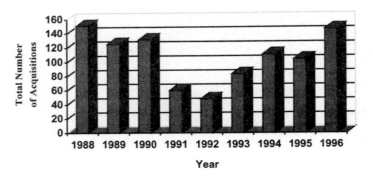

Source: Chapman Flood, *Annual Acquisitional Surveys*, 1993–96.

Acquisitional growth strategies are the most prevalent means of internationalisation amongst Irish companies. After organic growth strategies, mergers and joint ventures are the least popular methods of internationalisation for Irish companies (Chapman Flood, 1993; Donnelly, 1996). As O'Malley (1992: 38) notes, Irish companies have predominately "engaged successfully in international markets in the form of taking over foreign firms and becoming multinational companies". Irish companies, in the main, tend to pursue small to medium-sized overseas acquisitions, many of them "bolt-ons" to existing operations. The rationale suggested includes ease of integration, the minimisation of risk, the consolidation of market share and lastly a rapid return on investments (*The Sunday Business Post*, December, 1996). As the chief executive of a large manufacturing Irish MNCs explained:

> by and large 'greenfielding' takes a lot longer in order to get your money back. We found it much easier, much quicker to actually go off and buy an existing business (fieldnotes, Donnelly, 1996).

Recent reports, however, suggest a change in this trend with a number of Irish companies, including the Bank of Ireland, Allied Irish Banks, CRH and Independent Newspapers, announcing their largest ever acquisitions in 1996 (*The Irish Times*, December, 1996). Recognised as progressively important and having different requirements from foreign-owned firms, internationally trading indigenous companies have recently become the direct focus of State industrial policy initiatives (*National Development Plan 1994–1999*, 1994). The internationalisation of Irish companies is expected to continue given the limitations of domestic markets, a further opening of the economy, a shift in State policy toward the development of indigenous companies in international markets, the growing need to locate facilities close to the main overseas markets and the need to achieve critical mass to compete in the deregulated markets of the 21st century.

STRATEGY AND INTERNATIONAL HRM

One area of international business research has concentrated on identifying the methods by which firms seek to penetrate foreign markets, and the rationale for adopting their chosen foreign market entry strategy (for example, see McKiernan, 1992). Scandinavian research attempted to explain the process of internationalisation in terms of well-defined stages, with firms moving sequentially from exporting to licensing and then to foreign direct investment; each step involving greater commitment to the internationalisation process (Johanson and Vahlne, 1977; Johanson and Mattson, 1988). Such approaches to internationalisation have problems with recent developments in international business. First, these models have been complicated by the rapid growth, in the last decade, of collaborative arrangements such as international joint ventures and strategic alliances (Hendry, 1994). Second, with the upsurge in international joint ventures and acquisitions in the last decade (Hamill, 1992), many firms were able to effectively "leapfrog" the internationalisation process. This is particularly significant in the Irish context given the primary role of acquisitions in the foreign market entry strategies of Irish firms.

One of the central issues concerning companies with overseas operations is the balance between globalising forces and local market responsiveness (Bartlett and Ghoshal, 1989). Problems of control are exacerbated in international companies when operations are dispersed over considerable geographic and cultural distances and when the environment is complex and heterogeneous (Baliga and Jaeger, 1984). Edstrom and Galbraith (1977) suggest three modes of control: personal or direct control, bureaucratic control which relies on recording and reporting, and, lastly, control by socialisation where the functional behaviours and rules are learned and internalised by individuals. It has been argued, however, that control modes may change as the firm's strategy evolves over time. During the early ethnocentric or home-country focused stage of a firm's international involvement, parent country expatriates exercise tight control. As strategy becomes host-country focused or polycentric, there is a marked decline in the number of expatriates abroad and their function shifts to the communication and co-ordination of strategic objectives. Finally, with globalisation and the evolution of a globally-focused or geocentric strategy, there is a need for a broad range of executives with international experience (Adler and Bartholomew, 1991).

There is growing evidence to suggest that the international HRM policies of firms organised on a multi-domestic basis differ from globally integrated firms (Kobrin, 1992; Schuler et al., 1993). Other researchers have suggested linkages between product life cycle stage/international strategy and HRM policy and practice. (Milliman, Von Glinow and Nathan, 1991). With the recent emergence of the concept of strategic international human resource management (SIHRM) defined as:

> human resource management issues, functions and policies and practices that result from the strategic activities of multinational enterprises and that impact the international concerns and goals of those enterprises (Schuler, Dowling and De Cieri, 1993),

came a growing recognition that the success of global business depends more importantly on the quality of the MNC's human resources and how effectively the enterprise's human resources are managed and developed (Bartlett and Ghoshal, 1992).

INTERNATIONAL HRM: SOME IRISH EMPIRICAL EVIDENCE

This section summarises the results of a small-scale pilot study which examined the IHRM practices of five leading Irish international companies. The study was based on semi-structured interviews with the Human Resource or Personnel Director, based at corporate headquarters. The majority of the interviews were conducted in the early 1990s, with some follow up interviews in 1996. These companies were specifically chosen to include companies representative of both the manufacturing and service sectors. Three of the companies were international service companies (two in the financial services sector and one in air transportation). The other two were manufacturing multinationals (both in the Clay, Cement and Glass sector). All reported rapid growth of their international business operations in recent years.

There are four areas normally encompassed by the term International HRM. This section considers each in turn. The first is international staffing, an area which to date has enjoyed the bulk of research on IHRM. The second is expatriate performance and assessment. The third focuses on IHRM policies such as recruitment, selection training and repatriation. The fourth examines international management development.

International Staffing Policies and Practice

International companies face three alternatives with respect to the staffing of management positions abroad: the employment of Parent Company Nationals (PCNs), Host Country Nationals (HCNs), or Third Country Nationals (TCNs). The choice between the various alternatives is influenced by several factors, both internal and external to the international firm, which are discussed below. As Scullion (1995) outlines, there are a number of options open to MNCs with respect to their staffing policies: ethnocentric, polycentric, geocentric, mixed and ad hoc. Companies with ethnocentric predispositions will tend to favour the employment of PCNs, while companies with a polycentric value system will tend to employ HCNs (Heenan and Perlmutter, 1979). In regio- or geocentric international firms, overseas management positions may be staffed by TCNs. In practice, geocentric staffing policies are unusual even in the giant MNCs. Evidence suggests that in general Irish-owned MNCs tend not to adopt a geocentric approach to the management of their overseas operations, favouring instead a mix between the ethnocentric and polycentric approaches (Donnelly, 1996).

The international business strategy of the firm also influences staffing policies at the subsidiary level. Multinational integration strategies require a greater use of PCNs in order to control and co-ordinate integrated activities (Porter, 1986) and multi-domestic or nationally responsive strategies would require the use of HCNs to ensure sensitivity to local market and cultural considerations (Scullion, 1993). The availability of local management talent in host countries and government restrictions on the employment of local nationals are other factors influencing the choice of staffing policy, as are the relative costs of the alternatives. The characteristics of the subsidiary will also have an impact. The employment of PCNs will be greater in new subsidiaries, particularly in the start up phase. Similarly the employment of PCNs will be greater in greenfield sites as compared with acquisitions and in subsidiaries which are strategically important to the international company (Hamill, 1989).

There was considerable variation in the international staffing practices of the Irish companies interviewed. This was not surprising given the range of factors influencing the choice of staffing policy as discussed above. The financial services companies had a very clear ethnocentric policy, with a strong preference for the employment of PCNs in senior management positions abroad. By contrast, the employment of HCNs was the preferred policy in the two manufacturing companies. In the air transportation company there was no fixed policy and there was considerable variation across countries in staffing policy and practice.

The considerable differences in approaches to international staffing between the two financial services companies, was highlighted by their different responses to staffing following major international acquisitions in the 1990s. One of the financial services companies developed a senior management team combined of PCNs and HCNs. The main rationale for using Irish expatriates in this case was for development purposes, i.e. to develop future senior managers with the international management perspective and capability to run an increasingly international business. A very different approach was followed by the other financial services company. Post acquisition, the practice was to continue with HCN managers running the business. The company was very concerned with ensuring a non-hostile takeover, and felt, for political reasons, it was appropriate to continue with local managers rather than bringing in expatriates. In addition, the company was very satisfied with the quality and the performance of the HCN senior management in the acquired company.

The financial services companies also had a number of branches abroad, in addition to their recently acquired businesses, particularly in the US and the UK. In contrast to the staffing approach in the acquired banks, the senior management of the foreign branches were usually Irish expatriates. This is linked to the strategic marketing approach of the companies to focus on extended domestic markets in the UK and US, and the strong preference expressed by some major customers that top managers in host countries should be parent country nationals. In this context public relations and marketing were usually the key roles. Previous research had mostly ignored this factor because it has concentrated mainly on very large multinationals and has tended to neglect the service sector (Brewster, 1991).

As the two manufacturing companies moved beyond the early phase of internationalisation and adopted a highly decentralised approach to their international business, the firms shifted towards a polycentric staffing policy. A number of advantages of this approach were identified which were consistent with findings in the literature (Dowling et al., 1994):

1. Local managers were more sensitive to local culture and local market trends,

2. It helped to maintain the local identity of the business,

3. It helped to recruit and retain high quality HCN managers,

4. HCN managers generally cost less than PCN managers,

5. This approach was a better fit with the decentralised business approach.

Despite the tendency towards polycentrism in the two manufacturing companies, both firms continued to employ a growing number of expatriates. Similarly, in the air transportation company, there was a growing use of expatriates in the 1990s, following a period in 1980s when there was a move away from expatriate staffing in favour of HCNs, largely on cost grounds. The study identified a number of reasons for employing expatriates in Irish MNCs which were consistent with recent European research (Banai, 1992; Brewster and Scullion, 1997):

1. The lack of available management skills in some countries,

2. To retain control of local operations,

3. The need for specific product and business knowledge,

4. The training and development of local staff,

5. International assignments were increasingly seen as a central part of management development.

The increase in the use of expatriates in practice can be linked to the rapid increase in the pace of internationalisation experienced by Irish companies together with the development of new international business areas. This finding is consistent with the argument that an ethnocentric approach is particularly appropriate in the early stages of the internationalisation process (Zeira, 1976). A major challenge for the Irish companies in the next decade will be to adjust the staffing policies to the international evolution of the firm.

The Performance of Expatriate Managers

An important issue in the International HRM literature is that of expatriate failure, which is usually defined as the premature return of an expatriate manager (Dowling and Welch, 1988). The literature suggests that expatriate failure remains a significant problem, particularly for US multinationals, ranging between 25 and 40 per cent (Mendenhall, Dunbar and Oddou, 1985). Recent research suggests that these figures are somewhat exaggerated (Harzing and Van Ruysseveldt, 1995) and that expatriate under-performance is a far more frequent problem than failure of the type that requires repatriation (Scullion, 1995). A major conclusion which emerges from the present study is that the expatriate failure rate in Irish companies is similar to other European countries and is considerably lower than in comparison with US companies. None of the five companies reported expatriate failure rates in excess of 5 per cent and the majority (four out of five) had rates of around 1 per cent. Four reasons were given for the low Irish expatriate failure rate. First, Irish managers were felt to be more international in their orientation and more internationally mobile than some of their foreign counterparts. Second, international assignments were generally seen to be a key part of the overall management development process. Third, Irish MNCs were seen to be developing effective HRM policies in response to internationalisation. Fourth, the relatively small numbers of expatriates involved in smaller MNCs and the personal knowledge of managers resulted in more reliable selection.

Family-related problems were identified as the major reason for poor performance in an international assignment in Irish MNCs, a finding which is consistent with recent European research (Brewster and Scullion, 1997). In practice, however, Irish companies paid little attention to the family factor in relation to their selection decisions, notwithstanding the importance of this factor to the success of the international assignment (Mendenhall, Dunbar and Oddou, 1987). Finally the research illustrated the complexity of the issues surrounding the question of performance measurement in MNCs (Schuler et al., 1991). An important finding was that despite the growing tendency to see expatriates as key human assets, the criteria used for the performance appraisal of international managers had, in practice, received relatively little attention and indeed none of the companies had introduced separate appraisal systems for expatriate managers.

Repatriation

A significant finding of the present study was the identification of the repatriation of managers as a significant problem for Irish international companies. Whereas none of the five companies reported serious concerns with the performance of expatriates, four of the five companies said they faced or anticipated significant problems regarding the re-entry of expatriate managers. The research highlighted that concerns over re-entry may lead to low morale and a higher turnover of expatriates (Harvey, 1989; Scullion, 1994). A key problem for the Irish international firms was finding suitable posts for repatriates of similar status and responsibility to those positions they held abroad. It was anticipated that the repatriation problem would become more acute in future years because some companies expected to continue to expand overseas at the same time as undertaking rationalisation of domestic operations, thereby limiting opportunities at home. The research also highlighted other problems associated with re-entry such as loss of status, loss of autonomy, loss of career direction and a feeling that international experience is undervalued by the company (Johnston, 1991).

Despite concerns about the costs of expatriate turnover, none of the Irish companies had introduced formal repatriation programmes to assist managers and their families with repatriation difficulties. Similarly none of the companies had introduced mentor systems designed to assist the career progression of the expatriate manager. Three measures were, however, introduced to minimise the repatriation problem. The first was to reduce the duration of the international assignment as it was generally felt that repatriation problems were more acute in longer assignments. Second, companies were paying greater attention to the career planning of expatriates, and in particular were planning the return of expatriates earlier. Third, one of the financial services companies had begun to offer sabbaticals to some senior expatriates on completion of their international assignment.

INTERNATIONAL HRM POLICIES

Three of the five companies (the air transportation company, one manufacturing company and one of the financial services companies) claimed to have well-developed policies covering the recruitment, selection, pre-departure briefing, repatriation and compensation of expatriates. The other two companies were operating with a more limited set of guidelines in these areas.

Recruitment and Selection

The high costs of expatriate failure highlighted the importance of effective recruitment and selection procedures to the international firm. A key recruitment issue is whether firms recruit internally or externally and an important selection issue is whether the criteria used for selecting expatriates should be different from that used for domestic appointments (Scullion, 1994). None of the five Irish companies recruited externally for expatriate positions. They had a clear preference to recruit internally from their existing pool of management for these positions. Two main advantages of internal as opposed to external recruitment were cited by the companies. The first was knowledge of the individual and the family, which was particularly important for those companies establishing new international operations in the early phase of the internationalisation process. Second, was the growing tendency to use international assignments for career development purposes.

In terms of the selection criteria used for international assignments, domestic track record and general management and technical skills were the main factors considered (Tung, 1982). Four of the five companies, however, also took into account a wider range of factors including cultural empathy, family situation, previous international experience. Foreign language ability was important for younger graduates and the development potential of the graduate was increasingly important. For more senior expatriate appointments, the ability to operate independently and to develop cross-cultural leadership skills were seen as key factors (Scullion, 1992). However, while all companies felt that the effective selection of managers was vital to successful performance abroad, only one of the companies had introduced psychological testing for expatriates. It was felt that the candidates for such jobs would be well known to the company in a relatively small organisation.

International Briefing and Training

An effective briefing on the nature of the international assignment prior to departure was also regarded as important to the success of an international assignment (Ronen, 1989). All of the companies conducted briefings which usually involved interviews with senior managers to clarify the key objectives of the assignment. In addition, there was sometimes the opportunity to hold discussions with former and current expatriates who had knowledge of the country in question. This latter form of briefing was particularly valued by the managers because they could ask questions and learn from the experiences of their predecessors.

None of the companies had established their own cultural awareness training programmes. This was partly because the two most important foreign markets, the US and the UK were not felt to be so culturally dissimilar to the domestic culture. The relatively small size of the Irish companies was also a factor here. There were limited resources available at the corporate headquarters for training and development. Three of the companies used external training organisations to help prepare their managers for international assignments. One of the financial service companies sent senior international managers to leading edge courses run by world class business schools in the US. Four of the five companies adopted the approach of encouraging the manager and the spouse to visit the area prior to the acceptance of the assignment. This was felt to be an effective way of giving the managers and their spouses some real understanding of the conditions in the foreign country and of the nature of the challenges they would face in living in a foreign environment.

International Management Development

The effective implementation of global strategies depends, to a large degree, on the existence of an adequate supply of internationally experienced managers (Adler and Bartholomew, 1992). Scullion (1992) identified shortages of international managers as an increasingly important problem for British multinationals. There were growing concerns amongst some Irish MNCs that shortages of international managers and restrictions on managerial mobility were recently emerging as significant constraints on the internationalisation and growth strategies of Irish companies. In some cases the shortage of international HCNs shaped their preference for acquisitional growth strategies, with the retention of existing management a key factor. Shortages of qualified HCN managers was a particularly acute concern for the manufacturing MNCs due to the very rapid internationalisation of their business in recent years.

There was also growing recognition of the importance of developing effective international management development programmes (Scullion, 1997). Four of the five companies reported that they were spending more on international management education, particularly for top and senior management. The companies used a combination of internal and external international development programmes, one interesting feature of which in the case of the financial services MNCs was the use of leading foreign business schools in Europe and the US. Two of the five companies (one manufacturer and one financial services company) had introduced international HR planning, however, this development was at a relatively early stage in these companies. The key international HR issue facing these companies was the need to develop the next generation of top managers with the capacities to run an international business (see Box 12.2). International management development, succession planning and international career planning were seen as vital areas for the corporate human resource function in the international firm (Scullion, forthcoming).

CONCLUSIONS

The argument presented in this chapter suggests that International HRM is becoming increasingly important not only in the traditional giant MNCs but also amongst a growing number of medium-sized firms who have internationalised their operations in recent years. The preliminary evidence presented in this chapter suggests that a number of Irish MNCs, who in this case are amongst the largest Irish firms, have few serious problems regarding expatriate performance or expatriate management. The repatriation of expatriate managers back to Ireland was identified as a growing problem for Irish MNCs. The recruitment and retention of the high-quality HCN managers needed to manage effectively the acquired international businesses was a vital component of international HRM strategy in those companies committed to the policy of using local managers. More generally the integration of the acquired foreign businesses was a key challenge facing Irish MNCs.

In general all of the Irish companies in the present study were effective in international HRM, despite not following best practice in some areas such as the use of sophisticated selection methods and the use of tailored training programmes to suit the needs of a particular foreign assignment. There are two main reasons to explain this paradox. First, the use of internal recruitment in companies which have a relatively small population of expatriates facilitates the development of self-selecting, highly motivated expatriate populations. Second, the current selection and training procedures are adequate for the time being because they are only dealing with a limited number of international assignments. However, these procedures may become less effective as the nature of the firm's international involvement changes and the expatriate population grows (Forster and Johnsen, 1996). This suggests that further empirical research is required which charts the international HRM problems and issues which Irish companies face when they develop through the various stages of the internationalisation process.

A recent piece of research by Creaner and Monks (1996) examined the IHRM practices of eleven Irish international companies. Their research highlighted the need to develop more sophisticated theoretical frameworks for identifying the range of variables which impact upon human resource choices in international activities. Their findings also suggested that theories of internationalisation which have been developed from research in large MNEs do not adequately explain the approaches used in smaller firms. In particular the research suggested that smaller firms may need to be more flexible, adaptable and opportunistic than large MNEs. This suggests the need for a new research agenda in international HRM which is to establish better information about the role and management of HRM across frontiers in small and medium-sized international firms as well as in giant MNEs, to clarify and measure current developments and to place such developments in the context of more adequate theories of international HRM.

Box 12.1: The CRH Story: "Pioneering Abroad"

CRH plc was one of the first Irish companies to seek international expansion during the 1970s. Limited by a shrinking and highly cyclical domestic market, the group embarked on a path of geographical diversification to increase profits. Setting an objective to increase overseas earnings to 30 per cent by 1980, key people were assigned overseas with a brief to source potential acquisition opportunities. To minimise risk, CRH targeted potential growth regions where the language and business cultures were familiar. The UK and US markets were initially identified as meeting those prerequisites and in 1978 the first acquisitions were completed in these markets. Key to CRH's internationalisation success has been a number of factors — the establishment of specific acquisitional criteria; targeting of well-managed companies with a strong local franchise; small to medium-sized acquisitions; concentrating on building industry products; and the retention of local management. Currently there are twelve geographically dispersed semi-autonomous acquisition teams. Their local knowledge enables the Group to identify promising markets; source attractive potential acquisitions; carefully evaluate interested sellers; conclude mutually beneficial deals and integrate the new acquisition speedily into existing operations.

Source: In interview with CRH.

Box 12.2: International HRM Issues at CRH plc

When CRH plc, the international building materials group, was formed in 1970, it employed 5,400 people at 55 locations in 2 countries. Today it employs 21,000 people at 792 locations across 12 different countries. Enhanced by acquisitions of owner managed private companies, CRH currently has a mix of managers that includes owner-entrepreneurs, internally developed managers and highly qualified business development professionals. Given this pace of expansion, one of the greatest challenges identified by the group is the need to ensure that the rate and pace of business development is matched with appropriate management development. In particular, this has meant greater emphasis being placed on succession planning.

A core part of the head-office human resource function, succession planning, involves classical gap analysis — that is, the identification of future senior managerial needs of the group with current resources and the subsequent addressing of gaps in resourcing. The process at CRH began by piloting an approach to leadership competencies. Having identified 57 separate core competencies, programmes aimed at the development of such skills as results, planning, decision-making, teamwork, communication and creativity were outlined. By profiling future job requirements and individual career objectives, CRH hopes that future managerial group needs will be matched as the company continues to grow its operations.

Source: In interview with CRH.

References

Adler, N.J. and Bartholomew, S. (1992): "Managing Globally Competent People", *Academy of Management Executive*, 6: 52–64.

Baliga, B.R. and Jaeger, A.M. (1984): "Multinational Corporations: Control Systems and Delegation Issues", *Journal of International Business Studies*, 2: 25–40.

Banai, M. (1992): "The Ethnocentric Staffing Policy in Multinational Corporations: a Self-fulfilling Prophecy", *International Journal of Human Resource Management*, 3: 451–72.

Bartlett, C. and Ghoshal, S. (1989): *Managing Across Borders: The Transnational Solution*, Boston: Harvard Business School Press.

Bartlett, C. and Ghoshal, S. (1992): "What is a Global Manager?", *Harvard Business Review*, September/October: 124–32.

Brewster, C. (1991): *The Management of Expatriates*, London: Kogan Page.

Brewster, C. and Scullion, H. (1997): "Expatriate HRM: A Review and an Agenda", *Human Resource Management Journal*, 7(3): 32–41.

Chapman Flood (1996): *Acquisition Surveys 1993–96*, Dublin: Chapman Flood Corporate Finance in association with M&A International (Ireland) Limited.

Creaner, J. and Monks, K. (1996): Entering The International Market: Opportunities and Choices in Human Resource Practices, Dublin City University working paper.

Dineen, D. and Garavan, T. (1994): "Ireland: The Emerald Isle — Management Research in a Changing European Context", *International Studies of Management and Organisation*, 24(1–2): 137–64.

Donnelly, N. (1996): "The Management of Industrial Relations in Irish-owned Multinational Companies: Some Exploratory Findings", paper presented at the First Conference on *Management Research in Ireland*, University College Cork, September, 12–13.

Dowling, P.J. and Welch, D. (1988): "International Human Resource Management: An Australian Perspective", *Asia-Pacific Journal of Management*, 6(1): 39–65.

Dowling, P.J., Schuler, R.S. and Welch, D. (1994): *International Dimensions of Human Resource Management*, (second edition), Belmont, CA: Wadsworth.

Edstrom, A. and Galbraith, J. (1977): "Transfer of Managers as a Coordination and Control Strategy in Multinational Organisations", *Administrative Science Quarterly*, 22: 248–63.

Edwards, P.K., Ferner, A. and Sisson, K. (1996): "The Conditions for International Human Resource Management: Two Case Studies", *International Journal of Human Resource Management*, 7(1): 20–40.

Enderwick, P. (1986): "Multinationals and Labour Relations: The Case of Ireland", *Journal of Irish Business and Administrative Research*, 8: 1–11.

Forster, N. and Johnsen, M. (1996): "Expatriate Management Policies in UK Companies New to the International Scene", *International Journal of Human Resource Management*, 7(1): 179–205.

National Development Plan (1994): Government Publications, Dublin: The Stationery Office.

Gunnigle, P. (1992): "Management Approaches to Employee Relations in Greenfield Sites", *Journal of Irish Business and Administrative Research*, 3(1): 20–36.

Hamill, J. (1989): "Expatriate Policies in British Multinationals", *Journal of General Management*, 14(4): 18–33.

Hamill, J. (1992): "Cross-border Mergers, Acquisitions and Alliances in Europe" in Young, S. and Hamill, J. (eds.), *Europe and the Multinationals*, London: Edward Elgar.

Harvey, M.G. (1989): "Repatriation of Corporate Executives: An Empirical Study", *Journal of International Business Studies*, Spring: 131–44.

Harzing, A.W.J. and Van Ruysseveldt, J. (1995): *International Human Resource Management*, London: Sage.

Heenan, D.A. and Perlmutter, H.V. (1979): *Multinational Organisation Development*, Reading, Mass.: Addison-Wesley.

Hendry, C. (1994): *Human Resource Strategies for International Growth*, London: Routledge.

Irish Times, The, "A Record Year for the Big Business in Irish Businesses", December 28, 1996.

Johanson, J. and Mattsson, L.G. (1988): "Internationalisation in Industrial Systems — A Network Approach", in Hood, N. and Vahlne, J.E. (eds.), *Strategies in Global Competition*, London: Croom Helm.

Johanson, J. and Vahlne, J.E. (1977): "The Internationalisation Process of the Firm — A Model of Knowledge Development and Increasing Foreign Commitment", *Journal of International Business Studies*, 8(1): 23–32.

Johnston, J. (1991): "An Empirical Study of Repatriation of Managers in UK Multinationals", *Human Resource Management Journal*, 1(4): 102–8.

Kelly, A. and Brannick, T. (1985): "Industrial Relations Practices in Multinational Companies in Ireland", *Journal of Irish Business and Administrative Research*, 7: 98–111.

Kobrin, S.J. (1992): *Multinational Strategy and International Human Resource Management Policy*, unpublished paper, The Wharton School, University of Pennsylvania.

Lynch, J. and Roche, F. (1995): *Business Management in Ireland: Competitive Strategies for the 21st. Century*, Dublin: Oak Tree Press.

McKiernan, P. (1992): *Strategies of Growth*, London: Routledge.

Mendenhall, M. and Oddou, G. (1985): "The Dimensions of Expatriate Acculturation: A Review", *Academy of Management Review*, 10: 39–47.

Mendenhall, M.E., Dunbar, E. and Oddou, G. (1987): "Expatriate Selection, Training and Career Pathing: A Review and Critique", *Human Resource Planning*, 26(3): 331–45

Milliman, J., Von Glinow, M. and Nathan, B. (1991): "Organisational Life Cycles and Strategic International Human Resource Management in Multinational Companies: Implications for Congruence Theory", *Academy of Management Review*, 16: 318–39.

Monks, K. (1996): "Global or Local? HRM in the Multinational Company: the Irish Experience", *International Journal of Human Resource Management*, 7(3): 721–35.

O'Malley, E. (1985): "The Performance of Irish Indigenous Industry: Some Lessons for the 1980s" in Fitzpatrick, J. and Kelly, J. (eds.), *Perspectives on Irish Industry*, Dublin: Irish Management Institute.

O'Malley, E. (1992): "Problems of Industrialisation in Ireland" in Goldthorpe, J.H. and Whelan, C.T. (eds.) *The Development of Industrial Society in Ireland*, Oxford University Press for the British Academy.

OECD (1994): *Reviews of Foreign Direct Investment: Ireland*, OECD: Paris.

Porter, M. (1986): *Competition in Global Industries*, Boston, Mass.: Harvard Business School Press.

Roche, W.K and Geary, J.F. (1997): "Multinationals and Industrial Relations Practices", in Murphy, T.V. and Roche, W.K. (eds.) *Industrial Relations in Practice (Revised and Expanded)*, Dublin: Oak Tree Press.

Ronen, S. (1989): "Training the International Assignee" in Goldstein, I. (ed.), *Training and Career Development*, San Francisco, CA: Jossey-Bass.

Schuler, R.S., Fulkerson, J.R. and Dowling, P.J. (1991): "Strategic Performance Measurement and Management in Multinational Corporations", *Human Resource Management*, 30: 365–92.

Schuler, R., Dowling, P.J. and De Cieri, H. (1993): "An Integrative Framework of Strategic International Human Resource Management", *International Journal of Human Resource Management*, 4(4): 717–64.

Scullion, H. (1992): "Strategic Recruitment and Development of the International Manager: Some European Considerations", *Human Resource Management Journal*, 3(1): 57–69.

Scullion, H. (1993): "Creating International Managers: Recruitment and Development Issues" in Kirkbride, P. (ed.), *Human Resource Management in Europe*, London: Routledge.

Scullion, H. (1994): "Staffing Policies and Strategic Control in British Multinationals", *International Studies of Management and Organisation*, 3(4): 86–104.

Scullion, H. (1995): "International Human Resource Management" in Storey, J. (ed.) *Human Resource Management: A Critical Text*, London: Routledge.

Scullion, H. (1997): "The Key Challenges for International HRM in the 21st Century", in *Association of European Personnel Managers Handbook*, London: Institute of Personnel Managers Handbook.

Scullion, H. (1998) *The Role of the Corporate Human Resource Function in the International Firm*, forthcoming.

Sunday Business Post, The, "A Record Year for Mergers and Acquisitions", December 29, 1996.

Tung, R.L. (1982): "Selection and Training Procedures of US European and Japanese Multinationals", *California Management Review*, 25(1): 57–71.

Tung, R.L. (1984): "Strategic Management of Human Resources in the Multinational Enterprise", *Human Resource Management*, 23(2): 129–43.

United Nations (1993): *Small and Medium-sized Transnational Corporations: Role, Impact and Policy Implications*, New York: UN Publications.

Young, S. and Hamill, J. (1992): *Europe and the Multinationals*, London: Edward Elgar.

Zeira, Y. (1976): "Management Development in Ethnocentric Multinational Corporations", *California Management Review*, 18(4): 34–42.

13

HUMAN RESOURCE MANAGEMENT IN THE PUBLIC SECTOR

John O'Dowd and *Tim Hastings*

INTRODUCTION

One of the most significant developments in public sector management internationally over the last decade has been the adoption of private sector models of employee management, in particular the ideas and practices associated with human resource management. There is now considerable evidence of the application by governments of differing political hues of new models of employee management as part of a broader process of public sector reform (ILO, 1995; OECD, 1996). A number of political, economic and social factors have been identified as giving rise to these developments, in particular the intensification of international competition and the resultant pressure to reduce public sector spending, the constraints on public spending imposed by the European Union (EU), in the form of the Maastricht criteria, and the pro-competition and deregulation policies of the EU, which have had a particular impact on commercial state companies such as public utilities. Other significant influences have been New Right ideas especially on the role of the state and economic growth, and the rise of "consumerism" with its demands for better services and a focus on the needs of citizens as opposed to service providers (Ferner, 1994; Hastings, 1994; Roche and Gunnigle, 1995; Roche, 1996). Finally, there has been the widespread belief that private sector management techniques are superior to those being applied in the public sector.

It has been argued that a pattern of public sector reform initiatives has emerged in many, but by no means all, of the countries of the developed world. For example, Pollitt (1995), has identified a "shopping basket" of eight elements (cost cutting and bringing greater transparency to resource allocation, disaggregating traditional bureaucratic organisations into separate agencies, decentralisation of management hierarchies, separating the function of providing services from purchasing them, introduction of market-type mechanisms, performance management, departure from national systems of determining pay and conditions to local determination, increasing emphasis on service quality and customer awareness) which, notwithstanding national variations, have been deployed in whole or in part in most public sector reform programmes affecting core public services as well as commercial state companies. Collectively these elements have come to be known as the New Public Management (NPM).

The new models of employee management associated with NPM challenge existing systems of pluralist relations based on adversarial collective bargaining as well as the traditional models of personnel management. In Ireland these new models have found some level of expression in the Government's Strategic Management Initiative in the core civil service and in individual initiatives within different semi-state companies.

The backdrop to recent developments in Irish employee relations is the now eleven-year-old series of national economic and social agreements covering pay and social and economic developments. The latest of these agreements, *Partnership 2000* (1996), which was signed in January 1997, has as one of its central objectives the introduction of partnership models in both private and public sector employments. The platform provided by this centralised consensus has allowed for the development of new industrial relations and personnel approaches based on human resource thinking but within a distinctly pluralist setting or, as one study put it, alongside, rather than in place of, collective bargaining

(Gunnigle et al., 1994). In addition it has been argued that the traditional adversarial model of industrial relations that was typical of both private and public sectors for many years has been undergoing a process of fragmentation into a number of emerging and competing models of industrial relations and human resource management (Roche, 1996). It will be seen that while the public sector has continued until very recently as a site of predominantly adversarial industrial relations, a number of commercial state companies such as ESB, Telecom Éireann and others have begun to develop a more sophisticated approach based on the integration of strong trade unionism, a more strategic approach to competition, collective bargaining and the ideas and practices of HRM. Also, even more traditional core public services now face the challenge of implementing radical reform programmes within a framework of co-operative industrial relations and workplace union-management partnership. In this context many of the initiatives under consideration here have both industrial relations and human resource dimensions, both of which need to be fully comprehended to understand the distinctive character of the emerging model.

While there has developed a literature on HRM in the private sector (Gunnigle et al., 1994 and 1997) there is a distinct absence of data from surveys or from case studies of key aspects of organisational change such as work organisation, job design, or changing practices in industrial relations and personnel management in the public sector. This chapter seeks to outline, for the first time in some detail, individual human resource developments in the core civil service and the commercial semi-state sector and to discuss the limits and shape of these developments in the context of a highly unionised sector. In particular, we seek to explore whether the developments taking place at organisational level together with the direction of national policy point to a distinctive emerging model of Irish public sector human resource management.

Because the chapter takes an exploratory approach to developments, many of which are still in train, we have taken a broad approach to what constitutes a human resource management initiative. A more rigorous approach would rule out consideration of many initiatives, which are not specifically of the human resource variety, but are nevertheless developing under the influence of human resource thinking.

PUBLIC SERVICE INDUSTRIAL RELATIONS AND PERSONNEL MANAGEMENT

There are a number of respects in which private and public sector industrial relations and personnel systems have traditionally been distinguished from each other (Beaumont, 1992; Ferner, 1994; Weggemans, 1987) and, as will be seen below, it is a matter of some controversy as to whether or not such differences constitute insurmountable barriers to the application of private sector HRM in a public sector context. Public and private sector employments have traditionally had separate legislative provisions, usually, but not always, including a greater range of rights and protections for individual pubic service employees. For example, in Ireland since the late 1970s worker directors have been appointed by statute to the boards of both commercial and non-commercial semi-state companies while civil servants have had separate legislative provisions in areas such as dismissal. Centralised control of personnel and industrial relations practice and policy has usually served to ensure equity and unity in employment conditions within the public sector on the basis of governments acting as a "good employer". In the Irish context this has held true not alone for the core public service but for the wider public sector as well. In recent years, however, employee relations developments in the commercial state companies have begun to have more in common with the private sector than the core civil service.

Of particular significance for the conduct of industrial relations in the public sector is the dual role of government as political authority and employer. For example, successive Irish governments up to the 1980s accepted implicitly as an employer the principle of fair comparison between public sector and private sector pay levels as the basis of public service pay determination. There have also been cases, such as the threatened nurses' dispute in 1997, in which the government as political authority decided to make concessions in its role as employer in order to protect its positions both as employer and political authority. The interventionist role of the state in the industrial relations of the commercial state sector was also a noteworthy issue in the 1980s as this sector came under pressure from domestic and EU policy-makers to become more competitive (Hastings, 1994). The state, therefore, makes decisions through the political process that impinge upon its employer role. These decisions are based less on market criteria than on political and macro-economic considerations. This has clear implications for both the take up and exercise of strategic human resource management practice in the public domain in Ireland.

While there are many significant differences between the public sectors of the industrialised world in respect to industrial relations and personnel management, a number of common features may be identified. In addition to national pay systems there was usually a system of limited open recruitment, security of employment, and subsequent promotion within an internal labour market through a hierarchy of national grades with duties related to pay levels. Where negotiation took place this was usually highly formalised and centralised with a wide-ranging bargaining agenda. The personnel function tended to be highly centralised and concentrated on the administration of wages, promotions, leave, recruitment, etc. and on the formal processing of union claims and grievances. There were high levels of trade union density across nearly all occupations and professions with public sector trade union density in Ireland estimated at over 90 per cent (including powerful occupational categories such as teachers, nurses and other professionals who comprise a high proportion of public sector employees) compared to over 35 per cent for the private sector. Total public sector employment is set out in Table 13.1.

TABLE 13.1 PUBLIC SECTOR EMPLOYMENT, 1994–1997 ('000S)

	1994	1995	1996	1997 (March)
Civil Service	31.1	32.0	31.6	32.1
Defence Forces	14.3	14.0	13.1	13.2
Garda	10.8	10.7	10.7	10.7
Education	63.6	65.9	67.2	66.8
Regional Bodies	30.4	30.1	30.2	30.0
Semi-State Companies	63.4	63.0	62.1	61.6
Health	63.9	65.2	65.8	-
Total	277.5	280.8	280.8	-

Source: Central Statistics Office Statistical Release (1997), Dublin: Government Information Services.

At the same time it would be inappropriate to regard public service industrial relations as inherently different from the private sector (Gunnigle, et al., 1995: 92). In a review of industrial relations developments in Ireland, Roche (1996) locates public service industrial relations within the "adversarial" model which developed as the dominant national model. In the core public services such as the civil service, local government and health, and the education sector, unions and management have traditionally used conciliation and arbitration schemes to process industrial relations issues and as fora for employee consultation and involvement. In the commercial state sector it has been more common to use the private sector industrial relations machinery in the form of the Labour Relations Commission and the Labour Court. Significantly, for pay bargaining purposes the commercial semi-state sector is treated as part of the private sector in national pay arrangements such as *Partnership 2000*.

HUMAN RESOURCE THEORY IN THE PUBLIC SECTOR

One of the key questions facing both academics and practitioners alike is whether there is a generic concept of management, including strategic and human resource management, which can be applied to both the public and private sectors. It is not our intention to reach a final conclusion on this matter but to rehearse the arguments that have arisen in the literature so as to inform our discussion of the application of HRM in the Irish public sector at the end of the chapter. Such generic management theory underpins the prescriptive work of advocates of the NPM such as Osborne and Gaebler (1993) who argued that while there were important distinctions between the two sectors, the differences did not outweigh the similarities to the degree that a distinctive form of public sector management was required. Lawton and Rose (1991: 6-8) broaden the argument out and conclude that "it is often difficult to distinguish clearly between the two sectors and it may be more fruitful to examine organisational differences in terms of size, decision-making processes, structures and management style rather than concentrate upon which sector the organisation is in". Thomas (1996: 26), writing from a Canadian perspective, concludes "that it is possible to exaggerate the dissimilarities between public and private sector management". For example, there are domains of activity in the public sector where private sector techniques, when carefully applied, can be made to work — innovations in public service delivery methods over the last decade provide ample evidence of this.

Stewart and Ranson (1988: 121) representing a "differentialist" position refer to the principles of accountability, collective ownership and political control which underpin the public sector and suggest that strategic management in the public sector cannot be based on the competitive stance of different organisations as in the private sector. Rather they believe that strategic management in the public sector expresses values determined through the political process in response to a changing environment and that the public sector requires its own model. They characterise the dilemmas of strategy setting in the public domain in terms of resolving a number of conflicts. These include the conflict between the collective and the individual, a conflict that goes to the heart of human resource theory.

Rainey et al. (1976) in a "pre-HRM" article emphasise a number of points of difference between public and private organisations which cannot be ignored in any discussion of the application of HRM to public sector organisations. These differences include the following: a lower degree of market exposure which results in less incentive to introduce operational efficiencies and less access to bottom-line indicators; legal constraints which restrict the scope of authority of managers and encourage formalisation of rules and controls; political influences which mean that internal managerial decisions are open to external pressures; hierarchical authority relations which reduce the autonomy of administrative decision-making; weaker managerial authority over subordinates; constraints on merit systems and less innovativeness.

Storey (1992: 8-9) has distinguished between "hard" and "soft" models of human resource management. Within the "hard" approach employees are treated as just another input cost such as raw material, while "soft" HRM on the other hand focuses on the development of employees as individuals through training as the factor making the difference in the company's success.

In a discussion of human resource management in the public sector, Storey (1989: 57) takes as his starting point the break that emerged in the UK within the conventional wisdom of what he calls "post-Donovan proceduralism" of the late 1970s with its prescription to formalise rules, agreements and relationships which had been informal. Citing integration, the eliciting of commitment, a shift from collective modes of accommodation to ones based on the individual, and ownership by line managers, Storey says there are grounds for believing that there has been a measure of change in management approaches to these issues. While what he calls the "*ancien régime*" was marked by "firefighting" and reaction, the new order is supposedly quintessentially proactive.

Like Stewart and Ranson (1988), Storey considers the interplay between strategic human resource management and the political nature of strategic objectives in the public sector. The kernel of his argument is that successful human resource management in the public sector requires not only top management support but also political support from elected politicians (ibid: 61). But the adversarial nature of the party political system puts this continuity of support in jeopardy. A second brake on the widespread adoption of a fully-fledged human resource management approach in the public sector arises from the comparatively poor education and training of managers. A third problem flows from the fact that market forces cannot solely govern decisions about human resource utilisation and the levels of reward. While cautioning against the way in which techniques were "borrowed" from the private sector, Storey says the constraints against the widespread adoption of human resource management in the public sector should not necessarily be seen as insurmountable. Rather, he says they should be seen for what they are: indicators that principles and approaches refined originally within large and exceptional private organisations, such as IBM, should not be expected to translate easily into organisations in very different settings. His final verdict, based on UK experience up to the late 1980s, was that extensive discussion had taken place and diverse experimentation, but with a somewhat limited impact upon staff attitudes and behaviour.

Other writers on the State sector, however, see the changes that have occurred over the last ten years on a wider canvas. Pendleton (1993) attributes the amalgam of change and continuity in industrial relations on the British railways to the persistent tension within management as to whether confrontational or consensual means were the most effective way of securing change. Changes at workplace level, he argues, were not so much the outcome of new industrial relations strategies as the result of financial and organisational pressures brought about by commercialisation. Pendleton's conclusion (ibid: 67) was that changes on the railways owed more to the indirect effects of commercialisation than to explicit strategies to refashion industrial relations. Ferner and Colling's view (1991: 393) that increased efficiency can be seen as a precondition for, rather than a consequence of privatisation would seem to support this assertion about the dominance of a rising ethos of commercialisation over and above issues of ownership.

It is clear, then, that there are a number of fairly obvious differences between the two sectors. In the private sector performance is measured in market terms of profit and loss and appropriate management models derive from this market imperative. In the public sector, or at least those parts of it that do not have to trade commercially, performance cannot be measured in such quantifiable "bottom line" terms. There are political, consumer, legal and "professional" contexts in which the achievement of public sector organisational objectives can be expressed and measured. Values such as equity provide a broader concept of meeting public needs than the "consumerist" model of the free market (Lawton and Rose, 1991; Farnham and Horton, 1993; Moore, 1992: 363)

HRM IN THE IRISH CIVIL SERVICE

In 1996 the Irish Government published, to considerable public acclaim, a report titled *Delivering Better Government* (1996), which was written by a group of top civil servants at the Government's request. The report called for a high performance, open and flexible organisation, quality service to the Government and the public, maximum contribution to national competitiveness through effective human resource management systems including a new approach to performance management and a partnership between management and staff at all levels of the Civil Service. This emphasis on public service reform, including the reform of the systems of people management, derives from a recognition of the link between public sector performance and the overall performance of the economy (Yntema, 1993). Public administration affects national competitiveness in at least three significant ways. First, the size and cost of providing public services affects the level of taxation to be levied on the general population and determines the availability of resources for the competitive sector. Secondly, the efficiency (or lack of it) of the public sector affects the legislative and regulatory environment in which the competitive sector has to operate. Thirdly, the quantity and quality of service provision in areas such as education and training are significant factors in determining national competitiveness.

The Strategic Management Initiative (SMI)

Delivering Better Government can be seen as a distinctly Irish variant of this New Public Management (NPM), although it is too early to attempt a definitive characterisation at this stage. Nevertheless, it is important to note that successive Irish governments have, despite similar pressures on public spending as those experienced throughout the developed world, resisted the neo-liberal strain of NPM typified in the UK by a highly ideological approach "governed by the view that the private provision of public services is inherently superior to public provision and that individualism is both the antithesis of and superior to collectivism" (Kessler and Purcell, 1996: 208). The consensual approach to social and economic policy which was developed through the series of national programmes since 1987 and the absence of a significant neo-liberal strain in Irish politics have frequently been argued as reasons for this (Gunnigle et al., 1997: 225–7; Roche and Turner, 1994).

While the current wave of public sector reform began as recently as 1994 with the launch of the SMI by the then Taoiseach, Albert Reynolds, there were earlier attempts at public sector reform including the *Devlin Report* (1969) and the White Paper titled *Serving the Country Better* (1985). Prior to the launch of the SMI, a number of government departments, most notably the Revenue Commissioners and the Department of Social Welfare, had begun to introduce strategic planning processes and to reorient service delivery around the needs of the public in keeping with the "customer orientation" of the private sector.

The preparatory work on *Delivering Better Government* was carried out by senior civil servants, but in 1996 a National Coordinating Committee (NCC) was established by the Government to take responsibility for the implementation of the SMI with a wider representation from the Irish Business and Employers Confederation, the Irish Congress of Trade Unions, and other interests. It is worth noting that over this period all of the parties represented in Dáil Éireann, ranging from the Left to Right of the political spectrum, have been involved in one form of coalition government or another and that there has been significant continuity as governments changed on the issues of public sector reform and the partnership approach to industrial relations. All of the main civil service trade unions are represented on the new body.

Delivering Better Government calls for "a different approach to human resource management" with this latter term being used as if it required no definition and as if it was already in common usage in the civil service (which it is not). Box 13.1 sets out the general stance of the report on the development of the personnel function in government departments.

BOX 13.1. EXTRACTS FROM *DELIVERING BETTER GOVERNMENT*

"The Group (i.e. the National Co-ordinating Group of Departmental Secretaries who wrote the document) believe that the creation of a results-driven Civil Service clearly aligned with Government priorities and focused on quality of service will not be possible within the existing personnel structures. New structures for allocating authority and responsibility need to be accompanied by a corresponding modernisation in HRM. The Group believes that traditional personnel policies have had too narrow a focus and that a more proactive personnel management approach needs to be adopted. . . . The Group also envisage a significant restructuring of existing personnel systems arising from the redefinition of the role of the Secretary as the person who will have responsibility for managing the Department and for ensuring that responsibility is taken at all levels throughout the organisation."

"First, personnel management . . . needs to be more broadly defined since it tends to be mainly administrative in nature, with insufficient attention being given to resource planning, career management, staff development, workload distribution and, especially performance management. In short, the more developmental and strategic aspects of human resource management as now widely practised have not had a significant impact on public service management to date. Second, the degree of central regulation and control of the human resource function has increasingly been called into question, particularly in the context of the more effective operation of the administrative budget system . . . the Group accepts the increasing need to devolve greater autonomy and responsibility for . . . personnel resources from the centre to departmental managements. . . .

> The Group recommend, therefore, that: departmental personnel units reorient their activities and focus to: take a more strategic/developmental approach; and devolve responsibility for day-to-day human resource matters to line managers: this reorientation take place in tandem with a . . . process of devolving authority from the Department of Finance to departments generally . . . each department develop a HRM strategy linked to the overall strategy for the organisation. . . ." *Delivering Better Government* (pp. 32–3).

Despite the critical tone, *Delivering Better Government* accepts the current national pay and grading system as the basis for future developments. It implies that the unified structure does not constitute a sufficient constraint on management to warrant the introduction of a fully devolved system under which each department would operate independently by setting its own grading structure and conditions of service. Table 13.2 highlights the main changes proposed in *Delivering Better Government* and indicates how certain of these imply radical change from the current industrial relations and personnel systems.

TABLE 13.2: CURRENT PERSONNEL AND INDUSTRIAL RELATIONS SYSTEMS AND NEW APPROACHES IN *DELIVERING BETTER GOVERNMENT* AND *PARTNERSHIP 2000*

Current Systems	New Model
Ministerial legal responsibility for employment matters including recruitment and dismissal.	New legislation passed in June 1997 to transfer responsibility for personnel matters to Heads of departments.
Centralised recruitment via Civil Service Commission.	No proposal to change; review to take place.
Formal systems for consultation and negotiation.	Retain and within existing system develop formal mechanisms for greater direct employee involvement.
Adversarial culture and low levels of trust.	Develop co-operation through partnership and develop high trust relations. Reduce conflict through new conflict resolution machinery.

Negotiation of change through industrial relations machinery on incremental basis with compensation for co-operation with change.	Develop ongoing co-operation with change as the norm. Pay increases under local bargaining clause of *Partnership 2000* linked to verified progress on change agenda. Co-operation with change not a basis in itself for compensation.
Formal definitions of duties for each grade level and a hierarchical grading system.	Redefine lines of demarcation to increase employee flexibility. Reduce number of grades.
Limited open recruitment with permanency of tenure and little specialisation outside professional and technical occupations.	Extend external recruitment somewhat and modify future contracts to provide for atypical forms of employment.
Central control by Department of Finance of personnel and industrial relations issues.	Devolve responsibility to departments and within departments. Personnel sections to develop a more strategic role.
Low levels of innovation in work organisation and job design.	Encourage innovation.
A "good employer" model of employment relations.	Implicitly retain but modernise personnel through a "HRM" approach.
Low levels of staff training and development.	Upgrade significantly to three per cent of payroll costs.

Source: *Delivering Better Government* (1996) and *Partnership 2000* (1997).

The new National Co-ordinating Committee (NCC) had a number of working groups reporting to it. These groups prepared action programmes on the following issues: quality customer service, open and transparent service delivery, regulatory reform, financial management, information technology and human resource management. These working groups comprised senior civil servants and senior personnel from a variety of professional, voluntary and business organisations as well as trade union representatives.

The Human Resource Management Working Group identified a number of priority areas for action: managing performance including underperformance, the devolution of responsibility for

HRM to line managers within departments and from the Department of Finance to departments within the civil service itself, recruitment policy and practice, and training and development. There is a continuity of themes and proposals between the SMI texts and *Serving the Country Better* (1985) and the more recent document produced by the Department of Finance (1992) on the local bargaining clause of the Programme for Economic and Social Progress (PESP). This latter emphasised flexibility in grading structures, the importance of staff and trade union commitment to change, greater concentration on results and performance, better communications, and staff involvement in the setting of objectives. *Delivering Better Government* is not, therefore, an entirely original document in terms of the main ideas or proposals. What is different is that the 1992 document was very much an internal industrial relations text, whereas now these ideas have been promulgated publicly with the highest possible level of managerial and political support.

Each government department and office has now published a high-level statement of strategy under the direction of the NCC. In addition to these "official" documents there is the "unofficial" but nonetheless valuable and revealing report on strategic management (including human resource management) in the civil service which was written by a group of Assistant Secretaries and which draws in particular upon the experiences of Australia and New Zealand (McNamara, 1995).

The Assistant Secretaries' report (McNamara, 1995) is more forthright in its analysis of personnel matters in the civil service. It is highly critical of what it sees as an over-centralised personnel system. On the important issue of employee motivation the report notes that line managers have little or no control over the pay and conditions of staff and that monetary rewards are effectively taken out of the equation as far as motivation of staff is concerned, and that line managers are encouraged to opt out of dealing with their own staff because of the centralised approach to industrial relations. The report concludes that modern HRM practices are not only an enabling but a necessary condition for the

reforms of the public sector to succeed. A number of recommendations are made including: that HRM should be treated as a strategic issue driven by a central body; there should be an internally
integrated HRM policy covering everything from recruitment to
dismissal, with legal responsibility resting with the Secretary of
each department; human resource specialists should be recruited
for all departments; there should be more stress on training and
development; underperformance should be addressed and appraisal systems improved. There has been little public comment
on this report (see McKevitt, 1996 and O'Dowd, 1996). With the
exception of the call for a central body to drive HRM change
(based no doubt on the experiences of Australia and New Zealand)
all of the prescriptions of the Assistant Secretaries are repeated in
Delivering Better Government.

It is clear from this outline that, at least at face value, the Irish
government has made certain key choices in the development of
public service employment relations. Drawing upon the strategic
choice model developed for the public sector by Kessler and Purcell (1996: 211) these choices may be categorised as follows: employee development rather than cost minimisation; employee involvement and commitment rather than command and control;
and union partnership rather than the minimisation of the union
role. Since the launch of the SMI in 1994, a number of components
of a new strategy have been developed and integrated. These include the general thrust and direction of the reform agenda as set
out in *Delivering Better Government*, the facility to introduce new
forms of working such as teams which was secured in the "restructuring" agreements of the PCW, the subsequent development
of a detailed programme for the reshaping of the personnel function along HRM lines, the commitment by unions and management to modernisation and ongoing change in *Partnership 2000*,
the negotiation of a pay and partnership deal in *Partnership 2000*
which now provides for the implementation of all these elements.
At face value this would appear to be the most comprehensive and
integrated programme for change ever within the public sector

with substantial implications for change in the areas of personnel management and traditional industrial relations.

Box 13.2 below outlines a number of recent and current developments associated with the SMI which have a distinctive HRM "flavour". These changes were all negotiated under the present adversarial system. It has become clear, however, that the state, as employer, has become impatient with the slow pace of change and with the continuation of a "pay for change" stance on the part of trade unions. Thus *Partnership 2000* seeks to go beyond "pay for change" and to develop an approach based on ongoing co-operation but within a partnership system that gives unions and employees a greater influence over management decision-making. It is worth noting that the new Fianna Fáil/Progressive Democrat government introduced a new "implementation committee" in late 1997 to sustain pressure for change.

Delivering Better Government raises a number of important questions regarding the existing industrial relations and personnel systems and their capacity to accommodate a human resource management approach. What exactly are the implications of the introduction of human resource management into the public service as far as managers, staff and trade unions are concerned? To what extent can ideas and practices that were developed for use in a commercial context and in other countries be applied to the Irish public service? Are HRM and trade unionism incompatible, or is there a form of partnership between managers and trade unions which can become a new and viable *modus vivendi*? In the absence in the public service of the powerful market forces that have wrought such significant changes in the employment relationship in industry and services, what are the prospects of radical change being introduced into the Irish public service? Given the common perception that previous attempts at public service reform have not succeeded what are the prospects for this latest attempt?

BOX 13.2: EXAMPLES OF CURRENT OR RECENT CHANGES WITH A "HRM FLAVOUR"

Consumer-oriented Change

- Customer charters introduced by a number of departments including the Revenue Commissioners, Health and Agriculture and Food .

- More user-friendly opening hours and queuing systems in public offices. Agreements under PCW for more flexible opening hours.

- Localisation and decentralisation of services: e.g. the Department of Social Welfare's new one-stop-shop local office which was designed to have the most advanced technology, an integrated payments system and staff trained in customer awareness.

- SMI working group on Quality Customer Service is developing "best practice"

Development of HR strategies

- A consortium of departments has worked together to develop specific departmental HR strategies with Price Waterhouse as external consultants.

- SMI working group on HRM has developed action programmes on performance management, devolution of responsibility for human resource matters to line management, recruitment policy and practice, and training and development.

Work Organisation and Job Design

- Flexibility and change agreements under the PCW have provided for flexibility between certain grades and for new work forms such as teamworking, more flexible reporting arrangements within hierarchical structures, and more flexible working between administrative staff and professional/technical grades.

- Limited experimentation with new work forms such as teamworking (e.g. Valuation Office).

- Use of working parties in Department of Social Welfare to simplify procedures and reduce "red tape".

- Cross departmental teams such as the National Drugs Team.

Business Management Techniques

- Benchmarking exercise involving Geological Survey Offices in Dublin, Belfast and Stockholm.

- Accruals Accounting Project in Department of Transport, Energy and Communications.

- Business Process Re-engineering Project in Department of Social Welfare on Long Term Schemes.

Employment Contracts

- Heads of departments all have seven-year contracts.

- Limited use of temporary contracts.

- Agreement to amend contracts of future entrants agreed in PCW agreements.

- PCW agreements provide for formal systems for deployment of temporary and part-time staff.

Pay and Grading Developments

- Formal breaking of pay "linkages" under PCW.

- Some rationalisation of grades: e.g. amalgamation of "indoor" and "outdoor" Customs and Excise grades with general service grades in context of Single Market.

- Amendment of Conciliation and Arbitration Scheme.

- System of performance-related pay for Assistant Secretaries.

- PCW agreements provide for new pay "levels" with more flexible working between grades.

- Appraisal scheme for middle-managers linked to promotion system.

Organisation Structures

- New regional management structure in Department of Social Welfare as part of localisation development.

- Decentralisation of offices to provincial locations as part of economic strategy of governments.

- Establishment of new semi-state companies such as the Irish Aviation Authority.

HUMAN RESOURCE MANAGEMENT IN THE
SEMI-STATE SECTOR

The introduction of human resource management initiatives in the semi-state sector has been singularly uneven reflecting the disparity of management and union approaches within individual companies as well as the lack of a coherent Government policy to date to modify traditional adversarial approaches. The greatest pressures for change have come from anticipated or existing forms of EU deregulation and prevailing Government pressures to prepare the individual companies to meet head to head competition and the opening up of markets. These pressures have been most evident in the case of electricity and telephony.

As Roche (1996: 19) has noted, attempts to innovate not infrequently reflect little more than a conviction that throwing enough new initiatives at established practice might "make some impact and do some good". The greatest efforts at innovation, not surprisingly, have emerged in those companies facing the most immediate competitive threat and where traditional pluralistic bargaining is not capable of delivering the level of change required within the time available before markets are fully opened. In the ESB, for example, in the late 1980s the first significant attempt to break the hold that traditional collective bargaining operated on employee relations emerged in the section of the company most exposed to competition, namely the generation area (Hastings, 1994: 92). The background to the new initiative was the dawning realisation that the surplus capacity, which had allowed the company to live with certain restrictive work practices in power stations, was being progressively eroded as demand increased. Similarly, in TEAM Aer Lingus, the background to the dispute of summer 1994, which led to massive lay-offs and an innovative Labour Court recommendation which introduced new flexible working and upskilling, was a major "softening" in rates in the international aircraft maintenance market and continued heavy financial losses.

In Telecom Éireann, the company's strategic alliance and the opening up of the telephony market has led to managers being offered personal contracts in an effort to imbue the performance ethic at the highest level. In parallel, a strategic approach by the largest union in the company, the Communications Workers Union, and Telecom's requirements to short circuit the procedural delays in bringing in workplace change, has led to an innovative move to create an employee shareholding structure. Within this new structure, long cherished gains in working conditions and allowances were traded for an employee shareholding of up to 15 per cent and a partnership route to change. Within Telecom Éireann's mobile phone subsidiary, Eircell, the pressure for change stemmed from the Government decision to award the second mobile phone license to a private operator. The creation of Eircell as a standalone subsidiary, with a separate management structure, may also have been influenced by a desire to have a more responsive and flexible employee relations climate than its parent.

Distinctive HRM Initiatives in the Public Sector

The ESB, Telecom Éireann, Bord na Móna and Aer Rianta are four major semi-state companies where human resource initiatives are underway but at different levels of development and implementation. Industry de-regulation has been the major driving force in both the ESB and Telecom Éireann but the creation of change programmes have had a different genesis very much reflecting the more immediate competitive threat in the telephony area than the electricity market. In the area of telephony, however, there are currently over 40 organisations licensed to provide telecommunications and many of these are linked to major global operators *(The Telecom Partnership, 1997)*. Competition in the provision of infrastructure was introduced in July 1997 while full competition in telecommunications is now planned for December 1998. The pace and configuration of human resource initiatives reflects not alone the market situation of each company but the nature and structure of traditional bargaining relationships. This is especially the case in the ESB.

Table 13.3 sets out a range of initiatives that are presently underway in Irish semi-state companies.

TABLE 13.3: HUMAN RESOURCE MANAGEMENT INITIATIVES IN IRISH SEMI-STATE COMPANIES

Companies	Initiatives
ESB	Separate business units
	Fewer management levels and staff grades
	Up-skilling in power stations and distribution
	Management contracts
	Greater role for line managers
	Creation of corporate forum
	Partnership groups in all areas
Telecom Éireann	Separate Business Units
	Team briefing/leaders
	Management Contracts
	Flatter Management Structure
	Union/Management Strategy Group
	Employee Share Ownership
	Resource Value Analysis/career mobility
Eircell	Multi Functional Teams
	New Flatter Organisation
	Flexible working
TEAM Aer Lingus	Annualised Hours
	Flexible starting and finishing times
	Multi-Skilling between crafts
	Short term contracts
Bord na Móna	Company divisionalisation
	Autonomous Enterprise Units
	New products and services
Aer Rianta	Joint Union/Company Group
	Compact for Joint vision and goals
	Attempt to go "beyond bargaining relationships"

Sources: (i) Final Report of the ESB Joint Steering Committee (1993); (ii) Telecom Éireann (1997); (iii) Labour Court Recommendation No. 14552 on TEAM Aer Lingus

THE ESB

After a bruising almost week-long strike in 1991, ESB chief executive Joe Moran invited the general secretary of the ICTU, Peter Cassells, into the company to review the state of relationships between the management and the unions. In a key finding, the Joint Steering Committee, chaired by Peter Cassells, found that people throughout the company believed that shared objectives ("common cause") are an essential foundation for good relationships in ESB (1993: 8). The final review of relationships report was published in February 1993. The improvement in the internal industrial relations climate produced by this report, outlined in Box 13.3, allowed for a subsequent tripartite investigation of the ESB's cost structure, the Cost and Competitiveness Review (CCR) which comprised management, union and Government representatives.

The CCR process, which involved the shedding of 2,000 jobs, reductions in the number of grades and categories and greater devolution of authority to line management was aimed at preparing the company for the opening of the Irish electricity market to foreign competitors. It was preceded by a range of joint union management benchmarking studies which were completed in late 1994. The plan was accepted by the bulk of the staff in May 1996, ushering in one of the largest change programmes ever undertaken with the agreement of the unions in one of the country's biggest companies. The crisis in the company's industrial relations system which followed the 1991 strike, which unnerved both management and unions, led to the impetus for the Cassells Review (see Box 13.3) which subsequently prepared the ground for the Cost and Competitiveness Review.

The challenge for unions and management in the company is to maintain the momentum created by the recent series of changes of which the review of relationships report and the CCR process were major elements. Recent developments in the ESB very much conform to the type of "dualist" model outlined by Storey (1992: 258) in which the existing industrial relations system operates alongside a range of human resource initiatives which are aimed at engendering trust and flexibility.

BOX 13.3: THE FINAL REPORT OF THE JOINT STEERING COMMITTEE
ON THE REVIEW OF RELATIONSHIPS WITHIN ESB

This report believed that the continued success of the company as
a high performance public service firm meeting customer needs
and providing a fair deal for employees must be based on two key
factors — trust and shared objectives. The quality of relationships
was to be built on a commitment to the achievement of shared
objectives, mutual respect and high levels of trust between management, staff and unions. It urged developing an approach to industrial relations which was focussed on finding solutions,
greater involvement and participation by individuals and groups
in all aspects of the business. Two way communication at all levels and in all locations was also recommended. Where possible,
individuals were to align their career development requirements
with the needs of the company and contribute in accordance with
their ability to the achievement of shared ESB objectives. The
Committee found that in the past the roles of management and
unions had been characterised by an "isolationist" approach to
each other and it was essential that positive relationships built on
trust were established so that both management and unions could
radically review how they discharged their respective roles and
responsibilities. The report called for a new style of people management which recognises the need for openness and building
good working relationships with staff and trade union representatives. Managers were to be communicative, well informed, visible
and available, setting goals and providing support and encouraging debate and listening carefully to diverse opinions. Structures
were required at corporate, regional, departmental and generating station level to allow staff and unions make a meaningful input into the decision making process. A corporate forum was to be
created to provide a non-confrontational setting in which information on a wide range of issues could be shared and matters of
major significance could be discussed prior to decisions being
taken. A review of existing participative structures was also
called for to determine if they were capable of providing staff with
a meaningful input to decision making. It also called for a new
understanding of the role of industrial relations in the changing
business environment of the 1990s as well as regular meetings
between management and unions of a non-confrontational type.

Source: Final Report of the Joint Steering Committee, Review of Relationships within ESB (1993), Dublin: ESB.

One of the major barriers in this regard was getting agreement from almost sixty different categories of staff before the CCR process could be signed off, highlighting the difficulty of reaching agreement on a human resource change agenda in a union friendly environment even with the support of the top union leadership. Very few business environments would permit a negotiation period as long as eighteen months to settle an agenda aimed at preparation for outside competition. A central question within the Board, in view of the large measures of agreement reached on change, is whether the existing industrial relations system itself, which has as its apex the Joint Industrial Council, will be allowed "tick over" or be subject to serious review. Alterations to bargaining machinery and institutions have become synonymous with major change programmes in Britain, particularly under privatisation. This same question also applies to the other companies in Table 13.3, particularly Telecom Éireann, where the existing internal procedures have come under pressure from the breadth of management's change agenda and the immediacy of the demand for their introduction.

Finally, what is clear from the ESB is that the principle of partnership is regarded as a means to a more effective and efficient organisation rather than an end in itself. In other words it is seen as a vehicle for change rather than something ethereal and removed from the current agenda. A future deepening of the partnership approach within the ESB will require a continual flow of information on all aspects of the business as well as a framework, directed towards the future, to give it concrete expression.

TELECOM ÉIREANN

In late April 1997, the unions in Telecom Éireann, dominated by the Communications Workers Union (CWU), agreed a plan to transform the company into a world class business which provided a framework to reduce costs by £110 million over five years. The elaborate ninety-six page document, *The Telecom Partnership, A Framework for the Transformation of Telecom Éireann into a World Class Telecommunications Business*, provided for, among

other things, the creation of an internal jobs market for 2,500 surplus staff, the introduction of atypical working with extended
working hours for the bulk of staff from 8.30 am to 8.00 pm. It
also provided for new overtime arrangements for the 12,000
workforce where half of the overtime total would be paid in cash
and the remainder would be paid in time in lieu. As part of this
agreement, both management and the unions subscribed to a
shared analysis of the environmental and transformational needs
of the company and to the view that telecom companies are
changing from being national monopoly providers into global
players in fiercely competitive markets. In concrete terms, they
recognised that for Telecom Éireann this implied the need to reduce prices significantly on a continuing basis, the need to grow
the business and take advantage of opportunities to move into
new markets and the need to reduce the cost base. Agreeing to
locate the new agreement firmly within the wider *Partnership
2000* Agreement, both sides defined partnership as an "active relationship based on recognition of a common interest to secure the
competitiveness, viability and prosperity of the enterprise" (*The
Telecom Partnership*, (1997: 10)). Partnership structures were to
be set up at national level, business unit level and local level to
engage in collective problem solving and to advance a "Going for
Growth Strategy".

But after agreeing a fundamental change in the company's
bargaining machinery through the transference of all significant
disputes away from existing internal machinery to the Labour
Relations Commission or the Labour Court, major difficulties
arose in relation to a quid pro quo. Failure by the Government to
accept immediately the unions' demands for a 14.9 per cent
shareholding in Telecom, in return for the change agreed in the
transformation document, led to a stand-off with the leader of the
largest union in the company, David Begg. Begg, then general
secretary of the Communications Workers' Union, who attacked
the civil service for being less than fully supportive of the agreement. The Telecom agreement, he said, was like a "stamp that
never issued" (*Irish Independent*: May 3,1997). Agreement with

the unions on the structure and size of the employee shareholding was finally reached in May 1998 after considerable political involvement.

AER RIANTA

Unions and management in Aer Rianta have opted for what they call "process participation" as a means of improving communications and relationships and preparing the company for future technological and competitive challenges, particularly the ending of duty free sales. Rather than focusing on specific targets, goals or programmes, the arrangements are intended to be assimilated into the normal business process. This process form of participation avoids what the company/union group see as a situation where representative committees "would be looking for agendas." Working on the basis that the company's mission statement, philosophy, objectives and strategy have all been developed exclusively by management, the joint company/union group believe that these principles need to be revised to reflect the aspirations of staff members. The desire for participation is being given expression at different levels in the company through the creation of different groups. Regular work groups for people on the shopfloor, departmental groups, business unit groups, and a group at corporate level, were aimed at "ensuring that those employed in the organisation will know at every level how the important processes in the life of the organisation are managed" (Aer Rianta, 1996) Overseeing the whole process is the Joint Company/Union Group for Constructive Participation, which is intended to be the core development forum for constructive participation.

BORD NA MÓNA

Against the background of a 70 per cent fall in energy prices in 1985, followed by significant losses, a new management team moved in 1987 to preserve 2,200 jobs and shed 2,500 people in a major restructuring programme. With the co-operation of the trade unions the company introduced an enterprise scheme which allows staff to work in autonomous work groups within which earnings are based on performance and productivity. The company was later divisionalised and the research and development unit was expanded. Productivity eventually rose by something close to 75 per cent. The company later set out to emphasise a range of corporate values which included the customer, profits and staff. After a long process of participation and studying best practices world-wide, the board of the company adopted the value that "it is the right of staff to innovate and the duty of management to facilitate it" (O Connor, 1995: 119)

CONCLUSIONS

Any discussion of HRM in the Irish public sector must start with recognition of the almost total absence of research in the area coupled with the fact that many initiatives are still at a planning stage or only recently begun. These factors make any conclusions particularly tentative. Nevertheless, what evidence is available suggests that a variety of HRM approaches have taken root in the Irish public sector, posing significant challenges for unions and management. Early indications point to the bulk of initiatives being of the "soft" variety in both the commercial semi-states and the civil service and, in the context of continuing consensus on social and economic strategy at national level, this is unlikely to change significantly. At the same time there have been some notable cases of a "hard" HRM approach in commercial state companies such as TEAM Aer Lingus where the employment of temporary staff, the introduction of annualised hours and job shedding have featured on the employer agenda. Growing competitive forces and shortening time frames for the implementation of change in the commercial state sector may see management adopting harder approaches than in the core public services where similar time pressures do not apply at present.

The development of HRM initiatives in the semi-state sector very much reflects the competitive conditions with which each individual company has had to contend. EU deregulation policy and job shedding have been major driving forces behind changes but not all rationalisation within the sector has been accompanied by moves to reshape industrial relations along HRM lines. The "parent" departments, in particular the Department of Public Enterprise, have focused on broad strategic questions, most notably the achievement of viability and competitiveness, rather than seeking to provide prescriptive templates for the reshaping of industrial relations. At the same time particular partnership approaches such as those instanced in Telecom Éireann and Aer Lingus and, more recently the extensive employee participation schemes in Aer Rianta, have received general support from this department. The absence of a more proactive approach may seem unusual in the highly centralised Irish context and perhaps this reflects a stronger civil service confidence in the efficacy of market forces to bring about change as opposed to a "voluntarist" union-management approach. One observer, (Roche, 1996: 27), has noted that

> Ministerial interventions in semi-states . . . appear to point to an impatience or even scepticism regarding the attempts of unions and management to adjust to competition by re-shaping industrial relations practices along partnership lines.

Nevertheless, political control within the semi-state sector goes beyond the setting of corporate objectives and occasionally, but less frequently than heretofore, involves engagement with day to day activities, especially in the context of threatened disputes (Hastings, 1994).

It is not surprising, therefore, that civil service departments are encouraging the recruitment of chief executives from the private sector to the commercial state sector. This in turn has led to an alteration in personnel policy including the employment of personnel and human resource specialists well versed in the latest private sector developments and thinking. In the public service, however, the approach being taken at present centres on the professionalisation of the HRM function, without recourse to external recruitment but with hands on control from the pivotal Departments of the Taoiseach and Finance. In this context it is worth

pointing out that *Delivering Better Government,* written as it was
by a group of top civil servants, represents the emergence for the
first time of a distinctive "management voice" in the Irish civil
service that appears to be committed to radical public service reform. The new Public Service Management Act provides for former departmental secretaries becoming "secretaries general" with
a role akin to that of a chief executive. All the indications are that
these positions will continue to be filled from within the civil
service itself. One of the central questions in this regard is
whether major organisational and cultural change can be
achieved without introducing new blood at senior levels including
the increasingly important HR function within what have been
fairly inward and hierarchical organisations up to now. The idea
of professionalising the HRM function would also seem to cut
across the "generalist" traditions of civil service personnel management.

Whether or not human resource management can develop fully
in the context of national pay and grading systems in the civil
service and, by extension, in the wider public service, also needs
to be addressed. *Delivering Better Government* accepts the "unified
structure" of pay and grades across all departments. But it has to
be asked whether this is a definitive position or a recognition that
change on a core issue such as this needs to be approached in a
more circumspect manner over time. It is possible that a greater
degree of local level bargaining over the coming years will facilitate a move away, albeit a gradual and negotiated move, from entirely national pay and grading systems. The local bargaining
clause of *Partnership 2000* is likely to facilitate this. At the same
time the enduring power among public servants of arguments
from equity has been borne out in recent pay disputes under the
PCW, particularly those involving professional groups such as
nurses. In addition, it is likely that the Hay MSL consultancy
project on performance management will open up a debate on the
role of performance related pay in the civil service and whether it
should be managed locally or centrally. This debate is unlikely to
be defined solely along a union-management axis. In fact it is

likely that within the ranks of senior management there will be varying opinions as to whether or not the existing pay system needs to be radically altered to support a more performance-oriented culture. The introduction of a form of performance-related pay was one of several recommendations in the White Paper, *Serving the Country Better* (1985: 35) that never got off the starting blocks. On this occasion the issue is likely to test to the limits the ability of unions and management to work through a genuinely performance based system in the context of a partnership model. A central problem will be the conflict between the strong cost control function of the Department of Finance and the policy of devolving responsibility for personnel management and industrial relations to line departments.

Adapting to HR initiatives and demands has presented unions with a number of difficulties as well as opportunities. Initial union opposition to HR developments was very much based on a reaction to the distinctly anti-collectivist strands of Thatcherism and Reaganism with their focus on the individual and the dominance of market values. While traditionally unions have been hostile to HRM in principle as an inherently anti-union ideology, trade union policies since the late 1980s have been more receptive to new employee relation models. The clearest expression of this shift emerged in the *ICTU New Forms of Work Organisation* report (1993). In general, the whole area of the introduction of new flexibilities and new grading structures associated with HRM, has posed the greatest problem for unions. In the public service this resistance has surfaced in the form of repeated rejections of agreements that provided for atypical employment and other forms of flexible working. In the commercial state sector the creation of new grades and ending of demarcations also presented barriers to new models. One of the ironies of the current situation is that it has been the traditional industrial relations institutions, such as the Labour Court and the Labour Relations Commission which have, in the context of extreme competitive pressures and immediate crises, been to the forefront in sanctioning much of the HRM change in major State companies on foot of a largely mana-

gerial agenda, much of it crisis driven. In this context it is significant that increasing use has been made by a number of public sector unions of the LRC/LC system to settle pay disputes under the
PCW. It may well emerge that public sector unions will opt to
formally use the "private sector" LRC/LC as a permanent alternative to conciliation and arbitration leading to an institutional convergence of the public and private sector industrial relations systems.

The introduction of partnership models has itself given an impetus to the restructuring of traditional industrial relations approaches with the separation out of the areas of non-conflictual
relationships from traditional bargaining. This is best exemplified
in the communications forum in the ESB and in the proposed
partnership councils in Telecom Éireann. This shift has profound
implications for both the content and the process of collective bargaining throughout the entire public sector in that it is attempting to remove the most contentious elements of the bargaining
agenda, namely organisational and job-related changes, and
transferring these to a non-adversarial partnership process. Differences over such items as change and structure have in the past
been at the core of the adversarial model of industrial relations in
both the public services and the commercial state sector. This new
form of trade union involvement in management decision making
ultimately implies a much greater use of single-table bargaining
as well as questioning the basis for a multiplicity of unions. In the
past the multiplicity of unions in such companies as TEAM Aer
Lingus and the ESB has been seen as a factor influencing the duration of the change process.

In the Irish context, it would be wrong to regard traditional
pluralist industrial relations and the emerging human resource
model as mutually exclusive. For example, as we have seen, trade
unions have modified their positions in the light of practical experience, much of it obviously positive, of HRM being applied at
workplace levels. Cases such as Telecom Éireann, which include
such apparently incompatible bedfellows as union acceptance of
personal contracts for managerial staff, the ending of traditional

arbitration, and formal recognition by the company of the legitimate role of trade unions in management decision making, point to a more complex interaction between individualist and collectivist agendas than has been highlighted heretofore. This mix of individualism and collectivism appears to go beyond the apparent conflict between the individualism of human resource management and the collectivism of industrial relations. Industrial relations reform, unreconstituted traditional approaches and discrete HR initiatives of a "soft" or "hard" variety may be operating at different levels of an organisation, running in parallel in others or coalescing in ways that are not yet fully accounted for.

Government's endorsement of the partnership approach as a variant of soft HRM may be seen as a constraint on management choice in the personnel area. This may be more the case in the public service than in the commercial state sector. In the latter it appears that the nature of the relationship between these companies and their "parent" departments and the pressures of their competitive contexts provide for a greater degree of management freedom in the making of strategic choices. To a large extent, as already indicated, there has been a remarkable continuity of policy on the development of both the commercial state sector and the core public services between governments in the last decade. The three-year programmes have served to bridge policy gaps between governments and oppositions when changes of government took place. However, the question arises as to what would happen to the current accommodation in the absence of Government support for partnership.

The emerging shift from a dominant adversarial and pluralist model of industrial relations to one significantly influenced by the values associated with HRM and partnership suggests that the contours of the traditional "good employer" model are being redrawn. A distinctive feature of the development of HRM in Ireland has been its emergence through centralised bargaining and partnership. While the re-fashioning of public sector industrial relations is far from complete and while it may not lead to a complete convergence of private and public sector approaches, the indications are that the strength of internal and external pressure for change precludes a reversal to the old orthodoxies.

References

(a) Government Publications (all published by the Government Publications Office, Dublin)

1969: *Report of the Public Services Organisation Review Group (The Devlin Report)*.

1985: *Serving the Country Better: A White Paper on the Public Service*.

1991: *Programme for Economic and Social Progress*.

1994: Labour Court Recommendation 14552 on TEAM Aer Lingus

1994: *Programme for Competitiveness and Work*.

1996: *Delivering Better Government*.

1997: *Partnership 2000*.

1997: Central Statistics Office Statistical Release on Public Sector Employment.

(b) Books and Articles

Aer Rianta (1996): *Requisite Arrangements: Towards Constructive Participation*, Dublin: Aer Rianta.

Beaumont, P.B. (1992): *Public Sector Industrial Relations*, London: Routledge.

Department of the Environment (1996): *Better Local Government: A Programme for Change*, Dublin: Stationery Office.

Department of Finance (1992): Unpublished Memo of Understanding in Relation to the chapter on the local bargaining clause of the Programme for Economic and Social Progress.

Farnham, D. and Horton, S. (eds.) (1993): *Managing the New Public Services*, London: Macmillan.

Ferner, A. (1994): "The State as Employer" in Ferner, A. and Hyman, R. (eds.), *New Frontiers in Industrial Relations*, Oxford: Blackwell.

Ferner, A. and Colling, T. (1991): "Privatisation, Regulation and Industrial Relations" *British Journal of Industrial Relations*, 29(3): 391–409.

Final Report of the Joint Steering Committee (1993), Review Of Relationships within ESB, Dublin: ESB.

Gunnigle, P., Morley, M., Clifford, N. and Turner, T (1997): *Human Resource Management in Irish Organisations*, Dublin: Oak Tree Press.

Gunnigle, P., Mc Mahon, G.V. and Fitzgerald, G. (1995): *Industrial Relations in Practice*, Dublin: Gill and Macmillan.

Gunnigle, P., Flood, P., Morley, M. and Turner, T. (1994) *Continuity and Change in Irish Employee Relations*, Dublin: Oak Tree Press.

Gunnigle, P., Morley, M., and Turner, T. (1997): *Human Resource Management in Irish Organisations: Practice in Perspective*, Dublin: Oak Tree Press.

Hastings, T. (1994): *Semi-States in Crisis: The Challenge for Industrial Relations in the ESB and Other Major Semi-State Companies*, Dublin: Oak Tree Press.

International Labour Organisation (ILO) (1995): *Impact of Adjustment in the Public Services (Efficiency, Quality Improvement and Working Conditions)*, Geneva: ILO.

Irish Congress of Trade Unions (ICTU) (1993): *New Forms of Work Organisation: Options for Unions*, Dublin: ICTU.

Irish Congress of Trade Unions (ICTU) (1995): *Managing Change: Review of Union Involvement in Company Restructuring*, Dublin: ICTU.

Irish Independent, May 3, (1997): report on proceedings of the Communications Workers Union Annual Conference in Tralee.

Kessler, I. and Purcell, J. (1996): "Strategic Choice and New Forms of Employment Relations in the Public Service: Developing an Analytical Framework", *International Journal of Human Resource Management*, 7: 206–29.

Lawton, A. and Rose, A. (1991): *Organisation and Management in the Public Sector*. London: Pitman Publishing.

McKevitt, D. (1996): Strategic Management in the Irish Civil Service: Prometheus Unbound or Phoenix Redux, *Administration*, 43(4): 34–49.

McNamara, T. (ed.) (1995): Strategic Management in the Irish Civil Service: A Review Drawing on Experience in New Zealand and Australia, *Administration*, 43(2).

Moore, C. (1992): "Human Resource Management in the Public Sector" in Towers, B. (ed.) *Handbook of Human Resource Management*, Oxford: Blackwell Publishers.

O'Connor, E. (1995): "World Class Manufacturing in a Semi-State Environment: The Case of Bord na Móna" in Gunnigle, P. and Roche, W.K. (eds.), *New Challenges to Irish Industrial Relations*, Dublin: The Labour Relations Commission and Oak Tree Press.

O'Dowd, J. (1996): " Strategic Management: An Alternative View of Personnel", *Administration*, 43(4): 51–6.

Organisation for Economic Co-operation and Development (OECD) (1996): *Governance In Transition: Public Management Reforms in OECD Countries*, Paris: OECD.

Osborne, D. and Gaebler, T. (1993): *Reinventing Government: How the Entrepreneurial Spirit Is Transforming The Public Sector*, New York: Plume.

Pendleton, A. (1993): "Railways" in Pendleton, A. and Winterton, J. (eds.), *Public Enterprise in Transition*, London: Routledge.

Pollitt, C. (1990): *Managerialism and the Public Services*, Oxford: Blackwell.

Pollitt, C. (1995): "Justification by Works or by Faith?", *Evaluation*, 1(2): 133–54.

Rainey, H.G., Backoff, R.W. and Levine, C.H. (1976): "Comparing Public and Private Organisations", *Public Administration Review*, 36.

Roche, W.K. (1996): *The New Competitive Order and the Fragmentation of Employee Relations in Ireland*, Working Paper, Dublin: CEROP, Graduate School of Business, University College Dublin.

Roche, W.K. (1997): "Partnership: Myth or Reality?" a summary of concluding remarks at the IRN Industrial Relations Conference, *Industrial Relations News*, 11: 21–23.

Roche, W.K. and Gunnigle, P. (1995): "Competition and the New Industrial Relations Agenda", in Gunnigle, P. and Roche, W.K. (eds.), *New Challenges to Irish Industrial Relation*, Dublin: Oak Tree Press.

Roche,W.K. and Turner, T. (1994): "Testing Alternative Models of Human Resource Policy Effects on Trade Union Recognition in the Republic of Ireland", *International Journal of Human Resource Management*, 5: 721–53.

Stewart, J. and Ranson, S. (1988): "Management in the Public Domain", *Public Money and Management*, 8(1): 13–8.

Storey, J. (1989): "Human Resource Management in the Public Sector", *Public Money and Management*, 9(3): 19–24.

Storey, J. (1992): *Developments in the Management of Human Resources*, Oxford: Blackwell.

Telecom Éireann (1997): *The Telecom Partnership A Framework Agreement for the Transformation of Telecom Éireann into a World Class Telecommunications Business*, Dublin: Telecom Éireann.

Thomas, P.G. (1996): "Beyond the Buzzwords: Coping with Change in the Public Sector", *International Review of Administrative Sciences*, 62: 5–29.

Turner, T. and Morley, M. (1995): *Industrial Relations and the New Order: Case Studies in Conflict and Co-operation*, Dublin: Oak Tree Press.

Weggemans, H. (1987): "Personnel and Public Management" in Koomian, J. and Eliassen, K.A. (eds.), *Managing Public Organisations: Lessons From Contemporary Europe*, London: Sage.

Yntema, P. (1993): "Managing Human Resources in the Public Sector" in Koomian, J. and Eliassen, K.A. (eds.), *Managing Public Organisations: Lessons From Contemporary Europe*, London: Sage.

14

BUSINESS STRATEGY AND HUMAN RESOURCE MANAGEMENT

Geraldine O'Brien

INTRODUCTION

The central contention underpinning HRM is that organisations incorporate human resource considerations into strategic decision-making, establish a corporate human resource philosophy and develop a complementary and coherent set of personnel strategies and policies to improve human resource utilisation (see Gunnigle's chapter in this book). This linkage of people management issues and strategic planning processes is what is seen to differentiate Human Resource Management (HRM) from personnel management (Sibson, 1983; Storey and Sisson, 1993). Hendry and Pettigrew (1990) take the view that the focus on strategy and the link between business strategy and HRM constitutes the distinctive feature of HRM and provides the most productive focus for its study. Our concern in this chapter is with this central tenet of HRM, that is, the interplay between business strategy and human resource management.

To understand fully the different approaches to this question, it is first necessary to consider what is meant by the concept of strategy, recognising the fact that there is little agreement on the substance, nature and meaning of the concept (Gunnigle et al., 1997a). We will also look at the manner in which different commentators address the links between business strategy and human resource strategy. This will lead us to the question of whether the notion of business/human resource strategy integration is a conceptual construct or whether there is evidence to support the view that organisations *are* building a closer relationship between their business strategy and their human resource strategy? If there is evidence of such integration, can it be correlated with superior company performance?

THE CONCEPT OF STRATEGY

Storey and Sisson (1993) note that central to the very idea of HRM is the notion that it entails a more *strategic* approach to the management of people than do traditional personnel or industrial relations models. The supposition underlying most of the writing on the subject is that it is relatively easy to move from ad hoc, pragmatic management to strategic management.

> The principles appear very simple and the process apparently merely entails a series of logical steps. To move up to managing strategically therefore seems only to require the appropriate degree of will on the part of the managers concerned (Storey and Sisson, 1993: 52).

However, as they go on to point out, strategic HRM is problematical both at a conceptual and a practical level. The first set of problems arises with the concept of business strategy. Johnson and Scholes (1993: 10) define strategy as

> the *direction* and *scope* of an organisation over the long term: ideally, which matches its *resources* to its changing *environment,* and in particular to its *markets, customers or clients,* so as to meet *stakeholder* expectations.

Within this viewpoint, strategy is seen to operate at three levels: *corporate strategy* relates to the overall scope of the organisation, its structures and financing, and the apportionment of resources between various parts of the organisation; *business* or *competitive strategy* refers to how the organisation is to compete in a particular market, its approaches to product development and to customers; and finally, *functional* or *operational strategies* are concerned with how the various sub-units — marketing, personnel, manufacturing, and so on — contribute to the higher-level strategies (Walker, 1992).

We can also distinguish between "upstream" and "downstream" strategic decisions (Purcell, 1989). "Upstream", first-order decisions refer to the long-term direction of the organisation or the scope of its activities. These types of decisions will have implications for the type of people employed, the size of the firm and the technology required. These latter decisions can be classified as more downstream, or second-order, strategic decisions. According to Purcell (1989), choices on human resource structures and approaches are made in the context of downstream strategic decisions on organisational structure. These choices are themselves strategic as they fix the limits of employee relations management in the organisation, but they are likely to be crucially influenced by first and second-order decisions as well as by external factors such as legislation, trade unions and the labour markets. These are termed third-order strategic decisions.

Such definitions, Legge (1995: 97) warns us, are implicitly "presenting a normative model of what strategy *should be* rather than a description of the behaviours that *are enacted* under the loose label of strategy". The view of strategy as a formal and rational decision-making process, i.e. the *classical* perspective, has met with considerable criticism (Quinn, 1978; Mintzberg 1978, 1988, 1990, Pettigrew, 1977). These authors suggest that "rationalistic" models of strategy need to be replaced with "processual" and "incremental" models. The interaction of various external and internal factors compels managers to make continuous assessments and continuous adjustments. Managing strategy then becomes an interactive process. Mintzberg (1978, 1988), for example, points out that strategy is about "preferences, choices and matches" rather than being an exercise in applied logic. It is a shared perspective about future intentions — a "pattern in a stream of activities". He distinguishes between "realised" and "unrealised" strategies and between "intended" and "emergent" strategies. Strategies that are both intended and realised are "deliberate" strategies whereas "unrealised" strategies are those, that may be intended but are in fact never executed. As Hendry (1995) points out the distinction between content and process is particularly salient when it comes to strategy implementation for there may be many a slip between the plan and its implementation. Realised strategies, on the other hand, may emerge without the conscious design of the strategists, i.e. "emergent" strategies. Mintzberg believes that deliberate strategy hinders learning, while emergent strategy fosters it but precludes control.

As Whittington (1993) points out the "classical" approach is not the only perspective on the concept of strategy. He offers a four-fold typology in which approaches to strategy vary along two dimensions, namely, "outcomes", i.e. the extent to which strategy is aimed at profit-maximising outcomes or entertains other possible outcomes, and "processes", i.e. the extent to which strategy formulation is deliberate or emergent. He identifies four generic approaches to strategy formation, as illustrated in Figure 14.1.

FIGURE 14.1: MODEL OF GENERIC PERSPECTIVES ON STRATEGY

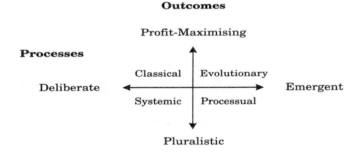

Source: Whittington (1993: 3).

In the "classical" approach, strategy is a rational process of deliberate calculation and analysis designed to maximise long-term advantage. For the classicists good planning is what it takes to master the internal and external environment. Strategies are seen as emerging from a conscious, rationalistic, decision-making process, fully formulated, explicit and articulated, a set of orders for others, lower down the organisation to carry out. As Whittington (1993: 15–17) puts it:

> plans are conceived in the general's tent, overlooking the battlefield but sufficiently detached for safety . . . the actual carrying-out of orders is relatively unproblematic, assured by military discipline and obedience.

The "evolutionary" perspective draws upon the ideas of population ecology, whereby

> the most appropriate strategies within a given market emerge as competitive processes allow the relatively better performers to survive while the weaker performers are squeezed out and go to the wall (Legge, 1995: 99).

Because of the uncertainty of the environment, this perspective considers the "classical" approach as often inapplicable and yet only organisations that have a profit-maximising strategy will survive. As managers do not control the situation, they can only make sure that the fit between strategy and environment is as efficient as possible (Lundy and Cowling, 1996).

In the "processual" view, there is a view that "both organisations and markets are often sticky, messy phenomena, from which strategies emerge with much confusion and in small steps" (Whittington, 1993: 22). From this perspective, a strategy may be identified in retrospect, as separate steps showing a loose coherence over time (Legge, 1995). Mintzberg's views outlined above and Quinn's (1978) notion of "logical incrementalism" fit well with this viewpoint. A second essential feature of the processual view is that it permits a micro-political perspective (Pettigrew, 1973; Purcell, 1989; Purcell and Ahlstrand, 1994), acknowledging that

> strategic decisions are characterised by the political hurly-burly of organisational life with a high incidence of bargaining, a trading off of costs and benefits of one interest group against another, all within a notable lack of clarity in terms of environmental influences and objectives (Johnson, 1987: 21).

The fourth perspective is the "systemic" one, which suggests that strategy is shaped by factors such as class, gender and national culture. In other words, strategic choices are constrained by the social system. Because of their social background or culture, strategists may well have interests other than profit-maximisation. Hence, for example, the very different strategic goals of US and Japanese companies, the former prioritising return on investment and share price increase, the latter preferring market share and proportion of new products (Abegglen and Stalk, 1985 cited in Legge, 1995). This, Whittington (1993) argues, reflects the different capital market structures of Japan and the US while the similarity between the UK and the US he attributes to a shared Anglo-Saxon culture that values individualism and free enterprise. Whittington summarises the systemic model by describing its strategy as "embedded", its rationale as "local", its focus as external but looking towards societies rather than towards markets. Finally Whittington (1993: 41) believes this to be the dominant perspectives for the 1990s because

> [the end of the] opposition between capitalist America and the Communist Soviet bloc should allow a more nuanced appreciation of the different textures of market economies and the rich variety of their linkages with the rest of society. The success of the Far Eastern economies, the entry of East European countries into the capitalist world and the closer interaction of West European countries are compelling proper appreciation of the diversity of practice within capitalist economies.

LINKING HRM WITH BUSINESS STRATEGY

What is meant by integrating HRM policies with business strategy and whether such linkage is feasible will, according to Legge (1995), depend very much upon the strategic perspective adopted. The logic of knowingly matching HRM policy to business strategy is only appropriate if one upholds the rationalistic "classical" perspective. If one takes the "processual" perspective there may be no clearly enunciated business strategy with which to match HRM policy. Hendry and Pettigrew (1990) suggest that there are limits to the extent to which rational HR strategies can be drawn up if the process of business strategic planning is itself irrational. From the "evolutionary" viewpoint the whole business of consciously matching strategy and HRM policy is a fantasy and not worth the effort because it is the market that will decide what is appropriate. The "systemic" perspective would suggest that the concepts of corporate and human resource strategies might be unfamiliar in some cultures. These differing perspectives are worth keeping in mind for when we look at the various efforts at linking business strategy and human resource management, because many of these efforts have relied heavily on a classical perspective of strategy with resultant difficulties.

As was pointed out above, one of the features that differentiates strategic HRM from "traditional" personnel management is the integration of HRM with business strategy. This vertical "fit", or integration between the environment, business strategy, and HR policies and practices, has been referred to as "external fit" by Baird and Meshoulam (1988) or "organisational integration" by Guest and Peccei (1994). The notion of "fit" begs a number of questions; for example, why is integration between strategy and HRM considered important and integration with what?

The focus on the integration of HRM with strategy is a direct outcome of the emphasis on "competitive advantage", the kernel of competitive strategy (cf. Becker and Gerhart, 1996). Competitive advantage is the sum of the capabilities, resources, relationships and decisions which allow an organisation to exploit opportunities in the market-place and to avoid threats to its desired position (Lengnick-Hall and Lengnick-Hall, 1990). Increasingly it is being acknowledged that the management of people is one of the key links to generating a competitive edge.

> People and how we manage them are becoming more important because many other sources of competitive success are less powerful than they once were. Traditional sources of success — product and process technology, protected or regulated markets, access to financial resources, and

> economies of scale — can still provide competitive leverage,
> but to a lesser degree now than in the past, leaving organ-
> isational culture and capabilities, derived from how people
> are managed, as comparatively more vital (Pfeffer, 1994a:
> 10–11).

Equally, the capacity to implement the changes called for in business strategies is dependent on people. As Walker (1992: 8–9)
points out "people, not companies, innovate, make decisions, develop and produce new products, penetrate new markets, and
serve customers more effectively".

Lengnick-Hall and Lengnick-Hall (1988) identify a number of
reasons why it is desirable to integrate human resource management and strategy. First, integration provides a broader range of
solutions to difficult organisational problems. Second, integration
ensures that human, financial, and technological resources are
considered when determining goals and assessing implementation
capabilities. Third, integration forces organisations to think consciously about the employees who are central to the implementation of policies. Finally, reciprocity in integrating human resource
and strategic concerns reduces the subordination of strategic considerations to human resource preferences and the overlooking of
human resources as an essential source of organisational competence and competitive advantage. This diminishes a potential
source of sub-optimisation.

Integration also refers to the synergy and fit across human resource practices as well as between those practices. Baird and
Meshoulam (1988) have described this latter complementarity as
"internal fit" or "horizontal" integration. They argue that organisational performance will be improved to the extent that organisations adopt human resource management practices that complement and support each other. This perspective implies that individual policies or practices "have limited ability to generate
competitive advantage in isolation," but "in combination . . . they
can enable a firm to realise its full competitive advantage"
(Barney, 1995: 56). Others (e.g. Kochan and Osterman, 1994; Pfeffer, 1994) are more inclined to suggest that there is an identifiable

set of best practices for managing employees that have universal, additive and positive effects on organisational performance while Youndt et al. (1996) maintain that the two approaches are in fact complementary.

Lengnick-Hall and Lengnick-Hall's (1988) point above about the reciprocity in integrating human resource and strategic concerns leads us to a consideration of the direction of the integration or "fit" between business or corporate strategy and HRM. Guest (1991) wonders if the fit should be to business strategy, a set of values about the quality of working life or should the stock of human resources mould business strategy? Are there, as Legge (1989) implies, inevitable conflicts between the different types of fit? Legge's assessment of attempts at fitting HRM policies to various typologies of strategic behaviour leads her to the view that HRM is seen largely as a third-order strategy deriving from second-order strategies, which in turn derive from first-order strategy. If this is the case, although they may be aligned, it is unlikely that HR strategies will ever be fully integrated. However, Legge (1995) questions, from an effectiveness and efficiency perspective, whether a grand integrated strategy is better than having no strategy. She maintains that a tight matching of HRM policies with business strategy may be both impractical and disadvantageous. Becker and Gerhart (1996: 789) also point to a potential downside of tight fit:

> Tightly coupled systems, because of their complexity and the high interdependence between system elements, may break down in unexpected ways, and they may not be very adaptable to change.

As an example, Legge (1995) points to models that seek to match management skills and incentives to particular competitive responses. She maintains that it would be preferable to develop managers who can perceive the need for and have the ability to respond appropriately to a range of competitive conditions, given the rate of environmental change. However, Becker and Gerhart (1996) point out that if strategic HR systems are genuinely aligned around business problems and operating initiatives, and that perspective is embedded in the system and the organisation, then all stakeholders will be anticipating system change as they see the business problems evolving.

Much of the emphasis in the discussion of vertical integration is on the growing importance of the *implementation* of strategy over its *formulation*. From this perspective, attention to HRM only occurs once the strategic direction has been decided, and while the two domains may learn from each other, strategic issues generally remain unaltered throughout implementation. As people are more adaptable than organisational strategies, the match between people and strategy is typically seen as unidirectional — from strategies to HRM practices that evoke employee role behaviours and, to changes in consequent organisation performance (Wright and McMahan, 1992). HRM is not then really portrayed as a measurable capacity from which strategic choices can be derived easily (Sparrow and Hiltrop, 1994).

Human resource strategies are functional strategies and typically functional planning follows a top-down process. However, Walker (1992) rightly contends that human resource strategies are different in that they are meshed with all other strategies; the management of people is not a distinct function but the means by which all business strategies are implemented. Human resource planning ought, therefore, to be an integral part of all other strategy formulation. Walker, based on Dyer's (1986) findings, has identified three different approaches to the development and implementation of human resource strategy (outlined in Figure 14.2). He believes that in a world where human resource plans are still often considered to be staff-driven operational and implementation plans, an aligned process would be a big step forward.

FIGURE 14.2: DEVELOPING AND IMPLEMENTING HUMAN RESOURCE
STRATEGY

Environment Assessment	Strategy Development	Strategy Implementation
Integrated Process		↑
Human resources considered as part of environmental assessment.	Business strategy covers all functional areas, including human resources.	
Alligned Process		Management of human resources: alignment of organisation, capabilities, performance management.
Parallel and interactive environmental assessment: human resource issues influence overall results.	Human resource strategy developed together with business strategy.	
Separate Process		↓
Environmental assessment focuses on human resources; past business strategy reviewed for inputs on human resource issues.	Human resource strategy developed as a separate functional plan (by staff, unit, company-wide or business unit).	

Source: Walker, (1992: 78) (based on Dyer, 1986).

Torraco and Swanson (1995) would go further than Walker and argue that today's business environment requires that the human resource function not only support the business strategies, but that it must take on a central role in the formulation of business strategy. This latter role must include "process control", that is, the capacity to influence the range of information used in making a decision, as well as "decision control" which is the ability to exert influence on the decision itself (Fischer et al., 1996). As Hendry and Pettigrew (1986: 7) put it:

> HRM [has] a role in creating competitive advantage, in which the skills and motivation of a company's people and the way they are deployed can be a major source of com-

petitive advantage. A company can methodically identify wherein its HR strengths lie and gear its HRM policies and business strategies towards utilising and developing these advantages. The HR skills that will be crucial for the future in its industry can be identified, and it can take steps to acquire these.

Dyer (1983, 1985), Eisenstat (1996), Beer (1997), Purcell (1994) and Fischer et al. (1996) argue that the HRM function should be integrated into the strategy formulation process as well as adjusting HR practices at the implementation stage. The adoption of strategic HRM is believed to require a highly competent and persistent strategic HRM champion. Consequently, they emphasise the importance of having a HR director at board level. They expect the HR function to be proactive and they look for coherence between all the practices and policies inherent in the organisation's strategy. According to Marchington and Wilkinson (1996) there is evidence that a HRM specialist on the board increases the probability that HRM issues will be considered in the formulation of strategic plans, whereas without such a presence these issues are more likely to be sidelined or inadequately discussed.

However, many organisations simply do not have the necessary type of HR leader (Fisher et al., 1996; Sparrow and Hiltrop, 1994). As Gratton (1994: 48) points out "Without the re-engineering of fundamental human resource systems, mission statements are destined to remain rhetorical". She maintains that a schism between rhetoric and reality exists in too many organisations, where the systems to select, induct, appraise, reward and develop simply conspire to focus, enable and sustain behaviours which run counter to the very core of the strategic intent. In part, the reasons for this schism, she argues, lie in the fact that in many organisations the business strategy is created in isolation and "handed down" to the HR professionals for implementation. This one-way process occurs because there is no HR representation at board level to create initial integration, members of the HR function have limited business awareness, or they operate in an administrative rather than a strategic role.

There have been many discussions about the role the HR function can play in strategy formulation and implementation but, equally, there are those who state that the HRM profession has not been able to build a convincing case for the strategic contribution of HRM. Fulmer (1992) states that too few general managers understand the role HR could play and human resource specialists have not been able to make a case for themselves because they lack the training for such a role. The skills they require to contribute to the long-term competitive success of their company are both technical and managerial (Fulmer, 1992, cf. Beer, 1997, Eisenstat, 1996).

Some of the comments regarding the role of the HR function could, of course, also be made in relation to line managers and their role in the achievement of strategic "fit". In the classical approach to strategy it is a case of making the right decision and then cascading this through the managerial hierarchy to shop floor or office workers, who then take the necessary action to meet organisational goal. However, many well-intended strategies have little effect because management practices are not aligned with them. Brewster et al. (1983) provide a number of examples from different industries which illustrate how the espoused policies of top-level management are ignored, amended or ranked in the face of conflicting pressures on organisations.

Each of the two pluralist perspectives on strategy shows up the conflict inherent in organisational life,

> whether this be due to tensions *within* management or to challenges which may be mounted from workers (either through trade unions or as individual employees working without co-operation) (Marchington and Wilkinson, 1996: 363).

This conflict may operate as a barrier to full vertical integration in practice. While the emphasis may be on achieving corporate or business objectives, this should be a process, in Quinn-Mills' (1983) words, of "planning with people in mind" taking into account the needs and aspirations of all the members of the organisation. Schuler and Jackson (1989) admit that it is unclear as to how feasible or desirable it is for workers to continually change as organisations find it imperative to change strategies more rapidly than before. They also point out that it is unlikely that firms will be able to change HRM practices proactively and singly unless they have significant power.

At the management level Marchington and Wilkinson (1996) have identified a number of potential difficulties. These include the fact that many middle managers and supervisors may not

- Identify closely with the goals of the employer

- See any value in being constrained by instructions from senior managers

- Believe that they will have senior management support

- Have sufficient time to undertake the HR aspects of their jobs

- Receive explicit rewards for undertaking the HR aspects of their jobs

- Have received adequate training to convert strategy into practice.

A further question is the extent to which managers actually have a genuine free choice of strategic position. Political forces within the organisation, as well as the competing coalitions with different self-interest, may prevent the take up of many strategic HRM practices (Pettigrew, 1973). For example, the existence of union agreements may limit the ability of the organisation to tailor HR policies and practices to the organisational strategy.

Brewster (1993) contends that HR strategies will be subjected to considerable environmental pressure — for example, in Europe, legislation about employee involvement. This may mean that HR strategies cannot be wholly ruled by business strategies. He also suggests that European HR managers may place less emphasis on a strategic role, in the first place, because, as a result of greater government involvement in regulating work life in many European countries, managers in general have less control and autonomy than is assumed in American models. At the same time, however, European managers can rely on a greater level of government support for the labour market, and in some ways this gives them more choices in the strategic HRM field (Brewster, 1993).

Kochan and Osterman (1994) have also highlighted the role of national institutional systems in constraining or facilitating the diffusion of HRM principles. Roche and Turner (1997) contend that national institutional systems may typically operate in a selective manner in constraining or facilitating the uptake of HRM policies rather than constraining or facilitating HRM policies *tout court*. For example, HRM policies in voice and flow management do not face strong constraints in the established institutional system. In other words, they may "go with the grain" of the wider institutional system of Irish industrial relations, in which unions and collective bargaining remain of pivotal importance. On the other hand, innovations in reward systems and work organisation may face stronger institutional constraints because they "go against the grain". This implies that attaining "internal fit" across different HRM policy areas is problematic. It is possible that short-term managerial pragmatism, combined with limited managerial skill, may predispose managers to "pick and mix" HRM policies, with little concern for consistency or "fit" (Storey, 1992).

We will turn in a moment to look at the approaches taken by various commentators to the question of business strategy/HRM linkage. But before doing this it is necessary to attend to a key feature of HRM. Storey (1987) points out that human resource management has its "hard" and its "soft" dimensions. The "hard" model emphasises the "quantitative, calculative, and business strategic aspects of managing the headcount resource in as "rational" a way as for any other economic factor" (Storey, 1987: 6). Its focus is ultimately on human *resource management*. The soft usage reverberates of the human relations movement with its stress on employees as a resource, a source of competitive advantage through their commitment, adaptability and high quality. Here the focus is on the *human resource* aspects of people management. The same term is thus capable of giving diametrically opposite sets of messages. Salaman (1992) points out that the different interpretations of HRM have consequences not only for how the individual is treated but also for the whole approach to the employment relationship. In the hard approach, ultimately staff are dispensable costs. The interests of the individual and the organisation are therefore always potentially in conflict. The soft approach, on the other hand, assumes that the relationship between employee and employer is one of mutual benefit; employees can be developed and empowered so that they realise their potential. This assumes the presence of trust on both sides.

Very often the different conceptual approaches to HRM are seen to reflect either a "hard" or a "soft" perspective. Marchington and Wilkinson (1996) note that an acceptance of the philosophy behind the "soft" approach would be likely to lead one to the absolutist or "best practice" models of human resource management. The alternative understanding of human resource management would focus one on the need to ensure that HRM strategies and practices are aligned with, and downstream from, business strategy; in other words, towards the contingency or matching models. However, Cappelli and McKersie (1987) believe that these rather different emphases are not necessarily incompatible and that, for example, most of the normative statements contain elements of both the "hard" and the "soft" models.

A further distinction that can be made between the contingency models and "best practice" models is the extent to which they are "open" or "closed" (Salaman and Mabey, 1995). For example, the contingency models have in common an important feature that distinguishes them from other approaches: they all maintain that the business strategy will determine the most appropriate form or context of HRM. These are open approaches *contingent* with respect to the characteristics of the "appropriate" strategy — there is no best way; it would simply be a suitable HR strategy. On the other hand, for many writers, the essence of HR strategies lies in the utilisation of a specific and limited range of policies (best practice) in every situation, which might be termed a closed view. The presumption, according to Salaman and Mabey

(1995), seems to be that the goals are necessary and valuable in every case, for every strategy and every set of conditions. This is not to deny that this approach also affirms that there should be a close, supportive and mutual relationship between business strategy and HR strategy. We will now look at the two main alternative perspectives on the link between business strategy and HRM, "Best Practice" Models and Contingency Models.

BEST PRACTICE OR "UNIVERSALISTIC" MODELS OF STRATEGIC HRM

Most notable among the "best practice" models are those put forward by the teams at Harvard Business School (Beer et al., 1984), at the Massachusetts Institute of Technology (Kochan et al., 1986) and at Stanford (Pfeffer, 1994a and 1994b). The thesis that "best practice" HRM might generate improved performance for *any* organisation, at least in the long term, has gained new currency with the recent writings of, for instance, Pfeffer (1994a), Osterman (1994) and Huselid (1995).

The roots of the Harvard model (Beer et al., 1984) are widely recognised as being in the human relations school, with a resultant emphasis on communications, teamwork and the utilisation of individual talents. Beardwell and Holden (1997) argue that the Harvard Business School's model is more flexible than the contingency models. The "map of HRM territory", as the authors (Beer et al., 1984) have described their model, acknowledges that there is a variety of "stakeholders" in the organisation, which includes shareholders, different groups of employees, the government and the community. Beer et al. (1984) point out that the formulation of HRM strategies has to recognise these interests and blend them as much as possible into the human resource strategy and ultimately the business strategy. This "neopluralist" perspective has been recognised as being useful in the study of comparative HRM (Poole, 1990) and has also made the model more amenable to "export" as different legal frameworks, managerial styles and cultural differences can be accommodated within it. The Harvard model has won a certain level of acceptance among academics and commentators in the UK, which has had relatively strong union structures and different industrial relations traditions from the United States. Notwithstanding, some academics have still criticised the model as being too unitarist while accepting its basic assumptions (Hendry and Pettigrew, 1990).

The core of the Harvard model is the responsibility and ability of managers to make decisions about the employment relationship that maximise organisational outcomes for key stakeholders. The approach taken to workplace relations emphasises

> unitary, integrative, individualistic systems, undermining workforce organisation or collectivist values as outcomes of management choices about the key HRM levers affecting workforce-organisation relations (Salaman and Mabey, 1995: 39).

There are six basic elements to the analytical framework of the Harvard model (see Figure 14.3). These are (1) situational factors; (2) stakeholder interests; (3) HRM policy choices; (4) HR outcomes; (5) long-term consequences; and (6) a feedback loop through which the outputs flow directly into the organisation and to the stakeholders.

The *situational factors* influence the choice of HR strategy. Management's strategic task is to make certain key policy choices in the context of the particular set of situational factors.

The *stakeholder interests* accepts the importance of "trade off", either explicitly or implicitly, between various interests, for instance between the owners' interests and those of the employees and their unions.

The model appears to submit that there is one superior set or bundle of *human resource management policy choices*, but the presence of multiple stakeholders will influence the specific choice of HR policy; in other words the choices result "from an interaction between constraints and choices" (Bratton and Gold, 1994: 21).

FIGURE 14.3: THE HARVARD ANALYTICAL FRAMEWORK FOR HRM

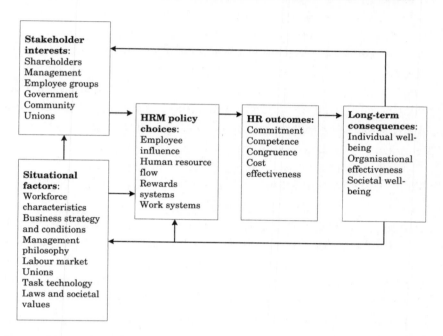

Source: Beer et al. (1984: 16).

If suitable choices are made, then valuable *HR outcomes* will follow. These include high employee commitment to organisational goals, a complementary and coherent set of HR policies, a competent workforce with high individual performance resulting in cost-effective products or services. The basic premise is that employees have talents, which are seldom fully utilised at work, and that they have desires to experience growth through their work.

The *long-term* consequences are at three levels, individual, organisational and societal. At the individual level, the outcomes are the psychological rewards received in return for effort. For the organisation, increased effectiveness ensures its survival. Finally, society achieves some of its goals, for example, high employment and economic growth, as a result of full utilisation of people at work.

The final element is the *feedback loop*. While the situational factors influence the HR strategic choices, the relationship can be two-way with the long-term outputs in turn influencing the situational factors, stakeholder interests and HRM policies.

Although the model allows for considerable variation and appears to contrast itself with situational determinism (Storey and Sisson, 1993), Guest (1987: 510) would maintain that it is an "implicit theory". The analysis of strategic choice contained in the model, with specified desirable outcomes of commitment, competence and so on, can be seen to be prescriptive (Boxall, 1992).

Guest (1987) has drawn on the Harvard framework to develop the "bare bones" of a theory. In a series of articles (1987, 1989a, 1989b, 1990, 1991), he defines HRM in terms of four key policy goals: high commitment, high quality, flexibility and strategic integration. He argues that only when a coherent strategy, aimed towards these four policy goals, fully integrated into business strategy and fully supported by line management at all levels, is applied, will the high productivity and related outcomes desired by management be achieved (Guest, 1990). By his own definition, Guest has devised a normative "theory" of HRM.

Guest (1987, 1989a) identifies four "preconditions" for the achievement of the HRM policy goals, namely a "greenfield" site with a carefully chosen workforce that has not been exposed to an "undesirable" industrial sub-culture; a highly professional management team, preferably Japanese or American; intrinsically rewarding work; and security of employment. In practice, however, high levels of competition can make the last of these difficult to achieve, if not impossible (Whipp, 1992). Furthermore, the Japanese style work and employment practices that are usually found in "greenfield" sites rarely appear to offer the main body of workers intrinsically rewarding work (Delbridge and Turnbull, 1992).

To what extent does the research support the "best practice" models by showing that there is an identifiable set of best practices for managing employees that have universal, additive and positive effects on organisational performance?

There is growing evidence, albeit still very limited, of the relationship between organisational effectiveness, corporate culture, and financial performance (Denison, 1990; Kotter and Heskett,

1992; Pfeffer, 1994a, 1994b; Collins and Porras, 1994). Effectiveness is much more than the aggregate talent of the organisation's employees. It is a function of the co-ordination around business processes that the organisation is able to develop (Beer et al., 1996; Ulrich and Lake, 1990). That co-ordination is in turn a function of the company's cultural context (Beer and Eisenstat, 1996).

A number of researchers have supported "best practice" predictions. Terpstra and Rozell (1993) proposed five "best" staffing practices and found a moderate, positive relationship between the use of these practices and organisational performance. Leonard (1990) found that organisations having long-term incentive plans for their executives had larger increases in return on equity over a four-year period than did other organisations.

Pfeffer (1994a) illustrates how five companies — Plenum Publishing, Circuit City, Tyson Foods, Wal-Mart and Southwest Airlines — all in highly competitive markets, with few barriers to entry, little unique or proprietary technology, and many substitute products or services and lots of bankruptcies, have managed to obtain returns of between 15,000 and 22,000 per cent over the past 20 years. This achievement has earned them *Money Management's* rating as the top five US companies for that period. According to Pfeffer, what these companies tend to have in common is that for their sustained advantage they rely on how they manage their work force.

Koch and McGrath (1996) studied 319 business units in the US. They reported positive and significant effects on workforce productivity in organisations that used more sophisticated human resource planning, recruitment and selection strategies. These effects were particularly pronounced in the case of capital-intensive organisations. They did not, however, study the inter-relationships between the human resource practices or the links with strategy.

How do human resource decisions influence organisational performance? In the simplest terms, according to Becker and Gerhart (1996: 780), "they must either improve efficiency or contribute to revenue growth". Traditionally, human resources have been viewed as a cost to be minimised and a potential source of efficiency gain. However, the new interest in human resources as a strategic lever that can have economically significant effects on a firm's bottom line is resulting in a shift of focus more toward value creation. The mechanisms by which human resource decisions create and sustain value are complicated and not well understood (Becker and Gerhart, 1996) and therefore measuring the outcomes of HRM is not without its difficulties. Armstrong (1994) studied 10 blue-chip companies, 8 of which could be described as "fully integrated", one was "moving towards integration" and the remaining one was "aligned". Two of these companies could point to a significant improvement in the ratio of added value per pound of employment costs, but the rest could not produce any quantifiable evidence, although they all seemed to think that HR was a good thing.

> I don't think you can point to pounds and pence and say "it's had this effect". It's virtually impossible to say that there's been an improvement in performance, an improvement on the bottom line, and that this is attributable to your human resource values; and I find it very difficult to imagine how you can positively measure it. Your real measure is just talking to people. It's very difficult to persuade accountants of that and I am an accountant (Managing Director quoted in Armstrong, 1994: 55).

No one could even estimate the size of their contribution, and Armstrong felt that it had to be accepted that the specific impact of HR strategies on overall performance is almost impossible to calculate (Armstrong, 1994).

However, despite the difficulties, we are seeing a shift towards defining measures of achievement in terms of ultimate impact on the issues defined. This requires definition of the specific measures to be used — the evidence required to determine the impact of the actions on the issue (e.g. turnover, personnel cost ratios, employee attitude indexes, productivity improvement, service quality or skill development). Becker and Gerhart (1996) identify many problems associated with measuring effectiveness and HR.

These include defining the unit of analysis, the measure of organisational performance, what HR practices to include and how they are to be measured.

There is evidence that sophisticated HR practices can have a direct bottom-line effect on organisational profitability. Huselid's 1995 report is fairly unique in that it quantifies the effects of what he termed "high performance work practices" on company performance. Marchington and Wilkinson (1996) point out that Pfeffer (1994b) and other UK writers (Storey, 1992; Wood, 1995, Wood and Albanese, 1995) who have looked at "best practice" HRM draw upon case study evidence or less extensive questionnaire survey results to generate their conclusions. On the other hand Huselid's study is based on a national sample of nearly one thousand US companies. Instead of focusing on a single practice (e.g. compensation), he assessed the extent to which companies used "best practices" in the areas of selection, performance appraisal, compensation, grievance procedures, information sharing, attitude assessment and labour-management participation (as measured by his HR Sophistication Scale). The indications are that these practices have an economically and statistically significant impact on both intermediate employee outcomes (turnover and productivity) and short- and long-term measures of corporate financial performance. For example, Huselid estimated that companies with HR sophistication levels one standard deviation higher than the average HR sophistication level of companies in the sample had profits per employee of approximately US$33,250 more than average companies. However, there was limited support for predictions that the impact of High Performance Work Practices on company performance is in part contingent on their interrelationships and links with competitive strategy.

Delery and Doty's (1996) study of 216 firms in the US banking sector also provided strong support for the universalistic perspective. Their results show that differences in HR practices are associated with rather large differences in financial performance. For example, for banks one standard deviation above the mean on each of three significant practices, financial performance was estimated to be approximately 30 per cent higher than it was for those banks at the mean. They contend that the results appear to be even stronger than Huselid's results.

Ichniowski et al. (1996) show in their review that most US studies that examine systems of HR practices have demonstrated that such practices, particularly where they are adopted in "bundles" or coherent packages, are associated with positive performance effects.

The Special Research Forum on Human Resource Management and Organisational Performance (cf: *Academy of Management Journal* 1996, 39 (4)) brings together seven studies that, at multiple levels of analysis, provide consistent empirical support for the hypothesis that HR can make a meaningful difference to a firm's bottom line (Becker and Gerhart, 1996). However, the UK findings are less conclusive. Wood and de Menezes (1998) in analysing the 1990 UK Workplace Industrial Relations Survey data viewed high commitment management (HCM) as a matter of degree in contrast to many writers who have tended to focus on HCM as a total package. Four progressive styles of HCM were discovered. Wood and de Menezes' research revealed no unique strong performance gains stemming from the use of HCM. It appears that exceptionally high users, in common with low users of HCM, do perform better than other organisations in terms of their profitability and ability to create jobs. Nonetheless, on other performance dimensions they found HCM had little effect. Wood and de Menezes suggest a number of potential reasons, related to the particular research methodology, for the absence of a strong association between HCM and many of the performance variables that they had studied. However, they go on to state that

> we clearly cannot rule out the possibility that there is no unique pay-off to using HCM, that is, that the results can be taken at face value. The implication of this would be that arguments for HCM have to be centred on equity rather than efficiency grounds (Wood and de Menezes, 1998: 508).

The different approaches taken by researchers with regard to unit of analysis and the measure of organisational performance make it difficult to cumulate research findings. According to Becker and Gerhart (1996) a further constraint is the fact that studies adopting the "best practice" perspective vary significantly as to the practices included and sometimes even as to whether a practice is likely to be positively or negatively related to high performance. For example, Arthur's (1994) high-performance employment system specifies a low emphasis on variable pay, whereas the high performance employment systems defined by Huselid (1995) and MacDuffie (1995) have strong emphases on variable pay. Another example comes from Pfeffer (1994) and Huselid (1995) who describe HR strategies that rely on internal promotions and provide access to employee grievance procedures as high performance employment systems whereas other studies (Arthur, 1994; Ichniowski et al., 1994) consider these practices as elements of more rigid HRM systems frequently associated with less productive unionised environments.

In addressing the research agenda, Becker and Gerhart (1996: 793) stress that future work on the strategic perspective, in addition to addressing the issues above, must elaborate on "the black box between a firm's HR system and the firm's bottom line". This would require the elaboration and testing of more complete structural models — for example, models including key intervening variables — that would help to rule out alternative explanations for an observed HR/firm performance link such as reverse causation.

Delery and Doty (1996) maintain that overall the level of support generated for universalistic predictions indicates that the universalistic perspective is a valid theoretical perspective for strategic human resource management theorists. Salaman (1992) asserts that the "best practice" approach exerts considerable influence because the policies and practices it promotes are frequently seen to be the answer to all organisational problems and the means by which any corporate strategy could be achieved.

TABLE 14.1: PRACTICES INCLUDED IN DIFFERENT AUTHORS' HIGH PERFORMANCE HR STRATEGIES

HR Practice	Kochan & Osterman	Huselid	Pfeffer	Arthur
Self-directed work teams	Yes		Yes	Yes
Job rotation	Yes		Yes	
TQM	Yes			
Contingent pay		Yes	Yes	Yes
Training		Yes	Yes	Yes
Information sharing		Yes	Yes	
Job Analysis		Yes		
Promotion from within		Yes	Yes	
Attitude surveys		Yes		
Grievance procedure		Yes		
Employment tests		Yes		
Formal performance appraisal		Yes		
Intensity of recruiting efforts		Yes	Yes	
Job design			Yes	Yes
% of skilled workers				Yes
Supervisor span of control				Yes
Social events				Yes
Average total labour cost			Yes	Yes
Benefits/total labor cost				Yes
Employee ownership			Yes	
Symbolic egalitarianism			Yes	
Wage compression			Yes	
Long-term HR perspective			Yes	
Measurement of practices			Yes	
Overarching HR philosophy			Yes	
Problem-solving groups/ quality circles	Yes		Yes	Yes
Promotion criteria (merit, seniority, combination)			Yes	
Employment security		Yes		

Source: Adapted from Becker and Gerhart (1996), Pfeffer (1994a) and Huselid (1995).

However, Storey (1992) has noted that towards the end of the 1980s commentators on HRM were trying to deal with the "dilemmas" in the management of human resources. Basically, this is reflected in a move from the tendency to prescribe the "how to" in managing employees to an approach which takes a more contingent view of the type of HR practices considered appropriate for particular organisations.

CONTINGENCY MODELS OF STRATEGIC HRM

As noted above the contingency perspective focuses on the need to achieve a match between the business strategy and the resultant parameters for HRM. In other words, the relationship between the use of specific HR practices and organisational performance is posited to be contingent on an organisation's strategy. Contingency arguments "are more complex than universalistic arguments because contingency arguments imply interactions rather than the simple linear relationships incorporated in universalistic theories" (Delery and Doty, 1996: 807). Three frames of references are often used: different "stages" in the development of the organisation; Boston Consulting Group (BCG) matrix; and linking HR strategies to different business strategies, e.g. Porter's "generic" competitive strategies.

Stages of Organisation Development Models

The first collection of models sets out to fit HR policies and practices to the organisation or business unit's stage of development. Stage of development can be characterised in terms of the organisational life-cycle, from start-up through to decline. Alternatively, it can be characterised in terms of the product or geographical diversity achieved (e.g. single product through to multiple products) and by the associated organisation structure (e.g. functional through to global organisation). Kochan and Barrocci's (1985) links between four stages of business life and the appropriate HR policies in terms of recruitment and selection, rewards, training and development and industrial relations are shown in Table 14.2.

Fombrun et al.'s (1984) model characterises organisations' strategy according to their product or geographical diversity and their organisational structure and then shows the particular configurations of HRM policies that are deemed suitable to each stage of development (Table 14.3). Thus, for example, in terms of training and development, a declining organisation would implement retraining and career consulting services (Table 14.2) while for a single product functional organisation, development will be unsystematic, relying largely on job experience (Table 14.3).

An alternative contingency model is that based on the notion of portfolio planning, the best known system being that developed by the Boston Consulting Group (BCG) (1970; Hedley, 1977).

BCG Matrix

There is a growing tendency for large companies to be diversified. Key issues facing the corporate office are on what basis to allocate capital within the business and, secondly, how to identify potential growth areas within and outside the organisation. This involves the use of portfolio planning, which has been defined by Hamermesh (1986: 10) as

> those analytic techniques that aid in the classification of a firm's businesses for resource allocation purposes and for selecting a competitive strategy on the basis of the growth potential of each business and of the financial resources that will be either consumed or produced by the business.

The purpose of the BCG model is to help the strategic planners classify the various business units in the portfolio against (1) the attractiveness or potential of the market for growth, and (2) its relative competitive position in terms of current market share (Hendry, 1995). The model (see Figure 14.4) leads to generalisations about corporate and business strategy.

TABLE 14.2: CRITICAL HUMAN RESOURCE ACTIVITIES AT DIFFERENT ORGANISATIONAL OR BUSINESS UNIT STAGES

Human Resource Functions	Life-Cycle Stages			
	Start-Up	Growth	Maturity	Decline
Recruitment, selection and staffing	Attract best technical/ professional talent.	Recruit adequate numbers and mix of qualified workers. Management succession planning. Manage rapid internal labour market movements.	Encourage sufficient turnover to minimise lay-offs and provide new openings. Encourage mobility as re-organisations shift jobs around.	Plan and implement workforce reductions and reallocation.
Compensation and benefits	Meet or exceed labour market rates to attract needed talent.	Meet external market but consider internal equity effects. Establish formal compensation structures.	Control compensation.	Tighter cost control.
Employee training and development	Define future skill requirements and begin establishing career ladders	Mould effective management team through management development and organisational development.	Maintain flexibility and skills of an ageing workforce.	Implement retraining and career consulting services.
Labour/employee relations	Set basic employee relations philosophy and organisation	Maintain labour peace and employee motivation and morale.	Control labour costs and maintain labour peace. Improve productivity.	Maintain peace.

Source: Storey and Sisson (1993: 61) (adapted from Kochan and Barocci (1985: 104)).

TABLE 14.3: HUMAN RESOURCE MANAGEMENT LINKS TO STRATEGY AND STRUCTURE

Strategy	Structure	Human Resource Management			
		Selection	Appraisal	Rewards	Development
1. Single product	Functional	Functionally-oriented; subjective criteria used.	Subjective measures via personal contact.	Unsystematic and allocated in a paternalistic manner	Unsystematic; largely job experience; single function focus.
2. Single product (vertically integrated).	Functional	Functionally-oriented; standardised criteria used.	Impersonal; based on cost and productivity data.	Related to performance and productivity.	Functional specialists with some generalistics; largely rotation.
3. Growth by acquisition (holding company) of unrelated businesses.	Separate self-contained businesses.	Functionally-oriented but varies from business to business in terms of how systematic.	Impersonal; based on return on investment and profitability.	Formula-based includes return on investment and profitability.	Cross-functional but not cross-business.
4. Related diversification of product lines through internal growth and acquisition.	Multi-divisional	Functionally- and generalist-oriented; systematic criteria used.	Impersonal; based on return on investment, productivity and subjective assessment of contribution to company.	Large bonuses; based on profitability and subjective assessment of contribution to overall company.	Cross-functional, cross-divisional and cross-corporate; formal.
5. Multiple products in multiple countries.	Global organisation (geographic centre and worldwide)	Functionally- and generalist-oriented; systematic criteria used.	Impersonal; based on multiple goals such as return on investment, profit tailored to product and country.	Bonuses; based on multiple planned goals with moderate top management.	Cross-divisional and cross-subsidiary to corporate; formal and systematic.

Source: Storey and Sisson, 1993: 63 (adapted from Fombrun et al., 1984).

Figure 14.4: Portfolio Planning Growth–Share Matrix

Market Share
(Relative competition position)

		High	Low
Market Growth (Business growth rate)	**High**	Star	Wildcat
	Low	Cash Cow	Dog

Thomason (1984) attempted to make links between the BCG ideal types and HRM. Purcell (1989) and Purcell and Ahlstrand (1994) have taken this work a step further. Purcell (1989) clearly sees human resource issues as downstream from first-order corporate and business strategies, and contingent on them also. The business strategy adopted is seen as deciding the appropriate human resource management approach that should be adopted by the organisations (Marchington and Wilkinson, 1996). The portfolio model has often been used within HRM to suggest particular requirements for managerial behaviour and employee resourcing, especially the choice of general manager for the business unit (cf. Hendry, 1995).

The appropriate human resource policies and practices for each BCG ideal type are presented as follows:

- *Stars* (high share, high-growth) are in a strong position. They require high levels of investment but their dominant position in the market often allows them to produce sufficient profits to finance further growth. Purcell (1989) portrays these organisations as increasingly using sophisticated human resource management designed by professional staff but implemented and managed by line management. These organisations' HR policies are likely to include employee relations based on high individualism, sophisticated selection and recruitment procedures, emphasis on training, individualised performance-related pay and above the market rate pay, regular and systematic appraisals and a strong emphasis on teamwork and communications. There will be a stress on new forms of employee representation and if unions are contemplated, it is likely to be on the basis of single union agreements. Purcell (1989: 67) suggests that in these units "technical and capital investment is matched by human resource investments".

- *Cash cows* (high-share, low-growth) produce large profits and positive cash flows. They only require moderate amounts of capital for themselves and the cash surplus is used to finance the stars and to help develop new businesses in growth markets. To ensure the order, stability and predictability that they require, they rely on structured systems of collective bargaining, job evaluation, and the adoption of modern sophisticated method of managing a highly unionised workforce. Depending on the strength of the performance-control system and the profit requirements of head office, cash cows can, however, sometimes slip into forms of indulgency patterns (Gouldner, 1954). Because the unit is profitable there can be a tendency to tolerate over-manning, restrictive practices and general inefficiency; there is little pressure for change and the costs associated with removing these customs and practices may be deemed too high.

- Cash cows are vulnerable to market changes and may fall into *dog mode* that is the worst of positions, with a low share of a slow-growing (or even declining) market. Here undoubtedly there is going to be pressure for change and cost cutting which may result in downsizing, layoffs, short-term working, greater control and an emphasis on downward communication.

- *Wildcat* (low-share, high growth) businesses compete in fast growing markets and are aiming to move up the experience curve ahead of the competition. These businesses need substantial capital investment over and above what they can produce themselves and yet they live in a very uncertain world. This type of unit will want to avoid most of the rigidities associated with larger, well-established organisations. Flexibility, particularly functional flexibility, is the key requirement. They will also want to avoid the high overhead costs associated with formal human resource policies and structures.

Purcell (1989) points to the fact that different businesses in the portfolio are treated as separate units, each requiring its own approach to people management. This differentiation rules out the possibility of having corporate institutional strategies in relation to non-economic matters such as values, standards and social responsibility.

> The management of human resources thus becomes an operational responsibility and brings with it the need to weaken or inhibit cross-unit comparisons and trade union interest in strategic management, while developing local, unit-based loyalties (Purcell, 1989: 69).

Legge (1995) also questions whether in such organisations it is possible to have a corporation-wide, mutually reinforcing set of HRM policies, in other words, "internal fit". Besides, she wonders whether this really matters in terms of organisational effectiveness when the level of integration in the organisation is only at the financial level and the business units are allowed a high level of autonomy.

> All that would then be required for congruence would be that each unit adopt policies that were consistent with its own business strategy and mutually reinforcing — irrespective of the extent to which they contradicted HRM policies pursued in other business units elsewhere in the corporation (Legge, 1995: 125).

Purcell (1989) does warn that to the degree that the emphasis is on short-run rates of return on investment and margin improvement, and that tight financial controls are placed on managers, it becomes harder at the unit level to develop and maintain long-run HR policies. Keep (1992) also stresses that short-term financial criteria may militate against longer-term strategic HRM devel-

opments such as investment in training. These pressures in decentralised organisations highlight two paradoxical elements of
strategic HRM; integration with strategy and devolution of HRM
responsibilities to line managers (Kirkpatrick et al., 1992).

On a broader front, portfolio schema have been criticised for
stifling organisational renewal rather than encouraging it (Porter,
1987) and for their damaging effects on the broader economy:

> [Product portfolio management], which was originally con-
> ceived as a device for determining priorities for an invest-
> ment portfolio, has been perverted into a device for killing
> certain businesses and boosting others, purely in order to
> maximise the corporation's financial results. (Ohmae, 1982:
> 142)

Porter's "Generic" Competitive Strategies and Human Resource Strategies

Schuler suggests that business strategies are most effective when
systematically co-ordinated with HR management policies and
practices (Schuler, 1987, 1988, 1989; Schuler and Jackson, 1987a,
1987b, 1989). He has drawn together and summarised the writings which are based on Porter's (1980, 1985, 1990) generic
strategies of cost leadership, differentiation and focus.

Porter suggests that there are three basic strategic choices
open to an organisation to secure "competitive advantage". These
are innovation, quality-enhancement or cost reduction. Schuler
and Jackson (1987a) suggest that each of Porter's three business
strategies requires a different set of "needed role behaviours" or
essential employee behaviour patterns. These behaviours are
shaped by the HR practices of the organisation. Schuler (1988)
elaborates 31 dilemmas which constitute the key "human resource
management practice choices" to elicit the required behaviour.
Those seeking advantage through innovation-driven strategies
are more likely to need a sophisticated or commitment-oriented
HRM policy making full use of human resources. In contrast, a
cost-led strategy is likely to call for efficient rather than full use of
human resources. Quality-driven strategies are less clear-cut but

will typically imply full utilisation of human resources. Schuler and Jackson's (1987a) model of employee role behaviour and HRM policies associated with particular competitive strategies is outlined in Table 14.4.

If the basic assumption of the contingency models that organisations adopting a particular strategy require HR strategies that are different from those required by organisations adopting alternative strategies is correct, then much of the variation in HR practices across organisations should be explained by the organisations' strategies. However, one must ask to what extent the research confirms the validity of these frameworks linking competitive strategy to HRM.

Validity of the Contingency Models

Beaumont (1993) has noted that although a number of general and specific hypotheses have come out of the conceptual discussions of the HRM issue, there has been relatively little systematic empirical research designed to determine the nature and determinants of the human resource management policy mix of individual organisations. Legge (1995: 116) maintains that given the reservations expressed about the rationalistic approach and conceptual limitations of the strategy models used in contingency models, "it is not surprising that they have been mainly employed at a normative level to derive prescriptions, rather than those prescriptions being empirically tests". She goes on to state that those who have attempted some empirical testing have produced very limited and fragmented evidence in their support. Gerhart et al. (1996) and Pfeffer (1994b) have also suggested that there is not a great deal of empirical support for the existence of an alignment between HRM and corporate or business strategy. On the other hand, Roche and Turner (1997) maintain that the empirical evidence on the importance of business strategy in shaping human resource policy does show it to have an impact. However, they do go on further to point out that the scale of the human resource strategy effect has been shown to be modest in the admittedly limited empirical literature to date.

TABLE 14.4: EMPLOYEE ROLE BEHAVIOUR AND HRM POLICIES ASSOCIATED WITH PARTICULAR BUSINESS STRATEGIES

Strategy	Employee Role Behaviour	HRM Policies
1. Innovation	• A high degree of creative behaviour • Longer-term focus • A relatively high level of co-operative behaviour • A moderate concern for quality • A moderate concern for quantity • An equal concern for process and results • A greater degree of risk taking • A high tolerance of ambiguity and unpredictability.	• Jobs that require close interaction and co-ordination among groups of individuals • Performance appraisals that are more likely to reflect longer-term and group-based achievements • Jobs that allow employees to develop skills that can be used in other positions in the firm • Compensation systems that emphasise internal equity rather than external or market-based equity • Pay rates that tend to be low, but that allow employees to be stockholders and have more freedom to choose the mix of components that make up their pay package • Broad career paths to reinforce the development of a broad range of skills
2. Quality enhancement	• Relatively repetitive and predictable behaviours • A more long-term or intermediate focus • A moderate amount of co-operative, interdependent behaviour • A high concern for quality • A modest concern for quantity of output	• Relatively fixed and explicit job descriptions • High levels of employee participation in decision relevant to immediate work conditions and the job itself • A mix of individual and group criteria for performance appraisal that is mostly short-term and results-oriented • A relatively egalitarian treatment of employees and some guarantees of employment security

	• High concern for process • Low risk-taking activity • Commitment to the goals of the organisations	• Extensive and continuous training and development of employees
3. Cost reduction	• Relatively repetitive and predictable behaviour • A rather short-term focus • Primarily autonomous or individual activity • Moderate concern for quality • High concern for quantity of output • Primary concern for results • Low risk-taking activity • Relatively high degree of comfort with stability.	• Relatively fixed and explicit job descriptions that allow little room for ambiguity • Narrowly designed jobs and narrowly defined career paths that encourage specialisation, expertise and efficiency • Short-term results orientated performance appraisals • Close monitoring of market pay levels for use in making compensation decisions • Minimal levels of employee training and development.

Source: Storey and Sisson (1993: 66) adapted from Schuler and Jackson (1987a: 209–13).

A number of researchers have shown links between organisational strategy and specific HR policies. For example, Balkan and Gomez-Mejia (1990) found association between organisation strategy and compensation policy. Rajagopolan and Finkelstein (1990) found that organisations' reward systems differed significantly and this difference was related to differences in their organisational strategy.

Buller and Napier's (1993) study of mid-sized firms went beyond most as it tried to relate links between strategy and HR to organisational performance. But their findings provide no clear evidence that strategy–human resource integration is related to firm performance, although there are suggestions that integrating HR activities with strategy may be more beneficial in mature rather than fast-growing firms. Against this, Fox and McLeay (1992, cited in Legge, 1995) in their study of 49 companies, drawn largely from the UK engineering and electronics sectors, found a positive relationship, over a ten-year period, between practices in the areas of recruitment and selection, management education, training and development, performance appraisal, remuneration and rewards and company-level career planning, as applied to managers, their integration with corporate strategy and financial performance, adjusted for sector average performance.

Schuler and Jackson (1987b) carried out a study of 300 firms in a variety of industries. Their results suggest that there are predictable relationships between organisational strategy and human resource management practices. By and large, these differences were consistent with Schuler's (1987) propositions. The analysis revealed that greater differences in HRM practices are found within organisations than across organisations, regardless of strategy. That is, organisations are likely to use rather different HRM practices with employees at different levels. Furthermore firms with more than one business are likely to have more than one set of HRM practices. Thus, a single firm with several businesses may have different conditions of employment to the extent that it has businesses operating with different life-cycle stages and pursuing different organisational strategies. Further analysis

(Schuler and Jackson, 1989) provided support for the hypotheses that human resource management priorities would differ for firms in the growth and maturity stages of the product life-cycle and that they would differ across firms using the competitive strategies of differentiation and cost-efficiency. Schuler and Jackson (1987b: 139) do point out that "these results do not prove that organisations systematically selected particular practices to match their strategy".

BOX 14.1: THE RELATIONSHIP BETWEEN BUSINESS STRATEGY, LIFE-CYCLE AND HUMAN RESOURCE MANAGEMENT IN THE IRISH FOOD INDUSTRY

Othman (1994) in his study of 119 firms in the Irish food industry set out to investigate the relationship between business life-cycle, strategy and HRM practices. The main hypothesis was that the HRM practice of firms is determined by their strategy. It was further hypothesised that the choice of strategy is constrained by the firm's business life-cycle (Schuler, 1989; Schuler and Jackson, 1989). Porter's (1980) model of generic strategy was used as the framework in assessing the firm's strategy.

The results showed that the hypothesised relationships were not supported by the data. There was no evidence to suggest that the specific HR practice typology proposed by Schuler (1989) is associated with Porter's (1980) generic strategy types among firms in the Irish food industry. The study found that contingencies such as the existence of a HR department and employment size are the more important predictors of HR practice.

The HR practices associated with firms having HR departments indicated a more formal, developed and long-term oriented practice. Othman maintains that the development of some of these HRM practices, e.g. the use of personality as a recruitment criterion, requires the presence of certain competencies and know-how and he suggests that the presence of a HR department provides organisations with these capabilities. More developed HR practices were also associated with larger firms. Othman maintains that the resources needed to establish a HR department and staff it with competent employees is more likely to be available in larger firms. Thus, their HR practice is more developed than in the case of smaller firms.

> The data showed that there was no obvious fit between busi-
> ness strategy and HRM strategy in the food industry at the time
> the study was undertaken. Othman concluded that considerable
> doubt must be cast on the role of strategy as the imperative in
> shaping HRM practice.

Source: Adapted from Othman (1994).

In further empirical work designed to examine Schuler's (1987) work on the Porterian model, Jackson et al. (1989) surveyed 267 organisations in the US. They report their results show clear differences in the HR practices used by organisations of different types. Furthermore the relationships between organisational characteristics and HR practices are substantially different for managerial and hourly paid employees. They found some support for the proposition that innovating firms adopted HRM practices that were broadly compatible with innovation but they also found that the practices varied with manufacturing technology, industry sector, organisational structure and size, and union presence.

As Dyer (1983: 165) says, "the acid test" is whether there are "identifiable combinations" of environments (and settings) and particular types of human resource strategies which "consistently yield better results than their alternatives". So the nature of the argument now strongly incorporates the concept of outcomes rather than relying largely on descriptions of styles or types of HRM philosophies and their links with competitive postures as was common in the late 1980s (Beardwell and Holden, 1997). An important difference between those adopting a "best practice" approach and those adopting a contingency approach is that the key concern for the former has been to show that high commitment management can contribute to organisation performance. On the other hand, the latter have been less concerned with performance than with seeking to establish that the types of HRM policies and practices adopted by organisations reflect their competitive strategies and other sets of (variable) contingencies. Legge (1995) maintains that this lack of measures of organisational perform-ance is a general weakness in the empirical studies of the contingency models. This point is accepted by Schuler and Jackson (1987b) who state that whilst they and others (e.g. Miles and Snow, 1984) have implied that a fit between HRM practices and organisational strategy is likely to be more effective than a lack of fit, this remains to be empirically examined. Legge (1995) argues that the evidence in relation to the Porterian model is inconclusive. Overall she argues that "a lack of longitudinal in-depth case studies in the American work, combined with a penchant for small-scale, low response rate surveys, gives only fragile empirical support — if that — for a weighty prescriptive infrastructure" (Legge, 1995: 117).

In the UK, the detailed survey work undertaken as part of the Warwick Company Level surveys (Marginson et al., 1988; Marginson et al., 1993) paint a more tentative and critical picture,

> recognizing the limitations of the rationalistic models of strategy and the complexities of disentangling the inter-reletationships between organisational strategy and HRM policies and between HRM policies and practices (Legge, 1995: 118).

Summing up, Marginson et al. (1993: 37) state:

> If one of the defining characteristics of human resource management is the explicit link with corporate and business strategies then this survey has failed to find it for the majority of large companies in the UK.

Despite the problems associated with the contingency models, they are useful in a number of ways. In the first place, the linking of appropriate human resource strategies with an analysis of business strategies does allow us to move beyond the prescription implied in the "best practice" models that organisations, irrespective of the market position or business strategies, should adopt particular HRM stances. Secondly, the models can assist HR practitioners to frame proposals which might be more appealing to senior line managers because they are seen to "fit" with the business strategy and conform with the criteria used by senior management (Marchington and Wilkinson, 1996). As such the models are useful as sensitising devices rather than as a technique for reading off the approach to be adopted.

Following on from our consideration of the research as to the validity of the various frameworks linking competitive strategy and HRM, the next issue to address is the extent to which a strategic or proactive approach to HRM in present in organisations.

STRATEGIC HUMAN RESOURCE MANAGEMENT — THE EVIDENCE

According to Gunnigle et al. (1997a) a problem in analysing changes in organisational approaches to HRM is that there is little consensus on the exact nature and extent of such change or how new developments contrast with more traditional approaches to workforce management. They are of the opinion that much of this confusion stems from the tendency to regard HRM as an essentially distinct and homogeneous approach, incorporating a specific policy and combination of personnel policies. However, practice seems to indicate that there are numerous variants of HRM, incorporating different approaches to workforce management (Keenoy 1990a).

Guest (1990) made an early attempt to assess the diffusion of HRM in the USA. He summarised a 1985 study by the Bureau of National Affairs in the US and concluded that "some companies are trying to innovate in the field of HRM, but there is no evidence to support the view that this is a general trend in American industry" (1990: 387). Guest's assessment is significant because he argues that in the US the central tenets of HRM are taken very seriously and, also, human resource management is a contemporary manifestation of the "American Dream".

Various case studies and surveys in the US and the UK illustrate that there is considerable innovation in the use of techniques to increase productivity and employee involvement in operational-level decision-making. Guest reports (1989b: 50) that

. . . at a significant proportion of foreign-owned green-field sites, management is pursuing some of the central features of HRM. These include flexible working, employee commitment and attention to high quality, which is partly reflected in the investment in careful selection and training.

However, it is not possible to say that HRM practices have been adopted widely across organisations in the USA and the UK. Bratton and Gold (1994) draw our attention to the fact that the total number of case studies in the UK and US claiming to be practising and moving toward HRM is relatively small. They go on to state that there is a distinct possibility that the overexposure of a relatively small number of cases gives the impression that more change is taking place than is actually the case.

While there is some hard evidence that a significant number of important UK organisations have adopted HRM practices, Keenoy (1990b) and Bratton (1992) argue that many of these techniques could exist within either an HRM or a traditional personnel management model, depending upon both circumstances and strategic choice. Among high technology companies, there is some evidence of adoption of HRM-style practices defined in terms of an emphasis on individual modes of job regulation and of high degrees of strategic integration (McLoughlin and Gourlay, 1992).

In the Workplace Industrial Relations Survey (Marginson et al., 1988) many respondents asserted that their organisations had an overall policy or approach to the management of employees but they found it very difficult to describe the features of this integrated approach. This led Marginson et al. to conclude that "the general weight of evidence would seem to confirm that most UK-owned enterprises remain pragmatic or opportunistic in their approach" (1988: 120). The second Workplace Industrial Relations Survey (Marginson, et al., 1993) gives an equally pessimistic appraisal of the likelihood of any general integration of human resource policies with business strategies. Furthermore this study indicated that the sets of policies associated with the "best practice" model were seldom encountered in practice (Millward, 1994). Wood and de Menezes (1998) in analysing the 1990 Workplace

Industrial Relations Survey data viewed high commitment management (HCM) as a matter of degree. Four progressive styles of HCM were discovered. They found the use of high commitment management in its entirety is still relatively rare in the UK but at the same time their study does suggest that organisations with medium or high levels of HCM are probably more prevalent than is implied by writers who treat HCM as an absolute concept.

Storey (1992) distinguished 25 key dimensions on which distinction can been made between strategic human resource management and traditional personnel/industrial relations. These dimensions were then used to track actual change in the employment methods of 15 mainstream British companies. While it was clear that there was extensive take-up of HRM style approaches, the authors also sound an important warning. If a critical test of HRM is an explicit and deliberate connection between HR strategy and corporate strategy, or evidence of a clear, people-focused strategy, then the research results do *not* support the notion that strategic human resource management is wide spread.

> Apart from an insistence on a customer orientation, most cases failed to show much in the way of an integrated approach to employment management, and still less was there evidence of strategic integration with the corporate plan (Storey and Sisson, 1993: 22).

It would appear that many of the initiatives arose for diverse reasons which Storey and Sisson (1993: 23) maintain might indicate the true nature of the HRM phenomenon, "that it is in reality a symbolic label behind which lurk multifarious practices".

Brewster and Smith (1990) who examined key trends in strategic HRM practices throughout the European Union reinforce the view that "a coherent human resource strategy, including an early strategic input on human resource issues, is found in only a small minority of those organisations that may be making some use of human resource management techniques" (Guest, 1990: 387). They found that "in many organisations human resource strategies follow on behind corporate strategy rather than making a positive contribution to it" (1990: 37). They also found that in the UK only 50 per cent of respondents claimed that the individual responsible for HR is involved in the development of the corporate strategy from the outset.

Roche (1998) reports that the incidence of commitment-oriented human resource policies in Ireland is modest. Using the Price Waterhouse/Cranfield International Survey (1992–93) data for Ireland, he tested a series of specific propositions as to the factors influencing the adoption of bundles of commitment-oriented human resource policies. The research confirmed that organisations with a relatively high degree of integration of human resource strategy into business strategy are very much more likely to adopt commitment-oriented bundles of HRM policies. High strategic integration increases the odds of adopting such policy bundles by some 20 times.

Gunnigle et al. (1997b), comparing the results of the 1995 Price Waterhouse/Cranfield International survey with the 1992 survey, reported that there are indications of a general trend towards greater HR strategy among organisations in Ireland. However, this trend is not evenly spread across organisations. Larger organisations are more likely to engage in formal business and HR strategy development. Furthermore, the survey found that the extent of formal strategy development is highest in US- and British-owned organisations. This finding is in line with previous studies on strategy development in US companies based in Ireland (see, for example, Gunnigle et al., 1994). Indigenous Irish organisations and those originating in other European Union countries have relatively lower levels of HR strategy development (Gunnigle et al., 1997b). But to what extent do such strategies get translated into work programmes and guidelines for the HRM function? It appears that while there is a heavy emphasis on strategy formulation this does not result in a commensurate emphasis on strategy implementation. Gunnigle et al. (1997b) suggest that this may reflect traditional difficulties in quantifying personnel objectives and strategies. However, there are variances according to organisation size. Over 80 per cent of large organisations responded positively on this dimension, in comparison to 42 per cent of smaller organisations. It appears that larger organisations require more explicit accountability in the HRM sphere than their smaller counterparts.

CONCLUSION

Our discussion started with the proposition that one of the key characteristics of HRM is the linkage between HRM strategy and business strategy. We considered what is meant by the concept of strategy and looked at the difficulties associated with business-HR strategy linkages. We examined "best practice" models that claim to show "how to" manage employees to ensure certain desired HRM outcomes. We also looked at a number of models which purport to show how HRM practices can be "matched" to the organisation's needs. Finally, we considered to what extent there is evidence to suggest a wide-scale adoption of strategic HRM.

In spite of the persuasive arguments in the literature calling for the integration of HRM and business strategy, empirical research does not give the proposition substantial support. While there is evidence of a wide range of HRM-type initiatives being developed in organisations, the evidence of a link between business strategy and HRM is far more limited. Even more limited still is evidence showing a direct link between integration and bottom line results. In view of this and the fact that establishing the preconditions necessary to ensure "fit" has been shown to be an extremely difficult task, one is left with the question "is the integration of business strategy and HRM critical or desirable?".

Guest (1990) considers the isolated and "piece-meal" diffusion of HRM practices as an indication of the failure of the concept. On the other hand, Boxall (1993) suggests that the "piece-meal" adoption of HRM practices may be a reflection of an incremental approach to change and is illustrative of a process of strategic learning going on in organisations. "If strategic HRM happens at all in any form it will be an evolutionary process, although this process may be accelerated by the pressure of change." (Armstrong, 1994: 55)

The processual model of strategy-making which is better grounded empirically (Legge, 1995) would suggest that integrating HRM and business strategy is a highly complex and iterative process, much dependent on the interplay and resources of different stakeholders. This point is supported by Othman's (1994) study of the Irish food industry that highlighted the fact that the adoption of HRM practices is affected by multiple contingencies. Kochan and Dyer (1993) maintain that the contingencies affecting the adoption of HRM practices go beyond internal variables and strategic considerations. They point to other external variables such as government policy, the adoption of the HRM practice by competitors, and the attitude of unions and industry associations as having an affect on the adoption of HRM practices. Such contingencies severely curtail the range of options avail to those who might wish to adopt a strategic approach to HRM.

However, Storey and Sisson (1993) contend that despite the various hurdles, managers who are prepared to question conventional wisdom do have an element of choice. But they stress that before embarking on initiatives, three critical points must be addressed. The first of these is that the business strategy must be capable of being translated into operational action plans. Second, it must be made absolutely clear to whom the responsibility for developing the strategy actually belongs; does it rest, for example, at corporate headquarters, the divisional office, or at each individual business unit? Third, some decision has to be made as to the overall thrust of the approach — will it, for example, aspire to match up to one of the "best practice" models or will it reflect in contingency fashion the particular need of the organisation?

It seems unlikely that one combination of "best practices" will be capable of ensuring the successful achievement of all types of strategy.

> Apart from anything else this would mean that a key value of the [HRM] approach — the selection of the *appropriate* form of [HRM] for a particular strategy — was replaced by a blanket solution. There would be no choice left (Salaman 1992: 58).

A set of practices that have individual, positive effects on performance may be a necessary, but not sufficient, condition for a larger effect on organisational performance (Becker and Gerhart, 1996). The final word can be given to Huselid (1995). Although he tends to favour the "best practices" viewpoint, Huselid does recognise that the efficacy of any practice can only be decided in the context of a particular organisation's strategic and environmental contingencies:

> All else being equal, the use of High Performance Work Practices and good internal fit should lead to positive outcomes for all types of firms. However, at the margin, firms that tailor their work practices to their particular strategic and environmental contingencies should be able to realise additional performance gains (Huselid, 1995: 644).

References

Abbegglen, J.C. and Stalk, G. (1985): *Kaisha: The Japanese Corporation*, New York: Basic Books.

Andrews, K.R. (1980): *The Concept of Corporate Strategy*, Homewood, IL: Irwin.

Argyris, C. (1992): "A Leadership Dilemma: Skilled Incompetence", in Salaman, G. (ed.), *Human Resource Strategy*, London: Sage.

Armstrong, M. (1987): "Human Resource Management: A Case of the Emperor's New Clothes?", *Personnel Management*, August: 30–35.

Armstrong, M. (1994): "Blue-Chip Firms With A Vision", *Personnel Management*, October: 48–55.

Armstrong, M. (1996): *Personnel Management Practice*, sixth edition, London: Kogan Page.

Arthur, J.B. (1994): "Effects of Human Resource Systems on Manufacturing Performance and Turnover", *Academy of Management Journal*, 37: 670–87.

Baird, L. and Meshoulam, I. (1988): "Managing Two Fits of Strategic Human Resource Management", *Academy of Management Review*, 13(1): 116–28.

Balkan, D.B. and Gomez-Mejia, L.R. (1990): "Matching Compensation and Organizational Strategy", *Strategic Management Journal*, 11(2): 153–69.

Barney, J. (1995): "Looking Inside for Competitive Advantage", *Academy of Management Executive*, 9(4): 49–61.

Beardwell, I. and Holden, L. (1997): *Human Resource Management*, second edition, London: Pitman.

Beardwell, I.J. (1992): "The New Industrial Relations — A Review of the Debate", *Human Resource Management Journal*, 2(2): 1–7.

Beaumont, P.B. (1993): *Human Resource Management*, London: Sage.

Becker, B. and Gerhart, B. (1996): "The Impact of Human Resource Management on Organisational Performance: Progress and Prospects", *Academy of Management Journal*, 39(4): 779–801.

Beer, M. (1997): "The Transformation of the Human Resource Function: Resolving the Tension between a Traditional Administrative and a New Strategic Role", *Human Resource Management*, Spring, 36(1): 49–56.

Beer, M. and Eisenstat, R.A. (1996): "The Silent Killers: Overcoming the Hidden Barriers to Organizational Fitness", Working Paper 97–004, Boston, Mass.: Division of Research, Harvard Business School.

Beer, M., Eisenstat, R.A. and Biggadike, R. (1996): "Developing an Organisation Capable of Strategy Implementation and Reformulation: A Preliminary Test" in Moingeon, B. and Edmondson, A. (eds.), *Organisation Learning for Competitive Advantage*, London: Sage.

Beer, M., Spector, B., Lawrence, P.R., Quinn Mills, D. and Walton, R.E. (1984): *Managing Human Assets*, New York: Free Press.

Blyton, P. and Turnbull, P. (1992): "HRM: Debates, Dilemmas and Contradiction", in Blyton, P. and Turnbull, P. (eds.), *Reassessing Human Resource Management*, London: Sage.

Blyton, P. and Turnbull, P. (eds.) (1992): *Reassessing Human Resource Management*, London: Sage.

Boston Consulting Group (1970): *The Product Portfolio Concept*, Perspective 66, Boston, Mass.: Boston Consulting Group.

Boxall, P. (1992): "Strategic Human Resource Management: Beginnings of a New Theoretical Sophistication?", *Human Resource Management Journal*, 2(3): 60–79.

Boxall, P. (1993): "The Significance of Human Resource Management: a reconsideration of the evidence", *International Journal of Human Resource Management*, 4(3), 645–64.

Boxall, P. (1994): "Placing Strategy at the Heart of Business Success", *Personnel Management*, July: 32–5.

Bratton, J. (1992): *Japanization at Work: Managerial Studies for the 1990s*, London: Macmillan.

Bratton, J. and Gold, J. (1994): *Human Resource Management: Theory and Practice*, London: Macmillan.

Brewster, C. (1993): "European Human Resource Management: Reflection of, or Challenge to, the American Concept?" in Kirkbride, P. (ed.), *Human Resource Management in the New Europe of the 1990s*, London: Routledge.

Brewster, C., Gill, C. and Richbell, S. (1983): "Industrial Relations Policy: A Framework for Analysis", in Thurley, K. and Wood, S. (eds.), *Industrial Relations and Management Strategy*, Cambridge: Cambridge University.

Brewster, C. and Smith, C. (1990): "Corporate Strategy: A No-go Area for Personnel?", *Personnel Management*, July: 36–40.

Buller, P.F. and Napier, N.K. (1993): "Strategy and Human Resource Management Integration in Fast Growth versus Other Mid-sized Firms", *British Journal of Management*, 4(2): 77–90.

Cappelli, P. and McKersie, R.B. (1987): "Management Strategy and the Redesign of Work Rules", *Journal of Management Studies*, 24(5): 441–62.

Cappelli, P. and Crocker-Hefter, A. (1996): "Distinctive Human Resources are Firms" Core Competencies", *Organisational Dynamics*, Winter: 7–21.

Chandler, A.T., Jr. (1962): *Strategy and Structure: Chapters in the History of the American Enterprise*, Cambridge, Mass.: MIT Press.

Collins, C. and Porras, J.I. (1994): *Built to Last: Successful Habits of Visionary Companies*, New York: Harper Business.

Delbridge, R. and Turnbull, P. (1992): "Human Resource Maximisation: The Management of Labour under Just-in-Time Manufacturing Systems" in. Blyton, P. and Turnbull, P. (eds.), *Reassessing Human Resource Management*, London: Sage.

Delery, J.E. and Doty, D.H. (1996): "Modes of Theorising in Strategic Human Resource Management: Tests of Universalistic, Contingency, and Configurational Performance Predictions", *Academy of Management Journal*, 39(4), 802–35.

Denison, D.R. (1990): *Corporate Culture and Organizational Effectiveness*, New York: Wiley.

Dyer, L. (1983): "Bringing Human Resources into the Strategy Formulation Process", *Human Resource Management*, 22(3): 257–71.

Dyer, L. (1985): "Strategic Human Resource Management and Planning", in Rowland, K.M. and Ferris, G.R. (eds), *Research in Personnel and Human Resource Management*, Greenwich, CT: JAI Press.

Dyer, L. (1986): *Human Resource Planning Practices*, New York: Random House.

Eisenstat, R.A. (1996): "What Corporate Human Resource Brings to the Picnic: Four Models for Functional Management", *Organizational Dynamics*, Autumn: 7–22.

Ferris, G.R. (ed.) (1996): *Research in Personnel and Human Resource Management*, 14, Greenwich, CT: JAI Press.

Fischer, C.D., Schoenfeldt, L. and Shaw, J.B. (1996): *Human Resource Management*, Boston, Mass.: Houghton Mifflin.

Fombrun, C.J. (1982): "Conversation with Reginald H. Jones and Frank Doyle", *Organizational Dynamics*, 10(3): 42–63.

Fombrun, C.J., Tichy, N.M. and Devanna, M.A. (1984): *Strategic Human Resource Management*, New York: John Wiley.

Fox, S. and McLeay, S. (1992): "An Approach to Researching Managerial Labour Markets: HRM, Corporate Strategy and Financial Performance in UK Manufacturing", *International Journal of Human Resource Management*, 3(3): 523–54.

Fulmer, W.E. (1992): "Human Resource Management: The Right Hand of Strategy Implementation" in Thompson, A.A., Fulmer, W.E. and Strickland, A.J. (eds.), *Readings in Strategic Management*, fourth edition, Homewood, IL: Irwin.

Gerhart, B., Trevor, C. and Graham, M. (1996): "New Directions in Employee Compensation Research" in Ferris, G.R. (ed.), *Research in Personnel and Human Resources Management*, 14: 143–203, Greenwich, CT: JAI Press.

Gouldner, A. (1954): *Wild Cat Strike*, New York: Harper & Row.

Gratton, L. (1994): "Implementing Strategic Intent: Human Resource Processes as a Force for Change", *Business Strategy Review*, Spring, 5(1): 47–66.

Gratton, L. (1997): "Tomorrow People", *People Management*, 24 July: 22–7.

Guest, D. (1987): "Human Resource Management and Industrial Relations", *Journal of Management Studies* 24(5): 503–21.

Guest, D. (1989a): "Personnel and Human Resource Management: Can You Tell the Difference?", *Personnel Management*, January: 48–51.

Guest, D. (1989b): "Human Resource Management: Its Implications for Industrial Relations and Trade Unions", in Storey, J. (ed.), *New Perspectives on Human Resource Management*, London: Routledge.

Guest, D. (1990): "Human Resource Management and the American Dream", *Journal of Management Studies*, 27(4): 377–97.

Guest, D. (1991): "Personnel Management: The End of Orthodoxy?", *British Journal of Industrial Relations*, 29: 2 June: 149–75.

Guest, D. and Hoque, K. (1994): "Yes, Personnel Does Make a Difference", *Personnel Management*, November, 40–44.

Guest, D. and Peccei, R. (1994): "The Nature and Causes of Effective Human Resource Management", *British Journal of Industrial Relations*, 32(2): 219–42.

Gunnigle, P., Flood, P., Morley, M. and Turner, T. (1994): *Continuity and Change in Irish Employee Relations*, Dublin: Oak Tree.

Gunnigle, P., Heraty, N. and Morley, M. (1997a): *Personnel & Human Resource Management: Theory and Practice in Ireland*, Dublin: Gill and Macmillan.

Gunnigle, P., Morley, P., Clifford, N. and Turner, T. with Heraty, N. and Crowley, M. (1997b): *Human Resource Management in Irish Organisations*, Dublin: Oak Tree/University College Dublin.

Hamermesh, R. G. (1986): *Making Strategy Work: How Senior Managers Produce Results*, New York: Wiley.

Hedley, B. (1977): "Strategy and the Business Portfolio", *Long Range Planning*, 10(1), February, 9–16.

Hendry, C. (1995): *Human Resource Management: A Strategic Approach*, Oxford: Butterworth-Heinemann.

Hendry, C. and Pettigrew, A. (1986): "The Practice of Strategic Human Resource Management", *Personnel Review*, 15(5): 3–8.

Hendry, C. and Pettigrew, A. (1990): "Human Resource Management: An Agenda for the 1990s", *International Journal of Human Resource Management*, 1(1): 17–43.

Huselid, M. (1995): "The Impact of Human Resource Management Practices on Turnover, Productivity and Corporate Financial Performance", *Academy of Management Journal*, 38(3): 635–72.

Ichniowski, C., Kochan, T., Levine, D., Olson, C. and Strauss, G. (1996): "What Works at Work: Overview and Assessment", *Industrial Relations*, 35(3): 299–333.

Jackson, S.E., Schuler, R.S. and Rivero, J.C. (1989): "Organisational Characteristics as Predictors of Personnel Practices", *Personnel Psychology*, 42(4): 727–86.

Johnson, G. (1987): *Strategic Change and the Management Process*, Oxford: Blackwell.

Johnson, G. and Scholes, K. (1993): *Exploring Corporate Strategy*, third edition, Hemel Hempstead: Prentice Hall.

Keenoy, T. (1990a): "HRM: A Case of the Wolf in Sheep's Clothing?" *Personnel Review*, 19(2): 3–9.

Keenoy, T. (1990b): "Human Resource Management: Rhetoric, Reality and Contradiction", *International Journal of Human Resource Management*, 1(3), December: 363–84.

Keep, E. (1992): "Corporate Training Strategies: the Vital Component?", in Salaman, G. (ed.), *Human Resource Strategies*, London: Sage.

Kirkbride, P. (ed.) (1993): *Human Resource Management in the New Europe of the 1990s*, London: Routledge.

Kirkpatrick, I., Davies, A. and Oliver, N. (1992): "Decentralisation: Friend or Foe of HRM?", in Blyton, P. and Turnbull, P. (eds.), *Reassessing Human Resource Management*, London: Sage.

Koch, M.J. and McGrath, R.G. (1996): "Improving Labor Productivity: Human Resource Management Policies Do Matter", *Strategic Management Journal*, 17: 335–54.

Kochan, T.A. and Dyer, L. (1993): "Managing Transformational Change: The Role of Human Resource Professionals", *International Journal of Human Resource Management*, 3(3): 569–90.

Kochan, T.A. and Barocci, T.A. (1985): *Human Resource Management and Industrial Relations*, Boston: Little, Brown.

Kochan, T.A., Katz, H.C. and McKersie, R.B. (1986): *The Transformation of American Industrial Relations*, New York: Basic Books.

Kochan, T.A. and Osterman, P. (1994): *The Mutual Gains Enterprise*, Boston: Harvard Business School Press.

Kotter, J.P. and Heskett, J.L. (1992): *Corporate Culture and Performance*, New York: Free Press.

Legge, K. (1989): "Human Resource Management: A Critical Analysis", in Storey, J. (ed.), *New Perspectives on Human Resource Management*, London: Routledge.

Legge, K. (1995): *HRM: Rhetorics and Realities*, London: Macmillan.

Lengnick-Hall, C.A. and Lengnick-Hall, M.L. (1988): "Strategic Human Resources Management: A Review of the Literature and a Proposed Typology", *Academy of Management Review*, 13(3): 454–70.

Lengnick-Hall, C.A. and Lengnick-Hall, M.L. (1990): *Interactive Human Resource Management and Strategic Planning*, Westport: Quorum.

Leonard, J.S. (1990): "Executive Pay and Firm Performance", *Industrial and Labour Relations Review*, 43: 13–29.

Lundy, O. and Cowling, A. (1996): *Strategic Human Resource Management*, London: Routledge

MacDuffie, J.P. (1995): "Human Resource Bundles and Manufacturing Performance: Organizational Logic and Flexible Production Systems in the World Auto Industry", *Industrial and Labor Relations Review*, 48: 197–221.

Marchington, M. and Wilkinson, A. (1996): *Core Personnel and Development*, London: Institute of Personnel and Development.

Marginson, P., Edwards, P.K., Martin, R., Purcell, J. and Sisson, K. (1988): *Beyond the Workplace: Managing Industrial Relations in Multi-Plant Enterprises*, Oxford: Blackwell.

Marginson, P., Armstrong, P., Edwards, P. and Purcell, J. with Hubbard, N. (1993): *The Control of Industrial Relations in Large Companies: An Initial*

Analysis of the Second Company Level Industrial Relations Survey, Warwick Papers in Industrial Relations, 45, Warwick: IRRU, School of Industrial and Business Studies, University of Warwick.

McLoughlin, I. and Gourlay, S. (1992): "Enterprise without Unions: Managing Employment Relations in Non-union Firms", *Journal of Management Studies*, 29(5): 669–91.

Miles, R. and Snow, C. (1978): *Organizational Strategy, Structure and Process*, New York: McGraw-Hill.

Miles, R. and Snow, C. (1984): "Designing Strategic Human Resource Systems", *Organisational Dynamics*, Summer: 36–52.

Millward, N. (1994): *The New Industrial Relations?*, London: Policy Studies Institute.

Mintzberg, H. (1978): "Patterns in Strategy Formulation", *Management Science*, 24, May: 934–48.

Mintzberg, H. (1987): "Crafting Strategy", *Harvard Business Review*, July–August: 66–75.

Mintzberg, H. (1988): "Opening up the Definition of Strategy", in Quinn, J.B. Mintzberg, H. and James, R.M. (eds.), *The Strategy Process*, New Jersey: Prentice Hall.

Mintzberg, H. (1990): "The Design School: Reconsidering the Basic Premises of Strategic Management", *Strategic Management Journal*, 11: 171–95.

Moingeon, B. and Edmondson, A. (eds.) (1996): *Organisation Learning for Competitive Advantage*, London: Sage.

Ohmae, K. (1982): *The Mind of the Strategist*, New York: McGraw-Hill.

Osterman, P. (1994): "How Common is Workplace Transformation and How Can We Explain Who Adopts It? Results from a National Survey", *Industrial and Labor Relations Review*, 47: 173–88.

Othman, R. (1994): *Strategic HRM: An Empirical Examination. Relationship Between Business Life-cycle, Strategy and Human Resource Management in the Irish Food Industry*, unpublished Ph.D. thesis, University College Dublin.

Peters, T. and Waterman, R. (1982): *In Search of Excellence*. New York: Harper & Row.

Pettigrew, A. (1973): *The Politics of Organisational Decision Making*, London: Tavistock.

Pettigrew, A. (1977): "Strategy Formulation as a Political Process", *International Studies of Management and Organisation*, 8(2): 78–87.

Pfeffer, J. (1994a): "Competitive Advantage Through People", *California Management Review*, Winter: 10–28.

Pfeffer, J. (1994b): *Competitive Advantage through People*, Boston, Mass.: Harvard Business School.

Poole, M. (1990): "Editorial: Human Resource Management in an International Perspective", *International Journal of Human Resource Management*, 1(1), June: 1–15.

Porter, M.E. (1980): *Competitive Strategy*, New York: Free Press.

Porter, M.E. (1985): *Competitive Advantage*, New York: Free Press.

Porter, M.E. (1987): "From Competitive Advantage to Corporate Strategy", *Harvard Business Review*, May–June: 43–59.

Porter, M.E. (1990): *The Competitive Advantage of Nations*, London: Macmillan.

Porter, M.E. (1996): "What is Strategy?", *Harvard Business Review*, November–December: 61–78.

Purcell, J. (1989): "The Impact of Corporate Strategy on Human Resource Management", in Salaman, G. (1992) (ed.), Human Resource Strategies, London: Sage.

Purcell, J. (1994): "Personnel Earns a Place on the Board", *Personnel Management*, February: 26–9.

Purcell, J. and Ahlstrand, B. (1994): *Human Resource Management in the Multi-Divisional Company*. Oxford: Oxford University.

Quinn, J. B. (1978): "Strategic Change: Logical Incrementalism", *Sloan Management Review*, 1(20): 7–21.

Quinn, J.B., Mintzberg, H. and James, R.M. (eds.) (1988): *The Strategy Process*, Englewood Cliffs, NJ: Prentice Hall.

Quinn-Mills, D. (1985): "Planning with People in Mind", *Harvard Business Review*, July–August: 97–105.

Rajagolan, J. and Finkelstein, S. (1990): "Effects of Strategic Group Membership and Environment Change in Senior Management Reward Systems", *Academy of Management Proceedings*.

Roche, W.K. and Turner, T. (1997): "The Diffusion of the Commitment Model in the Republic of Ireland", *Review of Employment Topics*, 5(1): 108–151.

Roche, W.K. (1998): *In Search of Coherent Commitment-Oriented Human Resource Policies and the Conditions which Sustain Them*, working paper, Dublin: Centre for Employment Relations and Organisational Performance, Graduate School of Business, University College Dublin.

Rowland, K.M. and Ferris, G.R. (eds.) (1985): *Research in Personnel and Human Resource Management*, Greenwich, CT: JAI Press.

Salaman, G. (1992): *Human Resource Strategies*, London: Sage.

Salaman, G. and Mabey, C. (1995): *Strategic Human Resource Management*, Oxford: Blackwell.

Schuler, R.S. (1987): "Personnel and Human Resource Management Choices and Organisational Strategy", *Human Resource Planning*, 10(1): 1–17.

Schuler, R.S. (1988): "Human Resource Management Practice Choices" in Schuler, R.S., Youngblood, S.A. and Huber, V.L., (eds.), *Readings in Personnel and Human Resource Management*, third edition, St. Paul, MN: West Publishing.

Schuler, R.S. (1989): "Strategic Human Resource Management and Industrial Relations", *Human Relations*, 42(2): 157–84.

Schuler, R.S. (1990): "Repositioning the Human Resource Function: Transformation or Demise?", *Academy of Management Executive*, 40(3): 49–60.

Schuler, R.S. and Jackson, S.E. (1987a): "Linking Competitive Strategies with Human Resource Management Practices, *Academy of Management Executive*, 1: 207–19.

Schuler, R.S. and Jackson, S.E. (1987b): "Organisational Strategy and Organisational Level as Determinants of Human Resource Management Practices", *Human Resource Planning*, 10(3): 125–41.

Schuler, R.S. and Jackson, S.E. (1988): "Customerisation: the Ticket to Better HR Business", *Personnel*, 65(6): 36–44.

Schuler, R.S. and Jackson, S.E. (1989): "Determinants of Human Resource Management Priorities and Implications for Industrial Relations", *Journal of Management*, 15(1): 89–99.

Schuler, R.S., Youngblood, S.A. and Huber, V.L. (eds.) (1988): *Readings in Personnel and Human Resource Management*, third edition, St. Paul, MN: West Publishing.

Sibson, R.E. (1983): "Strategic Personnel Planning", *Personnel Administrator*, 28(10): 39–42.

Sisson, K. (1994a): "Personnel Management: Paradigms, Practice and Prospects, in Sisson, K., (ed.). *Personnel Management*, second edition, Oxford: Blackwell.

Sisson, K. (ed.) (1994b): *Personnel Management*, second edition, Oxford: Blackwell.

Sparrow, P. and Hiltrop, J.M. (1994): *European Human Resource Management in Transition*, UK: Prentice Hall.

Storey, J. (1987): *Development in Human Resource Management: An Interim Report*, Warwick Papers in Industrial Relations, 17, Coventry: Industrial Relations Research Unit, Warwick University.

Storey, J. (1992): *Developments in the Management of Human Resources*, Oxford: Blackwell.

Storey, J. (1995): *Human Resource Management: A Critical Text*, London: Routledge.

Storey, J. (ed.) (1989): *New Perspectives on Human Resource Management*, London: Routledge.

Storey, J. and Sisson, K. (1993): *Managing Human Resources and Industrial Relations*, Buckingham: Open University Press.

Terpstra, D.E. and Rozell, E.J. (1993): "The Relationship of Staffing Practices to Organisational Level Measures of Performance", *Personnel Psychology*, 46: 27–48.

Thomason, G. (1984): *A Textbook of Industrial Relations Management*, London: IPM.

Thompson, A.A., Fulmer, W.E. and Strickland, A.J. (eds.) (1992): *Readings in Strategic Management*, fourth edition, Homewood, IL: Irwin.

Tichy, N.M., Fombrun, C.J. and Devanna, M.A. (1982): "Strategic Human Resource Management", *Sloan Management Review*, 23(2): 47–61.

Tomlinson, J. (1993): "Human Resources — Partners in Change", *Human Resource Management*, 32(4): 545–54.

Torraco, R.J. and Swanson, R.A. (1995): "The Strategic Roles of Human Resource Development", *Human Resource Planning*, December: 10–21.

Thurley, K. and Wood, S. (eds.) (1983): *Industrial Relations and Management Strategy*, Cambridge: Cambridge University

Tyson, S. (1995): *Human Resource Strategy*, London: Pitman

Tyson, S. and Fell, A. (1986): *Evaluating the Personnel Function*, London: Hutchinson.

Ulrich, D. and Lake, D. (1990): *Organizational Capability: Competing From the Inside Out*, New York: Wiley.

Walker, J.W. (1992): *Human Resource Strategy*, New York: McGraw-Hill.

Whipp, R. (1992) "Human Resource Management, Competition and Strategy: Some Productive Tensions" in Blyton, P. and Turnbull, P. (eds), *Reassessing Human Resource Management*, London: Sage.

Whittington, R. (1993): *What is Strategy and Does it Matter?* London: Routledge.

Wood, S. (1995): "The Four Pillars of Human Resource Management: Are They Connected?", *Human Resource Management Journal*, 5(5): 49–59.

Wood, S. and Albanese, M. (1995): "Can We Speak of a High Commitment Management on the Shop Floor?", *Journal of Management Studies*, 32(2): 1–33.

Wood, S. and de Menezes, L. (1998): "High Commitment Management in the U.K: Evidence from the Workplace Industrial Relations Survey, and Employers' Manpower and Skills Practices Survey", *Human Relations*, 52(4): 485–515.

Wright, P.M. and McMahan, G.C. (1992): "Theoretical Perspectives for Strategic Human Resource Management", *Journal of Management*, 18(2): 295–320.

Youndt, M.A., Snell, S.A., Dean, J.W. and Lepak, D.P. (1996): *Academy of Management Journal*, 39(4): 836–66.

Index